Performing Arts and Gender in Postcolonial Western Uganda

Eastman/Rochester Studies in Ethnomusicology

Ellen Koskoff, Series Editor
Eastman School of Music
(ISSN: 2161–0290)

Recent titles:

Gender in Chinese Music
Edited by Rachel Harris, Rowan Pease, and Shzr Ee Tan

Performing Gender, Place, and Emotion in Music:
Global Perspectives
Edited by Fiona Magowan and Louise Wrazen

Music, Indigeneity, Digital Media
Edited by Thomas R. Hilder, Henry Stobart, and Shzr Ee Tan

Listen with the Ear of the Heart:
Music and Monastery Life at Weston Priory
Maria S. Guarino

Tuning the Kingdom:
Kawuugulu Musical Performance, Politics, and Storytelling in Buganda
Damascus Kafumbe

New York Klezmer in the Twentieth Century:
The Music of Naftule Brandwein and Dave Tarras
Joel E. Rubin

Songs for Cabo Verde:
Norberto Tavares's Musical Visions for a New Republic
Susan Hurley-Glowa

The Kecak and Cultural Tourism on Bali
Kendra Stepputat

Walking with Asafo in Ghana: An Ethnographic Account
of Kormantse Bentsir Warrior Music
Ama Oforiwaa Aduonum

Intimate Entanglements in the Ethnography of Performance:
Race, Gender, Vulnerability
Edited by Sidra Lawrence and Michelle Kisliuk

A complete list of titles in the Eastman/Rochester Studies in Ethnomusicology
series may be found on our website, www.urpress.com

Performing Arts and Gender in Postcolonial Western Uganda

Linda Cimardi

UNIVERSITY OF ROCHESTER PRESS

Copyright © 2023 Linda Cimardi

All rights reserved. Except as permitted under current legislation, no part of this work may be photocopied, stored in a retrieval system, published, performed in public, adapted, broadcast, transmitted, recorded, or reproduced in any form or by any means, without the prior permission of the copyright owner.

First published 2023

University of Rochester Press
668 Mt. Hope Avenue, Rochester, NY 14620, USA
www.urpress.com
and Boydell & Brewer Limited
PO Box 9, Woodbridge, Suffolk IP12 3DF, UK
www.boydellandbrewer.com

ISBN: 978-1-64825-032-3
ISSN: 2161-0290 ; vol. 14

Library of Congress Cataloging-in-Publication Data
Names: Cimardi, Linda, author.
Title: Performing arts and gender in postcolonial western Uganda / Linda Cimardi.
Description: Rochester : University of Rochester Press, 2023. | Series: Eastman/Rochester studies in ethnomusicology, 2161-0290 ; 14 | Includes bibliographical references and index.
Identifiers: LCCN 2023008414 (print) | LCCN 2023008415 (ebook) | ISBN 9781648250323 (hardback) | ISBN 9781805430643 (pdf)
Subjects: LCSH: Ethnomusicology—Uganda. | Performing arts—Uganda. | Gender identity in music. | Gender identity in dance.
Classification: LCC ML3797.2.U4 C56 2023 (print) | LCC ML3797.2.U4 (ebook) | DDC 780.89—dc23/eng/2023
LC record available at https://lccn.loc.gov/2023008414
LC ebook record available at https://lccn.loc.gov/2023008415

A catalogue record for this title is available from the British Library.

This publication is printed on acid-free paper.

Printed in the United States of America.

Contents

List of Illustrations	vii
Foreword by Samuel Kahunde	ix
Acknowledgments	xi
Note on Language	xiii
Note on the Musical Examples	xv
Note on Online Audio and Video Material	xvii
Prelude: Encountering Local Culture in Western Uganda	xix

	Introduction: Approaching Gender and Performing Arts in Bunyoro and Tooro	1
1	"Traditional Dance Preserves Culture and Shows People How to Behave": *Runyege*, MDD, and Gender	32
2	Singing Marriage, *Runyege*, and Labor	64
3	"Women Aren't Supposed To": Instrument Playing in the Past and Today	101
4	Shaking the Hips, Stamping the Feet: The *Runyege* Dance	132
5	Narrating and Representing Local Culture: Theater in Songs and Dances	164
6	Trans-Performing and Morality in Cultural Groups	190

Postlude: Gendering Culture	221
Appendix I. Glossary of Terms in Runyoro-Rutooro	227
Appendix II. Historical Recordings from Bunyoro and Tooro	235
Author's Interviews	245
References	251
Index	269

Illustrations

Figures

I.1	Map of Uganda	3
1.1	Semantic areas of singing, instrument playing, dancing, and storytelling	35
1.2	*Kinyege* fruit with flower ovary containing the *maranga* seeds and *maranga* plant	37
1.3	Christopher Magezi in his workshop holding a pair of *binyege* rattles	37
1.4	Photograph of "a Nyoro dance" (from Lloyd 1907)	39
1.5	Gerrison Kinyoro recounting the origins of *runyege*	43
2.1	Presenting the *mukaaga* bridewealth	69
2.2	Entertainment during a wedding in Kibate	73
2.3	Joy Katusabe Bitamazire grinding millet on the *rumengo* stone	93
3.1	*Bagwara* group in Bugambe	111
3.2	School performance of African instrumental music	111
3.3	Percussionists accompanying *runyege*	119
3.4	Drummers during a school performance	128
3.5	Girls playing drums during a school performance	129
4.1	Two decorated gourds containing *tonto* beer at a wedding	141
4.2	Banana stamping process	144
4.3	Herbert Barongo dancing *runyege* men's part and detail of his footwork	145
4.4	Process of stepping on sorghum panicles and tray used to winnow cereals	146
4.5	Goretti Basemera dancing *runyege* women's part and detail of women's footwork	147

viii ❧ ILLUSTRATIONS

4.6	*Kutongora* performed by two dance couples	161
5.1	Rehearsals of a "traditional folk song" by Kahunga Bunyonyi Primary School	174
6.1	Women of the MASDRASS group performing *runyege* men's part	210

Note: When not specified in the captions under the pictures, the photographs were taken by the author.

Music and Dance Examples

2.1	*Kyera maino*	81
2.2	*Kamutwaire*	85
2.3	*Ke ke kamengo*	94
2.4	*Bituli bambi*	99
3.1	Patterns played by the two *ngoma* in Nyoro *runyege*	119
3.2	Patterns played by the two *ngoma* in Tooro *runyege*	121
3.3	Various patterns performed by *runyege* instruments in Bunyoro and Tooro	123
3.4	*Ngaabi* variations performed in Tooro	123
4.1	The men's first dance style in *runyege*	152
4.2	The men's second dance style in *runyege*	152
4.3	The men's third dance style in *runyege*	153
4.4	The women's first dance style in *bw'omu mbaju*	155
4.5	The women's second dance style in *bw'omu mbaju*	155
4.6	The women's third dance style in *bw'omu mbaju*	156
5.1	Section (1) of *Ceeku ceeku*	177
5.2	Section (2) of *Ceeku ceeku*	178
5.3	Section (3) of *Ceeku ceeku*	178

Foreword

As an ethnomusicologist and native of western Uganda, it is a great pleasure for me to present this work. *Performing Arts and Gender in Postcolonial Western Uganda* is one of the few books available to readers about the music and dance of this region. Drawing on years of extensive fieldwork and on the knowledge of the Runyoro-Rutooro language, the author explores and analyzes local repertoires and in particular *runyege*, the traditional performing art of the Banyoro and Batooro people of western Uganda. With both historical and ethnographic depth, she considers the multiple theories about its origins and the different views about the past and current role of its components: singing, instrument playing, dancing, and acting. The author focuses on gender as a fundamental element forging not only *runyege*'s normative structures and durable meanings, but also its coexisting inner flexibility and liveliness. Following the analysis of gender in *runyege* together with both the examination of broader gender notions in Bunyoro and Tooro through time and the impact of precolonial, colonial, and postcolonial cultural institutions, the reader is offered a view on the continuous redefinitions, simultaneous understandings, ongoing negotiations, and various embodiments playing out in this genre.

Performing Arts and Gender in Postcolonial Western Uganda shows the complexity and relevance of traditional African art forms not only as local heritage, but also as a potent means for expressing contemporary identities and articulating gender. This volume represents a precious contribution to both academic scholarship on East Africa and to the conservation of and reflection on cultural heritage of our local communities.

Samuel Kahunde, PhD

Acknowledgments

This book is the result of several years of research and sharing of ideas, insights, and perspectives with numerous people whom I had the good fortune to meet and who have generously contributed to this work in valuable ways.

My deepest and sincerest gratitude goes to the many people in Uganda who have participated in this research. This book would not be possible without their willingness to share their cultural heritage; their availability to play, sing, dance, and narrate; and their helpfulness in discussing their memories, perspectives, and understandings on gender and performing arts in Bunyoro and Tooro. They are too numerous to be mentioned here, but I hope that the presentation of their experiences and perspectives in the following pages will provide the reader with at least an impression of the importance of their collaboration and assistance with this research. With some participants, whom I remember with gratitude and admiration, I built a relationship of profound exchange and dialogue on both practical and theoretical aspects of my research. Isabarongo Issa Sunday and Isabarongo Stephen Mugabo, my research assistants and friends, have been fundamental in translating and mediating my encounters with Nyoro and Tooro culture and performing arts. They have been indispensable and valuable partners in carrying out fieldwork, and I owe them immense gratitude on both the human and scientific level.

I first began studying Nyoro and later Tooro musical cultures when based at the University of Bologna and I benefited from the supervision and advice of Donatella Restani, Nico Staiti, and Serena Facci. Serena has continued following the development of my work in the succeeding years, including reading the early drafts of this work—I am immensely grateful to her for her guidance, advice, and constant support. She was also instrumental in introducing me to the Italian Mission in Equatorial Africa, then directed by Cecilia Pennacini. I am thankful to the mission, which supported my research for many years and through which I first met dear colleagues and friends. In particular, Anna Baral has been a close friend and an invaluable reader and commentator on my work. Since my Bologna years, my former colleague Paolo Valenti has become a trusted friend.

The archival research that I conducted at Makerere University, at the MAKWAA (Makerere University Klaus Wachsmann Audiovisual Archive), and at the university's Main Library in Kampala has been fundamental to the advancement of this work. Especially during this time, I benefited from the valuable advice of Sylvia Nanyonga-Tamusuza and other colleagues based in Makerere University, in particular Dominique Makwa. I am also grateful to the late Peter Cooke, who counseled me, shared his research and documentation, and finally read and commented on my earlier papers connected to this research.

After finishing my doctorate and focusing for some years on Eastern European music and dance, I came back to the topic of this book thanks to Gerd Grupe, who encouraged me to translate the material and publish it in English during my time at the University of Music and Performing Arts in Graz in 2017–18. Since then, my Graz colleagues Kendra Stepputat and Sarah Weiss have provided me with helpful advice and inspired my work in academia. Damascus Kafumbe deserves my deep appreciation for his wise suggestions and sincere friendship.

I thank the Marian-Steegmann Foundation, which generously supported part of the publication costs of this book. My appreciation goes also to the University of Rochester Press and in particular to Ellen Koskoff and Julia Cook, who have followed the development of this book from its first proposal up to the final version. Finally, I want to express my sincere thanks to the two anonymous peer reviewers who contributed significantly to improvements in this book with their comments and guidance.

I have grown as a person, a woman, and a scholar in the course of researching and writing this book over the past fourteen years. I finished writing the first draft and later revised this book during the first and third wave of the Covid-19 pandemic, and during this time I enjoyed the solid and loving support of my husband Michael and now the pure joy brought by my baby daughter Nora, to whom I dedicate this book.

Berlin, December 2022

Note on Language

Runyoro-Rutooro[1] is the language of the Banyoro and Batooro people of western Uganda.

In this idiom, words have prefixes that specify the meaning of the stem. Thus, ru- usually identifies a language (like Runyoro-Rutooro); mu- and ba- (like Munyoro-Banyoro, Mutooro-Batooro) the singular and plural for persons; and bu- the place or region (like Bunyoro, while Tooro does not have a prefix). Prefixes are also used for adjectives (like kinyoro or kitooro), but here I will use only the stem with an uppercase initial letter for adjectives (like Nyoro) to simplify the reading. I use these typologies of terms, together with proper names, in roman type while other words and expressions in Runyoro-Rutooro appear in *italics*.

In most Nyoro and Tooro words, prefixes are preceded by a vowel (for instance Omunyoro, Abanyoro), which can be considered to function as an article. I retain this initial vowel only when I present song lyrics or quote sayings and proverbs; in all other cases I omit it.

In the transcription of Runyoro-Rutooro, I followed the orthographic norms described by Henry F. Miirima (2002). In particular, long vowels are written as double vowels or as diphthongs and triphthongs with the semi-vocalic letters w and y, while short vowels are written with a single letter. Differently from several other Bantu languages, modern Runyoro-Rutooro is no longer a tonal language (Kaji 2009; Rubongoya 1999); in only a few cases two different tones are used to differentiate the meaning of a word that would be written in the same way (Kaji 2018).

I specify here the pronunciation of some letters, as described by L. T. Rubongoya (1999), using the phonetic notation of the International Phonetic Alphabet:

A → /a/
E → /e/ or /ɛ/
I → /i/
O→ /o/ or /ɔ/
U→ /u/

---

1 In 1952, Runyoro-Rutooro was defined as one language (spoken by two ethnicities), part of the greater Runyakitara language family spoken in western Uganda (Miirima 2002; Rubongoya 1999).

xiv ❧ NOTE ON LANGUAGE

W (always as semivowel) → /u/
Y (always as semivowel) → /i/
C → /tʃ/
K → /k/
J → /dʒ/
G → /g/
H → /ɦ/
S → /s/
Z → /z/
NY (+ vowel or + semivowel and vowel) → /ɲ/
R and L (allophones) → /ɾ/ and /l/

Note on the Musical Examples

For the musical transcriptions in this book I use Western staff notation; however, I had to approximate the value of sounds in terms of both pitch and duration of the notes, since this kind of notation cannot illustrate Nyoro and Tooro music in detail.

In the percussion transcriptions, I have adopted the symbols employed by Sylvia Nanyonga-Tamusuza (2005) to indicate the different types of hand gestures or strokes on the drum's skin (a, b, c, d).

The notes with a square head (a) indicate a muted sound, obtained by pressing the palm in the center of the drum; this type of stroke is used mainly by the *ngoma* A to produce the low-pitched fundamental beat, which supplies the metrical reference for the other drums and for the dancers in *runyege*. The notes with a round head (b) indicate a banged sound, produced by beating the middle part of the drum skin with the palm but not the fingers and letting it resonate. The notes with a crosshead (c) indicate a stroke made with closed fingers in the middle area of the drum skin. These latter two kinds of strokes are mainly used by the *ngoma* B to perform the basic rhythmic pattern and its variations. The notes with a slashed head (d) indicate a slapped sound, corresponding to striking the drum with open fingers near the rim; this kind of stroke is characteristically used on the *ngaabi*, although it can also be employed by the *ngoma* B. Besides these symbols, black triangle noteheads (e) indicate the sound of the *binyege* leg rattles.

Note on Online Audio and Video Material

The audio (A) and video (V) recordings presented in the text can be found online at http://hdl.handle.net/1802/37373.

A1   *Kaisiki ija ontongole* performed by Gerrison Kinyoro (solo) and Stephen Mugabo (chorus). Kiguma (Tooro), May 11, 2011.

A2   *Kyera maino* performed by Korotirida Matama (solo) with Aberi Bitamazire and Godfrey Kwesiga (chorus). Muuro (Bunyoro), June 28, 2010.

A3   *Kamutwaire* performed by Korotirida Matama (solo) with Aberi Bitamazire and Godfrey Kwesiga (chorus). Muuro (Bunyoro), June 28, 2010.

A4   *Ke ke kamengo* performed by Dorothy Kahwa (solo). Muuro (Bunyoro), August 12, 2009.

A5   *Bituli bambi* performed by Gerrison Kinyoro (solo) with two other men (chorus). Kiguma (Tooro), September 9, 2010.

V1   *Runyege*, performance by Tooro Kingdom Cultural Troupe. Fort Portal (Tooro), 2012.

Prelude

Encountering Local Culture in Western Uganda

In the early morning of June 11, 2011, in the royal enclosure in Hoima, western Uganda, everything was ready to celebrate the *Mpango*, the anniversary of the enthronement of the Nyoro king, Solomon Gafabusa Iguru I. In the Kingdom of Bunyoro, a Ugandan traditional institution nowadays endowed with merely cultural power, this annual event is considered essential for representing and celebrating Nyoro identity, which is rooted in the local monarchy and cultural heritage and mainly expressed through royal rituals and traditional performing arts. The royal enclosure—an area including the royal palace, smaller buildings, and grazing fields for the royal herd—had been set up in the previous weeks to host the event. The space in front of the royal palace, a two-story white building constructed in the 1960s, was cleared and several gazebos were arranged to host special guests, dignitaries, and important religious, cultural, political, and business personalities from both the kingdom and the whole country. While this open space was public (though mostly reserved for dignitaries and invited guests), in more peripheral areas of the enclosure some special huts had been constructed according to traditional techniques. These huts were used for private royal ceremonies that took place during the preceding day and night. On the morning of the *Mpango* I was at the royal enclosure, ready to attend the hours-long celebration. This consisted of a varied program: the speech of the king, followed by speeches given by political and religious local authorities; the kingdom's anthem performed by the local brass band; the excited crowd greeting the arrival of the president of the Republic of Uganda, Yoweri Museveni, followed by his brief speech and the collective singing of the national anthem; the ritual procession of the main royal drum and other regalia from the nearby house of their custodian to the royal mound and then inside the palace; and the *Mpango* music played by the royal drums and side-blown trumpets (*makondeere*). The presence of the president, who attended the central part of the ceremony, and the playing and dancing of the *Mpango* music were the highlights of the event, which had attracted a few thousand people, especially from the surrounding villages and other towns of the kingdom

XX ❧ PRELUDE

but also from other parts of Uganda and neighboring countries like the Democratic Republic of Congo and Tanzania.

In this official celebratory frame, the traditional dance performances of the semiprofessional ensembles from the region as well as from other parts of the country offered interludes of entertainment between the more exclusive entries in the program. However, one performance among others seemed to attract the most attention from the audience, with reactions ranging from candid astonishment to amused embarrassment to annoyed disapproval. It was the *runyege* dance performed by a local cultural group, the Bunyoro Kingdom Culture Development Troupe, led by one of my main research participants, Christopher Magezi.

During my previous visits to Uganda, I had been told multiple times that *runyege* is the dance of the Banyoro—the genre with which the Nyoro people identify—although a very similar dance is performed in the neighboring kingdom of Tooro. *Runyege* is normally accompanied by drumming, singing, and clapping; dancing is organized in two distinct parts for men and women who, in the course of the dance, alternate group formations, solos, and interactions which resolve in the formation of couples, each composed of a man and a woman. *Runyege* is taught in local schools and forms a regular part of the repertoire of the semiprofessional ensembles in the region, like the group that performed that day in the royal enclosure.

On the one hand, local audiences often enjoy *runyege* performances in different venues, ranging from school festivals to wedding parties to shows in hotels to cultural celebrations. On the other hand, the royal music played by the *makondeere* that day was more rarely heard or danced to, since it was performed almost exclusively for the annual Mpango event. So, why were the Mpango attendees so intrigued by that *runyege* performance that they watched and commented on so eagerly? In my eyes, the performance was similar to others I had seen in other contexts, with comparable instrumental accompaniment, singing, dance style, and formations alternating on the dancing space. I could catch only a few words among the comments of the audience members seated near me, which focused on a woman or a man dancing. My research assistant Issa soon explained to me that one of the *runyege* dancers performing the women's part was a man, and this was why people were puzzled and made comments. Some among the attendees were surprised and wondered aloud if the dancer was a man or a woman based on his appearance and dance skills; others recognized the performer as a man and appreciated his dance abilities, commenting with a mixture of amazement and amusement that "he really dances as a woman"; others considered it inappropriate for a man to dance the women's part, especially in front of the king, at a time when the ensemble was supposed to display traditional Nyoro culture. As I started to understand on that occasion, it was very uncommon for a man, dressed in female attire disguising his male appearance, to dance the women's part in *runyege*. This performance was possible and accepted within the current stage conventions of *runyege*, but, at the same time, it somehow destabilized a number of assumptions about the local tradition, gendered body, dance structure, and performance dynamics.

This opening scene illustrates the topic of this book: how gender and local culture are bound to, articulated in, and negotiated through the traditional repertoires of music, dance, and theatre in western Uganda. Gender—inscribed and represented in *runyege*, the main genre I will discuss in this book—is one of the primary ways in which Nyoro (and Tooro) culture is preserved, handed down, and displayed. Although I focus on the areas of Bunyoro and Tooro, the observations I make are relevant beyond Eastern Africa in various other postcolonial contexts. Throughout my discussion, I demonstrate from different angles how the triad of gender, local culture, and performing arts interlock between past and present, in dialogue with as well as in opposition to issues characterizing the postcolonial period, touching on themes of tradition, ethnicity, biology, religion, morality, and sexuality. Different performing arts such as singing, instrument playing, dancing, and acting are among the topics discussed in this book as I analyze how they were transformed over time and are today recodified and staged in different contexts and in ways that use the heritage of the past to shape the present. Although these dynamics can be found in various global contexts, what is perhaps unique to Uganda is the extent to which the theatrical strategies and conventions—introduced through the festivalization and semiprofessionalization of traditional genres—codify and repeat conservative gender models while at the same time remaining intrinsically ambiguous in allowing the expression of alternative femininities and masculinities. While this contribution can be of significance for ethnomusicologists and anthropologists with an interest in the Global South, I consider my work relevant also for nonspecialists interested in the Ugandan context, since the dynamics I describe, with a close look at Bunyoro and Tooro, are part and parcel of national trends and debates on gender, identity, and ethnicity representation in a multicultural context, as well as on preservation and modernity of cultural heritage.

In the first two decades of the twenty-first century, a number of topical and political matters touching on issues of gender and sexuality, culture, and morality provoked fierce debate in Uganda. One, which also gained concerned attention internationally, was the Anti-Homosexuality Bill (also known as the "anti-gay" bill), which was approved in the Parliament after long discussions and soon after ruled invalid by the Constitutional Court in the 2010s. The bill seemed to be the result of a recent trend of conservative morality encroaching on society and politics. As argued by Alessandro

Gusman and Lia Viola (2014), to regain consensus Ugandan politicians have built on the "moral panic" created by the HIV/AIDS epidemic in the last decades and have legislated to regulate sexuality—not only through the Anti-Homosexuality Act but also with the Anti-Pornography Act. This is another law promulgated by the Ugandan Parliament and better known as the "miniskirt bill" since, in its first formulation, it banned the wearing of skirts that did not cover the knees. Supporting these laws was seen as giving emphasis to African and local traditions, on the one hand, and to morality inferred from religious prescriptions (both Christian, especially evangelic and pentecostal denominations, and Muslim) and colonial heritage, on the other hand. These elements articulate a discourse of self-legitimacy and opposition to neocolonialism—understood as foreign interests and influences on Uganda's internal politics and laws—shared, to varying degrees, by both the government and most of the population (Nyanzi 2013b and 2014; Sadgrove et al. 2012; Ssebaggala 2011; Vorhölter 2012; Ward 2015).

Tradition and culture are at the center of the debates around what is appropriate and what should be prohibited and condemned in gender and sexuality issues. As I was able to experience during my time in Uganda, these debates permeate the whole society, from the metropolis of Kampala to remote villages where the impact of national policies can be experienced. Through a politicized nostalgia of the good old times, local culture is mobilized in the discourses of power centers and among common people as the model of reference, as the mold of indigeneity opposed to exogenous "values" perceived as imposed, and as the source of inspiration to reconceive a viable future beyond the instability of present times. Usually through the constructed notion of "African identity," local tradition and culture serve as a powerful argument to invoke "good" models from the past and release the influential African moral positivity against what is perceived as foreign influences, but also to construct the destabilizing as alien (Nyanzi 2013b; Vorhölter 2012). The notion that a "good" and positive conception of gender is embedded in local culture marks the arguments of contemporary moralizing trends in Uganda and is blatantly evident in the debates around women's behaviors and nonheteronormative identities.

However, in multicultural Uganda, what tradition and culture are being referred to? Where are they located? Who—the government, local institutions, citizens, traditional performers—owns and/or represents them? How are the discourses surrounding these topics grounded in local cultures and which are the fulcra articulating these discourses?

Since the mid-1990s, Ugandan cultural institutions like precolonial monarchies have become more and more important loci of the experienced, as well as the imagined, tradition that incorporates cultural heritage and customs in the Ugandan political claustrophobia (Reid 2017). At the same time, traditional performing arts are also fundamental repositories of indigeneity and customs, a spring from which to draw examples as well as a tool to represent tradition and thus to negotiate and reshape its image. In several world cultures, the local village as opposed to the city is understood as the place where tradition resides, also in the form of traditional performing arts; in Uganda, tradition is perceived to be located in the plurality of peripheral cultural institutions like the kingdoms and villages that, together with their music and dance heritage, represent the various ethnicities of this multicultural nation. One such peripheral area is western Uganda, the regions known as Bunyoro and Tooro, where the broad phenomena that exist at the national level can be retraced in their local understanding and articulations. The way performing arts in these regions participate in these discourses and shape the node of tradition and gender is at the core of this book.

Introduction

Approaching Gender and Performing Arts in Bunyoro and Tooro

In 1993, when Ugandan President Yoweri Museveni and his National Resistance Movement (NRM) government restored the precolonial monarchies that had been abolished in 1967, most of the populations living south of Lake Kyoga rejoiced (Reid 2017). Since Independence, the central power had been in the hands of the dictatorial presidents Milton Obote and later Idi Amin, both from the northern part of the country, where institutions like kingdoms did not exist. As a Southerner and the leader of the guerrilla army that chased out the previous dictator thanks to the support of Southerners, Museveni understood the political and cultural importance of restoring the traditional kingdoms. To many people in Buganda, Bunyoro, Tooro, and Nkore, the abolition of the kingdoms had meant an abuse of power by the central government and the removal of institutions that were carriers of a long history and heritage (Karlström 1999; Kiguli 2001).[1]

While the Buganda Kingdom was so highly valued by British colonial administrators that its name was given to the entire Protectorate (Uganda being the Swahili version of Buganda), the most ancient kingdom of the African Great Lakes region had probably flourished in present western Uganda, in Bunyoro. According to some historians (Chrétien 1985 and 2000; Dunbar 1965; Majefe 1991), the Empire of Kitara originated in

---

1   The Nkore kingdom, located in Museveni's natal region, is the only one that has not been restored. The populations that did not recognize themselves in the ethnicities identified by the kingships had different attitudes towards precolonial monarchies, like the Bakonzo and Baamba populations, whose territories in the Rwenzori mountains had been included in the British-supported Tooro kingdom since the beginning of the nineteenth century. Tooro administration, marked by discrimination against Bakonzo and Baamba peoples, finished with the abolition of traditional kingdoms in 1967 and "was a cause of considerable rejoicing throughout the Rwenzori" (Doornbos 1970: 1129), although it did not signify the end of the Konzo and Amba calls for independence.

2 &❧ INTRODUCTION

that area and later expanded to include most of southern Uganda, eastern Congo, northern Tanzania, Rwanda, and Burundi, between 1300 and 1650. Over the centuries, independent kingdoms emerged from the empire and different languages developed, but the various monarchies retained common features and rituals defining royalty, as well as the traditional religious complex (*kubandwa*) marked by spirit mediumship (Pennacini 1998).

These traits also marked the putative successor of the Kitara Empire, the Bunyoro Kingdom, and the newest realm that emerged from it around 1830, Tooro (Fig. I.1). The people living in these two kingdoms, the Banyoro and Batooro, speak the same idiom of the Bantu interlacustrine linguistic group, the Runyoro-Rutooro, although minor pronunciation and lexical variants connote the two areas. Furthermore, because of their common past, Bunyoro and Tooro have a similar social structure, involving an extended royal family, a sort of aristocracy composed of the chiefs' families, and commoners, traditionally connoted as pastoralists (*bahuma*) or agriculturalists (*bairu*). As in other societies of the Great Lakes area, pastoralism was connected to the prestige and wealth derived from owning cows, while agriculturalists had a lower status in society (Doornbos 1970; Roscoe 1923; Taylor 1998). In precolonial times, a mixed system of agriculture and pastoralism, typical of the so-called Kitara Complex (Buchanan 1973), characterized the economy of both areas. During the second half of the nineteenth century, cattle decreased dramatically in Bunyoro because of raids, diseases, and the spread of ecological decay caused by continuous internal conflicts and wars against the British (Doyle 2006). As a consequence, agriculture became the main activity in Bunyoro with just a small proportion of the population dedicated to pastoralism (Beattie 1960: 1–2; Doyle 2006: 11–41; Torelli 1973). In Tooro the consequences of British colonization were not so dramatic, and rearing of livestock remained rather widespread (Ingham 1975; Taylor 1998). Today, agriculture is the main activity in both Bunyoro and Tooro, and cattle rearing is much less widespread, though still conveying high social status.

Nowadays, despite their numerous shared cultural and social traits, the Banyoro and Batooro consider themselves as separate peoples. The central claim in support of this is the existence of two distinct kingdoms, which are held to represent the identity of two different peoples. Since their restoration in 1994 as institutions with exclusively cultural prerogatives in the frame of the republican State, traditional monarchies have assumed the role of preservers and promoters of local culture. They are thus perceived as the source of original identity for the populations that identify in these institutions and their leaders, as well as the manifestation of a territorial delimitation and localized power in the multicultural national context.

The status of the Tooro and Nyoro kingships as separate entities consolidated during colonial times (ca. 1900–1962). Because of Bunyoro's fierce

Figure I.1. Map of Uganda by Kenton Ratliff. The sub-regions of Bunyoro and Tooro in western Uganda roughly correspond to the precolonial kingdoms' borders prior to 1967, except for Tooro, which by the 1960s included eastern territories connecting it with the Democratic Republic of the Congo.

resistance to the imposition of British administration, the strengthening of Tooro as an independent kingdom was fostered within the framework of the strategic interests of the Protectorate (Doornbos 1970). In Uganda, as in several other African countries (Amselle 1990; Amselle and M'Bokolo 1985), the colonial administration together with ethnographers such as John Roscoe, Lloyd A. Fallers, John Middleton, and Jeremy C. D. Lawrence contributed to the identification and construction of different ethnicities by tracing administrative borders, organizing surveys, and carrying out ethnographic work. The independent Ugandan state took up this colonial heritage of ethnicity identification and, also during the time of the abolition of the precolonial kingdoms, the different cultures of the country continued shaping their ethnic affiliation in relation to their neighbors, based on language, customs, and performing arts.

When the 1995 Ugandan Constitution ratified the restoration of the precolonial kingdoms as cultural institutions, it also opened the way to the recognition of other cultural entities that were acknowledged by local communities as being of cultural and social importance. Already during the colonial period, Ganda preeminence and privilege within the Protectorate had stimulated other populations, especially in the north of the country, to establish similar institutions in which they could identify and be represented in the multicultural context (Fallers 1961; Johannessen 2006; Mazrui 1970). The 1995 reform fostered a general run for the recovery of forgotten chieftainships and the creation of new similar institutions (Gardoncini 2010; Pennacini and Wittenberg 2008; Stacey 2008). Therefore, beginning in the mid-1990s, cultural institutions such as monarchies became crucial in the identification of peoples, territories, and local cultures. American historian Derek P. Peterson (2016) argued that monarchies also work as undemocratic constituencies and corporations. On the one hand, these institutions identify only with the main ethnicity in their territory, which under the leading party's (NRM) policies are administratively reconfigured as constituencies, and undermine minorities by denying them both cultural and political representation. On the other hand, while triggering a process of cultural revival that involves several aspects of social life including performing arts (Cimardi 2015 and 2017b; Pennacini 2011), monarchies have become like corporations that promote local heritage as branded product for tourism.

In connection with the cultural revival brought about by the restoration of traditional kingships, in recent years a renewed consideration for autochthony, indigenous traditions, and customs in contrast to foreign practices has emerged and grown ever stronger. The traditionalist attitude articulated following the ethnicities constructed during colonialism has given way to a new diffidence toward practices of the Global North that is at the same time a postcolonial critique of that heritage. This current of thought is of course not unique in Ugandan society and confronts the similarly widespread positive idea of "Western" customs as bringing modernity and well-being. While I do not wish to undermine this latter view or oversimplify the complexity of the various positionalities in Ugandan society, in this book I focus on the localist vision that is entrenched in cultural institutions, expressed and represented in traditional music and dance, and codified in the ethnic classification of the repertoires in the school festival system. Bunyoro and Tooro—through their monarchies, cultural heritage, and societies at large—are also involved in a local-global process of self-definition and confrontation. Although these two regions are today quite peripheral parts of the country in relation to central and southwestern Uganda (Buganda and Nkore), where most of the political, administrative, and economic activities are managed, they are more prosperous and nationally relevant than the northern regions, which are still suffering from prolonged insecurity and instability. In this sense, Bunyoro and Tooro are areas where national as well as local cultural phenomena find a dimension that can probably be representative of the whole country.

Gender in the Field

My interest in music from Uganda started in late 2007 with the research on Nyoro royal music that I undertook for my M.A. thesis (Cimardi 2008). Reading the literature on the region, I realized that, although western Uganda was considered the cradle of traditional monarchies through the Kitara Empire and Bunyoro as its contemporary heir (Chrétien 1985 and 2000; Mair 1977), no recent research on music had been carried on there. Studying royal music in Bunyoro was not only needed to cover a scholarship gap but also interesting in exploring how historical events such as the abolition and later restoration of the monarchy impacted on court music as well as how these processes affected other Ugandan regions.

Thanks to my supervisor, Serena Facci, I got in touch with the Ugandan ethnomusicologist Sylvia Nanyonga-Tamusuza, who welcomed me in Uganda, hosted me at her house during my first and last weeks in the country, and introduced me to Makerere University, the institution where she works in the capital city Kampala. Through her, I met Harriet Kasangaki, a Nyoro teacher who was by then also a music student at Makerere and could accompany me to Bunyoro.

In a busy and overcrowded taxi, Harriet and I traveled together northwest from Kampala. In Hoima, the main town in Bunyoro and seat of the Nyoro kingship, I settled into a small, tidy hotel in the town center where most of the customers were locals. Harriet suggested that one of the volunteers of the local branch of the Ugandan Red Cross Society, Issa Sunday, could help out during my stay because he had been part of a semiprofessional ensemble in the past as well as experienced in international cooperation through the Red Cross. Issa, who is a couple of years older than me, was at the time in his late twenties and lived in a village close to Hoima town. With great enthusiasm and energy, he started cooperating with me during my fieldwork on Nyoro royal music. At the same time, I became involved in the activities

6 ❧ INTRODUCTION

of the Ugandan Red Cross in western Uganda as a volunteer in their health campaigns in rural areas, advising on new activities and helping with fund-raising in my home country of Italy.

Investigating Nyoro royal music during the two months I spent in Uganda in 2008 made me aware of the limitations set on me because of my gender. Royal music is essentially performed by men, and parts of the ceremonies in which it is played are reserved for royal family members and selected men. Although as a foreigner I was perceived as a guest and thus respected and welcomed, some areas of royal music activities and practices remained inaccessible to me (as to any other female who is not part of the royal family), such as parts of the royal rituals or playing (or trying to play) some musical instruments (see chapter 3). Thanks to conversations with both male and female Ugandan friends and acquaintances, I also began to reflect on how gender was influential both in the local cultural heritage and in national policies as well as to question how my own gender could be perceived by my participants and condition my research.

The following year, I spent some more time in Bunyoro and started focusing on the traditional repertoires outside the royal context that are not marked by interdictions on women, but nonetheless strongly connoted by gender. Indeed, apart from some shared songs related to dancing and storytelling, traditionally there was a clear differentiation of songs for women and men, and even today the same division marks dances like *runyege*. While my initial interest was in women's performing expressions and practices in an effort to balance my previous work on royal music performed exclusively by men, my research later expanded to embrace various gendered performance practices, including those connoted as "for men" as well as those that are today less connoted by the performer's gender.

In 2010, besides visiting research participants and volunteering in Bunyoro, I traveled to the southern neighboring kingdom, Tooro, to research similarities and differences in the local repertoires of these culturally close regions. Together with Issa I traveled to Fort Portal, the main urban center in Tooro and headquarters of the royal palace, located on the highest of the numerous hills on which the town develops. Much richer in luxuriant vegetation than drier Hoima and more lively along its up-and-down roads, Fort Portal is the town where I spent the following weeks. There, I hoped to find a woman as a research assistant because I thought that this could facilitate new insights on gender.

Unfortunately, my attempts at establishing a relationship with a female assistant were not successful. Young women had difficulties in dealing with elders because their gender and age traditionally dictated that they were not in a position to lead a conversation, especially with male research participants. A recurrent perception I found among both women and men in western Uganda was that usually young women lacked the assertiveness to organize meetings and interviews, which is obviously connected to the social expectation about the deferential way they should relate to older people and men. More mature women, as had been the case with Harriet in Bunyoro, were too busy with their families, children, and daily work to have enough time to be my assistant. Here, too, gender appeared to be involved in shaping my research. Thanks to connections made by Issa with the local Ngabu za Tooro troupe, I met Stephen Mugabo, a percussionist and dancer in that cultural group, as well as a participant in cultural associations and local radio stations. Stephen offered to help me, not only as an assistant but also as a *runyege* teacher, and his performative experience and skills, which he shared with me during fieldwork, were valuable contributions to my views on the current Tooro traditional music and dance scene.

Overall, I spent around 12 months in Bunyoro and Tooro during multiple stays between 2008 and 2012, plus a short return in 2018. I was mostly based in the kingdoms' former capital cities, respectively Hoima and Fort Portal, where several of my research participants lived and from where I regularly visited the surrounding areas by mini-bus or, for shorter distances, *boda boda* motorcycle taxi. I also spent some periods in the administrative centers of the minor districts comprising the two kingdoms, in particular in the towns of Masindi and Kagadi in Bunyoro and of Kyenjojo and Kamwenge in Tooro. I normally stayed at small local hotels, preferring those that were low budget but had an electric generator, so that I could work on my notes or recordings even in the case of evening blackouts.

During fieldwork, Issa and Stephen were fundamental mediators as well as strategic organizers of my research. Especially in the first weeks, I needed to be introduced to the local communities by insiders who could explain the reasons for and purpose of my research. Although I improved with time, my knowledge of the Runyoro-Rutooro language was not advanced enough to sustain an articulate conversation, hence a linguistic mediator was required. Furthermore, my assistants were instrumental in establishing, through their acquaintances and by asking for information, connections with the people who then became my research participants, and their knowledge of the area was very useful in arranging the journeys to the various villages where the research participants lived. On some occasions, Bakar Abubakar in Bunyoro and Alice Basemeera in Tooro also worked as interpreters during my fieldwork.

Research participants also suggested other individuals for me to contact and meet, in a proliferation of connections covering most of the territory of Bunyoro and Tooro. I conducted interviews and recording sessions mostly at the residences of the people who had agreed to contribute to my research. The language used for interviews and recording sessions depended on the

8 &❧ INTRODUCTION

participants and the circumstances: with elders, Runyoro-Rutooro was generally spoken via translation or linguistic facilitation by my research assistants; with young people and other research participants who preferred it, I spoke in English and employed the local language only for specific terms. Together with Issa for Nyoro songs and Stephen for Tooro ones, I prepared translations of the lyrics based on the contextual explanations and clarifications of certain terms provided by the research participants.

When I did not get the opportunity to attend performances in locally organized events, or if I wished to have further documentation to facilitate analysis, I asked ensembles to perform in private sessions, and in order to document the "old" ways of performing songs remembered by elders, I sometimes set up specific sessions. Furthermore, to better understand the form and structure of Nyoro and Tooro *runyege,* I learned the basics of the two dancing parts and drumming: in Hoima with the ensemble Bunyoro Foundation Actors (in particular Salim Jamal) and Vincent Nyegenya and Monica Nyegenya, and in Fort Portal with the Ngabu za Tooro troupe (in particular Sylvia Karungi and Stephen Mugabo).

During my fieldwork, I met a number of individuals who possessed in-depth knowledge about the repertoires that I was researching. These experts were fundamental to my understanding of traditional Nyoro and Tooro repertoires: Christopher Magezi, an experienced performer and instrument maker from Bunyoro; Gerrison Kinyoro, an expert on Tooro music and dances; Jane Sabiiti and Jane Tibamanya, who sang over one hundred songs for me; Vincent Nyegenya, a connoisseur of Nyoro dances; and Kenneth Nyakairu, an authority on Tooro traditions.

Music and Local Culture

During my stays, the usual soundscape in Nyoro and Tooro everyday life was mainly composed of local and international popular music broadcast via the radio or mediatized through CDs and digital files. In towns such as Hoima and Fort Portal, shops, bars, and sometimes even street stalls, as well as mini-buses and households, played this music on their radios or digital players (laptops or mobile phones), populating the soundscape with a variety of local languages and English as well as a diversity of genres from gospel to hip-hop, from pop to traditional. While popular music is today the most commonly listened to and produced, traditional (royal or village) music is still highly regarded, not only in Bunyoro and Tooro but also more generally in Uganda. I focus in this book on the music, as well as the dance and drama, that is locally understood as traditional.

Royal music has a great cultural value for the Banyoro because of its exclusive association with the monarchy (marking its prestige), the historical and identity heritage attached to it (through the preservation of the stories of past kings and the connotation of royal rituals), and the peculiar characteristics of those repertoires (special instruments and songs). As seen in the opening scene in the Prelude, the *Mpango,* the main event featuring royal music, takes place just once a year to celebrate the anniversary of the king's coronation (Kahunde 2012a). The opportunities for ordinary people to enjoy royal music are clearly few and far between. However, local traditional music and dance not related to the kingship enliven a number of social and cultural events, as I experienced when Issa first persuaded me to attend a school festival. The yearly national school festival involves all schools in the country in a competition comprising several performance categories, including "traditional folk song" and "traditional folk dance." Similar performances are also part of the repertoire of semiprofessional groups, which typically perform both local dances and dances from other Ugandan cultures, as well as drama sketches.

At these school and group performances, my first impression was that their competitive and spectacular features had conditioned the repertoires, in the same way as other genres that had moved from participatory to representational settings in various global contexts (Nahachewsky 1995 and 2001; Turino 2008). Indeed, I could hear substantial differences between the way the songs were performed on stage and in elders' renditions. Today, traditional songs and dances are no longer performed informally in the course of daily life, and staged performances by schools and groups are the norm; only elders and middle-aged people remember the times when they used to perform them in the village. However, I encountered a great emphasis on "traditional" or "cultural" music in the description of the performances at school festivals and by cultural groups, both in public discourse and private conversation. Indeed, the discourse on tradition and culture was not only articulated in connection with royal music, but also in relation with other local repertoires. The same dynamics between elders' heritage and current performances, as well as the discourses involving the node of culture and autochthony, were evident in Tooro. As central as these discourses are in western Uganda, they progressively became more prominent in my research by connoting the repertoires I was focusing on, articulating the discussions about the old and the current performances, and finally defining the Banyoro in relation to the Batooro—and both of them in relation to the rest of Uganda and the world, in particular the Global North, which I represented in this specific situation.

Both in Bunyoro and Tooro, a recurring term in those debates was *nzarwa.* In a conversation with the music teacher Misinguzi and my assistant

10 ❧ INTRODUCTION

Issa (June 14, 2011), it was explained that this word refers to all the elements that characterize a community or ethnicity, that is, language, material culture, artistic expressions, and customs. In this sense, when speaking in English, they commonly translated *nzarwa* as culture. According to Margaret B. Davis (1938: 140), *nzarwa* means "home-born, native, aboriginal." So, the way this term was used by my research participants could be more precisely conveyed in English as local, autochthonous culture, as the emphasis on locality and indigeneity in determining the specificity of the heritage of the Banyoro and Batooro suggests. This is also made apparent when marking an identity border with neighboring peoples in Uganda, and in this case, my participants used the more precise locution *nzarwa yaitu,* "our culture." The local connotation of *nzarwa* emerges further in the opposition that appeared several times during my fieldwork: *bizina by'enzarwa* (musical pieces of the place), referring to local traditional music, and *bizina by'ebijungu* (musical pieces of the whites), meaning "Western" music (classical, Christian, or popular music from the Global North). A similar opposition between local/African and foreign/Western is usually invoked when discussing culture in general and with special reference to gender issues, as I argue in the following section. Although the local terms corresponding to the concept of tradition, *karukarukaine, kasigasigano,* and *karonkoronko* (Davis 1938: 319), are sometimes used in the official names of cultural groups, they were rarely used in the interviews I conducted in Runyoro-Rutooro through the linguistic mediation of my research assistants. Similarly, in the conversations I had in English on local music and customs, the word "culture" was preferred to "tradition." This would seem to indicate that history and transmission, which connote the handing over from generation to generation implied in the word "tradition," are considered as less relevant than the paradigm of locality central to the Nyoro and Tooro concept of culture. The use of "culture" in this sense is common among other Ugandan populations, and is also documented in Kenya, where the word "culture" is preferred to "tradition" in connoting performing arts, because the latter conveys the misleading idea of the immutability of the past (Kiiru 2017).

On the other hand, the Ugandan Ministry of Education consistently uses the adjectives "traditional" and "folk" to describe the repertoires performed at school festivals (e.g., "traditional folk song" and "traditional folk dance"). This derives from the international English used in the academia, as well as the school system, but it does not reflect local English, nor the local conceptualization of the repertoires themselves. However, because of the generalized use of "traditional" and "folk" in schools and festivals, these markers have been appropriated by some teachers, pupils, and troupe performers who are closely connected with the school arena of performing arts.

Although the ideas of history and transmission are not accentuated in the concept of *nzarwa* attached to traditional repertoires in Bunyoro and Tooro, my research participants noticed some changes that had happened over time to the traditional repertoires performed in the festivals and by cultural groups. During interviews and discussions on this topic, different degrees of awareness and evaluations of the changes that had occurred inevitably emerged. Old music teachers acknowledged that today the songs and dances in the school festival and as performed by cultural groups are different from how they were performed in the villages 30 or 40 years ago. A number of participants did not recognize as traditional some songs in contemporary performances because the words had been changed completely, but most considered that if it were not for the festival and the groups, their heritage would be lost. Younger teachers and educators acknowledge some transformations, but they do not deem them so important; they instead, as Banyoro and Batooro and as teachers, emphasize the urgency of preserving these repertoires—the local culture that is getting lost by way of westernization and influences from the Global North. Similar opinions are held by members of cultural groups, who see themselves as "culture lovers" and active members of the community because they perform a heritage that, with some improvements, can still be appreciated and loved by the people. The fundamental role of festivals and folk ensembles in recovering local repertoires, usually in connection with contemporary identity policy rather than in a strictly conservative manner, can be found in other global contexts, as well. For example, Lisa Gilman (2017) describes the Umthetho Festival in Malawi and its role in both reviving and inventing Ngoni tradition. In Mexico, where the Ballet Folklórico recovered and/or recreated dance repertoires that would otherwise have disappeared, the preservation of culture has contributed to the building of the Mexican national identity (Hutchinson 2009).

The need to preserve Ugandan heritage through performing arts is combined with the call to educate new generations, as well as adults who have grown up in the cities, about local cultures. The spectacularity of contemporary performances, coupled with their educative purpose, has brought about complex changes in the repertoires that at the same time are deemed to convey local culture. I am interested in understanding how these changes are impacting the way local culture is understood and, in particular, what image of culture is shaped and represented through the performances and how the culture-lab of performing arts interacts with gender conceptions and current moralist discourses.

12 ❧ INTRODUCTION

The Debates Surrounding Gender in Uganda

The traditional norms and expectations portraying ideal behaviors for most men and women are being confronted by women's present aspirations and the opportunities brought about by their income-generating activities, access to education, opportunities to travel, and life in big cities. During colonial times, these were mostly male prerogatives, but at least since the 1960s they have started to open up for women too, destabilizing the balance between genders that had been in place during precolonial and colonial times. I discuss the transformations in gender notions with greater detail in the next chapter, while here I focus on the contemporary debate about issues of gender and sexuality.

Since the 1990s, there has been intense debate across Ugandan society and academia about women and gender. Starting in the mid-1990s, Museveni's NRM government promoted policies directed at combating women's illiteracy, political invisibility, and poor medical care and introducing laws making school education compulsory for boys and girls, ensuring a quota of women in politics from the county to the national level (Mugenyi 1998). During the 2000s, the government shifted away from women-focused policies to the broader paradigm of gender equality. This approach included new measures that involved both women and men in addressing inequality, thus benefiting the whole population. However, the government and the local administration have been able to implement these policies only in part, and social as well as health projects receive significant financial support from international and missionary organizations (Reid 2017).

More recently, gender discussions have focused on the topic of homosexuality and involved several actors, from ordinary citizens to members of Parliament, from religious leaders to LGBTQ+ activists and academics, both at the national and international level. The discussion arose in 2009 in connection to a bill intended to reinforce sanctions against homosexuals.[2] In Uganda, most of the population seemed to approve of and support the bill;

---

2   "Sodomy" was codified as a crime "against the order of nature" during the colonial era and remained as such in the legislation of independent Uganda (Han and O'Mahoney 2014). The bill first drafted in 2009 explicitly addressed same-sex relationships, and specified and reinforced the punishments against them. The law signed by Museveni in 2014 prescribed penalties up to life imprisonment for people having same-sex intercourse, as well as the obligation to report people suspected of homosexual behavior (Nyanzi and Karamagi 2015). After it was ruled invalid by the Constitutional Court because it was not passed with the required quorum, some members of Parliament announced appeals against the nullification of the law, but, until the moment of writing, no further action was taken.

episodes of violence against homosexual persons were recorded in Kampala and the press and media galvanized a sentiment of homophobia.

Unfortunately, this is not only a Ugandan phenomenon since in recent years similar attitudes against homosexuality have been registered in neighboring countries, as well as on a global scale. International LGBTQ+ and human rights associations as well as politicians and governments gave resonance to the issue and took a clear stand against the Ugandan bill; international pressure manifested especially with the threat of withdrawing financial aid by governments of the Global North. Some sections of the Ugandan population perceived the international condemnation of the bill not only as unwanted interference in national matters but also as a manifestation of neocolonialism, of the continued influence of the Global North on Africa, to which foreign customs as homosexuality had been imported and imposed (Nyanzi 2013a and 2013b; Ssebaggala 2011; Vorhölter 2012).

Although homosexuality is not the focus of this book, it is worth analyzing the debate about it because of both its international relevance and the multiple similarities with the discussion on gender expectations and models in relation to tradition in Uganda, on which my analysis here is centered. In the discussion about the Anti-Homosexuality Bill, opposing viewpoints articulating the connection between Africanness and homosexuality emerged in Uganda. On the one side, supporters of the law—several politicians, religious leaders, and ordinary people—argued that homosexuality is un-African because it is contrary to African values and thus it must have been "imported" from the West, as were other cultural traits and behaviors. I often encountered this perspective during my fieldwork in Bunyoro and Tooro, supporting the theory that homosexuality was brought to Uganda by Arabic traders in the mid-nineteenth century, or more recently by whites. Murray and Roscoe (1998) and Epprecht (2008) documented the idea of homosexuality as being un-African in several African countries, where precolonial forms of nonheteronormative sexuality are strongly denied, as a consequence of the conversion to Christianity and Islam and the assimilation of religious as well as colonial stands against same-sex sexuality.[3] Conversely, Ugandan intellectuals opposing the law, like Sylvia Tamale (2007) and Stella Nyanzi (2013b), assert that homosexuality is not foreign to the continent since diverse forms of sexuality were present in precolonial Africa. In addition, morality, religion, human rights, and financial issues shape

---

3 Richard Ssebagala (2011) maintains that homophobia has exploded in Uganda as a consequence of the very discussion about homosexuality. In his view, talking about sexual matters outside the reproductive or health context is a traditional taboo in most Ugandan cultures and the exposure of same-sex relations in the public debate has caused homophobia as a rejection of these relationships.

14 ❧ INTRODUCTION

the perceptions of homosexuality as well as the debate on it (Gusman and Viola 2014). According to Nyanzi (2014), "The [anti-homosexuality] bill was drafted by Ugandans, but its genesis and support are intricately interwoven with a complex assemblage of local, continental, and global foreign influences, including the homophobic rhetoric of some African presidents, powerful collaborations with conservative US evangelicals, and the diffuse discourses of some bishops of the Anglican churches." The involvement of conservative American evangelical missionaries, usually connected to the US political right, has contributed to the increase in homophobia in Uganda through their influence on local evangelical pastors (Kaoma 2009; Sadgrove et al. 2012; Ssebagala 2011; Tamale 2007). This recent influence, however, has built its success on the preexisting local "moral panic" emerging from the HIV/AIDS pandemic, which saw sexuality as a source of immorality and sin that needed to be regulated, as Gusman and Viola (2014) have argued. According to Kevin Ward (2015), this moralized view of sexuality has been supported and disseminated by Christian leaders since colonial times through the local Catholic and Anglican Churches (Church of Uganda). More recently, since the establishment of the NRM government in the 1990s, Pentecostal-charismatic churches have developed greatly in the country and, also thanks to US connections and funding, pushed their discourses on salvation and condemnation of homosexuality through politics, media, and an increasing number of faithful (Bompani and Terreni Brown 2015).

This complex and multicentered discussion about homosexuality is the most evident component of broader sensitivities and tensions surrounding gender (involving women's equality and empowerment, alternative gender identities and expressions, nonnormative sexualities) and culture (connoted religiously, morally, and locally). Sexuality and morality, as conveyed by conservative Christian views, as well as gender and culture are strictly connected in widespread discourses that involve the bodies and behaviors of women, homosexuals, and individuals who do not conform to the social prescriptions for their genders by expressing alternative forms of femininities and masculinities. These tensions are furthermore complicated by the present neoliberal context and authoritarian state, where politicians are interested in maintaining international connections and funding by opening up to foreign investments and fostering human rights, but they also seek internal consent through bolstering nationalism and neocolonial resentment (Reid 2017). Especially in relation to gender issues, politics and civil society are in the the precarious position of supporting westernization, positively understood as changes derived from foreign influences and adapted to local conditions for a better society, and condemning neocolonialism, negatively seen as the forced imposition of practices perceived as incompatible with the local culture (int. Tina Bareeba: June 16, 2011; Vorhölter 2012). It is in a social context marked by these interrelated discourses that traditional performing arts are performed, discussed, and interpreted.

Although social and cultural practices in Uganda are intrinsically hybrid, gender, culture, and performing arts are usually conceived of and discussed between two polarities, one represented by the local, Ugandan, and African and the other constituted by the foreign, European, and Western. This polarization is typical of postcolonial Africa and functional to articulate discourses about (cultural, ethnic) difference, (historical) transformations, and (ambiguous, embraced, or contested) modernity. Especially in the African continent, this dyad structures the discussion about culture and its manifestations, as noted by Thomas Turino (2008: 127) in Zimbabwe and Lisa Gilman (2017: 165) in Malawi. However, as argued by Gilman, between these opposite poles there are a variety of positions, supporting or refusing at different degrees the local (seen as "ours" and positive, or as backward and unsophisticated) and the foreign (embraced as more advanced and carrying wealth, or feared and rejected as destroying local identity). This dichotomy is usually presented also in moral terms, attributing the "goodness" of practices and models to the African (often in relation to old customs perceived as positively conservative) or the European (normally in connection to Christianity). While I acknowledge the complexity of these different positions, in this book I give wider space to the discussion of the views that attach a positive moral and cultural value on the local, by focusing on traditional repertoires and their performers. At the same time, through my analysis of *runyege,* I aim to demonstrate how this genre incarnates the postcolonial intersection of past and present, locality and interculturality, conservation and innovation in the multiple values it conveys, as well as in its performance practice and style.

In this landscape, I consider the issue of Africanity fomenting the discourses on gender issues as connected with the idea of culture (*nzarwa*) of the Banyoro and Batooro. Indeed, both these concepts connote local customs, emphasize autochthony, and take a clear distance from practices perceived as foreign in the realm of gender as well as in performing arts. The contrast with what is (or is considered as) other, because it is different and distinct, informs this notion of the indigeneity in the concept of Africanity, as well as in *nzarwa*.

Defining Gender in a Postcolonial Context

These discourses in Bunyoro and Tooro, as well as at the national level, call for a postcolonial approach to gender. Similar to the Ugandan reactions to the Euro-American perspectives influencing the debate about the

16 ❧ INTRODUCTION

anti-homosexuality law, postcolonial speculation critically reconsidered some of the theories elaborated by women and gender scholars from the Global North (Amadiume 1987 and 1997; Bantebya Kyomuhendo and McIntosh 2006; Hanson 1992; Musisi 1992 and 2002; Oyěwùmí 1997; Scott 1988). Postcolonial African scholars like Ifi Amadiume (1987 and 1997) highlighted how representations of women in the Global South as passive and subjugated are ethnocentric and impose on women representations that are not part of local cultures. More generally, Nigerian sociologist Oyèrónkẹ́ Oyěwùmí (1997: 8) calls for a critical consideration of the continued dominance of the West in the production of knowledge in the study of gender in Africa. Some recent works in ethnomusicology have also dealt with gender and feminism in postcolonial contexts by discussing local models of femininity and masculinity that deconstruct assumptions on gender common in the Global North and explore the articulations of agency in national and diasporic dynamics (Downing 2019; Hutchinson 2016). Through the insights of this scholarship, I consider it necessary to understand the emic concepts of and perspectives on gender and to give voice to the different actors involved in the current debate, in relation to local, national, and international power centers. Especially Oyěwùmí's work (1997) directed my understanding of the construction of the category of gender and in particular of women. According to Oyěwùmí, "Western" notions of gender based on sex determinism have been absorbed by African colonized societies, thus erasing more situational and relational categories, as well as matriarchal values that offered paths of prestige for women. Similarly, the scholarship of Amadiume (1987 and 1997) and Bantebya Kyomuhendo and McIntosh (2006)—which analyze and deconstruct the multiple layers of gendered meanings and values across precolonial, colonial, and postcolonial Nigerian and Ugandan societies—guided my research on the connection between gender and performing arts across time.

Building on a body of scholarship that spans decades and deals with gender from a variety of perspectives (Ahmed 2006; Butler 1988 and 1990; Connell 2005; De Lauretis 1987; Gilmore 1990; Halberstam 1998; Murray and Roscoe 1998; Ortner 1997), I consider gender both as a theoretical concept and as an analytical perspective. I employ the notion of gender as a culturally constructed concept assigning a social identity to individuals, usually in relation to their biological sex and in a dynamic relationship with other categories that denote identity, such as race, age, and social status. These different characteristics of individuals contribute to the definition of their gender, which is thus marked by intersectionality (Crenshaw 1989). Furthermore, and this is of crucial importance for my domain of analysis, gender is performed, not given but acted and embodied, constructed by individuals through the iteration of movements, postures, and interactions in social and cultural contexts (Butler 1990). Since gender is built by repeated bodily practices, it may develop independently from biological sex, so sexual determinism should be overcome in favor of fluidity in understanding different connotations of gender identity and expression. Like other social categories, gender changes from one society, or even smaller community, to another, and it alters over time. Finally, gender, as a social category defining abstract models of individuals, involves a set of expectations that the wider community puts on individuals, who interiorize such models and are normally required to conform to them.

This theoretical framing allows me to explore historical notions of gender in western Uganda, which were more multifaceted in the precolonial era than today. As I discuss in the next chapter, in precolonial Bunyoro and Tooro gender did not follow the usual binary association with biological sex for some members of the royal family, and alternative masculinities and femininities were incarnated by traditional healers. In these cases marked by social status and religious matrix, the intersectional character of gender is clearly apparent. Through the fluidity embedded in my theoretical framing, I also aim to grasp the complexity of a cultural category that had, and still has in a different way, blurred and undetermined margins allowing tolerance or acceptance of "deviances" from normative expectations.

The notion of gender that I described does not define sexual orientation or intimacy, but using gender as an analytical tool can enable understanding of how forms of noncompliance with local gender models, as well as nonnormative sexual behaviors, can be experienced by individuals and interpreted by the broader society. Thus, a gendered perspective can help to differentiate among individuals' emotional and physical expressions regarding gender identity, sexuality, and public and private behaviors in relation to social expectations. In this book, my focus is not on sexuality, but rather on gender as a performance, identity, and expression emerging in the practice and discourses of traditional performing arts. Although sexual metaphors and allusions sometimes emerge from the analysis of songs' lyrics and from the *runyege* dance dynamics that I discuss in different parts of this book, sexuality was considered by my interlocutors as an embarrassing topic not to be talked of. I share Deborah Wong's (2015) criticism of the tendency of ethnomusicologists to avoid discussing sexuality on the basis that research participants do not mention it, which is usually a consequence of colonial prudishness and normative legislation; and I agree with her suggestion that there are effective methods of listening to and observing sexuality that would allow interesting new ways of exploring gender and music. However, to respect the privacy of my research participants and avoid unwanted attention with possible negative repercussions that may arise for those discussing

18 &◆ INTRODUCTION

their sexuality, I decided not to further expand my research to include sexuality in performing arts.

Also of relevance to my research has been the literature concerning music and gender in the African Great Lakes region, especially the work of Serena Facci (1998 and 2003, and with Cecilia Pennacini 2021) and Sylvia Nanyonga-Tamusuza (2002, 2005, and 2009). In particular, the book *Baakisimba* (Nanyonga-Tamusuza 2005) constituted, in conjunction with my conversations with the author, a starting point for my approach to gender in music and a model for researching the *runyege* music and dance genre. Nanyonga-Tamusuza's historical-ethnographic reconstruction of *baakisimba* and consideration of its current performances and the different gender conceptions that it conveys represented an important comparative paradigm in my research. Building on Nanyonga-Tamusuza's work, in this book I explore the centrality of local notions of gender and culture in the preservation, revival, handing down, and discourse of traditional performing arts in Uganda today.

Performing Arts or MDD: School Education, Festivals, and Groups

A wide literature has outlined how the European-derived concept of music does not have a precise correlation in Africa, and how singing and instrument playing should be considered in their interrelationships with other performing arts like dance and theatre, as well as storytelling, oral literature, and games (Agawu 2003: xiv; Blacking 1967: 16–17; Gilman 2009: 13; Kubik 2010: 9; Kwabena Nketia 1974: 24–26; Mabingo 2020a: 232; Stone 2002: 7). In Uganda, this cluster of arts is usually referred to by the umbrella term MDD: music, dance, and drama (Muyanda-Mutebi 1996: 23; Pier 2009: 5). Besides drawing from local ideas about the complex interrelation among traditional repertoires, the concept of MDD is intrinsically connected with music education in the Ugandan school system, the school national festival, and the practice of semiprofessional ensembles.[4] These institutions have developed since the 1960s in parallel with the elaboration of the concept of MDD and are today the main spaces where traditional performing arts, and the cultures they represent, are nurtured, shaped, and presented. For this

---

4   MDD was also the name of the department dedicated to performing arts in the main Ugandan tertiary education institution, Makerere University. The institute was renamed the Department of Performing Arts and Film in the early 2010s.

reason I introduce them here, focusing on their establishment during the 1960s, and I discuss them in more detail in the following chapters.

The urgency to reevaluate Africanness that emerged with Uganda's Independence in 1962 led to a renewed interest in traditional performing arts (Kubik 1968), which were regarded as instrumental in the construction of a national identity based on the harmonic coexistence of the different cultures in the country. During the 1960s, this process was common to several postcolonial African countries, among others Kenya (Franco 2015; Kiiru 2019), Senegal (Castaldi 2006), Malawi (Gilman 2009), Tanzania (Askew 2002: 13–14), and Zimbabwe (Turino 2008); while some decades earlier it had taken place in Latin America, for instance in Mexico (Hutchinson 2009; Shay 2002) and in Peru (Mendoza 2008). If these different experiences share the entanglement of nationalism with performing arts that were variously articulated as revival, institutionalization, or folklorization, the nationalist projects, actors, and types of institutions involved changed. Similar to the countries mentioned above, in Uganda the reevaluation of traditional performing arts was the result of the rejection of colonialism and search for African identity initiated by intellectuals and politicians in order to build a new independent nation. This project was necessarily multicultural, given the plurality of ethnicities enclosed in the national borders inherited from the colonial Protectorate. In Uganda, like in Kenya, it articulated through the top-down initiation of the teaching of traditional music and, later, dance in schools, as well as through the institution of a national school festival and a state ensemble. Although launched at a state level by politicians and intellectuals, these initiatives saw the deep involvement of local communities, who started to identify themselves in the genres indexed as representing their ethnicity, analogously to the situation that Turino (2008) described for Zimbabwe. Indeed, through the capillarity of school education and the national festival, the association of an ethnicity with one or more traditional genres strengthened and these genres became the symbols of the different local identities, and therefore fundamental to any claim for representation in the multicultural system of the country (Pier 2015).

Not only teachers and students but also local audiences and communities participated in the enthusiasm for the school festival, and the model of the national ensemble was copied locally by many groups that focused mostly on local musics and dances. The involvement of local communities and performers in the nationalist project through performing arts is comparable to other global cases, for instance to the folklorization of Cuzco repertoires in Peru. However, there the nationalist project was marked by the focus on Andean indigenous arts as symbols of national and possibly Pan-American identity (Mendoza 2008), while in Uganda the nation was interpreted as having been formed by a plurality of ethnicities represented by their traditional musics and dances. This is somewhat similar to the representation of national identity in Mexico that combines different indigenous groups, mestizos and Spanish expressions, although Mexican identity was built not through music school education and festivals, but mainly through the work of the national ensemble, the Ballet Folklórico de México, initiated by the dancer and choreographer Amalia Hernández (Hutchinson 2009; Shay 2002). Besides these points of connection and distance with other global experiences, it is worth considering more analytically how this became articulated in Uganda.

Music was at the center of the first attempts to capitalize on the great patrimony of traditional repertoires in the school system: local genres were mostly conceived of as instrument playing and singing, to the detriment of the dance and dramatic components integral to them. The European convention of music as separated from and of higher relevance than other Ugandan performing arts was rooted in the colonial and missionary disdain for dance (Mabingo 2017), and it influenced especially the early postcolonial time. In other parts of the world, like Indonesia, indigenous ontologies of performing arts were undermined in school education and the media, while in some contexts they continued to be understood and practiced as intertwined forms (Hood 2020). In 1964, the first music school was founded in Uganda, based at Makerere College in Kampala, and one year later the Teacher Training Department of the National Teachers' College in Kyambogo opened a music section, directed by British ethnomusicologist Peter Cooke. These two pivotal institutions paved the way for the inclusion of music in Ugandan schools. They were characterized by the teaching of both European and Ugandan music (the latter also taught about involving local musicians) and by candidate teachers' fieldwork in order to collect traditional music from their home areas (Cimardi 2019). A key figure in Ugandan music education has been the late Ugandan scholar Solomon Mbabi-Katana, who contributed greatly to the teaching of African repertoires in schools, both with his courses in Makerere University and Masindi Teachers' College and through his publications (Mbabi-Katana 1965, 1966, 1973, 1987, and 2002). The teaching of traditional music that he proposed was grounded on the classification of the repertoires, based on their culture of origin and their function; the simplification of intonation sometimes by assimilation to the European pitch system through transcriptions in the Tonic-Sol-Fa system; and the dramatization of the pieces in order to facilitate the pupils' comprehension of the meanings of the songs in different idioms. These features were later adopted in the Ugandan music syllabi, which registered minor changes until the 1990s, when all performing arts were formally included in school curricula and unified under the name "Music, Dance, and Drama."

In parallel with the flowering of music education, a national school festival of performing arts developed. Unlike in other East African countries, where national festivals followed on from the precolonial heritage of *ngoma* music and dance competitions (Gunderson and Barz 2000; Ranger 1975), in Uganda similar events are documented only in some northern areas of the country (Cooke and Dokotum 2000). The Ministry of Education of independent Uganda established the school festival of music, dance, and drama in 1962 (Nanyonga-Tamusuza 2003 and 2005; Pier 2015: 68–79) building on the model of the Anglican Namirembe Music Festival that since the 1940s had also included traditional local singing (Wachsmann 1946 and 1954: 43–44). The new annual festival was based on the principle of competitive selection as in Namirembe, and it also involved instrumental music and singing (Pier 2009: 50–51); later it expanded to include other categories such as dance and drama. Furthermore the national festival, also known as the school competition, was open to all the schools in the country—later on, participation became compulsory. Similar to the inclusion of music in higher education institutions and schools, the festival comprised both European and local categories. Its main purpose was to preserve and reevaluate local performing arts by training the pupils in their native musical traditions, but also, in a nation-building vision, to foster reciprocal knowledge and respect among the various cultures of the country. For this reason, in a progressive selection process from the county up to the national level, pupils came to meet pupils from different regions of Uganda (Pier 2009: 25–32).[5]

The need to rate performances as diverse as the various cultures of Uganda led not only to the formation of evaluation paradigms according to each category (e.g., traditional folk song, traditional folk dance, etc.), but also to the codification of the repertoires in a joint action with the research on performing arts going on in higher education institutions (Pier 2009: 31). This process took two main directions. On the one hand, the traditional repertoires of each ethnic group were classified according to their function and codified on the basis of their main formal characteristics, as well as adapted to the context of education by both mediating contents to make them relevant to students and erasing the sexual meaning of some repertoires (Nanyonga-Tamusuza 2003 and 2005). This process of codifying traditional repertoires in a conservative way, in particular eschewing elements connected to sexuality, is common to other postcolonial contexts, such as East Java (Sunardi 2015). On the other hand, the way was made

---

5   The idea that every ethnic group in the country, by then identified as "tribes," had a set of unique performing arts was inherited from the colonial ethnographic approach, which unequivocally connected one people to one culture (Cimardi 2015 and 2017b; Pier 2015: 76–77).

22 ❧ INTRODUCTION

for innovations that could "improve" the performances, by enhancing their spectacularity through creative melodies, patterns, dance figures, and formations and by bolstering their hold on the audience through the development of a narrative and the theatrical adaptation of the rendition (Cimardi 2019). Today, the two polarities of traditionalism and creativity are integrated into the school festival, and the organizers, teachers, pupils, and audiences perceive them as fundamental characteristics of the institution of the festival. Shaped by both the education system and the school festival, the concept of MDD is thus marked by authenticity, referring to the genuine local repertoires and traditions, and innovation, creating new appealing ways of presenting culture on the stage. This dynamic understanding of MDD underlies the definition by Ugandan dance scholar Alfdaniels Mabingo (2020a: 232) of Ugandan "cultural heritage dances" as "forms of dance with originations in Indigenous practices, which have continued to be adapted to emerging environments and spaces beyond their native environments of enaction." This vision also resonates with similar experiences in neighboring countries, particularly in Kenya where a similar competitive festival system developed (Kiiru 2017). More broadly, it also echoes the complex processes going on across the Atlantic, in South America, in the staging of tradition through the shift from participatory to presentational paradigms that involve postcolonial practices of hybridization to negotiate between tradition and transformation (Garcia Canclini 2005; Mendoza 2008). I discuss the standardization and parallel innovations introduced through the national school festival in Ugandan repertoires (especially in relation to *runyege*) throughout the following chapters.

A number of the best pupils who take part in the school festival go on to join one of the semiprofessional ensembles, normally called "cultural groups," which are popular all over Uganda. This kind of formation is common in most African countries and was modeled on Les Ballets Nationals of Guinea, which since the 1960s has been emulated in Uganda by the state ensemble Heartbeat of Africa (Hanna and Hanna 1968).[6] Indeed, in the

---

6   Anthony Shay (2002: 85–86) argues that, in contrast to Western ensembles of music and dance, the Soviet Moiseyev state company's representational strategies, which included non-European ethnicities and portrayed them in a positive light, resonated with the cultural and political concerns of the elites in postcolonial countries. For this reason, according to Shay, since the 1950s the Moiseyev state company was taken as a model for the foundation of national ensembles in countries of the Global South, including West African nations. Concerning the Ugandan national ensemble, besides the direct model of the Guinean national ballet, a clear reference to Moiseyev's model is not easy to retrace, although during its international tours—in the 1960s one of them involved the USSR (Hanna and Hanna 1968)—the Ugandan Heartbeat of

years immediately preceding and following Independence, in many African countries, state ensembles were founded as part of nation-building projects, such as in Malawi (Gilman 2009: 33–36), Senegal (Castaldi 2006), Kenya (Franco 2015; Kiiru 2019), and Zimbabwe (Turino 2008). Although these national ensembles were all characterized by the transformation of participatory repertoires in representational forms for the stage, different historical processes and political agendas of the nation states molded the specific directions taken by these projects. For instance, in colonial Zimbabwe the performances of spontaneous regional associations based in Harare township created the basis for indexically associating a social group with a musical tradition, which was then solidified through the broadcast of these associations' recordings promoted by the colonial government. These associations were later promoted in the rallies of the main nationalist party, where "in addition to being indices of their original regions, the various indigenous dances began to be associated with each other as a canon of 'traditional Zimbabwean dance'" (Turino 2008: 146). This canon was then taken over by the establishment of a professional state troupe performing different regional dances that came to be considered "national" dances. Zimbabwe and Uganda had a comparable system of indexing of ethnicity or region and traditional genre, and a similar national ensemble representing the cultural mosaic of the nation, based on the "rainbow ethnicity" paradigm adopted in several state dance ensembles globally (Shay 2002: 5). However, in Zimbabwe this process evolved differently from in Uganda because the indexing of ethnicity and traditional repertoires crystallized mainly through recordings and later political rallies in the former, instead of school education and festivals, as in the latter.

Considered the heir of the first state ensemble and the most popular cultural group in Uganda, the professional Ndere Troupe is today based in the capital city Kampala, where it manages its own cultural center. The Ndere Troupe includes performers from different areas of the country and in its colorful and carefully staged shows, mainly attended by tourists and wealthy Ugandans, it portrays the variety of Ugandan cultures through the staging of highly rehearsed and polished local dances (Asaasira 2015). Although internationally the Ndere Troupe is the representation of Uganda as a multicultural nation, domestically it is still perceived as showcasing, with a high degree of professionalism, the various local repertoires, in contrast to the Zimbabwean ensemble where a national dimension seems to overcome a regional one (Turino 2008).

Africa surely came in contact with other state ensembles, from which it might have drawn inspirations and models.

24 ❧ INTRODUCTION

The number of cultural groups that originated from the model of the Ugandan national ensemble increased constantly, even during the 1980s, despite the political instability of the country. Since the 1990s, cultural groups have flourished even more due to renewed national security, the cultural revival initiated by the restoration of traditional monarchies, and the possibilities of partnerships with NGOs (Barz 2006; Cooke and Kasule 1999). Besides participating in social and health projects promoted by these organizations, cultural groups are normally hired to perform at occasions like weddings, graduation parties, and the launching of new initiatives; the most successful among them even manage to hold weekly performances for a paying audience. In Bunyoro and Tooro, the repertoires of semiprofessional groups consist more of local dances, like *runyege*, than songs or instrumental music, but their shows also include pieces from other regions, as well as sketches and performances based on played-back pop music.

Unlike Buganda, where royal *baakisimba* can be danced in festivals (Nanyonga-Tamusuza 2005), in Bunyoro and Tooro neither the school festival nor the cultural groups normally perform repertoires connected to the kingship: royal music and dance are intended for the king and thus they are not meant to be performed in unrelated contexts. Although some attempts have been made to introduce royal music into performances by schools and cultural groups, the results have been limited and short-lived. In fact, the reintroduction of royal music after the restoration of the kingdoms has been conservative and based on the repatriation of old recordings (Kahunde 2012b). In this context, Nyoro and Tooro traditional music and dance performed at festivals and by cultural groups constitute both the space for and the matter of the discourse about the local culture in the contemporary arena. Traditional music and dance configure as dense aggregates of ideas, practices, perceptions, conventions, and discourses that navigate local, as well as national, perspectives, power centers, and interests. On stage, representations of local culture and gender are shaped, negotiated, and promoted.

Uganda as an Ethnomusicology Workshop: International Fame and Internal Impact

Focusing on performing arts in Bunyoro and Tooro, my interest in music and dance outside the royal context could not rely much on literature or previous documentation. Indeed, despite the cultural and historical relevance of western regions in Uganda, no in-depth research about Nyoro and Tooro repertoires has been carried out in the past. Besides Mbabi-Katana's booklet on *makondeere* side-blown trumpets used in royal ceremonies (Mbabi-Katana 1982) and the recent research by Nyoro ethnomusicologist Samuel

Kahunde on the revival of royal music (Kahunde 2012a and 2012b), only the recordings by Klaus Wachsmann, Hugh Tracey, and Peter Cooke document local musical traditions, mostly those related to the royal context.[7]

Klaus Wachsmann was among the first ethnomusicologists to conduct research in Uganda. Thanks to his role as director of the Uganda Museum, he carried out a vast campaign all over the country (1949–1954), producing more than 1500 recordings. Parallel results of his campaign were several photographs, some silent films, and the collection of musical instruments preserved by the Uganda Museum (Wachsmann 1956). Partly overlapping with Wachsmann's recording campaign was the one directed by South-African ethnomusicologist Hugh Tracey (1950–1952). Peter R. Cooke's research in Uganda spanned several decades, from the mid-1960s (with a far-reaching recording campaign between 1963 and 1968) until the 2000s. Cooke conducted research mainly in central Uganda, but also in the north and west of the country. Both Tracey and Wachsmann concentrated their attention on instrumental music and organology and privileged royal repertoires (Tracey 1958 and 1969; Wachsmann 1953), while Cooke's recordings feature more music and dance genres not connected to the kingship.

A focus on instrumental music has, in fact, characterized scholarship in Uganda. Since the 1950s, numerous researchers focused on the study of indigenous musical instruments, with special attention given to xylophone (*amadinda* and *akadinda*) music and royal repertoires (Anderson 1967; Cooke 1970, 1971, 1995, and 1996; Kubik 1960, 1962, 1964, 1969, 1985, 1992, and 2007; Wachsmann 1954, 1961, 1964, and 1971; Wegner 1990, 1993, and 1995). Thanks to the impact of these works, Uganda has become a sort of workshop for ethnomusicology on the African continent. Here, the discipline developed working tools, elaborated analytical interpretations, contributed to the study of musical instruments, and identified important investigation topics. The variety and complexity of Ganda and Soga instrumental repertoires and royal musicians' virtuosity, as well as the presence of xylophone traditions in other areas of the country that offered the possibility of comparison, certainly accounts for the amount of ethnomusicological scholarship on Buganda and Busoga. Also, the adaptability of Ganda and Soga xylophone music to a class environment (requiring at least two or three players per instrument) and to different levels of proficiency marked its success as a practical ethnomusicological course. In fact, xylophone music from Uganda, and Buganda-Busoga in particular, has today become part of the ethnomusicological canon and is taught in several universities in Europe and North America, along with West African drums and the Indonesian gamelan.

---

7   For more information about these three collections and the historical recordings from Bunyoro and Tooro, see Appendix II.

26 &❧ INTRODUCTION

However, the research focus on Ganda and Soga music together with the paucity of interest in the repertoires of other areas seems also to retrace the heritage of colonialism in the consideration of Ugandan societies and cultures, where Baganda were granted special treatment by the British and their territorial administration was chosen as the model for the indirect rule of the Protectorate (Fallers 1961; Johannessen 2006; Mazrui 1970). David Pier (2009: 10) also highlighted a lack of investigation of the power dynamics (not limited to the colonial period, but also involving postcolonial and present neoliberal times) in which ethnomusicological studies developed in Uganda. This resonates with Kofi Agawu's (2003) depiction of ethnomusicology as a child of colonialism, which follows, more or less consciously, the preferences and stereotypes imposed during the colonial period.

Notwithstanding the impressive and valuable literature on Ugandan music, several areas of the country did not attract academic attention until recently. This is the case of northern Uganda, which was ravaged by brutal guerrilla raiders led by the insurgent Lord Resistance Army (LRA) from the late 1980s to the end of the 2000s, when the rebels moved their incursions to neighboring countries. Only since the 2010s have new researches been conducted in the north of the country, especially among the Acholi population (Kibirige 2020; McClain Opiyo 2015). In Bunyoro and Tooro, the academic focus on instrumental and royal repertoires meant the undermining of vocal music and dance, and consequently a misrepresentation of women, who traditionally did not play musical instruments but sang and danced. My work addresses this bias and investigates how genders—normative manhood and womanhood, as well as alternative masculinities and femininities—shape and are shaped through traditional performing arts.

Positioning in and after the Field

Before introducing the different chapters of this book, it is necessary for me to discuss my own positionality, because my characteristics account for (most of) the knowledge I could gather, especially through fieldwork. In the field, I focused on presenting myself positively in order to be accepted by the community and the persons with whom I wanted to interact. To this end, I spontaneously adopted an attitude of modesty and self-deprecation, which specifically marked my position as a learner in need of others' availability for interviews and help in teaching me to dance and play the drums. This attitude was welcomed, but I soon understood that my gender and race were critical in defining my position in the field. As a young unmarried woman, gender (in connection with my age and marital status at the time) seemed to impose what I perceived as limitations on freedom of behavior and autonomy in conducting research, while as a white visiting scholar my race (also in relation to my education and status as a foreign guest) mitigated the strict application of some of those norms to me. Indeed, my whiteness and position as a visitor assigned me a high status—which I felt was forged by both the persistent effects of coloniality and old customs of hospitality— that allowed me flexibility when adopting (restrictive) expected behavior.

Thanks especially to Issa and Stephen, I understood that a number of "respectful" behaviors define a "good woman" in Bunyoro and Tooro. Women "are not supposed to" sit on a mat with their legs crossed, talk to men openly and directly in a confident way, whistle, leap over drainage ditches to cross the road, ride a bike, or climb a tree. On the other hand, they "are supposed to" dress, or more exactly to be covered, in a certain way (a knee-length skirt, a shirt that completely covers the belly and the sides), sit properly (with legs to the side), "show respect" to men and elders (kneeling to greet them, responding to their solicitations with shy tones, etc.).

The way these customs were conveyed to me in English through the phrase "(not) supposed to" surprised me. I was not told "you cannot" or "you are not allowed," probably because that would be considered too impolite toward a guest. Also, Issa and Stephen did not use the generic though authoritative "women do not" to describe women's gendered behaviors, possibly because they understood that "women do not" could have no specific meaning to a foreigner. All in all, the chosen expression "women are (not) supposed to" sounded to me like a mandate from a behavioral code referring to cultural customs and was also morally connoted: not respecting the prescribed behaviors would cause annoyance and disapproval.

Entering in the field involved, among other things, adapting my body (through posture and clothes) and my behavior (by being less physically dynamic) to fit the model of conduct prescribed for women. At the same time, my position in the field was also marked by race, being a white European, and by status as a foreign researcher having a higher education. These other characteristics allowed me to negotiate some of the expectations of my interlocutors, in particular, because of the status assigned me, I could be assertive in conversations and interviews.

Also, when discussing playing wind instruments or drums (especially the long cylindrical drum *ngaabi*) and dancing with leg rattles, my participants said that "women are not supposed" to do these activities, which are traditionally limited to men. Nowadays, especially through the school festival, the society is more flexible, so girls can and do play pipes, sometimes play the drums, and dance with rattles. However, these practices are not common in semiprofessional ensembles composed of both male and female adults: this flexibility applies to girls in schools (especially when no boys are available) but only in very limited ways to adult women. Indeed, when I myself wanted

28 &. INTRODUCTION

to learn the basics of drumming and rattle dancing, it caused some uneasiness. Several of my encounters with instructors, performers, and groups took place in the open air, mostly in bright and spacious compounds, and the sound of instruments or the rumor that a visitor was around usually attracted neighbors and passersby. The curiosity of seeing what was going on was often accompanied by the chuckling of the gathered watchers when I asked to play the drums and dance with rattles, or when I attempted to do so. While these things are unusual for a woman, nobody said I could not try them; I did, however, feel that it was perceived as being rather odd, not only because of my gender but also because of my race, since a white woman performing was a totally unexpected and uncommon view. Certainly, my standing as a white visiting scholar had some bearing upon my research participants' willingness to help me and facilitated my teachers' kind availability to teach me drumming and men's *runyege*. However, my teachers' attitude (as well as the attitudes of other observers) was veiled by curiosity and hilarity that was not solely connected to the strangeness of a white person playing local drums or performing local dances. I realized that the expectations of my success in performing were quite low: my female body was deemed not strong and resistant enough to sustain drumming and rattling. As I could retrace several other times, the prescription "women are not supposed to" was accompanied by an explanation based on biological assumptions about the possibilities of male and female bodies. Together with culture, "nature" is evoked to explain social and musical divisions that mark roles in society as well as in performing arts, as will emerge clearly in the following chapters. My positioned learning experience hence became instructive not only in order to understand musical and choreutic structures but also to experience and navigate how gender categories are constructed and negotiated.

The reflexivity accompanying my fieldwork was greatly stimulated by conversations with my research assistants. Cooperating with Issa, we developed—from our different positions—a focused mindfulness of the Nyoro society and culture. As an insider and a worker in the social and health field in western Uganda, Issa contributed through our countless discussions on my research to the substance and depth of my understanding of community and relational dynamics at the basis of Nyoro social phenomena and gender issues. On the other hand, he told me that, since our first collaboration, he experienced and understood some local customs and music genres differently than he had done before, when he took them for granted. Indeed, by answering my naïve or critical questions and discussing the encounters we had together in the field, he began to reflect on the meaning of some Nyoro traditions, cultural expectations, and music. Thanks to our shared reflexivity, I was able to investigate, negotiate, and understand the knowledge I gained, especially about gender and postcoloniality.

During our work together, Stephen became also my partner for the last two years of my research in Uganda, and, besides the personal value attached to it, our relationship as a couple afforded me greater insights into the complex negotiations inherent in gender relations. In both our research and romantic relationships, these negotiations revolved mainly around the uneasiness connected not only with linguistic and cultural challenges, but also with our uneven power positions in conducting interviews and recordings. This brought to the fore our different gender expectations and behaviors while meeting research participants and regarding the diverse roles and competence in leading conversations or technically executing recordings. Aware of the potential complications and pitfalls of relationships developing in the field that are described in the literature (Kulick and Willson 2015), I do not think that this relationship negatively influenced my fieldwork; to the contrary, it was an opportunity for personal, couple, and scientific growth. Furthermore, the fact that our relationship was not shown openly, as is common among unmarried couples in Uganda, helped to deepen our private conversations around the problems we faced in public and contributed greatly to my reflections on gender expectations and intersectionality in couple relations.

My positionality is relevant also in the writing process. I am mindful of the challenges of representation that this work entails, given my external position to Ugandan society and my status as a white European from a former colonial power, especially in consideration of the recent shift in the field of ethnomusicology stimulated by Danielle Brown's 2020 open letter on racism and colonialism in the study of music. In writing this book, I tried to strike a balance between giving space to local voices, stances, and understandings and presenting my own interpretations of musical, cultural, and gender issues—interpretations that I do not want to overshadow different local understandings. In this perspective, I followed Sarah Weiss's (2006: 8) approach of reporting the direct words and stories of research participants with their plural and sometimes contradictory views, as well as other sources that the reader can interpret directly with the aim of "avoiding a monologic exegesis"—the common risk of scholars writing about people other than themselves, especially when there is a power imbalance between the researcher and the participants. Although in several parts of my work I generalized some descriptions or reported research participants' normative illustrations in order to discuss and theorize widespread phenomena and practices, I also foregrounded my ethnographic experience, following Jane Sugarman's (1997: 36–37) example that allowed her to represent the various individualities emerging from the field and reduce exoticizing in writing. Ellen Koskoff's (2014: 102–103; 139) reflections on the endeavors of ethnomusicological writing on gender in portraying the different and mobile

30 &❧ INTRODUCTION

positionalities of the scholar and the participants as they interact in the field as well as in the interpretation that the researcher gives as an author guided me in describing, reporting, and interpreting. I am aware that the representation I give cannot be complete and that in the end it is the result of my own understanding and hence it may not be shared by all my research participants. I hope, however, that in reporting and describing multiple voices, performances, and phenomena I managed to give the readers at least an impression of the complexity of the interrelation between gender, performing arts, and local culture in western Uganda.

A Path across Traditional Performing Arts

The various components of the constellation of Nyoro and Tooro performing arts—singing, instrument playing, dancing, and acting—comprise my investigation of local culture and gender in western Uganda in the following chapters. In chapter 1, I use the genre *runyege* to illustrate the intermedial nature of the performing arts among the Banyoro and Batooro. The current performing arts scene in Uganda includes singing, instrument playing, dancing, and acting, and I briefly explore how these different components are bound together with ideas and perceptions of gender. I then weave together historical and ethnographic data to demonstrate the ways in which gender conceptions have changed from precolonial times to twenty-first century Uganda.

In chapter 2, I focus on singing, in particular wedding and work songs, through which I navigate the internal divisions between repertoires for women and men. Moving between the past as remembered and retold by elders and my ethnographic experience in the field, I work to extract the main stylistic traits as well as information about the roles and expectations for men and women in society, which emerge as strictly binary.

Chapter 3 is dedicated to instrument playing with a comparison between the old practice, documented by historical recordings and elders' memories, and the current one, mainly represented by school and ensembles' performances. I concentrate in particular on drums and their embedded masculinity, which has transformed over time through the opening up of drumming to girls and women.

In chapter 4, I present an analysis of *runyege*'s two separate dance parts, based on different local narratives. Furthermore, I explore the ways in which binary gender notions and expectations are encoded in movement, from basic steps to creative stage figures, both individually and through the physical interactions between couples. By drawing widely on interviews and discussions with dancers, dance teachers, and audience members, I show how local gender conceptions emerge as grounded in the narratives, interpretations, perceptions, and embodiment of the dance itself. It is through the national school festival that many, perhaps most, young Ugandans engage with traditional culture, and in this arena the meaning and style of traditional performances are conveyed through various theatrical paradigms.

In chapter 5, I analyze narration in singing (composing a story that binds together different songs) and representation in dance (recreating gendered and courtship dynamics through creative dance figures and acting) as fundamental performing devices used to reproduce discourses about tradition and gender in the school festival.

Chapter 6 looks at how these theatrical paradigms are applied in the performances of semiprofessional ensembles and highlights how in *runyege* dancing both a normative discourse about gender and a conterdiscourse contemplating alternative masculinities and femininities find their space of expression.

In the postlude, I recapitulate the articulation and interconnectedness of gender and performing arts in western Uganda and I consider the present negotiations in music, dance, and drama (MDD) from a postcolonial perspective by recontextualizing them within the stark contemporary debate about gender across Ugandan society.

Chapter One

"Traditional Dance Preserves Culture and Shows People How to Behave"

Runyege, MDD, and Gender

"Traditional dance preserves culture and shows people how to behave." This was a fairly typical answer to the question "What do you think about traditional music and dance?" from an anonymous questionnaire that I submitted to S6 Kibiito Secondary School students (Fort Portal, September 14, 2011).[1] In the summer of 2011, as part of my fieldwork, I decided to collect information from among the Nyoro and Tooro youth about their perceptions of and opinions on traditional repertoires and gender relations. It was important to explore the perceptions of young people, who primarily learn these repertoires in school, to counterbalance the data I had collected from elders, who still remembered songs and *runyege* as performed in the villages. In fact, the population of Uganda is composed mainly of young people: in 2020, 46% of Ugandans were under the age of 14[2] and most of them have learned, or are learning, traditional repertoires at school, especially by participating in the school festival, or through cultural groups, by watching their shows or actively performing. This answer given by one secondary school student is especially significant because it clearly connects the issue of attachment to local culture with the notion of proper behavior. What consistently emerged from the students' responses, as well as in

---

1   With the agreement of the teachers, I presented the questionnaire in schools in Bunyoro and Tooro, to be completed by students outside class time. The students could choose whether to participate and, to avoid any possible discrimination or bullying, the questionnaire was anonymous. After reading the responses, I had an open group conversation with the students involved to expand some of their answers and discuss recurring themes.

2   https://www.statista.com/statistics/447698/age-structure-in-uganda/ (accessed on December 23, 2021).

interviews and conversations with other research participants, was the perception of traditional performing arts as being fundamental heritage conveying the customs (including language, clothing, staple foods, social activities, and good manners) of local cultures. This is indeed the approach that informs the pedagogical philosophy of several teachers who consider traditional dances as the basis through which to pass on traditional culture (Mabingo 2017). The representativeness of local culture and the identitarian attachment to it is essential in the multiethnic Ugandan context where, drawing on the colonial legacy of identification of ethnicities later implemented in the performing arts through the schools' festival institution, every culture or ethnicity is believed to have specific performing arts that connote it (Cimardi 2015 and 2017b; Pier 2015). Furthermore, when discussing the focus on behavior in relation to traditional repertoires with students, most of their comments concerning "proper manners" and "good morals" referred to the seemly conduct expected of women, in terms of clothes, appropriate ways of greeting, and showing respect to men; there were also comments directed at men, to do with the payment of the traditional bridewealth and providing economically for the family. These elements implied a critique of the present in relation to the past as portrayed in traditional MDD, where women were properly "covered" in their long skirts, knelt while greeting men and elders, and respected their husband's decisions, while men gave several expensive goods to the bride's family and were caring breadwinners. As in Ugandan public discussion, most of the tensions related to behavior emerging from the questionnaires concerned gender relations and the positive model of local culture was contrasted with the perceived corrupted present. Significantly, these anxieties about good gendered behavior appeared in discussions with students on traditional MDD; in fact, gender crosses many aspects of the performing arts, at the same time structuring them and being represented by them.

This chapter discusses the connections between performing arts and gender in western Uganda. In the first part of the chapter, I present the multiple dimensions of MDD as they are articulated within *runyege* by describing the multifaceted nature of this genre, which comprises the playing of instruments, singing, dancing, and theatre. Notwithstanding the intermediality of *runyege* where all the various performing components are interconnected, I progressively introduce each one of them, in order to analyze their role within the genre and show their relation to gender models. In exploring one of the narratives about *runyege*'s origins, I report its historical roots that consistently show the pervasiveness of gender conceptions, as well as the persistent value of this genre in contemporary western Uganda. Gender structures *runyege* through the divisions of the roles in singing, dancing, and instrument playing; at the same time, the genre conveys the representation

34 CHAPTER ONE

of what are considered as traditional gender models, although spaces for negotiation and performers' agency are also there (see in particular chapter 6). In the second part of the chapter, I focus on gender and I weave together historical and ethnographic data to demonstrate the ways in which gender conceptions have changed from precolonial times to twenty-first century Uganda. From historical sources, as well as from scholarly work about women and on homosexuality, a variety of performances of gender connoting the precolonial times comes to light, while the gender model established during the colonial era is strictly binary and heteronormative. The effect of the Victorian morality of the colonial period extended to post-Independence and, I argue, that gender binary is today perceived as traditional and local. It is mainly this idea of gender that is conveyed, represented and, at the same time, strengthened through the practice of performing arts, such as *runyege*.

Runyege as a Paradigm of Performing Arts in Bunyoro and Tooro

While the idea of MDD is inherent in the national policies on performing arts, especially through the national school festival, the concept is also employed locally by the actors involved in education and semiprofessional troupes. Along with MDD, they often also use denominations in the local language, Runyoro-Rutooro. The word *kizina* (pl. *bizina*) defines a musical piece, be it a song or an instrumental piece. This unique word shows the close relationship between vocal and instrumental repertoires: the latter are normally derived from the sung melodies. However, the related verbs are different: to sing is expressed with *kuzina*,[3] but to play an instrument is *kuteera*, whose first meaning is "to beat," revealing a percussive conception of instrumental practice.[4] Besides singing, *kuzina* also means to dance and the noun *mazina* indicates a dance.

The semantic areas referring to singing, playing, and dancing partially overlap as verbs and nouns, and they appear as an articulated cluster that cannot be reduced to the eurogenic dichotomous ideas of music and dance (Fig. 1.1). In this frame of interconnected words, the third element of MDD,

---

3   In Tooro, I also came across the verb *kujenga* referring exclusively to singing Huma male repertoires, in particular the songs for cattle, as reported also by Davis (1938: 54).

4   Klaus Wachsmann (1954: 1–2) considered the contrast between instrumental melodies interpreted as speech (because of the local tonal languages that deeply shape melodies) and rhythmic patterns based on "a physical experience" to be widespread in Uganda.

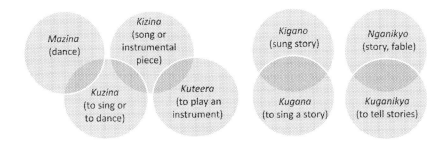

Figure 1.1. The semantic areas of singing, instrument playing, dancing, and storytelling.

drama, seems not to fit. Indeed, I could not find a translation or a similar concept in Runyoro-Rutooro. However, traditional sung stories, *bigano* (sing. *kigano*), combine singing with storytelling and enhance the narration and impersonation of characters through music. *Bigano* are entirely sung stories, usually in a call-and-response form, with no use of speech. Similar to, but distinct from, *bigano* are the *nganikyo* tales (sing. *ruganikyo*) that also contain a song, which normally has an important dramaturgic function in the plot. It is through storytelling, which combines narration and singing, that drama is understood to be part of the constellation of arts that, at a national level, is labeled as MDD.

The multiple dimensions of MDD are present in *runyege*, which is paradigmatic of the entwined knots binding together not only the various performing arts, but also gender in contemporary Uganda. Indeed, in *runyege* all instruments are traditionally played by men, while the singing is mostly performed by women. Furthermore, the *runyege* dance is characterized by two distinct parts for women and men dancers, the latter wearing the typical leg rattles (*binyege*, sing. *kinyege*) that make this genre immediately recognizable all over Uganda. Finally, the narrative dimension of *runyege* includes gendered interaction in the formation of couples.

Although *runyege* is not the only traditional genre in the region displaying these characteristics (see chapter 4), there are several reasons why I chose to focus on it. First, *Runyege* is certainly the most renowned music and dance genre from western Uganda, at both the local and the national level. It was usually mentioned in the interviews and conversations that I had in the field as being the most typical genre of the region and is frequently performed by local school groups, as well as by folk groups from both western Uganda and other parts of the country. This means that there are frequent opportunities to collect information about *runyege* and attend performances of it, which allowed

36 &❧ CHAPTER ONE

me to gather consistent documentation. Second, *runyege* is a genre shared, with some minor variations, by the Banyoro and Batooro and it is identified as Nyoro/Tooro throughout the country. In this sense, it can be seen as a means to investigate the processes involved in defining traditional repertoires among ethnicities that identify themselves as different in the national arena. The Banyoro and Batooro take a great pride in *runyege* as the distinctive genre of culture of the region, and this stance emerged several times during my field-work when research participants located this genre in the national landscape, as well as when they positioned it in relation to the wider music and dance genres available today in Uganda. Fundamental in the contemporary value given to *runyege* is its consideration as a repository of the local culture of the Banyoro and Batooro. This local culture finds, in my opinion, one of its main expressions in the representation and practice of gender.

Gender conceptions intersect in *runyege* in multiple ways and they are shaped by collective discourses, performance practices, representation conventions, and individual understanding and interpretations. To investigate these diverse levels, in the first part of this chapter I introduce the various components of *runyege*: instrumental accompaniment, dancing, acting, and singing.

Nyege—in Various Ways

The use of *binyege* leg rattles by male dancers was first documented in a photograph from the early twentieth century report by Albert B. Lloyd (1907; Fig. 1.4) describing his "adventures" along the Nile River. *Binyege* are leg rattles composed of a series (from four to six) of seed-shells lined on sticks and held together by a semiflexible structure of leather thongs or cloth, which allows the dancer to tie them around his calf, above the ankle and below the knee (Wachsmann 1953: 324 and 334). The energetic stamped steps of the men's dance make the *binyege* rattles resonate and thus mark the rhythmic accompaniment of the *runyege* dance.

The fruit from which the rattles are made is also called *kinyege* and it is produced by the *munyege* tree (*Oncoba routledgei*). The performer, instructor, and instrument maker Christopher Magezi from Bunyoro explained to me how *binyege* are made (int. Magezi: March 1, 2008). The *munyege* fruits (Fig. 1.2) are boiled, hollowed out through two holes carved on opposite sides, and then dried. Then, the hard seeds of the native plant locally called *maranga* (*Canna indica*, Fig. 1.2) are put inside the dried fruit. After that, other cuts are made on the external surface of the *munyege* to boost the sound. Finally, thin wooden sticks are inserted through the holes in the dried fruits, to hold the lines of rattles together, which are then connected to form the leg rattle (Fig. 1.3).

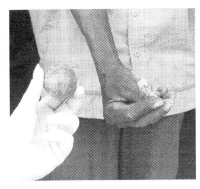 

Figure 1.2. Left: the round *munyege* fruit and the flower ovary containing the *maranga* seeds. Right: the *maranga* plant (*Canna indica*).

Figure 1.3. Christopher Magezi in his workshop holding *binyege* rattles. Hoima (Bunyoro), 2008.

As in the past, musical instruments are today made by men. These include not only the *binyege* rattles, which are indispensable in *runyege*, but also the other instruments used in the accompaniment, which today includes three drums, and sometimes the *ndingidi* one-string fiddle and *ngwara* side-blown trumpets (these latter instruments are played in Bunyoro only). Whereas drum construction requires a craft specialization (Roscoe 1923: 228–229), according to Magezi no advanced skills are needed to produce *binyege* and the necessary raw materials are native to the area and readily available. For this reason, in the past it was the norm that the (male) musicians built their

38 &❧ CHAPTER ONE

own instruments. Today, because of the professionalization of instrument building as part of craftsmanship, this is no longer so, and most performers buy their instruments. On the other hand, it is common that the craftsmen specializing in musical instruments are also musicians, as well as music instructors in schools and ensembles, like Magezi.

The various instruments used in *runyege* were traditionally played only by men, but the use of *ndingidi* and drums has become more open to girls and women (see chapter 3). This notwithstanding, I have never met or even heard of a female instrument maker, not even for the *binyege* rattles, which do not require special expertise. Indeed, the building, playing, and teaching of musical instruments are traditionally, and mostly still remain, a male domain. In particular, *binyege* are strongly characterized as manly instruments and they are an essential part of the men's dance costume. Tying together *runyege* rhythmic accompaniment and dance, *binyege* are considered masculine because it is traditionally deemed that only men possess the strength and stamina required to stamp and jump in *runyege*, making the rattles resonate.[5] Indeed, female bodies are considered too weak and delicate to perform such powerful movements: the manly tradition associated with musical instruments is thus reinforced by the argument of sex-connoted physical characteristics, which supports an exclusivity of use determined by gender, a feature that can be found cross-culturally (Doubleday 2008; Koskoff 2014).

A Love and Courtship Dance

Runyege is normally described as a dance (*mazina*) and—similar to other contexts like Malawi (Gilman 2009: 13), where dance is chosen as a denomination condensing different performing arts—the dance component seems to be of greater importance than singing and music playing (*kizina*) in defining the genre. Several traditional music and dance repertoires in Uganda are labeled as "dance"; and dance, with its visual, motion, and aural elements, seems to absorb most of the attention of both the performers and the audience. Today, *runyege* is commonly presented, locally as well as in the national arena, as "a love and courtship dance." This characterization is reinforced by the plot followed by most *runyege* performances: after the initial joyful collective dancing, the men display their skills and vigor in dancing to win the women's hearts, who respond to their solicitations with a gentle and flexible dance, and finally, couples are formed. Courtship in *runyege* can be seen as the articulation of a dual action: the men's ostentation in displaying their

---

5   A similar concept characterizes the *esyonzhoga* rattles of the Banande of eastern Congo (Facci 2003).

Figure 1.4. A photograph of "a Nyoro dance" (Lloyd 1907). Men and women are arranged in opposite lines and *binyege* leg rattles are worn by male dancers.

abilities and beguiling their chosen partner, and the women's initially shy and flattered and later openly joyful dancing in response to this cajolement.

The earliest visual documentation of *runyege* is most probably the earlier-mentioned photograph from the early twentieth century (Lloyd 1907; Fig. 1.4), in which *binyege* rattles can also be seen. Here, a row of men and a row of women dance while facing each other, suggesting a dance dynamic related to gender. However, the dancers seem to be adults, not young people involved in courtship. Magezi (int. June 29, 2011) remembered that anyone stirred by the moment of celebration could join a *runyege* dance, including married people. This suggests that *runyege* was not exclusively reserved for young people as a way to meet a partner, although this could happen.

The English description of *runyege* as being "a love and courtship dance" was echoed by my research participants, from musical experts to schoolchildren, and from music teachers to performers (int. Kagaba: May 11, 2011; int. Majara: August 12, 2009; int. Nyegenya: August 18, 2018; int. Kabutuku: August 30, 2018). However, I was not able to find an equivalent of "courtship" or a similar concept in the local language that would deliver

40 ❧ CHAPTER ONE

an analog meaning in Runyoro-Rutooro.[6] This suggests that this description of *runyege* could have emerged as a way to present the genre to foreigners, not Runyoro-Rutooro speakers, or in contexts (like schools and higher education institutions) where English is the current idiom. Indeed, the performance practice of this genre has progressively moved away from the participative performance context of the village and has adapted to new settings, such as school festivals and the variety of venues and occasions where cultural groups provide entertainment. The possible effect of this migration is that some of the meanings of *runyege* have been altered through a process of selection and adjustment. The teaching of this genre in schools has meant that, along with other Ugandan traditional repertoires labeled according to their most salient aspects, *runyege* was classified according to a typology principle. This classification, usually based on a eurogenic conception of dances, tended to flatten the multiple meanings of these genres by imprinting on them a univocal description. So, *runyege* was included in the category of "courtship dances," while other traditional genres were labeled as "war dances," "praise dances," or "initiation dances." At the same time, like other Ugandan repertoires (Nanyonga-Tamusuza 2003 and 2005), some of *runyege*'s content was adapted for young performers, by emphasizing the courtship element, as a sort of platonic ritual. In its new form the element of "love" remained implied (and sexuality unmentioned).

Since 2008, I have attended numerous *runyege* performances in very different contexts: school festivals at different levels of the competition, weddings, kingdom anniversaries, cultural receptions, shows in support of humanitarian and health projects, and touristic events. For many of these performances, I was also able to attend the rehearsals and so gained further insights into the modalities of staging *runyege*. In general, I was struck by the intensive formalization that courtship dynamics had in those performances: they regularly featured two rows of men and women facing each other, individual solos in the center of the stage, the progressive formation of couples, and a collective happy ending marked by speed and energy in couple dancing. Moreover, I observed that this development of *runyege* dance is the same as another genre connoted as a courtship dance, the *ekikebi* dance of the neighboring Bakonzo people (Facci 2009; Mbabazi 2003) and, more generally, a climax characterizes the final part of all dance performances in the current school festival.

---

6   Stephen Mugabo (int. August 31, 2018) suggested *mazina gw'okwegonza* as a translation of "dance of love." Davis' dictionary (1938: 125 and 260) includes *ngonzi* and *kugonza* as translations for "love," but no translation for "courtship."

This format of *runyege,* which involves the interaction of the dancers through courtship, is locally understood as a theatrical dynamic, as actions in a scene conveying dramatic content, as I discuss in more detail in chapter 5. In this sense, the theatre element is considered an integral part of *runyege,* together with music (instrumental and vocal) and dance. As an important part of the spectacularity of the performances, this dramatic component is a requirement for traditional repertoires in the national school festival and in *runyege* it has taken the form of a codified and accentuated courtship procedure.

Similar to other traditional genres that have undergone a process of revitalization or revival, elements of continuity with the past, as evidenced by photographic documents, and hints of recent changes, as suggested by present performance contexts and music teachers (int. Kabutuku: August 30, 2018; int. Nyegenya: August 18, 2018), appear to be tightly intertwined in *runyege.* In order to understand its development, I tried to trace its roots with the assistance of local music and dance experts.

Runyege in Emic Narratives: A Song in a Story

Among the several people I talked with about *runyege,* a few were able to offer an explanation of its origins. While the idea of a connection of *runyege* with blacksmith work (int. Nsamba: February 25, 2008 and July 31, 2009) emerged, it was not corroborated by other participants (int. Muhuruzi: February 27, 2008; int. Majara: August 12, 2009) on the basis that this interpretation relates only to the loud beating rhythms, and not to dance movements, besides the fact that *runyege* songs rarely refer to the work of blacksmiths. On the other hand, several traditional music experts pointed out that banana beer (called *tonto* or, less commonly, *marwa*) parties were occasions where *runyege* was most frequently performed and connected the dance movements to the actions necessary to prepare banana beer, in particular to the squeezing of bananas by stamping on them, a procedure not dissimilar to traditional Mediterranean grape crushing (int. Majara: August 12, 2009; int. Nyegenya: June 22, 2011; int. Magezi: June 29, 2011; int. Kinyoro: May 11, 2011, and August 31, 2018; int. Kabutuku September 5, 2011, and August 30, 2018).

In particular, Gerrison Kinyoro, a great expert on Tooro music and dance, told me a story about how *runyege* developed (int. May 11, 2011; Fig. 1.5).

> *Runyege* originates right from the squeezing of bananas to get out the juice. Whereby someone who was squeezing the bananas almost failed to produce what? Juice. And then, that someone stamping the bananas got tired, of course, and then, to encourage him, those who were around started singing, so that he gets *nsande* [banana juice]. So he continues,

42 ❧ CHAPTER ONE

with the hope that it will produce juice. And, as they started singing, he of course started stamping according to what? To the rhythm being sung:

Samba[7] samba tugende	Stamp [your feet], stamp and let's go
Chorus: *Samba* (repeated after each verse)	Stamp
Samba obundi ebirajwa	Stamp, maybe they will release [juice]
Samba n'amani maingi	Stamp strongly
Obundi harumu mpurumura	Maybe [among the bananas] there is *mpurumura*[8]
Mpurumura eyanguha kujwa	*Mpurumura* releases juice fast
Obundi harumu ekiterre	Maybe there is *kiterre*
Kiterre kimya kurungi	*Kiterre* releases [the juice] well
Osambe osambe okurungi	Stamp, stamp well
Osambe n'amani maingi	Stamp strongly
Obundi alimu enyamaizi	Maybe there is *nyamaizi*
Enyamaizi egenda mpora mpora	*Nyamaizi* releases [juice] slowly
Enyamaizi tayanguha kujwa	*Nyamaizi* does not release [juice] fast
Obundi harumu enkenge	Maybe there is *nkenge*
Enkenge tayanguha kujwa	*Nkenge* does not release [juice] fast
Samba samba bagenzi	Stamp, stamp brothers
Ebitooke byaitu birajwa	Our bananas will release [juice]
Dora akafuro kakaija	Look, foam is coming
Obundi kaniko karajwa	Maybe that means that [the juice] will arrive soon
Linda akafuro kakaija	Wait, foam is coming
Samba n'okumbya kumbya	Stamp and turn it
Obundi ebitoke birajwa	Maybe the bananas will release [juice]
Osambe boojo osambe	Stamp, please, stamp
Dora ensande kayaija	Look, juice is coming
Samba n'okumbya kumbya	Stamp and turn it
Samba byona birajwa	Stamp, they will all release [juice]

---

7   I did not find linguistic connections between the verb *kusamba* (to kick, stamp) used in *runyege* and the Brazilian and Angolan *samba* music and dance genres. Since *samba* as a genre is considered to have roots in various dances from Bantu language areas, it would be interesting to investigate possible shared vocabulary in the future.

8   *Mpurumura*, as well as *kiterre*, *nyamaizi*, and *nkenge*, are the local names for different varieties of bananas.

Figure 1.5. Gerrison Kinyoro recounting the origins of *runyege*. Kiguma (Tooro), 2012.

| *Ensande osambe kurungi* | The juice, stamp well |
| *Samba n'amani maingi* | Stamp strongly |

So, in that form, one was stamping and then the juice started coming out. Then, of course, they had juice, they had to follow all the process of fermenting the beer. Then, after three days, when they got the beer and were drinking, they remembered the song and started singing as they drank.... But then it was picked up by younger men, who continued to sing it when? Maybe when they gathered together ... and then they had to invent the *binyege*, those are fruits from the *munyege* tree. Then [they] made up sets of *binyege* which they tied on the legs. Maybe they started shaking ... then they would hear that sound and think: how about putting them on the feet? So, they did and started singing and dancing. [...] and they called the dance *runyege* from the *binyege*.

In this narrative about *runyege*'s origins, an improvised song to encourage a man squeezing the juice out of beer bananas explains how a connection between this activity and music/dance was created. According to Kinyoro's telling, the song was later recollected and sung again, and the men started dancing while remembering the squeezing of bananas as described in the song. In particular, the movements of stamping on the fruits to squeeze the

44 &❧ CHAPTER ONE

juice out were amplified by using leg rattles, an element that is fundamental both in the music and in the dance components of *runyege*. Even today, dancing the men's part is called *kusamba* (lit. to kick; to stamp) *orunyege*, while the instrumental component of the dancing can be referred to with the expression *kuteera ebinyege* (to beat, play the leg rattles). The centrality of men's steps and the leg rattles is evident in the very term *runyege*, based on the root (*-nyege*) of the word *kinyege*, leg rattle. However, in Kinyoro's story singing also emerges as a founding element of the genre, giving variety and (melodic as well as topical) content to the performance.

The Tooro musician and performer Stephen Kabutuku (int. September 5, 2011, and August 30, 2018) narrated a similar story to me. Once a man visited a friend, who offered him *tonto* beer and, to show his appreciation, the guest started to stamp his feet alternately on the floor, imitating the banana squeezing process, and singing a song of appreciation. Meanwhile, the women of the house had ground the sorghum to be added to the banana juice for fermentation. According to Kabutuku, the actions taken by men and women to produce *tonto* beer were the basis for the two distinct dance parts for dancers.

Although there is not unanimous agreement on the origin of *runyege*, the narratives connecting this genre to the making of banana beer seem to be the most complete and coherent (see more in chapter 4). This notwithstanding, they are a reconstruction of the present and seem to explain in retrospect the main elements of the dance and, at the same time, display the persistent importance of banana beer as a cultural symbol. Indeed, *tonto* beer is considered central in representing and sustaining the most important forms of Nyoro and Tooro social life. First, banana beer was and still is a vital element in the exchange of gifts that takes place during wedding ceremonies and is thus representative of one of the honored means of creating new alliances.[9] *Tonto* beer was drunk at specific times during the wedding ceremony, in which an exchange of considerable amounts of beer took place between the two families. While nowadays the weddings are not divided into several phases as in the past (see chapter 2), banana beer is still considered indispensable to hold a wedding, as a good both to gift and to consume together during the celebrations. Second, especially during the harvesting season, banana beer was drunk at different festive occasions, like when eating the first meal prepared with freshly harvested millet or when a family had many ripe bananas and decided to prepare beer. On these occasions, neighbors and friends freely joined the parties and enjoyed the beer supplied

---

9   As they did not produce it themselves, Huma pastoralists, for whom *tonto* was necessary both to obviate food prohibitions and to fulfill wedding rituals, had to obtain it from Iru agriculturalists (Elam 1973).

by the host. These parties are rarely held today and, for this reason, I did not have the chance to participate in any, nor heard of one taking place while I was in Uganda. However, this does not negate the association of *tonto* with social bonding through exchanging, sharing, and redistributing wealth. In fact, *tonto* beer emerges as fundamental in establishing and maintaining relations with relatives, neighbors, and friends both in the sense of cultivating peaceful relationships and consolidating reciprocal bonds of cooperation. These are the main elements of Nyoro and Tooro relational ethics: the gatherings and parties at which this drink was consumed were indeed social occasions to reinforce the sense of community. And this is most probably the reason why banana beer is considered a symbol of cultural value even today, as marking a friendly and sharing community, while the traditional celebrations where it was consumed have changed, like weddings, or have progressively become rarer, like beer parties. Besides symbolizing and thus preserving the value assigned to social exchanges and wealth sharing as it was in the past, *tonto* beer continues to represent this sense of sociality and community for the Banyoro and Batooro in the present, multicultural national Ugandan context.

I offer more details of the origins and meaning of different aspects of *runyege* in chapter 4. For now, it is worth emphasizing that research participants who connected *runyege* to *tonto* production linked the actions performed by men and women in preparing the beer with the separation of dance roles for men and women. The dance movements were associated with the actions used to squeeze bananas (the men's part) and to prepare sorghum to be added to the banana juice (the women's part). The connection between a dance genre and a work activity is common in traditional dances, especially in Africa. According to Judith L. Hanna (1973: 168): "Many African peoples have dances which mime traditional occupational behaviors important to the local economy. The dances serve as media to give work instruction and provide practice in the various required movements, strengthen muscles used in the work, and develop endurance." As a division of labor based on a dual gender conception is reflected in the two separate parts, broader ideas concerning gender are represented in the dancing style.

Womanhood and Manhood in Gendered Moves

The women's part in *runyege* is connoted by the shaking of the waist and hips, which finds a direct reference in the local names for it. In Bunyoro, the women's part of the dance is called *mugongo* (lower part of the back, lumbar region), and dancing the women's part is *kucweka* (to rush; to become broken,) *omugongo*, thus referring to their speedy shaking of the lower part

46 &❧ CHAPTER ONE

of the back and the waist. This expression also has another meaning, directly connected to womanhood: *kucweka omugongo* in the sense of "breaking the lower back" alludes to a girl's first menstruation. On the other hand, in Tooro the women's dance part is referred to as *bw'omu mbaju* (of the sides, ribs), indicating the hip-waist area and its movement in dance. This is similar to the (Afro)Caribbean, where women's hips and waist have great significance in relation to both dance and sexuality (Blanco Borelli 2016). While English-language literature tends to focus on hips, though, the term usually used in Caribbean popular music is *cintura*, waist. Analogously, when describing the women's part in *runyege*, my research participants preferred to use the English term "waist," which is closer to the meaning of the terms in the local language.

Discussing dance meaning, Andrée Grau (1993: 24) argued that "in people's conscious activity of making sense of the world of signs and symbols, social conventions and acquired habits of perception influence their selection of relevant cues and their understanding of what they see and hear." Similarly, many Banyoro and Batooro people related features of the women's dance in *runyege* with some characteristics considered specific to womanhood, in particular grace, elegance, and prettiness. These features emerge notably in the movement of the legs and feet as well as the waist area. Several research participants observed that women walk slowly, taking small steps, while men move with energy and leap with long strides. The smallness of women's steps was frequently pointed out to me, along with observations that traditionally women did not dance with their legs stretched out, not even when the tempo was very fast (int. Kinyoro: May 11, 2011).[10] The emphasis on women's waist movement reflects the Nyoro and Tooro conception of the female waist and hips as the physical elements connoting womanhood. My research participants observed how the women's waist movements are accentuated by their buttocks, which are bigger than men's. Kinyoro (int. May 11, 2011) observed that "the softness … in the waist of a woman, especially when she is dancing, attracts the man, especially seeing how the waist is moving." According to Gafabusa Hairora (2003: 56), in *runyege* dance, "the women emphasise the waist to appeal—'okuchwa omugongo,' a key image used to perpetuate traditional perceptions that relate women to sexuality and procreation." This is confirmed by some research participants, for whom the flexibility needed to perform the nimble hip and waist movements mirrors agility during sexual intercourse and, indirectly, denotes fertility. The waist shaking thus represents the central element in the local conception of womanhood. Finally, the physical endurance that a woman needs to perform the

---

10   In the past as well as today, a woman who stretches her legs out while seated or walking was considered not to be decent.

hip bobbing and waist shaking for an extended period is a demonstration of her stamina in physical activities and, hence, in work.

Not only is womanhood reflected in dance, but manhood is, too. The energy and strength needed to perform the men's steps, and the physical stamina required for the duration of a performance (*runyege* can be danced for 5 to as long as 20 minutes) are mentioned by both the Banyoro and Batooro as expressions of masculinity. Indeed, many elders and dance instructors referred to men's virility as the vigor and force they put into dancing. The muscular strength displayed in *runyege* is a central element in the local conceptualization of masculinity, as it is expressed by the concept of *manzi* ("brave man, hero," see Davis 1938: 91), which condenses the ideas of strength, vigor, and braveness associated with being a man (*musaija*). From this perspective, the connection with the brewing process is significant as it is primarily a men's activity, in which women participate marginally, as it is among other Bantu societies, like the Bagisu of eastern Uganda who use a millet-brewed beer during the *imbalu* circumcision ritual (Khamalwa 2012; Makwa 2012).

According to Hanna (1988: 88), the symbolic devices of concretization (characterizing the main narrative of *runyege*'s origin), stylization, and metonym emphasize the ideas about manhood and womanhood and, in this way, they contribute to the process of "sex role scripting,"[11] that is, the social construction and dissemination of gender knowledge. Based on the perception that people have of *runyege* dancing and on the various narratives about the origin of the two dance parts, it appears that they are significantly connected to traditional gender conceptions among the Banyoro and Batooro.

Has the gender conceptualization in Bunyoro and Tooro always been so clearly associated to biological sex as an inseparable binary? How is this present interpretation of *runyege* related to wider discussions on tradition in society and the recent concern about morality? A look backward at gender in Bunyoro and Tooro, and more recently Uganda as a whole, is required not only to understand the connections of the MDD complex with men's and women's roles and performances but also to contextualize the present discourse on tradition, which ties together performing arts and gender in contemporary Uganda. In the following pages, I reconstruct past gender concepts in Uganda and specifically in Bunyoro and Tooro, based on scientific historical and ethnographic literature, as well as through the critical reading of missionaries' and explorers' writings.[12]

---

11   For Hanna's definition of the concept of "sex role scripting," see Hanna 1988: 75.

12   Data on the precolonial period emerges mainly from ethnographies and various typologies of field reports and accounts published until the 1920s, which

48 &❧ CHAPTER ONE

Gender in Precolonial Times:
Common Men (*Basaija*) and Women (*Bakazi*)

In precolonial Bunyoro and Tooro, gender categories were more diverse than today. While two genders determined by biological sex shaped the lives of most of the population, this was not true within the royal family and, among commoners, there were also alternative femininities and masculinities not complying with hegemonic models.

The broad majority of Nyoro and Tooro individuals were considered as part of two main genders: men (*basaija*) and women (*bakazi*). These two categories were univocally connected to biological sex and, to apply R. W. Connell's terminology (2005: 77) to this binary, they constituted the "hegemonic" forms of masculinity and femininity that sustained and legitimized patriarchy. Education within the family and social expectations were crucial in defining and connoting the meaning of being a man or a woman. In Bunyoro and Tooro, young boys and girls were brought up similarly and great emphasis was placed on respect for parents and elders in general. In particular, the father had a high degree of authority: "as head of the family and household, he is the most important person in it. He is the *mukama* (the master and owner) of everybody and everything it contains; even property apparently at the disposal of his adult sons is ultimately his" (Beattie 1957: 327). At around 10 years old, children's tasks started to be differentiated according to their sex and they accompanied the parent of the same sex in his/her daily activities (Nyakatura 1970; Roscoe 1923: 259–264; Taylor 1998: 40–42, 46).

In the patriarchal and exogamous Nyoro and Tooro society, daughters were destined to leave their natal family while sons established their new household near to their father's, similar to the practices in other contexts marked by exogamy and patrilocality, like Prespa Albanian communities (Sugarman 1997: 155, 171–172). After her wedding, a daughter moved to another house and became part of another family where she would bear children that belonged to her husband's clan. In this sense, daughters were referred to as *baana bw'ahara,* children of far away, meaning that they would leave, while sons were *basigazi,* those that remained (int. Kasenene:

---

are based on information collected from local elders and refer to ancient customs. Aware of the interpretation problems connected to both colonial documentation and scientific literature because of its partiality and of the power discourses it conveys (Mudimbe 1988; Musisi 2002: 107; Schoenbrun 1993), I tried to handle these various sources with consideration for the background, thinking, and purpose of the authors and to compensate for their bias by comparing different sources.

September 06, 2011; Taylor 1998: 31–33). Male children would indeed establish their own house near their father's and live there with their wives, who would produce children that belonged to their father's clan. Sons would thus become *nyineka*, which means both owner of the house and head of a family (Davis 1938: 138; Taylor 1962).[13] Marriage defined the passage of boys and girls to adult age and their definitive inclusion in a specific gender category (men or women), in which belonging had until that moment been incomplete (Mukasa-Balikuddembe 1973; Roscoe 1923). Weddings were complex ceremonies that spanned over several weeks and were preceded by multiple encounters between mediators of the two families. Later, a formal introduction (*kweranga*) of the groom to the bride's family was held and, after the bridewealth (*mukaaga*) was paid, a ceremony for "giving away" the bride and "taking her to groom's house" (*kugaba* and *kugabura*) was held. Several songs were performed by the two parties in the various stages of the wedding (see chapter 2).

The values associated to hegemonic masculinity were proactivity, vitality, and authority. The ideal man was incarnated in the figure of the *manzi*, a strong and valiant man, who was respected in society, to which he contributed by interpersonal connections, and in his family, which he established through marriage, led, and protected. After marriage, a man had wider freedom than before: if the first wife was chosen by his family, then he could autonomously decide to have other wives and, although the consent of the first wife was considered important, it was not necessary, and polygamy was widespread. According to Mukasa-Balikuddembe (1973: 71), "the traditional husband... is an authoritative master to his wife whose relative freedom developed at her natal home has been curtailed on the day of her marriage." As British anthropologist John Beattie (1960: 57) wrote about Nyoro society, "the high status of a household head is particularly marked in his relations with his wife or wives, for men are always superior to women." The authority of husbands over wives was just part of the broader authority of men over women, which was an integral idea of traditional Nyoro and Tooro society. It is significant that the myth about the disappearance of the Bacwezi, demigods who reigned over the Kitara Empire, mentions the insubordination of women as one of the elements

---

13   The Tooro literature scholar Isaac Tibasiima (2009: 125) differently interprets the concept of *nyineka* by considering it literally as "mother of the home" and thus as a women's attribute, while he describes the husband as the *mukama w'eka*, the lord of the home. Tibasiima's interpretation is an isolated case in relation to the information I gathered from research participants and in the literature.

50 & CHAPTER ONE

threatening their reign (Fisher 1911: 108–109; Nyakatura 1973: 34).[14] The authority of parents over children was comparable to the authority of men over women: the mainstream understanding considered women to be as immature and irresponsible as children and thus in need of men's supervision.

Hegemonic femininity was connoted by acceptance and deference, but also by essential (re)productive power. Through marriage, a woman passed from being under the authority of her father to that of her husband, to whom she had to be deferential (Beattie 1958: 10); her sexuality and work were at his disposal, since the husband was considered to be the owner of the children and the agriculture products. On the other hand, although considered of a lower status than that of men, the functions of nurturer and food producer associated with femininity, understood as complementary to the prerogatives of masculinity, were considered essential for the survival and continuation of society. Furthermore, to women's sexuality and fertility (in particular to sexual intercourse, menstruation, and giving birth) were associated several beliefs and taboos (Roscoe 1923) that show how feared was the power of femininity and, for this reason, contained through restrictions—a trait recurring among other patriarchal cultures around the world. In precolonial western Uganda, there seemed to be an ambivalence toward femininity, analogous to the situation that Christina Sunardi (2015) describes for precolonial Java, which comprehended both the positive consideration of women's economic and reproductive roles connected to food and children production and the negative view of their sexual (and in East Java also martial) power that could destabilize men's position in society.

---

14 Myths and legends describe three dynasties that reigned over the Empire of Kitara, from which the present Bunyoro and Tooro people descend. After the time of the godly Batembuzi, the dynasty of semigods called Bacwezi lists only three kings. During the reign of the last of them, Wamara, several "evil forebodings" affected him and his brothers, such as losing the respect of their subjects and in particular of women and servants, their grazing herds being attacked by evil creatures, and their kraals being raided (Nyakatura 1973: 34–37). To understand why these unfortunate events were striking them, Wamara consulted two diviners who, through the anatomical analysis of a sacrificed calf, confirmed the negative premonitions and predicted that it was the time for the Bacwezi to leave Kitara. The Bacwezi are said to have then "disappeared" into natural places like lakes and mountains that are still today tied to their memory and cult as spirits. From the son of one of Wamara's brothers, Kyomya, and a woman from Buruli (northern Bunyoro) arose the Babiito dynasty, which still reigns in both Bunyoro and Tooro.

Among agriculturalists (*bairu*) as well as among pastoralists (*bahuma*), a neat division of labor according to gender existed. Among pastoralists men were in charge of the pasture, care, and milking of cattle, while women were not allowed to deal with cows but had to take care of the calves, handle the milk, and make dairy products (Taylor 1962: 57). Among agriculturalists, women did most of the work in the fields, which were exclusively owned by men, who dealt with clearing and preparing them for cultivation (Taylor 1962: 29; int. Sebala, Bitamale, and Rwakaikara: June 23, 2010; int. Kinyoro: July 29, 2012). So men's involvement in agriculture was occasional, while for women it was (and in many rural areas still is) daily.

A dual value system connected to working activities differentiated on the basis of gender was typical of agricultural Bantu societies (Remotti 1993: 29) and can be traced in Bunyoro and Tooro, too. Women's cultivation activities (digging and weeding) did not require any specific knowledge—indeed they were also carried out by children—and, although they were essential for the survival of the family, they were considered simple and rudimentary. On the other hand, men's activities, like building a house, clearing fields, and hunting, were considered more significant because they required more muscular strength and specific skills.

All in all, men held a higher position than women in society, as is typical of patriarchal systems, like Prespa Albanians (Sugarman 1997). As for the Prespas, the gendered division of labor and space and the important role of women at home probably contributed to women's acceptance of the system by redirecting their attention away from inequality in relations with men to same-gender power relations determined by age (young vs. old women as wives and mother-in-laws or as first and second wives) and to the complementarity of men and women.

The differentiation of roles within the family and society at large, the concepts of authority and respect, the division of labor, and the different values assigned to the various tasks were thus connected to two specific gender categories. Adult males and females became respectively men and women through marriage and they were associated with different skills, behaviors, and attitudes, which were cultural and social constructions, but whose concrete expressions were commonly considered natural, as manifestations of biological sexual differentiation. These ideas about womanhood and manhood expanded to the whole society during the colonial time and, accompanied by Victorian strict morality, froze into a normative gender binary that is considered today as traditional, as I discuss in the following pages. Now, it is important to highlight that this traditional-colonial gender binary permeates the conception as well as the common perception of *runyege*—the narrations of *runyege* origins on the basis of different activities for women and men, the limiting of instrument playing to men only,

52 ❧ CHAPTER ONE

and the two dance roles reflect these categories—while the two categories in turn emerge as a model for a good performance. Since these forms of masculinity and femininity were (and with limited discontinuities still are) hegemonic, I use them as the main polarities in my analysis of gender in Uganda and this allows me to identify also precolonial alternate, minority masculinities and femininities, which is the point I make in the following discussion.

Other Femininities and Masculinities in Precolonial Society

Besides the main dual gender conception applying to most of Nyoro and Tooro society, there were significant alternative cases of females with a special status as well as nonhegemonic masculinities. According to Melvin L. Perlman (1966: 567), in Tooro a woman whose father died with no sons could become his heir—a position that traditionally involved not only the acquisition of his material wealth including land, a house, and cattle but also his social status. If a female heir married, the husband would move into her house and she would thus become *nyineka*, household head. In her position as her father's heir and householder, she had property and authority, could make decisions, and her status was as high as that of a man. Only a poor man who could not afford to pay the bridewealth would marry a *nyineka*: such a marriage would be degrading for a man, who would not be independent, as a man should be, by living in a woman's house and being subject to her authority. In this case, while the female heir and her new husband maintained their gender as woman and man, they performed alternative forms of femininity and masculinity, where some characteristics of hegemonic womanhood (being subject to men's authority after the payment of the bridewealth) and manhood (owning a house, land, and cattle) were in part swapped. These forms of femininity and masculinity were minoritarian because it was rare for a man to die without sons and have his daughter inherit, but they were nonetheless socially accepted as necessary to grant every man a heir.

Another case of individuals that blurred the neat dual gender conceptualization were the *babandwa* (sing. *m(u)bandwa*), mediums of the traditional cult (Doyle 2007; Pennacini 1998; Perlman 1966; Roscoe 1923; Taylor 1962). Because of their centrality in preserving both the health and spiritual wellness of the community and of their ritual importance, *babandwa* had a high status and were greatly respected (Beattie 1969: 161 and 169; Berger

1973 and 1995).[15] For historian Iris Berger (1981: 23), "Mediumship also offered women a share in the prestige and prerogatives of men, a rare occurrence in these male dominated societies." Although mediums could be male or female, the majority were females (Beattie 1969: 160; Berger 1981: 22–23) and they could not marry because, through the initiation to mediumship, they wedded the spirit by whom they were possessed (Berger 1973 and 1981). An elderly woman that I met in 2011 in Kagadi (Bunyoro) had been a *mubandwa* until she converted to Christianity. She told me that she never married because, as a medium of her clan's spirit and hence in charge of the spirit's house, she was not supposed to move to the house of the husband's clan. So she was also a *nyineka*, a household head, or an *omukuru w'eka*, elder of the house, as she said. On the one hand, female *babandwa*'s status as women was supported by this sort of mystic marriage, the spirit being their husband, and by mediums' focus on fertility issues; on the other hand, their ritual status denied them one of the main features of womanhood: childbearing. Indeed, according to Pennacini (1998: 125), mediumship involved the waiver of motherhood: female mediums thus chose chastity because giving birth and raising children were considered impure, incompatible with the spiritual presence that inhabited them. Male mediums were also married in an otherworldly union to a spirit, which meant they could neither marry a woman nor have children. This defined for male *babandwa* a special form of masculinity connoted by feminine traits as wives, for example, taking care of the house and the needs of the spirit. Male mediums derived their high position in society not from the typically masculine authority exercised on wives and children, but from their spiritual power. The role of *babandwa* mediums in Nyoro and Tooro precolonial societies recalls the one of Korean shamans, who were predominantly females who held respected and important religious roles, granting them freedom of behaviors beyond gender expectations during rituals, as well as a higher status than their husbands in case they were married (Koskoff 2014: 51). However, in contrast with Korean male shamans perceived as marginal to mostly feminine shamanism, in Bunyoro and Tooro male and female mediums were both highly respected.

---

15   It is not clear if there was equality between male and female mediums. Scholars have different opinions: according to Pennacini (2009: 341) "regarding gender, which creates fundamental barriers of inequality within Great Lakes society, *kubandwa* breaks the rules: an initiated woman can practice exactly as a man. Through religious initiation she can reach a status that in normal life is obtained only by men, a position which is conceived as that of a chief exercising a mystical power." Other scholars (Beattie 1957; Doyle 2007; Taylor 1998), however, note that in *kubandwa* higher positions (especially as *museegu* medium initiator) were held by men.

The cases of female *nyineka* and *babandwa*, on one hand, and of female *nyineka*'s husbands and male spirit mediums, on the other hand, illustrate that, during the precolonial period, there were forms of femininity and masculinity alternative to the main dual gender model applying to the majority of the population. The peculiar connotation of these forms of masculinity and femininity was established through status and was also relational. In other words, they mainly depended on the prestige acquired by owning a house and hence leading a family (household head's status) or by the ability of dealing with ritual power (medium's status), and on the position of the individual in the wedlock marked by an imbalanced power relation between the roles of husband (the spouse who pays the bridewealth and is in a position of superiority, or the spirit) and wife (the spouse who is paid for and is relegated to a deferent position, or the medium). It is important to emphasize that no contempt was attached to female *babandwa* for not fulfilling all the requirements of womanhood, be it to be subject to male authority or to produce children; rather, they enjoyed peculiar respect because of the prestige connected to their status. The same could be said for male *babandwa*. Because of the masculinity attached to their status as heirs and *nyineka*, women living in their own houses were also held in esteem, although their simultaneous roles as childbearers (wives) and household heads (husbands) could cause some friction. Finally, men who married female heirs and went to live with them, thus implying that they could not afford to build their own house and voluntarily chose to live under the authority of a woman, had a low status and could be disparaged by the community.

A woman whose high status and privileged position are still very respected today, is the queen mother (*Nyin'omukama*, lit. mother of the king). In precolonial times, kings had several wives (*bago*, sing. *mugo*) and many children. The succession to the throne was not decided before the death of the suzerain but was marked by struggles and even wars between the royal children. When one of them grabbed power, his mother became *Nyin'omukama*. With a ceremony similar to the king's coronation, she acquired a status very close to that of the monarch. She received a dynastic drum, her own palace, cattle herds, and lands on which she administered justice (Roscoe 1923: 145–149). Although she had properties and authority, her relationship to her child was still maternal, connoted by advice and protection. Indeed, despite the authority she could exercise, she was (and is) conceived of as a woman: it is because of motherhood that she obtained power.

In precolonial Tooro and Nyoro societies as well as in neighboring Buganda (Kiguli 2001: 160), there were also cases of females conceived of as being men. The daughters of the king, *babiitokati b'engoma* (sing.

mubiitokati w'engoma),[16] were brought up similarly to their brothers and were not supposed to get married. According to Roscoe (1923: 168–169), the upbringing of the *babiitokati b'engoma* involved chores reserved to pastoralist girls, but also those typical of Huma boys, and indeed they were referred to as boys. Because of their rank, they were conceived of as men (*basaija*), they could not get married and hence subject to a man's authority, and at their death they were buried in the position reserved for men (Roscoe 1923: 143, 175). Their conception as female men was strengthened by the fact that, although they were allowed sexual freedom, they were forbidden to produce children (Beattie 1971: 101; Roscoe 1923: 171; Speke 1863: 534).[17] Being conceived of as men meant that the two main requirements defining womanhood (being a wife subjected to male authority and a mother producing children) did not apply to them. The high status of the *babiitokati b'engoma* determined their gender as men, which was reinforced by the way they were addressed, their upbringing, behaviors during royal ceremonies, and powerful roles in the kingdom.

The only female of the royal family to be conceived of as a woman was the official sister of the king, *Kalyota* or *Batebe*, who was indeed buried in the position reserved to women (Roscoe 1923: 143, 175). The *Kalyota* was chosen by the king as the head of the women of the Babiito clan outside the royal family, in parallel to one of the king's brothers who became the head of the clan's men with the title of *Kwiri* or *Musuga* (Beattie 1971). In this sense, Beattie (1971: 103) considers the *Kalyota* as the female counterpart of the male royal power. The idea of a dual-gender system where womanhood and manhood, incarnating complementary principles, counterbalance one another in power position and society seems to be common also in other African societies.[18]

---

16 The royal clan in Bunyoro and Tooro is Babiito. A member of the Babiito clan is a *mubiito* and a female a *mubiitokati.* The belonging to the royal family is indicated by the specification *w'engoma*, i.e. "of the drum," the symbol of power and of the monarchy (see chapter 3).

17 During the procession of the royal drums and regalia at the *Mpango* royal ceremony, the *babiitokati b'engoma* are the only females who stand like men and do not squat like women (int. *Nyin'omukama wo Bunyoro:* March 26, 2008). Finally, some of them were also local chiefs, like the famous Koogere that ruled in Busongora, Tooro (Dipio 2009; Taylor 1998: 215).

18 For a discussion and comparison of the roles of princesses and queen mothers in African and especially in the interlacustrine kingdoms, see Mair 1977: 50–52. Specifically on the Ganda society, see Schiller 1990. On music, gender, and power in West Africa, see Scharfenberger 2011.

56 &⧫ CHAPTER ONE

Table 1.1. Gender categories in precolonial Bunyoro and Tooro

	Males	Females
Commoners	Men	Women
Children of the king	Men	Men (except for the *Kalyota*)

This outline shows that a fundamental difference according to social class, or blood ancestry, namely being part of the king's lineage, marked a gender for females that was not in line with their biological sex.[19] Because the *babi-itokati b'engoma* were addressed and respected as men, it seems that they inhabited the role of "men" as the gender category marked by prestige and status, rather than being understood as a third gender separated from men and women.

Although these various gender identities as well as different forms of masculinity and femininity during the precolonial times are documented by different sources, the literature does not mention any relations that were not heterosexual.[20] This resonates with Epprecht's (2008: 34–39) argument that early sources about Africa (but also much later, following a centuries-long pattern) depict it as a completely heterosexual land, where marriage and reproduction were the capital values and norms in the society. This representation contributed to establishing an image of a heterosexual Africa, which ignored several manifestations of sexuality that would not fit into it.

Colonial Gender Models

The imposition of the British Protectorate (1894) on the area that later became Uganda and the foundation of Christian missions led to significant changes in Nyoro and Tooro societies. By signing agreements with colonial authorities the traditional kingdoms lost their effective powers, extensive agriculture products (cotton, tea, coffee) acquired a new central role in the economy, big cities like Kampala developed, and a money economy replaced barter (Taylor 1998). Furthermore, Christian evangelization engaged in founding and running schools, as well as against the traditional religion by

---

19   Unlike what is documented about neighboring Buganda (Nanyonga-Tamusuza 2005 and 2009), for Bunyoro and Tooro the sources do not clearly describe the king's authority as "man above all men," in relation to whom all other males were conceived of as women.

20   On the other hand, it is well documented that, at the end of the nineteenth century, the Ganda king Mwanga had homosexual relations with male pages at his court (Kiguli 2001: 170–172).

proclaiming it heathen and satanic and forcing its repression in collusion with the colonial government.

The colonial period was profoundly shaped by the British administration and missionary evangelism views on the roles of men and women and on sexuality. The work by Bantebya Kyomuhendo and McIntosh (2006) on Ugandan women throughout the last century is fundamental in understanding the changes in gender models during the colonial period. While their research, as well as other historical and anthropological literature, focuses on the transformations in gender that affected mostly women, from this scholarship it is possible to deduce also the changes impacting masculinities.

Transformations in Nyoro and Tooro gender notions were due to both the internal social and political transformations of those societies and the changes brought by colonization with the result that, on one hand, the gender binary was reformulated by erasing several of the variants in the precolonial one; on the other hand, this new model was flexible enough to incorporate new figures that had developed through social transformation. What remained unaltered was the authority of the husband and father within the family, fitting well with the colonialists' late Victorian morality. The mainstream European vision of African women framed them as wives and mothers and this paradigm of domesticity was propagated especially through the Church and schools (Musisi 2002: 99 and 107). Bantebya Kyomuhendo and McIntosh (2006: 14–15) also emphasize how the Victorian patriarchal morality of the early nineteenth century, supported by British as well as by Ugandan men, strengthened existing gender patterns, molding what they call the "Domestic Virtue model":

> In an attempt to define women's position in a way that would reestablish patriarchal control, male leaders—both African and British—formulated a model of how a good woman should act and what her duties were. This domestically focused set of gender assumptions contained multiple elements. All women were expected to marry and provide services for their husbands, and they were to bear children and care for them. They had practical duties in the household, including providing food (usually growing it themselves), and they were to remain within the compound or fields. A woman was supposed to be submissive to male authority—especially that of her husband—and deferential when dealing with her husband's male relatives and other men in the community. Women did not make decisions except about minor domestic matters [...] if a woman went out into the world on her own, she might legitimately be regarded in sexual terms.

This model, charged with the conservative views of Christianity and European civilization and advantaged by the diminishing power of traditional monarchies and spirit mediumship, negatively affected the minority

58 &# CHAPTER ONE

masculinities and femininities of the precolonial time. As it happened in other colonized societies like Java (Sunardi 2015; Weiss 2006), a part of the past forms of masculinity and femininity virtually flattened into the main gender binary, whose normativity was reinforced during colonization; at the same time, because of the patriarchal character of colonial domination, the previous possibilities for feminine power reduced. In Uganda, the pervasive influence of the Domestic Virtue model provoked a substantial change in the gender of the *babiitokati b'engoma*, the female members of the royal family. According to Beattie (1960: 30–31), whereas in the past "it would have been unthinkable for persons of such a high status to assume the markedly subordinate status of wives," from the 1950s onward they started to marry (although to rich men and without payment of the bridewealth) and to have children, hence they embraced the colonial model of femininity univocally connected to sexual determinism. It should not be forgotten that, in many cases, the transformations in gender notions caused by colonialism overlapped ongoing changes like those documented by Rhiannon Stephens (2013) in central-eastern Uganda, where already by 1900 royal women such as the queen mother and the princesses started to acquire a mainly symbolic role deprived of political and economic power, which was absorbed by men.

Christian missionaries were strongly engaged in evangelizing and fighting against the traditional religion, which they considered demoniac (Mukasa-Balikuddembe 1973: 30), thus a massive conversion of the population and the consequent radical reduction of *babandwa* spirit mediums took place. Many male mediums converted and formally abandoned the *kubandwa* mediumship, or they continued to practice, but married and founded their own family. In this way, they abandoned the feminine masculinity associated to male mediumship and assumed the role of the family head, which was connected to the hegemonic masculinity of precolonial times and privileged in the colonial society. The desire to be part of a modern faith and to adapt to the model of a good woman as wife and mother (as the only gender model appropriate for a female) led many female mediums—the majority of *babandwa*—to convert, marry, and have children, although some continued practicing in secrecy. Describing similar patterns in the African Great Lakes region, David L. Schoenbrun (1993: 39–40) observes how the colonial power also acted in disempowering female spirit mediums as sources of ritual power, with the purpose of recentralizing political power in the hands of men. However, in more or less public and manifest ways, the legacy of female *babandwa* seems to have been sustained during the past two centuries as a form of feminine agency related to both the spiritual and physical health of the individuals and their communities. In the tradition of "public healing," mostly performed by women as female *babandwa* and spread across different African counties—from Uganda (Berger 1981) to Liberia, from South Africa to the Gambia (McConnell 2020)—Berger (2014) sees the roots and models of later women's movements reaching even to contemporary women's associations engaged in both individual health and social well-being.

The diminishing of traditional mediumship cults had also an impact on the *kubandwa* music repertoires, which today are almost forgotten. Considered heathen and immoral, they are not performed by cultural groups. Very rarely school festival performances include some of these repertoires, like the songs for twins, but in moralized versions with any references to sex and genitals removed. The religious and moral condemnation of precolonial spiritual practices has contributed to the erasing of the memory of the special masculinities and femininities connected to the *kubandwa* cult. The result is that now only the gender model of married men and women is portrayed in the repertoires performed at festivals and by ensembles, meaning that what is presented constitutes only a selective (and biased) image of the tradition.

In the space of a few decades, the dissemination of the Domestic Virtue model in Bunyoro and Tooro erased the precolonial conception of female heirs and household heads, *babiitokati b'engoma* female men, and *babandwa* female mediums by aligning them with the features of the "good woman." In comparison to the precolonial era, this model allowed all females to enjoy motherhood, but in denying the possibility of alternatives, it de facto imposed the condition of wives and mothers on all female subjects. At the same time, this model implied a parallel paradigm for "good men" based on marriage, leadership in the family, and authority over the spouse and the offspring. This strengthened the hegemonic form of masculinity of the precolonial era and canceled the vision of celibacy as an acceptable and honorable status derived from spirit mediumship, while it increased the negativity associated to men married to female householders. This meant that marriage was the needed condition to be a real man and this required the payment of the bridewealth to the spouse's family—a condition that, under the transformed economical and labor conditions of the colony became more and more expensive, hence difficult to secure. In this context, while under the shared local and British patriarchy the colonial gender model consolidated men's power position in society, it put a great deal of pressure on men to obtain money and goods for the bridewealth and made masculinity very dependent on economical resources. A viable but definitely minoritarian alternative for what concerns marital status and offspring was the celibacy and chastity prescribed to Catholic priests, monks, and nuns—figures whose respected religious status compensated the lack of (earthly) spouse and children (Nanyonga-Tamusuza 2005).

According to Bantebya Kyomuhendo and McIntosh (2006), the Domestic Virtue model remained valid throughout the twentieth century and adapted to changing social conditions by admitting variants to the original model. The first variant concerned the access to education and so to professions in the colony. Men, and especially men from the local elites, had been the missionaries' primary target for education. Initially, it was religious education connected to the conversion to Christianity and it implied reading and writing, which ensured men with influent positions in the colonial administration and in the missions; later new technical schools started to fill the need of manpower of the colony and thus granted more men the access to salaried jobs. From the 1920s, the missionaries' will to increase the number of literate Christians stimulated the opening of girls' schools. Girls' education was different from boys' and it had an emphasis on domesticity, thus justifying traditional and conservative ideas in the transformation of Ugandan society. However, female education and associations should not interpreted exclusively through the domesticity paradigm, indeed, as shown by Aili M. Tripp and Sarah Ntiro (2002), women reemployed the skills acquired through such training and associationism also in their work environment and in politics. Moreover, education enabled some women, especially those from high-status families, to be employed as teachers and nurses, giving them greater freedom of movement and income. Bantebya Kyomuhendo and McIntosh (2006: 81–83) describe this change in women's opportunities as a variant gender model, which they label "Service Career." An educated woman could leave the house to work but had to pay for someone to fulfill the domestic requirements, for example, work in the fields, household chores, and childcare. However, notwithstanding education and the possibility to work outside the domestic context, women were still subject to men's authority, which remained unaltered. While this variant only applied to high-status Ugandan women, most women remained attached to the basic Domestic Virtue model. According to Perlman (1963: 55), in rural Tooro girls' education was not greatly supported by the families and in particular by the fathers. They suspected that education would make their daughters feel independent and undermine their paternal authority, so they did not consider it a good investment, especially since girls were destined for marriage and domestic work.

From the 1930s onwards, the number of Ugandan men involved in salaried work in factories and cities increased. Through their salary, men could provide for the basic commodity needs of the household, and this reinforced their authority as household heads; furthermore, their work, as it was in the past, was more valued than women's domestic activities. Since some purchasable goods became a basic demand of wives to their husbands, masculinity became more dependent on earning a salary and exposed to market economy. On the other hand, the migration of men to urban centers left women at home to run all of the activities and in charge of the household decisions, thus allowing them more freedom and empowerment. However, an additional aspect of men's absence from home was an increased suspicion toward the respectability of lone women, who could be accused of being prostitutes. This, together with the dependency on salaried work in the colonial economy, made the model of a "good man" defined by marriage as authority in the family and breadwinning more precarious and this instability afflicted many couple unions.

In the decades before Independence, the number of women who lived alone increased exponentially. Oftentimes, this was due to men's work migration, but many women lived alone because they had been abandoned by their partners. Indeed, traditional marriage had become less common given the higher demands for the bridewealth that were usually hard to meet by bachelors, but also due to the instability of couples provoked by changed gendered expectations and thus a weaker commitment to establish a union. Instances of concubinage became more and more frequent and did not result in long-term unions (Beattie 1958; Perlman 1963). The last years before Independence saw an improvement in the legal status of women, which, at least on paper, was made equal to men's in terms of rights and penalties, such as the right to vote (Perlman 1966: 582–584). Finally, the conversion of many Ugandans to Christianity meant, if only in theory, the rejection of polygamy that would possibly bring more parity within marriage. Indeed, Beattie (1960: 55) wrote that in Bunyoro: "Most marriages are monogamous, but Nyoro still like to have two or more wives if they can afford it, and even Christians sometimes have another wife besides their 'church' or 'ring' wife." In the next chapter, I will return in more detail to the topic of marriage considering the continuities and discontinuities between the traditional weddings remembered by my elder research participants and the present ceremonies that I got the chance to attend.

During the late colonial time as well as across the postcolonial era, the formation and dissemination of women's associations—many of which can be seen as developing the engagement of precolonial female therapists in individual and social well-being (Berger 2014)—contributed to make the hegemonic Domestic Virtue model slightly more flexible for women. Initially connected to religious contexts, like the Anglican Mothers' Union consecrated to cultivate the devotion and domestic values of good wives and mothers, women's associations have had different focuses historically, from civil and political engagement to collective income-generating activities and social commitment. As a space to develop feminine sociability, skills, cooperation, and values, these associations have been very important for Ugandan women and society at large. In chapter 6, I discuss these groups with greater detail.

62 &❧ CHAPTER ONE

The Culture in Gender

The Domestic Virtue model, based on earlier local ideas, stabilized after decades of colonial rule and survives, with minor alterations, to this day. The varied gender conception of the precolonial past marked by the intersectionality of biological sex, religious status, social rank, and relational position has largely been erased. It flattened into a twofold gender notion, where femininity and masculinity are based on biological determinism and grounded in patriarchy, which accepts a small degree of empowerment of women providing that motherhood and respect for men are retained as pillars of womanhood. While in contemporary and globalized Uganda alternative gender models of course exist, they remain quite marginal and minoritarian. On the other side, because it incorporates earlier gender conceptions, the "traditional" model is today considered by many in the positive light of "good tradition" and connoted as ancient, autochthonous, and genuine.

Nowadays, domestic virtue is still a gender paradigm defining good women. By complementarity, it defines a good man as respected, authoritative, and interactive in social contexts from which he draws and develops economic and social means. This gender binary, rooted in precolonial mainstream gender notions, but made normative and rigid during colonization is what is perceived as traditional today and, as such, it emerges in traditional arts in western Uganda, and in *runyege* in particular. However, two issues emerge in the connection of MDD, gender models, and culture. The repertoires that are currently performed the most frequently, such as *runyege* and folk songs, are an expression of what, for lack of better terms, can be defined as village or secular music. Are these repertoires representative of the whole Nyoro and Tooro culture and tradition as they are portrayed? The royal repertoires are today performed almost exclusively in the context of the annual royal anniversary (*Mpango*). In spite of more complex gender categories that could emerge from royal rituals and repertoires, involving spirit mediums and female *nanga* zither players, most of these figures have been lost and today the image of *Mpango* ritual and the musical landscape is dominated by male officials and musicians. So, in which ways do the gender categories represented in the current performances of village repertoires account for local culture?

Another issue involves the development of MDD in the decades since Independence through a process of codification and adaptation to different performance contexts and social conditions. How did these repertoires change over time and according to which trajectories? What are the messages of traditional performances in contemporary Uganda? What discourses shaped the codification of these repertoires regarded as traditional? Are there conditions and spaces that allow negotiations and transgressions of the traditional performance and gender paradigm?

In the chapters that follow, I address these issues through the analysis of the various components of MDD: music (singing and instrument playing), dance, and drama.

Chapter Two

Singing Marriage, *Runyege,* and Labor

S: *Kaisiki ija ontongole*   Girl, come and dance with me
ndakugurra ebinyobwa   I'll buy you peanuts

C: *Eee eee eee eeee*

S: *Obw'oliba otasekire*   If you do not laugh for me
engambo yange oligiba   you'll never hear me talking

C: *Eee eee eee eeee*

S: *Kinyantale omwa Zaliya*   In Kinyantale at Zaliya's
zukoma zaburwa ekisenya   they dried up and nobody collected them

C: *Eee eee eee eeee*

S: *Kyemerire nikiseka*   He is upright and laughs
n'akanyungu omulino   with a pipe between his teeth

C: *Eee eee eee eeee*

S: *Kulyamu ki omwa Zaliya?*   What do you eat at Zaliya's?
Kulyamu ki omwa Kumaraki?   What do you eat at Kumaraki's?
Kulyamu ki omwa Kumaraki?   What do you eat at Kumaraki's?
Kuragira ebidoodo byonka   Just amaranth

C: *Eee eee eee eeee*

S: *Abanikire omwanule*   Those who they are drying
enjura entahinda niyo egwa   the unexpected rain is the one that hits

C: *Eee eee eee eeee*

In 2011, Gerrison Kinyoro and Stephen Mugabo performed—respectively as solo (S) and chorus (C)—this song (**A1**), which is typically used in *runyege*, to illustrate how different topics could be simply juxtaposed, especially when the chorus did not convey a specific meaning (here it is just vocalized singing). Because of the lively community dimension of *runyege* performances of the past, extemporaneous variations in solo lyrics were needed to keep the performance interesting. So the soloist usually developed the first verses by drawing inspiration from the performance context, but they could also make reference to current news or quote proverbs. In some cases, they could do this within the same song, jumping from one subject to another while maintaining the same melody, as is the case in this song.

The first part (*Kaisiki ija otongole…*) evokes the context of the *runyege* dance: the singer invites a girl to dance, promising her a small present and urging her to enjoy the dance, otherwise he will not talk to her. That the solo voice is a male one is clear because the dancing partner is of the opposite sex (*kaisiki*, girl) as *runyege* gendered dance parts prescribe; furthermore, it is the male dancers that take the initiative, choose, and win over their dance partners. The female dancer was expected to smile shyly and to accept the invitation to dance, as the lyrics describe. Kinyoro pointed out that, in this case, this invitation is also, implicitly, an invitation to become a couple outside of the dance (int. May 11, 2011 and August 31, 2018). This kind of allusive reference to sexuality would be understood by the performers and the spectators. The second part of the song (*Kinyantale…*) suddenly shifts the theme and reports a topical occurrence. A wealthy man called Zaliya had firewood ready to be collected, but nobody took it. Kinyoro explained to me that this is an allegoric way of speaking (*ruhenda*) and is usually used to covertly express criticism or to refer to sex, things that were perceived as offensive, inappropriate, or vulgar. In this song, the dried wood alludes to Zaliya's daughters, who were ready for marriage, but he did not want them to get married, and so they remained at the paternal house. According to Kinyoro, *runyege* singers used *ruhenda* expressions in order to criticize people who might be present or to make sexual allusions. As I discuss below, in past rural Bunyoro and Tooro, an unmarried woman was seen as a sort of aberration. In the song, the word "daughters" is not used and there is no linguistic clue that young women are the subject of the lyrics, they are just referred to using the metaphor of dried things that remain there. The mocking tone of these lyrics—conveying a mixture of regret and disapproval directed toward Zaliya—is evident to interpreters of *ruhenda*. This critique continues by saying that in Kinyantale only bitter vegetables—amaranth leaves—are eaten, no millet, green bananas, or meat as in other families. Finally, Zaliya's situation is put in relation to the dance through the use of a proverb, "the unexpected rain is the one that hits," suggesting that the dancers should make sure that their partner will stay with them and not dance with someone else. This warning to dancers to keep their partners applies to *runyege* dancing as well as to life and, indeed, the story about Zaliya admonishes the young not to be without a partner, unless they want to be laughed at by the community.

66 ❧ CHAPTER TWO

The lyrics of this song condense several of the topics that weave together in this chapter. First, the binary normativity inscribed in this piece, requiring everybody to find a heterosexual partner, is inscribed in traditional wedding songs. Second, the gendering of *runyege* dance parts has an equivalent in the singing roles of solo and chorus. Finally, the gendered duality in singing and dancing is just an aspect of broader divisions that partition tasks, work, and position in society according to gender, as the working songs demonstrate.

The traditional songs that I consider in this chapter are no longer performed within the communities as they once were, but they are sometimes presented at the school festival, in the "traditional folk song" category, and are occasionally still performed by cultural groups. Many social changes intervened during the last century and transformed life conditions of Banyoro and Batooro, and Ugandans more broadly, thus causing the decadence of some sung repertoires, especially those related to weddings and to work. To understand the changes intervened in the music performed at weddings, I start with an ethnographic description of a contemporary Nyoro traditional wedding and discuss the social changes that influenced its present significance as well as the role of the repertoires performed and played in today's ceremonies. I then present and analyze some traditional songs, two about weddings, a typical *runyege* song, and two songs about work, which I collected from Nyoro and Tooro elders. In terms of content and occasions at which they are performed, these repertoires describe a set of customs and gender relations that, if not so active today, still mark rooted gender conceptions and relations. Indeed, the gendering of some of the repertoires is frequently underscored by the performers and is usually upheld in contemporary performances at festivals. Through the songs explored in this chapter, I also highlight some of the main traits of traditional repertoires. In particular, I consider their structure, singing features, different genres, and musical styles that were typical of the Huma pastoralist culture and the Iru agriculturalist one. Some of the musical features that emerge from the elders' performances are especially relevant in relation to the current performances of "traditional folk songs" by schools and cultural groups, which exhibit substantial changes.

A Nyoro Traditional Wedding Today

In April 2008, I was invited together with Issa to the wedding of John, the son of one of my main research participants, George Muhuruzi. I had met Muhuruzi multiple times during that spring and conversed with him about royal music, which he knew very well in his role as *mukuru w'ebikwato*, the custodian of the royal regalia. However, I had not met his son nor the bride-to-be, Maureen. Muhuruzi said that the ceremony for his son would be interesting for me because I could see how a wedding was carried out in Nyoro culture. The event would be conducted on two different days. The first one, a Friday, included the traditional introduction (*kweranga*) of the groom and his relatives to the bride's and the giving away (*kugaba*) of the bride to her new family. For this long ceremony, masters of ceremony, a photographer, a videographer, and a local cultural group—the St. Joseph Kolping Troupe—were hired. On the second day, the following Sunday, a Christian wedding (*buswezi*) was celebrated in the Anglican cathedral in Hoima, followed by a reception in a garden in town where the nationally famous ensemble Ndere Troupe performed.

The first day was particularly interesting, because it involved the traditional part of the wedding to which Muhuruzi referred. Following Issa's advice and my previous experience in attending another local wedding, I wore a colorful long dress that looked very elegant, but had the downside of not allowing fast and flexible movements. I knew that Muhuruzi was happy to have me as a guest, not as a fieldworker, so I had to dress appropriately and was not expected to record. Issa shot videos of the ceremony, which I used to reconstruct the events, as I took a few pictures while seated or moving around with the groom's party. When we arrived at Muhuruzi's house on Friday morning, all the relatives and guests of the groom were gathering and loading various gifts on trucks and cars to travel to the bride's paternal house. I traveled with them and, as we approached her house by foot, a cultural group sang a traditional welcome song and performed *runyege* dance for us. The yard in front of the house was prepared with two sets of gazebos in rows facing one another and a number of chairs ready for the guests, some of whom were already seated on the bride's side. In the center of the yard, a space was left empty for the masters of ceremonies—specialists in traditional weddings who are hired by each family to mediate between the two parts, as male relatives used to do in the past. Ribbons and flowers embellished the gazebos as well as the small tables in front of them and other decorations adorned the area, surrounded by loudspeakers. Later, neighbors and children arrived from the environs and sat on the grass and on mats around the gazebos.

The ceremony comprised speeches and verbal exchanges between the two masters of ceremonies who, as individuals not part of the families involved, have the role of officiating the wedding as a commitment of the couple and their families. The masters of ceremonies formally introduced the two families to each other, in particular the groom, who was announced as being there to look for a "child," implicitly referring to his wife-to-be. The bride's party then invited their "daughters" to come out because they were looked for. This was done pretending not to know which "child" the groom is

68 ❧ CHAPTER TWO

looking for, as it was in the past when the introduction ceremony truly represented the first time that the groom met the bride's relatives. Elegantly dressed, some girls and women of the bride's family (sisters, cousins, nieces, and aunts of the bride) slowly walked out from the house to the middle of the yard to the sound of popular love songs played by loudspeakers, such as *Gunuma* by Sofia Nantongo.[1] After dancing briefly they sat, facing the groom's party, on the mats placed there. The groom's representative thanked the ladies and their family, but admitted that the child they were looking for was not there. The bride's representative asked for a small gift (an envelope was given to one of them), and then was sent to look for other daughters, while the first group walked away accompanied by played-back songs. This repeated another two times, with different groups of ladies and requests for gifts, until the bride appeared in the last group.

At that point, the groom, accompanied by other members of his family, walked toward the bride, put a bead necklace around her neck and gave her a basket of flowers. The love song *Nakatudde* by the popular singer Maddox accompanied this moment while the photographer took close-up portraits. Then the groom went back to his seat and, on the track *Nassanga* by Geoffrey Lutaya, the bride was escorted toward the groom and pinned a cockade on his jacket. After walking together around the yard to be seen by all the guests as a new couple, the bride retired again.

Afterwards, gifts for the bride's family (*mukaaga*)—consisting of pots of banana beer and crates of other drinks, baskets containing food products, closed envelopes, and other presents, such as goats—were set in front of the bride's party. As a member of the groom's party, I participated with other women in carrying on my head these gifts, nicely packed in traditional baskets, as men carried the crates with drinks and other bigger presents. While we were transporting the presents, the other guests were entertained by played-back songs, such as *Olunaku luno* by Sylver Kyagulanyi, and a comic sketch performed by some members of the cultural group. The sketch closed with a *runyege* dance based on celebratory joy songs.

Afterwards, the gifts were accepted and appreciated by the bride's party and then she appeared again with a group of female relatives and sat on the mats in the center of the yard. The groom then approached her and put a ring on her finger and asked her to marry him. This moment was also accompanied by two well-known love songs, *Nsanyuka nawe* by Blu 3 and

---

1   This and the following songs by Ugandan artists that are mentioned are all in the Luganda language, which is different from Runyoro-Rutooro, though with a certain degree of mutual intelligibility. Nationally, the Luganda language is the most used idiom in media, information, and music industry; this is why speakers from other ethnicities, like the Banyoro and Batooro, can understand it quite well.

SINGING MARRIAGE, *RUNYEGE*, AND LABOR   69

Figure 2.1. Presenting the *mukaaga* bridewealth. The author (center) with the other women of the groom's party getting ready to carry gifts, part of the bridewealth, to the bride's party. Bunyoro, 2008. Photo by Issa Sunday.

Nkuweki by Irene Namubiru. Then, the groom's father, Muhuruzi, gave a speech on the newly established relation and alliance between the two families, their lineages, and clans, the Basiita and Babiito, which are among the most prestigious in Bunyoro.

Later the bride, in a different flower attire, and her female party reached the table where a big cake was displayed. As the groom approached her, the song *Yiga musajja* by Sofia Natongo played and, after a short countdown, the bride and groom cut the cake together—a moment that was accompanied by the song *Congratulations* by Cliff Richard and foam confetti sprayed into the air by the bride's female relatives. After the groom's father formally welcomed the bride as part of the new family, the groom finally embraced her, and he received the royal certificate acknowledging the legitimacy of their union as individuals belonging to different clans, sanctioning their civil marriage. This ended the ceremonial part of the traditional wedding, which was followed by a big meal served to all the guests, and entertainment by the cultural group, featuring also *runyege* dance, which lasted till the evening.

Muhuruzi had stressed that this was a traditional Nyoro wedding. Clearly, he meant to contrast this ceremony following Nyoro culture to the one held two days later according to the prescriptions of the Anglican Church and to

"Western" wedding standards, a type of ceremony that was introduced during colonization and then evolved following the worldwide globalization of Euro-American customs (including inherent patriarchal values) and capitalism (Sugarman 1997: 325–326). The "Western" wedding standards involved a mass in which the bride, in a wide white wedding gown, was taken to the altar by her father, followed by a celebration in a restaurant or reception hall, where the two families and their guests shared a grand meal and entertainment. John and Maureen's traditional wedding followed the main parts of Nyoro ceremonies as described in the literature (Beattie 1958), which involved the introduction (*kweranga*) of the groom, the offering of what was normally referred to in classical anthropology as the bridewealth or brideprice (*mukaaga*), and the giving away (*kugaba*) of the bride. This structure, as well as its inner stages, was similar to those of other ceremonies I observed in Bunyoro and Tooro. The engagement ring given by the groom to the bride during the traditional ceremony, while recurrent in many contemporary ceremonies, is not reported in the ethnographic literature. It seems to be an adoption within the traditional structure that allows interpreting the *kweranga* and *kugaba* not as a self-contained ceremony, where the socially and culturally approved union of a new couple is certified, but as an engagement ceremony that also needs the official wedding in the church, which will involve other rings for both spouses, to be effective in religious terms.

On the one hand, performing arts and especially popular songs define the main stages of contemporary wedding celebrations, as their presence in John and Maureen's ceremony shows. On the other hand, although not performed at weddings anymore, the sung repertoires associated with traditional weddings are alive in the memories of elders, as I discuss in the following pages. Furthermore, the latter are revived, adapted, and represented by children at the school festival and in some stage performances of the cultural groups. To understand the changes in the type and significance of music in today's weddings, I now trace the transformations of gender relations and couple unions that occurred in the last century and contextualize the meanings of today's traditional weddings and the role that the performing arts play in them.

Couple Relations, Gender Balance, and Weddings in Postcolonial Times

During the twentieth century, the number of marriages established through traditional weddings decreased for a number of reasons, mostly tied to the spread of capitalism worldwide. Social changes like the money economy; improvements in education, making children freer from authoritative parents; and men's labor migration and its impact on households all had an effect on men's and women's expectations of marriage and, more generally, on couple relationships. In the 1950s, this started leading to unstable marriages, informal unions not involving the *mukaaga* bridewealth, increasing divorce rates, and people forming stable partnerships at an older age (Beattie 1958; Perlman 1962 and 1963). Indeed, because of the instability of couples, the investment in traditional marriages became riskier, since in the case of divorce the *mukaaga* had to be returned. Furthermore, scholars report that payment of the bridewealth in cash instead of the traditional cows caused the commodification of marriages as well as the rise in costs (Doyle 2006: 214; Perlman 1966: 572). The debasement of women's status followed, as they could be equated with a tradable good, while for men this meant an increased dependence on salaried work and the capacity to save for a long time to accumulate enough money for the bridewealth. Similar to other societies across the Global South, until recent decades, it was mainly wealthy and educated people who had a religious wedding (including the traditional *mukaaga* payment) in one of the Abrahamic religions. This was a less flexible type of union since it involved fidelity and the commitment to monogamy (the latter for Christians only).

The 1970s were marked by the spread of militarism, in terms of the increased presence of the army and violence in everyday life, as well as by the hypermasculine ideology promoted by Idi Amin's regime, where manhood was characterized by physical and armed supremacy that manifested in particular against women (Decker 2014). At the same time, the regime repressed women's freedom by inhibiting their access to and participation in the public sphere, restricting their role to mothers segregated at home, and conservatively codifying what was deemed appropriate for them to wear (Bantebya Kyomuhendo and McIntosh 2006: 162). This notwithstanding, single mothers providing for their children through small trade started to be socially accepted. Bantebya Kyomuhendo and McIntosh (2006: 178) identify this emerging social view as a variant of the Domestic Virtue model and they term it the "Petty Urban Trade version." The increased instability of couples had made it necessary for lonely women to earn an income to support their children. In contrast with the past low reputation of women working alone in urban environments, single mothers providing for their children began to be positively evaluated and included in the category of good women together with married women. Socially acceptable job opportunities for women, which had been introduced during the colonial era, allowed them to earn an income and spend time outside the house, a situation common in other postcolonial contexts. Bantebya Kyomuhendo and McIntosh (2006: 264) argue that "Within the families, their [men's] place as household head and sole decision-maker was undercut by women's ability to generate their own income. Men's

72 ❧ CHAPTER TWO

position as authority figures within the community was threatened by women's involvement in the public domain."

Since the 1990s, the NRM government initiated several reforms targeting gender equality that allowed women to challenge their subjugated position in society by promoting their education and political participation.[2] In 1997, the Universal Primary Education plan made primary education compulsory for both boys and girls, thus granting access to schools to many girls, while in the past the education of boys had taken precedence. The same year, a new law prescribed a woman in every council at the county and district level, and seats for women in Parliament were equally encouraged. These reforms notwithstanding, Bantebya Kyomuhendo and McIntosh (2006: 195–197) report that women's involvement in politics is still subjugated to men's authority and women's political initiatives are usually undermined. Furthermore, Aili Mary Tripp (1998) argues that local councils flattened political activities and absorbed other forms of associations, including women's groups. Finally, the same scholars (Bantebya Kyomuhendo and McIntosh 2006: 200; Tripp 2002) denounced the Government for not supporting other reforms for equality, like the Domestic Bill, meant to protect women's rights in matters such as divorce and parental responsibility, and the Land Act, granting women the right to inherit land.

According to Tina Bareeba, Kibaale (Bunyoro) Field Officer of Ugandan NGO Forum for Women in Democracy (FOWODE), equality between women and men in the family and community is still a long way from being achieved, although institutions like hers are engaged in promoting it (int. June 16, 2011). In Bunyoro and Tooro, the idea that a woman has to "give respect" (*kumpa kitinisa*) to a man is still widespread. *Kitinisa* means "glory, honor, respect, reverence, pomp" (Davis 1938: 79) and men usually receive it from women, not vice versa. During my conversations in the field about women's emancipation, several people expressed annoyance at women's empowerment, which they saw as threatening men's position as leaders, as well as "spoiling our nature, our culture" (*kusiisa buhangwa bwaitu*). This latter discourse, grounded in postcolonial tensions and articulated in gender issues, interprets women's empowerment as the deterioration of local culture brought about by senseless westernization or a strain of neocolonialism. This

---

2   Besides aiming to gain the support of half of the voting population, Museveni's policies to stimulate women's emancipation reflected the decisions taken at the Forth UN Conference on Women held in Beijing in 1995, which pushed measures to improve women's position in society. This conference had a significant impact on motivating the policies, also supported and supplemented by the action and funds of NGOs and foreign governments, in favor of women all around the African continent, as Lisa Gilman (2009: 186–187) documents for Malawi.

SINGING MARRIAGE, *RUNYEGE*, AND LABOR ❧ 73

Figure 2.2. Entertainment during a wedding in Kibate (Bunyoro), 2008. On the left, a performer dances to pop music coming from the loudspeakers in front of him. The bride's family, seated under the gazebo, follows the performance. Standing on the right, the master of ceremonies waits to continue the ceremony.

unease is also in evidence at the national level, in the recent law known as the Anti-Pornography Act which, along with banning nude pictures, forbids women to wear skirts or shorts that do not cover their thighs to the knee.

Returning to couple relationships, in the present precarious landscape, unions established simply by living together and having children allow more flexibility than the traditional wedding because only the couple is involved and no bridewealth is required. Only if the couple is stable is a traditional wedding organized involving both families. For these reasons, traditional weddings are rarer than in the past and usually happen once a couple has lived together for some years and already has children. In contemporary western Uganda, the traditional wedding does not mark a change of status of the bride and groom as in the past, but it is rather the public confirmation and demonstration of a union involving the couple, their families, and clans, which sometimes have never met before the ceremony. For this reason, as it was for John and Maureen's traditional wedding, the main components of the *kweranga* introduction and the *kugaba* giveaway have retained their essence. Although couples also marry in churches or mosques, it is the

74 ❧ CHAPTER TWO

traditional marriage that is recognized as the "real" one by the relatives, who formally get to know each other through the *kweranga,* and in the *kugaba* officially acknowledge that the bride is becoming part of a new family.

While weddings like John and Maureen's follow a traditional structure, most of the music accompanying the ceremony was not Nyoro old songs, but Ugandan popular music. Romantic songs of renowned Ganda artists created the affective and contemplative background for the various stages of the search of the bride among her female relatives, her discovery by the groom, their reciprocal gift exchange, and formal engagement. This musical accompaniment seems to convey the understanding of these moments as a (reenacted) quest for love depicted with the emphatic terms, captivating melodies, and passionate rendition of romantic popular songs that describe the emotions, sentiments, and relationships of present Ugandan society. Music thus gives a contemporary reading of the traditional ceremony— which essentially featured a man who wins a woman away from her family to found his own family—allowing it to fit in today's changed couple relationships and social expectations that emphasize romantic emotions in marriage.

Given the contemporary meaning of traditional weddings, old Nyoro and Tooro songs depicting a bride who leaves her home to face difficult challenges in a new family, or a groom who comes back home as a man because he got his wife, do not reflect the present-day situation. For this reason, traditional wedding songs are not performed by the family or the hired cultural groups. Today's bride and groom are already adults, who usually live together and have their own children. The emotionality in traditional songs lay in the separation of the bride from her relatives and the destabilizing changing status of the couple, as I will discuss below. This no longer happens and a couple's decision to marry, usually after years of shared life, takes on the meaning of love and lifelong commitment. The emotional charge of the wedding is channeled through popular romantic Ugandan songs (in Runyoro-Rutooro, or more frequently in Luganda language), which accompany important stages of the ceremony or are lip synched by the members of the cultural groups. Through these romantic songs the eurogenic idea of love, also present in most of the Ugandan songs, resignifies part of the ceremony as manifesting the individual choice of the reciprocal commitment of the bride and groom. While traditional wedding songs expressed the voices of the members of the two families, contemporary romantic songs move the focus onto the newlyweds. In these songs, the feelings of love, affection, and desire are conveyed as expressing the bride's and the groom's sentiments and it is through these songs that the contemporary significance of a traditional wedding, as the commitment of two individuals, emerges. Finally, in John and Maureen's traditional wedding as well as in most of the weddings I attended, the only song by an American singer, "Congratulations" by Cliff

Richard, accompanied the other element besides the engagement ring that was clearly adopted from Global North weddings: the cutting of the cake. This song disrupted the contemplative ambience created by other songs to break in with a joyful exultation for the newly formed couple.

Consistently with other ceremonies I observed, the only traditional Nyoro music in John and Maureen's wedding was *runyege*—sung, played, and danced by the hired cultural group. It was not performed during the pursuit of the bride, although the dance involves choosing a partner and forming a couple, but it marked, through the meaningful lyrics of the accompanying songs, the joyful moments of the ceremony, such as the welcoming of the guests, the celebration after the acceptance of the bridewealth, and the final exultation after the welcoming of the bride into her new family. The energetic display of physical stamina involved in *runyege* dancing and the final moments of finding a dance partner does not fit the romantic and emotional affect that dominates other moments of the ceremony, which are accompanied by popular love songs.

Contemporary weddings in western Uganda retain traditional structures and elements but also resignify them through a use of music drawn in part from the local tradition, and also from new popular forms of national success. Nevertheless, Nyoro and Tooro wedding repertoires are sung today in staged performances by school pupils and, seldom, by cultural groups. The reference for these performances are the old ceremonies as they are preserved and interpreted in the memories and recollections of the elders. In the next sections, I discuss traditional weddings in the past and their connected songs.

"Where There Are Cows, There Is a Child": Traditional Weddings and Songs

Traditional wedding songs depict gendered relations and customs that in essence are still considered central in the local culture. Before the religious and economic transformations of the twentieth century changed social customs, weddings marked the passage from childhood to adulthood among the Banyoro and Batooro (Nyakatura 1970; Roscoe 1923: 264–283).[3]

---

3   Roscoe (1923: 260–263) also mentions a ceremony involving the removal of the six front teeth in the lower jaw, which marked the puberty of boys and girls and their being ready for marriage. I have found no information about this practice during my fieldwork nor in other written sources and I suppose it disappeared long ago and was performed mainly among the pastoralist groups that were the main informants for Roscoe's ethnography.

76 ❧ CHAPTER TWO

Through marriage, a male became a man: he built a house for his wife and future children and thus became *nyineka*, head of the family (Davis 1938: 139). Having just a house (*nju*) was not enough to make a man out of a male, it was a wife and children that would make it a family, a home (*ka*). For a girl, marriage meant leaving her father's house and moving to her husband's, thus becoming *nyinenju*,[4] mistress of a house (Davis 1938: 139). Considering the great importance placed on premarital virginity, the wedding marked the beginning of a woman's sexual life and her procreation potential (Roscoe 1923: 272–273; Taylor 1998: 25). A married woman created a home by generating and taking care of a family: both the term *muka*, wife, and *mukazi*, woman, are derived from *ka*, home. Furthermore, as in other languages around the world, *mukazi* is also broadly used with the meaning of wife, showing how fundamental marriage was in making a female a woman.

The different status of women (as brides and wives) and men (as grooms and husbands) was manifested during the wedding. The groom had an active role in taking the bride and in bringing her to their new house, while the bride's role was more passive, as she was taken away by a man. This dissymmetry is encoded in the language as it still used today: a man "marries" (*aswera*), a woman "is married" (*aswerwa*). The individuals who did not marry and did not have children were marginalized and mistreated by the community (Roscoe 1923: 239), and people used denigrating expressions to refer to them. For instance, an unmarried woman was called *kadiba,* from the verb *kudiba* "to be left over, remain unsold" (Davis 1938: 23) with the diminutive prefix *ka,* alluding to the immature condition of this person. In the local wedding dynamic where men "take" women, an unmarried woman is seen as a leftover and is treated with pity, as were Zaliya's daughters in the song opening this chapter. Although subordinate to her husband, a wife had a higher status than an unmarried woman (Taylor 1998: 34).

Among the various types of Nyoro marriages, ranging from the ideal traditional marriage to less formalized kinds of union (see Beattie 1958), I focus here on the traditional type because the sung repertoires mostly refer to that kind of wedding ceremony. In virilocal and exogamic Nyoro and Tooro societies, the wedding marked not only the change of status of the newlyweds, but it also established a bond between the two families and their clans (Mukasa-Balikuddembe 1973; Taylor 1998: 105–111). This bond was not egalitarian: the bride's family was in the position of "giver" of a girl to the groom's "receiver" family, and this meant losing a daughter. The "receiver"

---

4   In Tooro, the term *nyinabwenge* (lit. mother of knowledge), probably deriving from the neighboring Runyankore language, is also used with the meaning of *nyinenju* (Davis 1938: 139).

family would offer many goods to the bride's family, but they would never be considered enough to compensate for the girl having to leave her natal family. This uneven power relationship between families reflected mainly on the husband, who was expected to be respectful toward his wife's family and to carry out services for them. The gifts given to the bride's family as bridewealth consisted mainly of cows and banana beer. In the words of the chorus of a well-known Tooro wedding song, *Ekiruma ente nikyo ekiruma omwana*, "Where there are cows, there is a child," showing the close association between cattle and girls/brides. The word used in Runyoro-Rutooro for the bridewealth is *mukaaga*, which literally means "six" and refers to the customary number of cows offered by the groom's relatives. To the Western gaze, the custom of bridewealth has been interpreted as a form of trade of women between clans (see, for instance, Lévi-Strauss 1969). Also, Beattie (1957: 329) describes the status of a Nyoro daughter in these terms:

> Her father does not regard her, as he does his sons, as a potential source of more members of his line: her children will be born elsewhere to another *ruganda* [clan]. So she is in a sense a negotiable good, and the bridewealth her father receives for her will help him to obtain a wife for her brother or another of her male agnates, perhaps even for her father himself. In marriage her feelings are little considered, and even today fathers often attempt to compel their daughters to remain with husbands whom they dislike, because they are unwilling or perhaps unable to return the money received for her.

Such views have been contested by some Africans scholars, like Oyèrónké Oyěwùmí (1997: 51–52), and they do not correspond to the local understanding of the *mukaaga* custom as was explained to me in the field. From the Nyoro and Tooro perspectives, the traditional six cows would never compensate for the loss of a daughter: she was not a slave to be sold and bought, but a child raised by her clan that would contribute with a new family to another clan. In this sense, the gifts to the bride's family are not a payment, but rather the expression of gratitude to those who brought her up and agreed to let her go, as well as a sort of reparation for their emotional loss. This local understanding is found in various sources about Bunyoro and Tooro (Roscoe 1923: 267; Taylor 1998: 34) and my research participants confirmed it. In particular, two Tooro elderly ladies, Kabuzi and Nyakato (int. August 29, 2011), told me that in the past the *mukaaga* was an appreciation on the part of the groom's family for all that had been done for the bride and, during their youth, there was not the commodification of this custom as there is now.

Various phases marked traditional weddings of the past (Beattie 1958; Mukasa-Balikuddembe 1973; Nyakatura 1970; Roscoe 1923). These included several preliminary meetings between members of the two families,

78 ❧ CHAPTER TWO

in which the fiancés were not involved.[5] They sometimes met each other for the first time during the ceremony of formal introduction (*kweranga*) of the groom's family to the bride's. The *kweranga* was a delicate function, which required reverence and a display of subordination on the part of the groom's relatives while requesting the girl. If it was successful, a ceremony to "give away" (*kubaga*) the bride was organized at her paternal house and ended with the newlyweds moving to the groom's house. As I described previously, today this main conception of the marriage remains, but the various phases are condensed into one event including both the "introduction" and the "giving away."

As no traditional songs were performed at the weddings I attended in Bunyoro and Tooro, it was thanks to elders that I was able to record wedding songs and investigate their meaning. Songs associated with the wedding functions are usually referred to as *bizina by'obuswezi* or *bizina by'okuswera*. This repertoire is wide and most of the songs are connected to specific moments of the wedding ceremony, but they were not gender-specific: both women and men could sing them.[6] The position of the performer to the wedding couple was fundamental: the groom's family and the relatives of the bride performed very different songs. On the whole, the wedding repertoire shows the different connotations and effects of the wedding that cause the transformation of the bride and groom into adults. At the same time, wedding songs express the ambivalence of the newly established relationship and bond between the two families.

On several occasions in 2009 and 2010 I visited the house of the late Aberi Bitamazire in the village of Muuro, near the town of Masindi (northern Bunyoro). Bitamazire was an old musician, locally known as *Ngoma Munana*, "eight drums," because he could play several *ngoma* and *ngaabi* drums by himself (int. August 13, 2009). At his house, his sister Korotirida Matama performed as a soloist various wedding songs while Bitamazire with her nephew Godfrey Kwesiga sang the choruses. Among these songs were the two presented here, which are representative of both the changing status of the bride and the groom and the different perspectives of their families.

---

5   Both fiancés could, however, refuse to marry the person chosen by the families.

6   Some songs were known in geographically circumscribed areas; in particular, in Tooro, Bahuma people performed the songs referred to as *ngoma ny'abahuma*.

Crying for the Loss of a Child: The Bride's Side

The song *Kyera maino* was used in the past when the family had to say farewell to their daughter, who was led away to start a new life in another house. The song presents the qualities of the girl and expresses the sorrow of her family at the separation, as well as concern about the challenges that the new wife will most likely face in her new house.

This song has a standard call-and-response form, in which the solo verses change and the chorus remains the same throughout the performance. Normally, the first solo verses remain the same from singer to singer, both verbally and musically, since together with the chorus they identify the song. Then, after the first verses, the soloist improvises to fit the occasion. It is also common that the final note of either the solo or the chorus—as in this case—overlaps with the beginning of the following line. In this rendition (**A2**), the soloist Korotirida Matama sometimes also sings the beginning of the chorus to amplify it with her voice, since only two other people, Aberi Bitamazire with Godfrey Kwesiga, were singing it.

C: *Kyera maino, galija gakoyere*	White teeth, they will return dirty
S: *Kyera maino, ogenzere nigeera*	White teeth, you go now when they are white
S: *Kyera maino, omwana wange ogu*	White teeth, that child of mine
S: *Kyera maino, kanincura omurungi*	White teeth, let me cry for the good one
S: *Kyera maino, otahaga otaroga*	White teeth, you have not done witchcraft
S: *Kyera maino, ogenzere okuroga*	White teeth, you go and do witchcraft
S: *Kyera maino, otahaga otaiba*	White teeth, you did not steal
S: *Kyera maino, ogenzere okwiba*	White teeth, you go and steal
S: *Kyera maino, kanincura omwana*	White teeth, let me cry for the child
S: *Kyera maino, ai kangambe*	White teeth, ai, let me say
S: *Kyera maino, maama kanculege*	White teeth, mama, let me cry
S: *Kyera maino, caali nogenda*	White teeth, please, you go
S: *Eee, caali nogenda*	Eee, please, you go
S: *Eee, ogenzere okwiba*	Eee, you go to steal

S: *Eee, ogenzere murungi*	Eee, good one, go
S: *Eee, caali murungi noterwa*	Eee, please, the good one will be beaten
S: *Kyera maino, obundi nibasamba*	White teeth, they will sometimes kick you
S: *Eee, caali ogende*	Yes, please, go
S: *Eee, caali maama nincura murungi*	Yes, please, mama, I cry for the good one
S: *Kyera maino*	White teeth

The moment of bidding the bride farewell was emotionally charged for both the family and the girl. In this song, the parents and relatives bewail her departure, in a manner similar to lament songs of this kind of repertoire in other traditions (Facci 1996; Staiti 2012). The song is structured around the verse repeated by the chorus "White teeth, they will return dirty" (*Kyera maino, galija gakoyere*), which I presented only at the beginning of the verbal transcription. In this piece, the bride is referred to through the synecdoche "white teeth": her pure white teeth represent both her beauty and her physical health. This is the condition in which she leaves the paternal house, but when she will return to visit her family, she will have dirty teeth, she will be ugly and weak. The verse of the chorus thus depicts effectively and concisely the condition of a new bride. The soloist's lines describe the difficult situation that the bride-to-be will face in her new house. There she will be a stranger and unjustly accused by her in-laws (and possibly cowives) of witchcraft and theft. Her faults will be punished with punches and kicks. The family's pain at the girl's departure involves not only the separation from her but also empathy for the challenges of her new status.

The comparison of the bride's situation in her paternal home with the one in her marital one recurs in several Nyoro and Tooro wedding songs. The soloist, Korotirida Matama, performed numerous songs presenting the destiny of a bride in a very negative light. She explained to me that that was indeed the situation of girls in the past. According to her, for a girl her wedding was a traumatic event: she would cry because of the suffering of her family as she was leaving and, after the celebrations at the groom's house, her in-laws would retaliate for the treatment received during the wedding from her family (int. Matama: June 29, 2010). Bitamazire and Kwesiga, who sang the chorus, also remarked that men usually choose a wife because of her beauty, but after the wedding they do not take good care of her and she wastes away (int. Bitamazire and Kwesiga: June 29, 2010). In her first account of her stay in Uganda, British missionary Ruth Fisher (1904: 38)

Musical Example 2.1. Transcription of the first verses of *Kyera maino* performed by Korotirida Matama (solo) and Aberi Bitamazire with Godfrey Kwesiga (chorus).

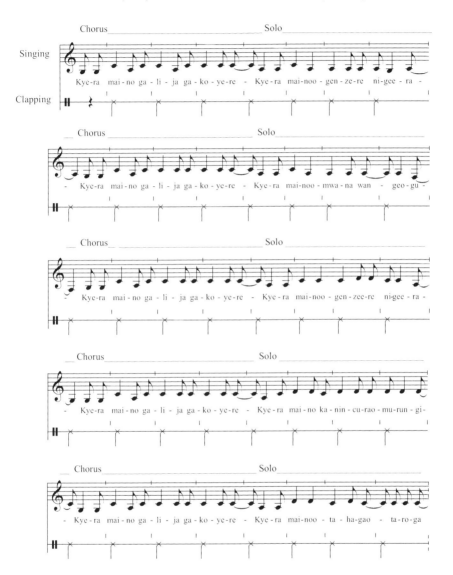

82 ❧ CHAPTER TWO

described local women's view of marriage thus: "They say it has two arms. One brings a home, protection, and presents of clothing and rejoicing. The other shuts the door of liberty; it brings work, and that means sorrow. The thought of the latter predominates on the wedding day." While Fisher's accounts are marked by a colonial and missionary perspective, this description of how women saw marriage nonetheless resonates with the elders' memories and with the words of this song.

Although old sources and the memories that elders presented to me emphasize the negative effects of the wedding for the bride, these seem to be only one of the diverse implications of the wedding for the bride's party and of the multiple meanings conveyed by songs. My impression is that both elders and missionaries stressed the bride's traumatic experience of the wedding and early marriage life in contrast to later conditions. On the one hand, nowadays several women live with their partners for some time and have children before an official ceremony is organized, so the wedding does not mark a significant change in young women's life by involving the departure from her paternal family and home as was the case decades ago. On the other hand, the influence of Christianity on Ugandan society supported a more equalitarian conception of marriage based on monogamy and mutual cooperation, which generally improved the condition of wives compared to the past.

Furthermore, the emphasis that the bride's relatives placed on the difficulties of married life and depicted in many songs can also be understood more broadly, as emblematic of the relationship between the two families. In the first place, the antagonism of the bride's relatives toward the groom's family: although the wedding created a bond between them, they remained strangers, people of another clan. The daughter that grew up in the loving circle of her family was a *mwana w'ahara,* a child of far away, destined to leave her home as a bride and become part of another family that was viewed with diffidence. The song, indeed, depicts her departure as permanent, both emotionally and conceptually, although the new wife could periodically visit her original family. The loss of a daughter could not be compensated for by the *mukaaga,* but required continuous care through the deference of the groom. Second, because of this unequal exchange between the two families, the groom's relatives would always be in a subordinate position to the bride's, as several proverbs show (Beattie 1977). Hence, describing the groom's family in pejorative terms strengthened the feeling of superiority of the bride's relatives in relation to the other family.

Finally, the songs for the bride have an educative value, as among the Basoga of eastern Uganda (Bukaayi 2009). By leaving her family, the bride became a woman and she would have to prove capable of managing a new household and dealing with her in-laws, who would probably, at least at first, treat her unfairly. By giving birth to children, her position as a wife would be consolidated. Through the offspring, she would be accepted by her in-laws and respected as a mother, though remaining subordinate to her husband and male relatives. Through these songs, with verses conveying bitterness, the bride's family not only showed her their love in the moment of parting but also prepared her for the inevitable challenges of being a wife.

Celebrating a New Family: The Groom's Side

According to the recollections of the elders that I consulted during fieldwork, the mood was very different when the groom arrived home with his bride—his relatives traditionally performed cheerful and celebratory songs. Their joyful feeling derived from having their boy return home as a man, but also from welcoming the bride, whose appearance was usually praised. At this point in the wedding ceremony, there was no trace of the diffidence and malice that the bride's relatives had predicted, possibly because of the festive character of the celebrations. Still, several of my research participants emphasized that this did not mean that frictions and issues with the new wife would not emerge within her new family. While the opposition between the sorrow of the bride's party and the joy of the groom's is globally common in societies marked by patriarchy and virilocality (Sugarman 1997), the descriptions of most of my research participants seem to generalize events of the past quite univocally, without presenting a space for alternatives in the wedding narrative. By stressing the tensions that past weddings generated, they seemed to emphasize how this tradition was different from today's ceremonies. Participants underscored the bride's family's preventive complaints while also saying that at her arrival at the groom's she was welcomed, showing the deep involvement of both families in the wedding and the latent hostility between them, as can occur between two groups of strangers. Indeed, the main difference between traditional and present-day weddings is that the relevance of traditional ones lay in the interactions and exchange between two previously unrelated families, while today the focus is on the newlyweds, two individuals who choose each other and involve their families to acknowledge this fact. This shift of emphasis in weddings is also echoed by the music involved: today, love songs depicting the sentiments of the couple, and in the past, different songs for the two families describing the effects caused by their opposed positions.

The song *Kamutwaire* ("He got her," **A3**)—performed in 2010 by Korotirida Matama, Aberi Bitamazire, and Godfrey Kwesiga—depicts the groom's family point of view: their satisfaction in welcoming back their boy, now a man. It has a call-and-response form and joyful character: most songs with these features also accompany *runyege* dancing; it was indeed common to dance while celebrating the newlyweds' arrival home.

84 &♥ CHAPTER TWO

The chorus is entirely yodeled (*kuhugura*) and performed also by the soloist Matama, whose voice strengthens Aberi Bitamazire and Godfrey Kwesiga's singing, as in the previous song. The different vowels employed (*e, i, u*) in *kuhugura* are associated either with high (head voice) or bass (chest voice) notes. The change of vowel helps to select the harmonics to connote the different timbric colors of high and bass notes, like in yodeling from the Alpine region or in central Africa, for instance among the BaAka (Fürniss 1991). This specific song has been taught in Nyoro schools for performance in the national festival, as well as adapted as a thanksgiving song for pupils. While the chorus in these school renditions maintains the use of vowels, there is no real yodeling, as part of an ongoing transformation of *kuhugura* into simple vowel-singing, which I discuss with more detail further on.

Matama and Bitamazire (int. June 29, 2010) explained to me that in the past they performed this song on the arrival of the groom at his house with his new bride, or when the bride was leaving her house to thank her family and, by praising the groom, showing that she had married well. The lyrics commend the groom and exalt his return home with a wife:

S: *Kamutwaire kamutwaire*	He has taken her, he has taken her
C: *Eeeyi ee ye*	[yodel]
S: *Ogende n'oserra*	Go and seek
S: *Omwana kamutwaire*	The child got her
S: *Akoojo k'eisomero*	The [educated] boy of the school
S: *Akoojo k'eidinda*	The boy of the pleat[7]
S: *Webaale murungi*	Thank you, good one
S: *Webaale okwija*	Welcome
S: *Olesere omwana*	You have brought a child
S: *Omwana w'engonzi*	A child of love
S: *Acumbege n'alya*	Always cook and he eats
S: *Omwana wange ogwo*	That child of mine
S: *Omwana bw'agenda*	When the child goes
S: *Omwana kamboine*	The child saw
S: *Nsimire omurungi*	I have appreciated the good one

---

7   *Idinda* literally means a "pleat"; the plural form *madinda* also means "xylophone" (Davis 1938: 48 and 88). My research assistant Issa interprets the line *Akoojo k'eidinda* as meaning "the special boy."

Musical Example 2.2. Transcription of the first lines of *Kamutwaire* performed by Korotirida Matama (solo) with Aberi Bitamazire and Godfrey Kwesiga (chorus).

In contrast to the bride's side, the wedding songs of the groom's relatives normally express joy and excitement. As is the case here, the lyrics usually refer to the fact that the boy came home with a child (woman), meaning that he is now a man. A wife allowed a man to "gain respect," her subordinated position supported the status of manhood, with its authority and power. I previously mention that a wife is fundamental in the production of the house and the home by bearing children and providing food for the household. Thanks to his wife, a man became *nyineka*, owner of the house and head of the family. Because of her essential role in defining a man as such and her

86 ❧ CHAPTER TWO

contribution to the family and the clan (through her work and children), the bride was welcomed as a member of the extended family. However, the new family expected hard work and deference from her and would reprimand and punish her if she made mistakes. Indeed, submission and obedience were considered fundamental characteristics in a wife. Such a woman would be described as *murungi*—a word coming up in this and other songs about the bride. Its translation to English is challenging because it means both "good person" and "beautiful person" (Davis 1938: 112). This double connotation of *murungi* resembles that of the Greek word καλός, which in relation to a person can mean pleasant appearance as well as moral virtuosity, somehow implying that inner goodness reflects in outer beauty. After much discussion with my research assistants, I decided to use "good" in the translations of the songs because of the importance of demeanor over attractiveness in the qualities of a wife that was stressed by numerous research participants. The same point was made by British anthropologist Beattie (1977: 89): "Banyoro are quite explicit about the ideal wife's virtues, among the most valued of which is submissiveness. In theory at any rate, good character is preferred to physical beauty."

Just as an unmarried woman was seen as deserving of pity, so the condition of a single man was, and in a way still is, considered regrettable. Some proverbs reported by Margaret B. Davis (1941: 123) illustrate this: *Ey'muhuuru tegira mucwe*, "the bachelor's meat has no gravy." Such a man does not have a woman to cook for him and he lacks tasty food and proper nutrition. This saying shows the solitude of a single man and, at the same time, emphasizes men's need to have a woman at their side who carries out those chores that are considered womanish, like cooking. Davis (1941: 122) reports also the proverb *Okwikara busa oswera okujuma*, "rather than remain a single, marry a nagging woman": even an undesirable wife, one who does not show deference to her husband, is better than being single. Indeed, a bachelor or a deserted husband was disdainfully called *muhuuru*, from the radical *huuru* "thin, feeble person" (Davis 1938: 46, 104), thus underlining his ineptitude as a man.

Wedding songs like *Kamutwaire* are nowadays performed almost exclusively at the school festival. Here, the performance of a "traditional folk song" is a sequence of various songs connected so as to weave a narrative, as I discuss in chapter 5. In the case of a "traditional folk song" about the traditional wedding, different wedding songs are performed one after the other in order to depict the successive elements of the ceremony, from the desire of a man to get married, through the bride's family's perspective, to the final euphoria when he arrives home with a wife. The songs' suite closes with a song like *Kamutwaire*, which develops to a joyful climax including *runyege* dance. *Runyege* songs and dance could indeed be performed to mark the celebrations at the groom's—a function that they maintain in contemporary weddings—but the performing contexts and underlying meanings of *runyege* songs were not limited to that, as I discuss in the following.

Singing *Runyege*: Past and Present

Combining data from historical recordings and the recollections of elders, *runyege* emerges as a genre that could host a great variety of sung repertoires and topics. The most common performance context for *runyege* were banana beer parties where beer songs[8] usually accompanied the dancing. In addition, *bigano* story-songs, wedding songs for the groom (as previously shown), and welcoming and rejoicing songs (like those performed at contemporary weddings) could also be used in *runyege*.

In both Wachsmann's and Tracey's recordings,[9] when call-and-response singing accompanies dancing, women mainly performed the chorus, while the soloists were invariably men. The documentation does not clarify whether male soloists were the norm during the 1950s and 1960s, or whether it was just a matter of contingency. According to some of my research participants, it was possible for a woman to lead the singing, although it was not very common in the past. Indeed, the soloist's preeminent role in the performance, speaking out freely before performers and onlookers, seems hardly compatible with the notion of hegemonic femininity as being marked by shyness and modesty. The different roles of solo and chorus are reflected by the local terminology: the soloist is called *mutongerezi,* "the one leading the song," or *musumukirizi,* "the one connecting the words," and the chorus is called *banukuzi* or *bakugarukamu,* "those who answer." In village performances, the *runyege* soloist could freely navigate diverse topics by combining verbal improvisation with proverbs, or drawing on other songs with a similar structure or theme, as in other African musical cultures such as among the Banande of eastern Congo (Facci 1996). The soloist could also sing about topical events, as highlighted by Torelli (1973), and could spur the dance

---

8   Among Tracey's recordings, *Obugambo bunsemerire ngalyara* and *Obundiba ntaizire* are described as "drinking songs": they deal with banana beer parties and are accompanied by *binyege* and clapping (Tracey 1973b: 297). Two other pieces (*Kotabijuba* and *Abagenyi baizire*) are presented as "*engwara n'orunyege* dance songs for men": the first song criticizes a person who does not accomplish his tasks, such as clearing weeds; the second one welcomes visitors (Tracey 1973b: 299).

9   Most historical recordings of *runyege* and other rattle dances feature instrumental accompaniment only (see chapter 3), while sung accompaniment is more rarely featured.

88 &❧ CHAPTER TWO

on or express social disapproval or criticism. The soloist was hence a leading figure in the performance and enjoyed great agency and freedom of expression—qualities traditionally associated with masculinity.

The soloist's autonomy moved within the frame of the melodically and verbally consistent chorus repetition. In most of the call-and-response songs that I recorded, the lyrics of the chorus depicted or referenced the song's content. In historical recordings of sung *runyege*, usually the chorus did not feature lyrics but vowels sang with a rapid switching between chest and head voices—the technique usually referred to as yodeling and locally known as *kuhugura*,[10] which is used also in the song *Kamutwaire* presented above. As Wachsmann's and Tracey's historical recordings document,[11] yodeling seemed to be quite widespread in Bunyoro in the mid-1950s, but not documented for Tooro. Wachsmann (1956: 4) briefly mentions yodeling as characteristic of Bairu agriculturalists' singing. For Peter Cooke (email April 3, 2012) yodeling was typical of the area of Bunyoro facing Lake Albert[12] because of the exchanges of the local Bagungu (population considered part of the Banyoro) with the groups living on the other side of the basin, in particular in the Ituri forest, who employ yodeling in their singing. Also Solomon Mbabi-Katana (int. June 30, 2011) considered yodeling characteristic of Iru singing and noticed that it was less and less practiced already during the 1970s.

Indeed, during my fieldwork, I was not able to find many people still able to perform it. Those who could yodel were mainly elders from northern Bunyoro like Matama, while in Tooro yodeling was not known, even in the past. In the historical recordings and the repertoires I recorded from elders, *kuhugura* yodeling was used in a variety of vocal repertoires, including

---

10   Far less frequently I heard the verb *kuhirimba* used to refer to this vocal technique, especially when performed by women. Differently from *kuhugura*, which is translated as yodel (Davis 1938: 45), this second term is not reported in Davis' 1938 dictionary.

11   Yodeling features in Wachsmann's recordings in Mbogwe of call-and-response songs for dancing (*Ensolima ikaija n'Abajungu, Mukunge mulise, Ayarungire abakazi kakarunga, Mukunge Stefano, Kawairanga,* and *Kahara niwe ow'omuyaga*) and in all of his recordings among the Bagungu community in Butiaba along Lake Albert. In Tracey's collection, yodeling is present in the recordings made in Hoima and Hoima District: call-and-response songs for dancing (*Obundiba ntaizire, Ayahangiri abakazi, Mukunge Stefano, Kawairanga, Muli baripiya,* and *Kaburora akaiba muhogo*) and solo songs accompanied by the *kidongo* harp (*Amarwa tinganywa, Omukungu nakan-yagwe, Ekyoma kyabora, Rwakyesiga ensolima,* and *Kigara kyamsiriba*).

12   Lake Albert is the colonial but, even today, official name of the water basin known as Nyanja Mwitanzige ("lake locust killer") in Runyoro-Rutooro.

wedding, *runyege,* and religious songs. Today, it is rarely used in the chorus of modern performances. Young performers in schools and ensembles seem to be unfamiliar with this vocal technique and normally perform choruses that maintain simplified melodic lines without any changes in voice range. Yodeling as a specific technique seems to be disappearing and, through the school festival and the ensembles' practice, vocalized choruses are becoming the new "traditional" model.

It is hard to understand why yodeling is almost no longer performed today and is being replaced by simple vowel-singing that is considered by some schoolteachers to be *kuhugura.* Yodeling was not attached to a specific genre of songs that were abandoned, as it could have been if it were used only for songs related to the traditional religion condemned by missionaries; on the contrary, it was used for different songs of the Iru culture. My impression is that yodeling may be subsumed by the influence of Western vocal techniques (church singing and popular music) combined with an homogenization at a national level through music education and the school festival. *Kuhugura* vocal technique from Bunyoro is an isolated case in the singing arena of Uganda, together with the undocumented and marginalized vocal repertoires of the Batwa from south Uganda and northern Rwanda. The dissemination of church singing and popular music combined with the absence of a singing technique similar to *kuhugura* being taught in schools or featured at the national festival (Twa repertoires have not been acknowledged yet) has most probably led to a propensity to perform songs without switching between vocal registers. Also, the attention of the jury at school festivals seems more focused on considering the appropriate regional language (category "traditional folk song") and dance style (category "traditional folk dance") than on other elements of singing, like vocal emission and technique. Therefore, the conservation of this specific singing technique was not stimulated in schools and, consequently, in semiprofessional groups, whose members learned to perform traditional repertoires mostly at school.

Schoolchildren at the school festival and members of cultural groups are the contemporary performers of the songs used to accompany *runyege,* as well as of other traditional songs. Since *runyege* is no longer performed informally in the villages, the performers learn the songs at rehearsals in preparation for a show. The changes in performance contexts as well as in the performers' training and age have brought about transformations not only in singing style, such as the abandonment of yodeling, but also in the lyrics and the singing roles. The topics of the songs now rarely involve beer or current events, but rather reflect the feelings of joy and happiness inspired by the occasion—most often a wedding or the arrival of visitors—and deal with friendship and love. The current focus on such topics seems to have led to the interpretation and representation of *runyege* as a joyful and courtship

90 &❧ CHAPTER TWO

dance, which is today the most common view of this genre, both locally and in Uganda generally.

Furthermore, the gendering of soloist and chorus as masculine and feminine roles is not as strong as in the past. On the one hand, in staged performances some song subjects covered in the past, such as beer drinking, are deemed inappropriate for schools. In addition, verse improvisation containing social critique has lessened. These transformations provoked the decrease of the freedom connoting the masculinity associated to the soloist's role. On the other hand, performances in girls-only schools required female soloists, and this practice spread to semiprofessional ensembles; today girls and women sing the solo part. Currently, in schools and cultural groups the choice of the soloist is determined not by gender but mostly by the vocal power of the singer, whose voice has to rise above the instrumental accompaniment.

Gender still determines singing roles in other repertoires, in particular those related to work activities, which I discuss in the last part of this chapter.

Labor Division, Food Processing, and Cattle in Work Songs

In Runyoro-Rutooro, work (*mulimo*) refers specifically to agricultural work; indeed, the connected verb, *kulima,* means "to cultivate, to dig" (Davis 1938: 146). However, the label of work songs is today employed in the Ugandan school festival to identify, among the "traditional folk songs," the repertoires about various productive activities. I have adopted this broad idea of work to discuss both labor division and some of the related repertoires.

The past diversity in Nyoro and Tooro society including the agriculturists (Bairu), who made up most of the population, and the minority of pastoralists (Bahuma) survives in some of the songs remembered by the elders. Because of the ecological crisis that decimated the cattle herds in early colonial times (Doyle 2006), in Bunyoro the Bahuma pastoralists and their culture almost disappeared, while Huma tradition was kept alive in Tooro. This is where I was able to record songs related to cattle rearing. Livestock was very important as moveable property in the whole interlacustrine region (Chrétien 2000) and, for this reason, cows were praised in songs (*bizina by'ente*). These songs were performed only by men, in praise of their herd. Cattle were men's property, and leading the cows to pasture, protecting and taking care of them, and milking them were considered men's tasks. Women, however, preserved the milk and prepared dairy products such as butter and cow ghee.

SINGING MARRIAGE, *RUNYEGE*, AND LABOR 🙰 91

Gendered labor division also existed among the Bairu and several sung repertoires were connected with working activities. Men performed some specialized activities like pottery and smithery (Nyakatura 1970; Roscoe 1923), and Torelli (1973) reported that smiths sang to coordinate their work. Men also fished and hunted (Roscoe 1923: 315–322) and some repertoires are related to these activities.[13] Men's contribution to agriculture was mainly limited to clearing the fields and taking care of the beer banana trees. Beer bananas and beer production were indeed considered men's work. Women (and children) did most of the work in the fields: digging, planting, weeding, and harvesting. Women's activities were, and in part still are, connected to the cultural space of the home, *ka*, in contrast to *nju*, house. While a *nju* is a mere building, *ka* is a dwelling that requires maintenance (cleaning and supplies), but also a family that needs cooked meals and care. In this sense, the idea of womanhood as connected to reproduction is tied to the space of the home: a woman produces children and the food for the family. As in other societies in the world, for instance the Albanian Prespa (Sugarman 1997: 177–178), a distinction between private and public spaces connected to gender also marked Nyoro and Tooro society, especially in the past. Among both the Bahuma and the Bairu, the home and family fields and their connected activities (food production, children bearing and raising) connoted femininity; the open and public spaces of the grazing fields, bushes, and the village with their associated activities (cattle rearing, hunting and forest work, pottery and smithing) marked the domain of masculinity. However, this separation was not absolute since men collaborated in both the fields (preparation of the land and care of a special type of bananas in the plantation) and the house (building and structural maintenance).

Staple and vegetable cultivation, processing of agricultural products and cooking were women's responsibilities. Especially in the past, it was taboo for a man to cook or even to watch his wife cooking, and if he refused to eat it was a grave offense to his wife, who could use this as a reason to leave him (Torelli 1973: 471–473). The kitchen (*icumbiro*) is a woman's domain and exclusively a feminine space. Both in old huts and in most of today's brick houses, the kitchen is a separate room that men are not supposed to enter. Even today, the kitchen is a place where a woman can seek refuge in case of conflict or a fight with her husband; she can be safe there since a man would never enter; doing so would undermine his masculinity and could even lead to him being rejected by his clan (int. Iraka: June 28, 2010; int. Muhuruzi:

---

13 Wachsmann recorded songs related to hunting (recordings in Bwanswa in 1954: *Empuunu, Engabi*, and *Hunting omuso*), and the horns and whistles used during the hunt. In the areas where men still hunt, such as Kibaire (central Bunyoro), horns are still used today.

92 &❧ CHAPTER TWO

March 25, 2008). Iru women usually sang during their working activities and their repertoires are mainly related to cereal grinding, firewood collecting, and child care (lullabies).

In the following sections, I analyze an Iru women's song for millet grinding and a Huma men's song in praise of cows.

A Women's Grinding Song: *Ke ke kamengo*

While grinding millet, it was common for Nyoro and Tooro women to sing songs related to the cereal and the processing of it. Finger millet (*buro*) was the basis of the local diet. Ground and mixed with cassava flour, millet was, and is, cooked with water to produce a sort of polenta (*karo*). While today women often have their cereals ground at an electrical mill, in the past millet was normally ground on a sloped stone (*rumengo*), on which the woman would press and grind the grains using a smaller stone.

Millet grinding songs were common in both Bunyoro and Tooro since every woman used to grind millet for her family and singing made this daily activity lighter and faster. These songs were sung alone and usually made mention of the *kamengo,* a diminutive form of the *rumengo* grinding stone, showing the affective connection to the tool connoted as feminine. One of these songs is *Ke ke kamengo* (**A4**), which I recorded in Muuro sung by Dorothy Kahwa. Kahwa was an old Nyoro woman who remembered these songs from her younger years, although she said that she had not sung them for probably fifty years (int. August 13, 2009).

Every verse of the song corresponds to four main beats. While singing, Kahwa beat regularly on a table (small triangle above the notes in the transcription). She was trying to imitate the rhythm of rubbing the millet on the grinding stone, which her sister-in-law Joy showed me later (Fig. 2.3). Singing helped not only to mitigate the monotony of grinding, but it also regulated the pace. Indeed, the main beat of the song was synchronized with the manual movement. Since the onomatopoeic syllable *ke* [ke] or *ce* [tʃe] recurs as an imitation of the sound produced on the grinding stone,[14] the words also keep the singing connected with the physical activity of grinding. Finally, in every verse of the song, the second part (*kamengo kaseere bali*) is repeated uniformly each time, while the first part features verbal and melodic

---

14 The opening verse, repeated during the song, contains the alliteration of the sound [k] which, besides marking the onomatopoeic *ke,* is due to the phenomenon of alliterative harmony. This is typical of Bantu languages, where verbs (here *kaseere*) inflect like the noun to which they refer (*kamengo*), thus producing the repetition of the same consonants.

SINGING MARRIAGE, *RUNYEGE*, AND LABOR 93

Figure 2.3. Joy Katusabe Bitamazire showing how to grind millet on the *rumengo* stone. Muuro (Bunyoro), 2009.

variations. The internal structure of the verses thus seems structured as a sort of call-and-response. In chapter 5, I present a version of this piece performed by children at the school festival, where these elements of the song's structure are split up between soloist (call) and a choir (response).

The lyrics further show the connection of women with the grinding stone and their role within the family:

Ke ke, kamengo kaseere bali	Ke ke, grinding stone grind for them
Kambaseere, kamengo kaseere bali	Let me grind for them, grinding stone grind for them
Mubatikire, kamengo kaseere bali	Put the water on the fire, grinding stone grind for them
Baana balye, kamengo kaseere bali	The children eat, grinding stone grind for them

Muteke mu, kamengo kaseere bali	Pour it, grinding stone grind for them
Muteke mu ensaano, kamengo kaseere bali	Pour flour into the water, grinding stone grind for them
Ke ke, kamengo kaseere bali	Ke ke, grinding stone grind for them

Musical Example 2.3. Transcription of the central lines of *Ke ke kamengo* performed by Dorothy Kahwa. The notes without head denote the sounds missing when the performer inhaled because of lack of breath; the lyrics syllables corresponding to these missing notes are given anyway.

The song addresses the grinding stone, telling it to grind for "them," the family and children for whom the woman is making the flour. The verses also give instructions (probably directed to her children) to prepare the boiling water into which the millet flour will be poured to obtain the *karo* polenta. Different from other women's working songs in sub-Saharan Africa reported for example by Gerhard Kubik (1999), in this specific case there is no reference to a women's condition or an expression of her feeling. However, this element can be traced in other millet songs, as well as in lullabies. In this piece, the woman is somehow integrated with the grinding stone in shared sounds, rhythm, and purpose: processing cereals in order to prepare food for the family.

Bizina by'ente: Men Praising Cows

In Tooro, some repertoires of the Huma pastoralist culture were documented in historical recordings[15] and are still remembered by a few elders and sometimes performed by cultural groups. Among these are the *bizina by'ente* (songs of/for the cows),[16] which were exclusively performed by men. To understand these repertoires, the value assigned to cattle in Huma culture, and among the Bantu populations of the African Great Lakes region more generally, must be understood. According to French historian Jean-Pierre Chrétien (2000), besides providing food (milk, ghee, meat) and other valuable resources (hide, horns, dung) for the community, cattle played a crucial role in the symbolism of human relations. They allowed men to weave interpersonal relations (marriages, alliances, and friendships) and to remedy social tensions, as among other neighboring societies practicing agriculture, like the Banande of Congo (Remotti 1993). While bulls were sometimes bred (for stud) and calves supplied most of the meat; cows were seldom slaughtered because they provided milk, which was a staple of the Huma diet, and could produce more cattle. For this reason, cows

---

15 Wachsmann, Tracey, and Cooke recorded the *kizina ky'ente* commonly known as *Bwasemera obugenyi bw'omunywani wange* with different lyrics. This song thus appears with different incipits: Wachsmann recorded it in Kisomoro as *Kabusemere obugenyi bwa munywani wange;* Tracey in Bukuuku in two versions with the "titles" *Bwasemera obugenyi bw'omunywani wange* and *Ilemere abagorra nsonga ilemere;* Cooke in Butiiti, also in two versions, as *Kabusemere* and *Mweyanze.* Cooke also documented another song for cows: *Mbere mwaruga.*

16 Occasionally also called *bijengo.* According to Davis (1938: 71), this word is from the neighboring language Runyankore, and means "recitation in praise of brave deeds." However, the related verb *kujenga* also means "to sing cattle songs" (Davis 1938: 54).

96 ❧ CHAPTER TWO

were used as movable assets for social and economic exchanges as well as a sign of wealth. This view was shared by my research participant Kenneth Nyakairu (int. July 22, 2010), who depicted cows, women, and friendships as being highly valued in traditional Tooro. He also described them as being closely interrelated: with cows, a man could afford the bridewealth and get a wife, or help economically someone who would then become his friend; he could ask a friend for cows or, if he had a daughter, he could get cows as bridewealth.

Among the Bahuma, the authority of men over women, their status, and decision-making capacity also derived from owning cattle. This gendered asymmetry emerges also from the analysis of Huma songs (besides *bizina by'ente*, also women's *nanga* and men's *ngabu* poems) by Tooro scholar Isaac Tibasiima (2009). In considering power relations in local repertoires, he showed how gender imbalance surfaces as an established setting not only through the gendering of the singing genres but also through the relational positioning of the singing persona, who has, however, some possibility of negotiating her situation. Besides their symbolism connected to social relations, Chrétien (2000) also observed that cows have a preeminent value in terms of social standing. Cattle ownership established the status of men and their families by showing their prestige. In this sense, Bahuma pastoralists were perceived as a sort of aristocracy by the majority of the Bairu agriculturalists.

The importance of cattle is reflected in *bizina by'ente*, songs that describe cows' beauty and express their value in the local economy and society. Traditionally, men as the owners of cattle performed these repertoires, which included detailed depictions of cows' coats, horns, behavior, and genealogy.[17] Cattle is the subject of other male vocal repertoires among pastoralist populations in East Africa, like the *oli* songs of the Di-Dinga from South Sudan documented by Felicia McMahon (2007: 86–115). While these repertoires too are rich in descriptions of the cattle through specific terminology and convey a praising of the animals through the affection of their owners, they are dedicated to bulls and not to cows. Some Nilo-Saharan populations of East Africa like the Di-Dinga, indeed, connect each boy with a specific bull through a "bull name," the name of the calf that the boy is given by his father (McMahon 2007: 89–90). The Di-Dinga *oli* bull songs praise this first bull that every boy is gifted and associates with. As the calf grows, the boy also grows up and becomes an adult through the male initiation ceremony, where he is supposed to perform his *oli* song (McMahon 2007: 106). The

---

17   However, I also recorded some songs for cows that commented on topical events, probably following the popularization of these repertoires among Bairu.

variability of the sex of the cattle praised in the dedicated vocal repertoires in East Africa seems due to the different structure of the societies expressing them. While Nilo-Saharian pastoralists were traditionally homogeneous and nonhierarchical populations structured according to age-groups that involved male initiation and the association of boys with bulls, several Bantu populations of the region were historically heterogeneous and hierarchical (composed by higher status pastoralists, like the Bahuma and Bahima in southwestern Uganda or the Tutsi in Rwanda and Burundi, among a majority of lower-status agriculturalists) and did not have age-groups or specific initiation rituals into adulthood. Hence, Nilo-Saharan boys identified with bulls and sang about them in songs that were especially created by each boy for his initiation and that remained as a personal song when he became a man (McMahon 2007: 90, 106). In contrast, among the Bantu populations it was adult men who sang about their cows: by owning the movable assets represented by cows they could perform the social practices essential in defining masculinity, that is, marrying and establishing alliances and friendships, as well as showing their status as pastoralists or as wealthy men, if they owned large herds.

I present here a *kizina ky'ente* that Gerrison Kinyoro (solo) performed with two other men (chorus) at my request. The singers were not very familiar with the song, which also has a changing chorus, and this uncertainty can be heard in the recording (**A5**).

In this song and the others that I documented in Tooro, the melismatic singing, rich in ornamental notes and considered typical of Huma culture, is not employed, unlike the *bizina by'ente* in historical recordings. This is probably due to the progressive integration of the Bahuma with the Bairu because of the reduction of pastoralism, and the popularization of these repertoires in the area. A Huma trait that persists is the peculiar call-and-response form, more elaborate than the common alternation between a changing solo part and a fixed chorus. In the song, the first two solo lines and choruses are repeated almost identically, while the third lines of both the solo and the chorus are different. In other words, the soloist sings the same line the first two times alternating with the chorus. The third time, both the solo and the chorus parts are fixed and recur in the same musical and verbal form (S: *Obumba nintahya*, C: *Nteera enkomi irangira*) every three verses throughout the whole song. This special call-and-response form seems to create a sort of strophic structure according to the scheme:

S1-C1, S1-C1, Sx-Cx; S2-C2, S2-C2, Sx-Cx; S3-C3, S3-C3, Sx-Cx; S4-C4, S4-C4, Sx-Cx.

98 &❧ CHAPTER TWO

This structure can also be seen in the lyrics of the song:

1) S: *Bituli bambi*	Bituli, really
C: *Ogu muhesi w'ebyoma*	The smith of metals
S: *Bituli bambi*	Bituli, really
C: *Ogu muhesi w'ebyoma*	The smith of metals
S: *Obumba nintahya*	When I go home
C: *Nteera enkomi irangira*	I click my tongue loudly
2) S: *Sisisi bambi*	Sisisi, really
C: *Ogu mwoki w'amakara*	The one who produces charcoal
S: *Sisisi bambi*	Sisisi, really
C: *Ogu mwoki w'amakara*	The one who produces charcoal
S: *Obumba nintahya*	When I go home
C: *Nteera enkomi irangira*	I click my tongue loudly
3) S: *Ibamba lya siina*	The smooth skin of the dark brown cow
C: *Ehagirekwo na taha*	She is really satisfied and goes home
S: *Ibamba lya siina*	The smooth skin of the dark brown cow
C: *Ehagirekwo na taha*	She is really satisfied and goes home
S: *Obumba nintahya*	When I go home
C: *Nteera enkomi irangira*	I click my tongue loudly
4) S: *Mayenje gagaaju*	The brown spotted cow and the brownish one
C: *Ehagirekwo na taha*	She is also satisfied and goes home
S: *Mayenje gagaaju*	The brown spotted cow and the brownish one
C: *Ehagirekwo na taha*	She is also satisfied and goes home
S: *Obumba nintahya*	When I go home
C: *Nteera enkomi irangira*	I click my tongue loudly

The soloist, outstanding connoisseur of Tooro music and friend Gerrison Kinyoro, explained that the song praises the cows' beauty, their genealogy, and the fact that they are well fed after grazing (int. September 10, 2010). Clicking the tongue to call the cattle is something that shepherds typically do and the song's protagonist mocks smiths and charcoal producers as people of inferior status. In the lyrics, the different color patterns of the cattle's coats are described using a rich variety of specific words in Rutooro.

Musical Example 2.4. Transcription of *Bituli bambi*, performed by Gerrison Kinyoro (solo) and male chorus.

Furthermore, the cows have proper names, like *Bituli* and *Sisisi*, which were used to address them, as in the first lines of the song.[18]

When I attended the school festival, there was no opportunity to hear *bizina by'ente* in the "traditional folk song" category. This category has a different theme every year—for instance, work, marriage, or traditional religion—and *bizina by'ente* repertoire, like other Huma praise songs, does not fit well into any of them. This is an example of the influence exerted by

---

18 In neighboring Nkore, Bahima pastoralists also have repertoires, called *birahiro*, praising cows. However they are not sung but rather declaimed. Similar to Tooro songs, Henry F. Morris (1964) describes the content of these repertoires as praising not the economic value of the cows, but rather their beauty, grace, and matrilineal genealogy.

100 ❧ CHAPTER TWO

the festival's selection process, in terms of its categories and guidelines, on the practice of traditional repertoires and how they are being passed on to the next generation. On the other hand, Huma praise songs, like women's *nanga* repertoires, have been performed and recorded by a number of artists and groups in Tooro (see chapter 6).

In this chapter, I explored how gender reflects and shapes sung repertoires. Presenting the use of songs in contemporary traditional weddings, I reconstructed backwards in time the changed role of marriage in Bunyoro and Tooro and the relevance of different songs in the wedding ceremonies. Analyzing how elder singers recall and perform traditional songs, I explored the opposing emotional perspectives of the bride's and the groom's families in building a new social bond and the impact of the marriage on women and men. Gendering in singing emerges from the discussion of the songs' subjects and the different singing roles that exist in call-and-response pieces. Through the songs that deal with various forms of work, I explored activities that are codified as feminine or masculine and the values associated with them in terms of gender models and social spaces. The hegemonic gender binary emerges as strictly encoded in performance practice, content of the song, and discussions about gender in the community. I connected these elements, together with some of the musical features of these repertoires, with the current practice, which I will analyze in detail in the context of the school festival (see chapter 5).

In the following chapters, I return to *runyege* and focus on two other performing arts: instrument playing and dancing.

Chapter Three

"Women Aren't Supposed To"

Instrument Playing in the Past and Today

In 2008, while researching Nyoro royal music, I was introduced to a *bakondeere* ensemble (sing. *mukondeere*) from the village of Kibiro, on the dry and salty shores of Lake Albert in Eastern Bunyoro. The group played the *makondeere* side-blown trumpets (Mbabi-Katana 1982; Wachsmann 1953: 351–359) using the interlocking or hoquetus technique, common in similar ensembles in Central African Republic (Arom 1985).[1] Since the group had only recently formed, some of my questions sought to investigate the discontinuities in the practice of *makondeere* playing due to the suppression of the Nyoro monarchy between 1967 and 1994 (Kahunde 2012a).[2]

L: Can people from other parts of Bunyoro join the group?

B: Other people are allowed, anyone is allowed to join the group, from anywhere in the world.

L: And women?

B: No, not women.

L: So a *muzungo* [white] man can play [the *makondeere*] at the *Mpango* for the king?

B: If you are a man, even a *muzungo* man, you can play *makondeere*.

---

1   The interlocking technique is also used for playing other musical instruments in the African continent such as xylophones or lamellophones like the *mbira*, but more generally it is identified by Turino (2008) as a frequent feature of participatory performance, since it helps create social synchrony and can symbolize belonging.

2   Int. March 8, 2008. This collective interview was carried out through the mediation of Issa Sunday, who translated my questions (L) as well as the answers of the *bakondeere* of the Kibiro group (B). This transcription of the interview is based on Issa's translations on the spot.

L: During the *Mpango* as well?

B: Yes, also during the *Mpango*.

L: Has it always been like this?

B: If the person can play *makondeere* and respects the culture, he is allowed to play.

[…]

L: Why can everybody but women play *makondeere*?

B: In the culture of Bunyoro, a woman is not supposed to play *makondeere*, or to play *ngoma* [double-skin cylindroconical drum].

Until the abolition of the monarchies in the late 1960s, the various groups of *bakondeere* belonged to particular clans, were based in specific villages all around Bunyoro, and took turns to serve as royal musicians at the court (Wachsmann 1953: 356). When the groups were revived in the late 1990s–early 2000s, the elders, like Francis Kiparu in Kibiro, started training new musicians. Because of the scarcity of volunteers, they welcomed anyone interested, no matter the clan or village of origin. Hence my question about whether any Munyoro could join the *bakondeere*. I was surprised when the *bakondeere* said that any person (*muntu*) could join their group: even a white (*muzungo* or *mujungo*) man was allowed to play—but not a woman, that was out of the question. My interest in this openness to whites was not addressed directly by the *bakondeere*, and I suppose that in the past there had been very few occasions—if any—when a white man had played with the *bakondeere* for the king. However, the *bakondeere* emphasized that it is possible, for anyone (a man) who knows how to play and "respects the culture" to perform in front of the king for the annual ceremony of the *Mpango*. Local culture is thus open to others, to foreigners, to whites, as long as they learn and respect it. In this context, local culture does not only imply knowing the *makondeere* playing technique and repertoire, but also knowledge of the code of behavior at the royal court, especially in the presence of the king. On other hand, notwithstanding this openness, the traditional exclusion of women in the playing of royal music (not only the side-blown trumpet but also drums) remains exactly as it was in the past: "in the culture of Bunyoro, a woman is not supposed to play *makondeere*, or to play *ngoma*." While today musicians' clan affiliation and origin have no bearing on joining a royal band, gender divisions still deeply connote instrument playing and define local culture. It would be unthinkable for women to play royal musical instruments because accessing instruments so profoundly connoted as masculine would mean that they disrespect, or are challenging, the pillars of local culture: gender binary division and men's dominance over instruments.

INSTRUMENT PLAYING IN THE PAST AND TODAY &♦ 103

Furthermore, gender appears a stronger paradigm than race in defining the individuals who are allowed to play instruments. It is not the belonging to a specific clan or Nyoro ethnicity, not being Ugandan or Black that marks instrument playing as part of the "culture of Bunyoro." Rather this culture and tradition of playing instruments are defined by adherence to the gender normativity that defines access to instrument playing as masculine. Even in postcolonial times, Nyoro and Tooro heritage represented by traditional instrument playing is not articulated along the paradigm of race but according to gender.

If "culture" explains why "women are not supposed to play," nature also emerges in the current discourse articulating the normativity that shapes instrument playing. Particularly in relation to drum playing, research participants referred to women's physical weakness as a reason why they do not play instruments—an explanation that can be found cross-culturally sustaining men's exclusive access to music instruments (Doubleday 2008: 18). Recurring responses to my questions about how females' bodies could be unable to play instruments mentioned the fact that women's arms are not strong enough and their hands are too soft to be able to hit the hard hide of drums. However, while royal music has seen a very conservative revival, where masculinity is still strongly identified with instrument playing, for other genres, like *runyege*, new performance contexts have opened up and altered the normativity of instrument playing. Today in some schools and in the ensembles affiliated with women's associations, females are the majority, if not the only, performers and, in order to perform traditional repertoires, they have to play instruments. The opening of instrument playing to women and girls, in a cultural context that traditionally prohibited them to play, is not unique to Bunyoro nor to Uganda and, in the last decades, can be traced to different contexts across the globe (Koskoff 2014: 131–132). What is rather unique about Uganda is that, while accompanying traditional genres with instruments, female musicians have to dress as men, in particular in school contexts. The use of masculine costumes for instrument playing is connected to the respect of culture: it shows that the performers know tradition (e.g., men play instruments) and that they respect it by visually representing it on stage. This means that although the gendering of some instruments—those not associated with royal music—has undergone a partial transformation in order for them to be played by females too, a normative representation of culture is still presented on stage. This representation based on the use of costumes stands in a clearly ambiguous relation to explanations naturalizing why women and girls traditionally did not play instruments.

In this chapter, I explore the complex contemporary nexus between musical instruments and gender by focusing on the role of instruments specifically in *runyege,* where instrument playing is one of the components of the genre, together with singing, dancing, and acting. Adopting an historical perspective, I trace the continuities and changes in the gendering of instruments and performers, from the strict normativity marking the past practice as masculine to the more flexible sense of masculinity connoting instruments today as they are also played by females. I first present the instruments used in older Nyoro and Tooro village and royal music and then I compare the instruments featured in historical recordings of *runyege* with early twenty-first-century practice. I use the drums in *runyege* as a case study to investigate their gendering in the past and how the interdiction of women was articulated. I concentrate on two main directions of analysis, both of which connect power in its varied forms with masculinity, thus articulating the local form of patriarchy. First, I describe the rooted conception of drums as symbols of power (as kingship, communication, and leadership). Then, I analyze the rhythmic, timbrical, and structural roles of drums in *runyege* as demonstrating a masculine capability to lead, articulate, and set the pace of the whole performance. Finally, I discuss the current performances that have opened up instrument playing to females, examining how instruments' and performers' genders are negotiated to fit into the present performance contexts and how costumes both allow and negate female musicians.

Royal and Village Intruments: Approaching *Runyege* Music

In what we can term as "village" music, as opposed to royal music, instruments were also generally played by men. Furthermore, most musical instruments used in the royal context have a parallel in village music like *runyege.* The conceptual difference between royal and village instruments is marked by local terminology (Table 3.1), by the association with different repertoires, and, in the case of double-skin cylindroconical drums, also by the playing technique.

The *binyege* rattles and the *ndingidi* tube-fiddle are typical of village dances and music and thus they are not found among royal instruments; for this reason I have not included them in the table.[3] The very rare *nseegu* flutes (Wachsmann 1953: 344–347) are known in the royal and the village

---

3   It should be noted that xylophones, widely used in other regions of Uganda, were not played by Batooro. In Bunyoro they were not common and only the Nilotic group of the Baruli in northern Bunyoro used them, while in southern Bunyoro some xylophones were adopted from neighboring Baganda (Anderson 1967; Wachsmann 1953).

INSTRUMENT PLAYING IN THE PAST AND TODAY   **105**

Table 3.1. Comparison of the local names of Nyoro and Tooro
musical instruments in the royal and village contexts
(when not specified, the plural form is identical to the singular).

Instrument typology	Local name for royal instrument	Local name for village instrument
Big double-skin cylindroconical drum	*Mpango* (royal drums proper) *Ntajemerwa* (court drums)	*Ngoma*
Small double-skin cylindroconical drum[i]	*Ihuuru* (pl. *mahuurru*)	*Kagoma*
Single-skin drum	*Ntimbo* (short, cup-shaped head) *Ngaija* (long, cup-shaped head)	*Ngaabi*[ii] (long, mostly cylindrical head)
Side-blown trumpet	*Ikondeere* (pl. *makondeere*)	*Ngwara*
Composite cone-flutes	*Nseegu*	*Nseegu*
Trough zither	*Nanga*	*Nanga*

Notes:

[i] This type of drum was also used, played with sticks while hanging from a tree, in twins' rituals.

[ii] The *ngaabi* is usually referred to as *ngalabi*, a term probably adopted from the Luganda language but nowadays also common in Bunyoro and Tooro. In the rare performances requiring the musicians to walk around, the *ngaabi* can be played while hanging on the drummer's shoulder.

religious contexts by the same name, but they have different repertoires according to their use in court ceremonies and entertainment or for spirit mediumship rituals.

The only exception to men's exclusive access to musical instruments in Bunyoro and Tooro was the *nanga* trough zither that used to be played by women (Wachsmann 1953: 389–393) in the village context as well as at the royal court.[4] Women of Huma pastoralist origin played it and it was probably through royal wives (*bago*, sing. *mugo*) and court female servants (*baranga*, sing. *muranga*) that the use of the instrument spread in the royal context,

---

4   The very connotation of this instrument as feminine in Bunyoro, Tooro, and the southern neighbor Nkore deserves more research in the future, especially in a comparative perspective extended to the broader region, where the trough zithers are played by men, such as in Rwanda and among the Bakiga and Acholi in Uganda.

106 ❧ CHAPTER THREE

since several of them came from pastoralist clans (Cimardi 2013). *Nanga* zithers were played by one or more women who were properly seated with legs folded to one side, while singing praises for the lover or husband (in the village context) and for the king and his dynasty (at court).[5] Following Ellen Koskoff (2014: 122–126), *nanga* playing and praise songs can be understood in the light of the gender ideologies associated to women playing instruments in courtship and court contexts. In particular, in the village context, *nanga* playing in the typically feminine sitting position with legs bent to the side and *nanga* songs describing the devotion and fondness of the singer for her lover or husband seem to fulfill the "idealized notions of proper female behavior and 'feminine accomplishments' within private settings that would not compromise their social status" (Koskoff 2014: 125). In the court context, these same elements can be applied to the royal wives. On the other hand, female royal servants—who also performed *nanga* and were usually concubines of the king (Davis 1938; Roscoe 1923)—combined musical and sexual roles at the court and had relative freedom, as did courtesans in different musical cultures around the globe (Koskoff 2014: 124–125).

The historical recordings of the 1950s documented the *nanga* zither in only a few pieces played at the royal palace, while most *nanga* repertoires were only vocal, suggesting that already by then the instrument was at least rare among the commoners. The progressive abandonment of the *nanga* zither is probably connected with the fading of Huma cultural habits as a consequence of the drastic reduction of pastoralist lifestyle started at the end of the nineteenth century (Cimardi 2013). The instrument finally disappeared also from the royal context, surely due to the suppression of traditional monarchies in 1967. Today the *nanga* zither is not played by Nyoro and Tooro women anymore, if not among the Basongora—a small pastoralist community historically related with the Batooro, but claiming recognition as a separate ethnicity, also using the *nanga* as part of the cultural revival supporting this demand. In present Bunyoro and Tooro, only a few

---

5   In 1950 Tracey recorded four *nanga* pieces in the Tooro village of Bukuku: *Enanga rwanzira, Kawanyita wagenda, Ayemere Kasunau nwanzi,* and *Kyanda.* According to him, "*nanga* songs are composed by the women in praise of their men folk and are commonly sung at weddings" (Tracey 1973b: 306). In turn, Wachsmann documented *nanga* pieces dedicated to past kings in Fort Portal royal palace in 1954 and in his notes defined them as either *nanga* or songs for the Bacwezi (first legendary dynasty of the kings in western Uganda). Four of them are just sung (*Song of the enanga ya bacwezi type, Kanusuke ntahe agabera, Song of the Ekizina kya bacwezi type,* and *Rwamaliba ya Babito*) and three are accompanied by the *nanga* zither: *Enanga ngaju ya omukama wa Toro* (usually known as *Kabonekiire*) played by a royal wife, and *Mujuma ya mugenyi* and *Ikangaine ya Kyebambe* performed by a royal princess.

vocal *nanga*, mostly about love, are remembered by elders and performed at the school festival and by cultural groups (see an example in chapter 6), and the old connection of this sung repertoire with the zither remains in the use of the verb *kuteera* (lit. to beat, used for instrument playing) instead of *kuziina* (to sing; to dance) to mean "singing a *nanga* song" (*kuteera nanga*). Conversely, the *nanga* zither was neglected by cultural institutions and initiatives that involved the revival and support of instrument playing both in the royal and village contexts. While certainly related to its rarity already in the 1950s, the absence of *nanga* playing from the contemporary scene of traditional performing arts in western Uganda reinforces the image of musical instruments as traditionally played by men only.

Going back to the local differentiation between village and royal instruments, this notion is echoed in the disparate paths that royal and village music have taken over the last few decades. The revival of royal music in Bunyoro after the monarchy's restoration has been quite conservative: the repertoires and playing techniques have been taught and practiced from what was remembered by elders and following historical recordings from the 1950s (Kahunde 2012b), royal music's ceremonial role during the *Mpango* and other official occasions has been restored, and the selection of the musicians is still restricted to men, though of any clan. On the other hand, the practice of village genres like *runyege* has been very dynamic in recent decades due to its inclusion in the competitive system of the school festival and in the staged performances of cultural groups.

Runyege's freedom from royal ceremonies and protocols, its inclusion in the school festival system as the main dance of the Banyoro and Batooro, and its adoption by local and national cultural groups have pushed its development toward standardization as a genre and simultaneously fostered its internal flexibility and variety to fulfill the requirements of current stage performances. If one compares present-day *runyege* performances with those featured in the recordings from the 1950s and 1960s by Wachsmann, Tracey, and Cooke, various transformations emerge.

Dealing with this audio documentation has been complex and challenging for me. Unlike royal music that shows great continuity between historical recordings and today, some of the pieces described as *runyege* or rattle dances were unrecognizable to me on the basis of the present performances that I am familiar with. What first surprised me were sizeable differences in instrumentation. Whereas today a set of three drums (two *ngoma* drums and one *ngaabi* drum, see Fig. 3.3) and *binyege* rattles provide the rhythmic accompaniment, in the historical recordings only the leg rattles were consistently employed. Also, the melodic accompaniment showed discontinuities, primarily the absence in today's *runyege* practice of *ngwara* side-blown trumpets.

108 &# CHAPTER THREE

Furthermore, I was able to only sporadically make out the rhythmic patterns I was taught as defining *runyege*. For this reason, I also listened to the pieces recorded in Bunyoro with the renowned Nyoro musician and dancer Christopher Magezi. To him, several pieces that were generically described as *runyege* were in fact *iguulya*, and he was not able to clearly identify some other pieces, which he considered in an old rattling style that is different from today. The identification of a piece as *runyege*, the written documentation about the historical recordings, as well as the way both experts and nonexperts term the contemporary performances, is usually unspecific, if not sometimes misleading. Indeed, both in the historical recordings and in present performances, *runyege* is often used as an umbrella term for all the genres employing *binyege* leg rattles (including, in addition to *runyege, iguulya, ntogoro, rusindi*, and *kagoma*) as well as indicating the specific genre, which can feature different rhythmic patterns according to the geographical area. For instance, with reference to the basic rhythmic patterns defying the various genres, Magezi explained to me that what is called *runyege* in his hometown Masindi, northern Bunyoro, is identified as *iguulya* in Hoima, central Bunyoro.

Notwithstanding the historical and present ambiguity in univocally defining it, *runyege* has been progressively codified along with its adoption in the school festival as the main dance for the Banyoro and Batooro in the national multiethnic context. As I discuss below and in the following chapters, during the more than sixty years' history of the festival institution, a progressive standardization and codification of the genre has developed in relation to instrumentation, topics of lyrics, and dance style. At the same time, its connection with other genres involving the leg rattles but different basic rhythmic patterns has been maintained. In contemporary performances that require musical variety to entertain the nonparticipating audience or jury, other related genres (in particular *ntogoro* and *iguulya*) are connected to *runyege* in a sequence, or the rhythmic patterns differentiating the various genres can be combined or follow each other as variations. Through the process of codification of *runyege* as a macro-genre and the parallel preservation of other local genres usually included under the *runyege* label, *runyege* has become standardized in instrumentation, topics of lyrics, and dance footwork and therefore clearly identifiable in the national context, but also flexible in its employment of different basic rhythmic patterns, thus satisfying the need for variety required by staged performances.

Integrating what was audible on the recordings with the interpretation of the accompanying notes and other historical sources, as well as investigating *runyege* performances of the past through the recollections of the elders and comparing them to current practice, are thus central procedures in tracing continuity and changes in instrument playing and the gendering of musicianship from the 1950s until the present day.

Runyege's Instruments in Historical Recordings

Tracey, Wachsmann, and Cooke documented *runyege* and other rattle dances in Bunyoro,[6] but only Cooke made recordings of these dances in Tooro. The notes accompanying these recordings are inconsistent in documenting the names and genders of the performers. In the documentation on Wachsmann's recordings, when no names are given, there is no clue about the gender of the musicians. Women are mentioned only when they participate as dancers or chorus singers in the performances. Similarly, in his seminal work on Ugandan instruments, Wachsmann rarely specifies the gender of musicians. Besides saying that the Uganda drum and the tube fiddle are played only by men, he mentions the gender of the performers only in special cases where the instruments happen to be played by women, like the double-skin cylindroconical drum played by the king's widows in Buganda or the *nanga* zither in Nkore, Bunyoro, and Tooro (Wachsmann 1953: 274, 390), letting us infer that the norm was for instruments to be played by men. The documentation of Tracey's field recordings (Tracey 1973b) mentions the performers' gender, and once again women are featured just as singers (in the chorus, not as soloists) and dancers; Cooke's recording notes document a similar situation. What emerges from the historical recordings is that during the 1950s and 1960s instrument playing was a men's domain, as was the case not only in other neighboring cultures, like the Baganda (Nanyonga-Tamusuza 2005), the Banande of eastern Congo (Facci 1986/1987 and 2003), or the BaAka of the Central African Republic (Kisliuk 2011), but also in the majority of musical performances worldwide (Koskoff 2014: 122–123).

The main instruments used in *runyege* in historical recordings are the *ngwara* side-blown trumpets (only in Bunyoro), *ndingidi* tube-fiddle, and *firimbi* or *nsiriba* whistle. Their use in the past is different from today and it is worth looking at the traditions in relation to the changes that occurred over time.

---

6   Nyoro dances are documented quite abundantly by Wachsmann and Tracey in their variety of styles and instrumentation. Apart from Bagungu's dances in Butiaba from the shores of Lake Albert, their recordings concentrated on central and southern Bunyoro (in the areas of the present Hoima and Kibaale Districts), but the northern area (Masindi District) was not covered. I suppose that rattle dances were documented in Bunyoro only because they interestingly involved the accompaniment of the *ngwara* trumpet and yodeling, neither of which are used in Tooro. Another element that may have led to the lack of *runyege* documentation in Tooro is the secrecy which, according to Kinyoro (int. May 11, 2011), connoted *runyege* dancing in Tooro prior to its reception within music and dance festivals in the 1960s.

110 &❧ CHAPTER THREE

Similar to their royal equivalent, the *makondeere*, the *ngwara* were played by Nyoro ensembles of at least five instruments, more commonly seven (two instruments doubled at the octave), performing in interlocking style. The *ngwara* normally subsumed the whole melodic part, thus excluding singing—only a few of Tracey's recordings document singing with the *ngwara*. According to the group of *bagwara* from Bugambe (int. April 13, 2008; Fig. 3.1), these instruments were employed to accompany *runyege* on special occasions, like weddings or the installation of the heir of a late *ngwara* player.[7]

When I met the Bugambe group in 2008, two elderly musicians had started teaching new members how to play the *ngwara* that, like the *makondeere*, had been neglected for a long time. Since the *ngwara* players also served as *bakondeere* in the royal court, the abolition of the monarchy meant that they could play only at private ceremonies and, over time, the practice faded. Also, *ngwara* as secular instruments accompanying *runyege* were not included in the school festival and ensemble system and interest in playing them only started again with the cultural revival fostered by the restoration of the kingship in the mid-1990s. The *ngwara* revival was conservative, as for *makondeere*, and for this reason *ngwara* playing is not as versatile as other instruments used by cultural groups. Indeed, the Bugambe group is different from other semiprofessional ensembles (the so-called cultural groups) because it is made up only of musicians and does not include *runyege* dancers. Still today the few active *ngwara* groups in Bunyoro are composed only of men, maintaining the old normative practices that defined instruments as a male domain.

In some historical recordings, the *ndingidi* tube-fiddle, sometimes together with singing, provides the melodic accompaniment to *runyege*. According to Wachsmann (1958), the *ndingidi* started to be played in Uganda in the early 1900s, and in the 1950s was still perceived as a quite recent instrument. It was however very popular and employed both in *runyege* and to accompany solo singing. The *ndingidi* used to be played by men only: Wachsmann (1953: 405) writes that "in [Bu]Ganda the lighter kind of music is played and associated with it. No woman will ever play it." From the 1960s, the *ndingidi* was included in the school festival system and adopted by the national ensemble to accompany singing and dancing, as well as in instrumental African pieces, compositions orchestrated for Ugandan instruments (Pier 2015). For this reason, the *ndingidi* had to be adapted to the school context. This implied "refining" the content of the songs associated with it so as to make them suitable for young performers, as well

---

7   The Acholi, neighboring the Banyoro in the North, also have *ngwara* trumpets that were played during harvesting time (Wachsmann and Kay 1971): the association of *ngwara* with the rejoicing and celebration related to harvesting is also widespread in Bunyoro.

Figure 3.1. The *bagwara* group in Bugambe (Bunyoro), 2008.

Figure 3.2. A school performance of "African instrumental music." On the right, a female pupil plays the *ndingidi* tube-fiddle together with a male pupil. Hoima (Bunyoro), 2009.

as recodifying the instrument's gendering by moderating its masculinity, since some of the pupils were girls in girls-only schools (Fig. 3.2). In this sense, the gendering of the *ndingidi* as masculine progressively lessened, in particular in the school context. However, this is not the case in cultural groups, where it is still usually played by men. Also, in women's associations' troupes, if the performers are all female the *ndingidi* is not usually used and the melodic part is left to the singing only.

112 &❧ CHAPTER THREE

Possibly the most interesting element in the 1950s *runyege* recordings is that, unlike today's practice, drums are rarely used and the rhythmic accompaniment is performed by leg rattles only.[8] Unfortunately, it is not possible to know if those recordings are really representative of *runyege* performances as they were by then or if the exclusive use of rattles was a peculiarity related to those specific recording contexts, like the nonavailability of drummers during the recording sessions or the collector's choice of dropping the drums because their sound would drown out the leg rattles. Certainly, in the past *binyege* rattles were the main accompaniment to dance, since they were and are central in both the rhythmic and choreutic components and the whole music-dance complex is organized around them. However, *ngoma* drums are also fundamental in African Great Lakes cultures and they were most probably used in the region before the introduction of *binyege* rattles. Indeed, some old sources—though not mentioning *runyege* specifically— report the contemporary use of drums and leg rattles for dancing. As early as the early 1900s, Lloyd (1907: 75–76) described the use of drums to accompany a Nyoro dance where male dancers wore leg rattles. Similarly, Swiss missionary Torelli (1973: 523) reports the simultaneous employment of one or more drums, and at times rattles and a whistle, in Tooro dancing. Also elders, like Kinyoro (int. July 29, 2012), remember from their childhood that drums accompanied dancing.

In Bunyoro, Wachsmann's recordings from Kipolopyo, as well as a *ntogoro* piece, *Kanyooma*, recorded in Butoti by Cooke, feature brief interludes of the whistle (locally known as *firimbi*) with a syncopated pattern in relation to leg rattles or signaling a change in the dance-rhythmic pattern. In Tooro, the whistle (called *nsiriba*) also featured in dances (Torelli 1973: 523), in which, according to Kinyoro (int. July 29, 2012), it was used to rouse dancers and to guide them into the dance's climax. Also for the whistles, the documentation of recordings provides no information about the performers' gender and we are led to assume that they were men. Today the whistles are normally not used in *runyege,* but their signaling and "modulating" function, essential in structuring and coordinating the dance, is performed by the *ngaabi* single-skin drum.

All in all, the 1950s recordings suggest a nonstandardized rhythmic accompaniment of *runyege*: it was possible to dance with rattles only, but sometimes drums and a whistle were involved. Cooke's 1964 and 1968 recordings, however, usually feature one *ngoma* or *ngaabi* drum together

---

8   In Wachsmann's collection, drums feature only in some rattle dances (some of which are called *kalihwa*) of the Bagungu community in Butiaba, near Lake Albert. Only two recordings from the area of Hoima that Tracey labeled as *runyege* feature *ngabi* drums: *Abagungu* and *Nzaireki akatera empihi.*

INSTRUMENT PLAYING IN THE PAST AND TODAY &* 113

with the leg rattles. Most probably drums started to be used consistently in *runyege* after Wachsmann's and Tracey's recordings, in connection with traditional music teaching in schools and the activities of semiprofessional troupes, two contexts that Cooke documented. In these cases, the use of drums seems to help the coordination of the ensemble and foreruns the current *runyege* practice where the rhythmic instrumentation is fixed: leg rattles for male dancers and three drums (two *ngoma*, one *ngaabi*).[9]

Most of the differences between *runyege* in historical recordings and today can be explained by the considerable changes that traditional performances underwent during postcolonial times. Although the context in which the historical recordings were made most probably required some degree of organization of the performances, during the 1950s and 1960s *runyege* playing and dancing was still performed as a participatory form on a community basis, as some elders among my research participants remembered from their childhood. However, informal performances of *runyege* seem not to take place anymore today and indeed I did not attend any during my time in Uganda, nor had my research participants in recent years. Since the mid-1960s with the institution of the school festival and the formation of the first national ensemble, several Ugandan traditional genres started to be performed in more formalized settings. Over time, these became their main performance contexts and today *runyege* is mostly performed by cultural groups or school troupes on stage. Their performances are marked by a formalized setting with a neat division between performers and audience; the organization of the pieces and the parts to be played or danced by the performers; and spectacularization through the use of customs and choreographed formations on stage. The elaboration of *runyege* and similar rattle dances for the stage has most probably caused the revision of its instrumental component. On the one hand, the need to teach *runyege* in schools and within the cultural groups brought about the codification of the rhythmical patterns as well as the formation of new ones connected to creative dance figures. On the other hand, the *ngwara* trumpets were dropped because of their link to banned royal music, while the rhythmic section needed organization and leadership to coordinate the dancers; hence drums became central.

The very inclusion of *runyege* in the festival system involving schools as well as semiprofessional ensembles has produced a recodification of the gendering of musical instruments. It is in particular the two types of drums (*ngoma* and *ngaabi*) used in *runyege* that underwent a negotiation of their masculinity because of their no-longer-exclusive association with male performers. In the following sections, I describe the many-layered connections

---

9   If only one *ngoma* is available, two different rhythmic parts can be played on the same drum.

114 &◆ CHAPTER THREE

of drums with power, authority, and leadership as elements socially, culturally, and musically marked as masculine, thus establishing drums as symbols of patriarchy. Finally, I discuss the transformations, triggered by the school festival institution, in the masculinity associated to these drums.

The "Uganda Drum": Power and Its Articulations

Ngoma (and their royal equivalent *mpango*) are double-skin drums, but only the upper membrane is hit, while the lower one serves to hold the lacing. The type of *ngoma* drums used in western Uganda is widespread in various regions of the country (like in Buganda: Kafumbe 2018). Klaus Wachsmann (1953: 369) adopts the term "Uganda drum" to refer to this type of membranophone in order to cover the internal diversity of the specimens in the country.

In Uganda, these kinds of drums are highly valued and respected (Kafumbe 2018; Wachsmann 1953). Unlike other musical instruments, in Bunyoro drums were not made by the musicians themselves, but by specialized craftsmen who knew the special techniques and materials required to make them (Roscoe 1923: 230–231). Indeed, every Uganda drum contains a "heart" or "soul," *mutima,* or, for royal drums, *ikura,* a "wonderful unseen thing" (Davis 1938: 50; Roscoe 1923: 231). All over the African Great Lakes region,[10] the object inside the drum was secret and only the constructor knew what it was. Facci (2007) notes how the respect and reverence given to the drum is also due to the secret part that it holds inside: its function is not sonic, like a sort of internal rattle to enrich the instrument's sound, but rather ritual. In Bunyoro and Tooro, the heart of the drum could be a knotted piece of animal skin or a small stone and, in the case of royal drums, it could combine different materials on which sacrifice blood had been poured (Roscoe 1915: 87). Even today, when the skin of a drum is worn or breaks, the craftsman replaces it with a new one but the inner object remains the same, assuring the continuity of the instrument, and its identity, in time.

In the former kingdoms of the African Great Lakes region, double-skin drums symbolize power and are treated with reverence (Facci 1996 and 2007; Remotti 1989 and 1993; van Thiel 1966–1967; Williams 1936–37; Wymeersch 1979). First, they represent royal power: in Bunyoro and Tooro the kingship is identified by the main royal drum.[11] Although organologically identical to *ngoma,* royal drums are deemed different; they are called

---

10   About the *mutima gw'engoma* in Rwanda, see Hertefelt and Coupez 1964; in the neighboring Ankole: van Thiel 1977; among the Banande: Facci 1996.

11   Testifying to the permanence of the drum as a symbol of the monarchy is the fact that, since the late colonial era, *mpango* drums feature in the Nyoro and Tooro royal coats of arms.

mpango and are considered sacred. All *mpango* are given a personal name and have their own distinctive rhythmic pattern (*mubaro*). There is one main *mpango* in each kingdom (in Bunyoro the main *mpango* is Nyalebe and in Tooro Kajumba), and there are royal drums dedicated to individual kings, each with a *mubaro* characterizing their reign. Finally, there are other minor royal drums (Wachsmann 1953: 371–372) and the court drums *ntajemerwa*. Both in Bunyoro and Tooro, even today the main *mpango* is employed during royal rituals, like the anniversary of the coronation also called *Mpango* and the ceremonies held for the New Moon, although today the latter are rarely performed. The special respect given to royal drums is also evident in the way they are played: *mpango* are struck with wooden sticks and they do not touch the ground, usually by means of a belt slung over the player's shoulder, while *ngoma* drums are placed on the ground and played with the hands.

In precolonial times, on the death of a Nyoro king, the royal drum Nyalebe was turned upside down to represent the suspension of the order of the royal rule; indeed, when a suzerain died, a succession war among his children started. The winner was the prince who could seize Nyalebe and turn it back to its normal position; in fact, coming to the throne is called *kulya engoma*, lit. to eat the drum, suggesting that the king incorporates the drum's power in his body. The ascension ceremony of the new king was then marked by him beating Nyalebe with sticks nine times (K. W. 1937; Nyakatura 1973), a number considered lucky in western Uganda. If the drum did not sound while the prince was beating it, he could not be king (Fisher 1911: 120). The main symbolic actions structuring the ascension ceremony are repeated annually during the *Mpango* anniversary, which has its fulcrum in the king hitting the main royal drum with nine strokes.

It was the royal drum that held the authority to legitimize a suzerain and hence it was from the royal drum that the king derived his power. Passed down from king to king, the royal drum has marked the patrilineal descent of the monarchy and incarnates patriarchal power. According to Nyoro traditions (Nyakatura 1973), the main royal drum Nyalebe was handed over to the current Babiito dynasty from the previous one of semigods, the Bacwezi: it was the drum that maintained the continuity of the kingdom, even during a dynasty change. This conception of the drum as a symbol of temporal continuity is common in interlacustrine Africa. In this regard, Remotti (1993) highlights how drums, as well as capital cities, shape the conception of time by both granting continuity through the main royal drum and delineating the reigns of the different suzerains, each of whom had his own drum. Finally, the Babiito that are also members of the royal family as princes and princesses are called with a reference to the drums: *Babiito* (mas.) and *Babiitokati* (fem.) *by'engoma* ("of the drum"). As discussed in chapter 1, in precolonial times

116 ❧ CHAPTER THREE

princes and princesses were gendered as masculine and indeed drums and royal power are interpreted as masculine in Bunyoro and Tooro.

Royal drums as enduring symbols of the monarchy have their human counterpart in the king. The potency associated with royal drums is reflected in the authority and leadership of the king; the reverence the drums are given is that which a king deserves. This potency, authority, and reverence are masculine as the king is, but more generally they are characteristics proper of manhood in traditional Nyoro and Tooro culture, and so associated to varied degrees with all men.

Besides the connection with the kingship, the power symbolized by the drum is also rooted in its capacity to communicate at a distance and thus to mobilize people. Indeed, most of the royal drums are not played for music making, but "beaten, hit" (*kuteera*) to spread information or issue orders.[12] The pattern associated with royal drums (*mubaro*) is indeed the codified timbric-rhythmical transposition of a word or a sentence, which can be about the kingdom or a message to call people for a particular activity (Mbabi-Katana 1984: 342). In this way, drums were also employed during the war to gather men for protection from an attack, to signal the position of soldiers, or to send messages to them. It was not only the king who had drums to be used in case of war (Nyakatura 1973: 189); the army leaders also had their *ngoma* (Roscoe 1923: 307). Furthermore, when they were appointed, local chiefs were given a drum and a spear by the king (Roscoe 1915: 88) and they "would then coin a definite slogan or motto [*mubaro*] which could be regularly communicated to his people as a drum message" (Mbabi-Katana 1984: 342). There was no dialogue between different drums as was the case in other parts of Africa, but rather a one-sided communication from top to bottom, a communication marked by a relation of power: in this sense, the drum worked as a tool to govern space and people. In the Nyoro and Tooro traditional understanding, it would be unthinkable for a woman to beat a drum to mobilize people at her will. Drums are beaten by men: authority and power as masculine descend from the king to local chiefs and army leaders. Because of their masculinity, they are entitled to use the drums' sonic power to exercise control and mobilization in the kingdom: by beating drums, they share, and contribute to build, royal authority.

---

12   While to beat or hit drums is a literal translation of *kuteera ngoma*, the verb *kuteera* is locally used to mean instrument playing, be the instrument blown, plucked, shaken, or hit. I use the literal translation of *kuteera* only with reference to the specific a-musical functions of Nyoro and Tooro drums. This is not meant to reinforce negative ideas about African music as requiring little skill or relying on brute force, but rather to mark a difference with drums' musical uses, which I describe with the verb "to play."

The masculinity of the drummers is reflected in the parallel gendering of the drum. As the symbol of power marking the rank of the king, army leaders, and local chiefs, all positions held by men, the drum also stands for patriarchal power. In this respect, it is significant that the mother of the king (*Nyin'omukama*), who is accorded prestige and honor second only to the king himself, has her own royal drum, but she cannot hit it. During the royal ceremonies held at her residency on the occasion of the *Mpango* anniversary, she touches the drumsticks nine times but does not beat the drum, as her son the king does. This confirms both the gendering of the drum as masculine and the femininity of the queen mother, who has such a high status for the very reason of generating the king, hence for her feminine fertility.

Nyoro and Tooro social hierarchy led from the king, through local chiefs, to the head of the family, the *nyineka*, who owned a *ngoma*.[13] As husband and father, the *nyineka* was the most respected person in the family and his authority was uncontested. As a Nyoro proverb says, *Ateza nyineka, empaka aziragira*: "the one who disagrees with the head of the house sleeps hungry." The association of the drums (both royal *mpango* and village *ngoma*) with the potency, leadership, and authority of men is confirmed also by Wachsmann (1953: 374), who states categorically that "Uganda drums are beaten by men." These views about the masculinity of drums and of drum players as males resonate with Veronica Doubleday's reflections on gender and musical instruments: "Male musicianship is intimately connected with masculinity, and when men maintain musical instruments as their exclusive cultural property, they make assertions about masculine identities and roles [...] There is also a political dimension to male public instrumental performance, and prestigious male instrumental ensembles have frequently sustained and enhanced images of male authority and leadership" (Doubleday 2008: 17). In Nyoro and Tooro culture, it is men who play drums and thus express their masculinity as connoted by power and authority. The *ngoma* are viewed as masculine instruments and the leadership they represent runs parallel to their essential musical function in contemporary *runyege*, which I discuss in the next section.

Runyege's Core: The Basic Rhythmic Patterns of the *Ngoma*

The two double-skin drums employed in the present *runyege* have two distinct functions: the *ngoma* (A) with its lower sound keeps the fundamental

---

13 Stephen Mugabo (int. March 16, 2012) told me that during the 1980s his father played his *ngoma* in the village, but that it was rare to know someone who had a *ngaabi* drum.

118 &❧ CHAPTER THREE

beat; the second *ngoma* (B) with a higher pitch performs the basic rhythmic patterns. The role of both *ngoma* in present *runyege* is fundamental to the performance: the two drums give the performers the main metric reference and constitute the connecting tissue of the various rhythmic parts. Conversely, this means that *ngoma* (A) drummers have the power to dictate the pace of the performance by deciding the speed of the main pulse and that *ngoma* (B) drummers have the authority to coordinate the rhythmic parts of the performance, as well as the freedom to make variations. Once again, power, authority, and freedom as attributes of masculinity within the local culture's normativity connote both the *ngoma* drums and their players.

In Bunyoro and Tooro, I had lessons with various *runyege* performers and instructors. As I discuss below, nowadays girls in all-girls schools learn to play instruments, including drums, and teachers are usually open to teaching female pupils how to play drums in mixed schools together with their male schoolmates. After learning at school, some women keep playing drums in semiprofessional ensembles, especially the *ngoma*, when there are no male performers available. This opening of drumming to females constituted the condition in which I was able to learn to play the drums. Furthermore, my education and status as a guest were factors in the respect afforded me by my instructors and hence in their considering teaching me an important task, or at least a useful and relevant experience for their profession. Finally, my position as a foreigner as well as a learner contributed to my instructors' willingness and friendliness to teach me as schoolteachers treat both boys or girls—probably with even more patience because I needed more tutoring and practice and had many questions.

In this section, I present the patterns played by the two *ngoma* in Bunyoro and Tooro and consider the role of these drums in the whole performance. The drumming patterns I learned, as well as the dance steps, are slightly different in the two regions. Also, within each region interpretations are multiple and I base my description of the basic rhythmic patterns of *runyege* on what my teachers (in Bunyoro: Vincent Nyegenya and Salim Jamal; in Tooro: Gerrison Kinyoro and Stephen Mugabo) taught me, as well as on the interviews and discussions with *runyege* experts (in Bunyoro: Christopher Magezi and Vincent Nyegenya; in Tooro: Gerrison Kinyoro and Stephen Kabutuku).

In Bunyoro, the *ngoma* B can perform two different patterns (Mus. Ex. 3.1). Usually it plays a four-stroke pattern, which some performers associate with the word *bitakuli*. This pattern provides the rhythmic background for both the *binyege* rattles and the *ngaabi* motifs and variations. Alternatively, the *ngoma* B can perform a three-stroke pattern like the *binyege* rattles. This last pattern is considered the basis of Nyoro *runyege* because it characterizes the main step sequence of the male dancers (see chapter 4). It is associated with the term *nkaceka*. While performing the *nkaceka* and the *bitakuli*

Musical Example 3.1. The patterns played by the two *ngoma* in Nyoro *runyege* (after Vincent Nyegenya): while *ngoma* A keeps the stable basic pulse, *ngoma* B can perform the patterns *bitakuli* or *nkaceka*.

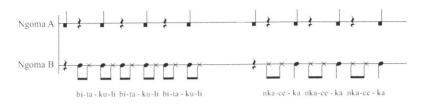

Figure 3.3. Percussionists of the Bunyoro Foundation Group accompanying *runyege* in Hoima, 2009. From left to right: Moses Muhuza performing *runyege* rhythmic patterns on *ngoma* B drum, Moses Alituha keeping the basic beat on *ngoma* A, and the late Herbert Barongo playing the *ngaabi* (C) cylindrical drum while holding it in its usual position, leaning on the drum performing the basic beat.

patterns, the drummers can switch between them and make variations. Furthermore, the duration of the strokes can slightly change as a result of rhythmic variation; in particular, in *nkaceka* the last stroke is sometimes a bit longer, while in *bitakuli* the last two strokes can be faster.[14]

My research participants explained that the words connected to the drum patterns reflect the sound of the strokes on the drum. Indeed their transposition on the drum seems to follow the vowel length and sometimes also the "color" of the vowels, while the relative pitch is not so relevant because of the rarity of tones in modern Runyoro-Rutooro. However, the interpretations of the words traditionally associated with the rhythmic patterns are different. The three-stroke pattern word *nkaceka* means literally "I became weak" (Davis 1938: 20), but it is hard to explain the connection of this with the drumming or rattle dancing that shows men's strength. Majara (int. August 12, 2009) was alone in suggesting that it could be connected to the effort and consequent physical weariness of men who are stamping while dancing. However, the root *ceka* is very close to the verb *kucekeca* (Davis 1938: 20), meaning "dance, leap," and the double sense of "dance and sing" and "have no strength" can be found in another verb, *kujenja* (Davis 1938: 54). On the other hand, the four-stroke pattern word *bitakuli* simply means "sweet potatoes" (Davis 1938: 8) and my research participants who used this word-rhythmic pattern could not point to any connection with *runyege*.

According to the music expert and teacher Gerrison Kinyoro, in Tooro *runyege* proper is based on the three-stroke pattern *bangatu*, performed by both the *binyege* rattles and the *ngoma*. However, since in Tooro present *runyege* incorporates the disappearing dance *obw'omu mbaju*, sometimes the *ngoma* B can perform the pattern typical of this dance, while the *ngaabi* C plays the pattern *bangatu*. The *obw'omu mbaju* pattern comprises four strokes and is associated with the word *kuturuba* or *katurumu* (Mus. Ex. 3.2). Kinyoro translated the word *katurumu* as "we are here" and he interpreted it as an invitation to join the dance: "we are here, join us and dance." On the other hand, I could not find any explanations for the meaning of *katuruba*, which can possibly be a transformation of the original *katurumu*

---

14 In Wachsmann's and Tracey's *runyege* recordings from Bunyoro, where no drums were employed, the *nkaceka* pattern is barely distinguishable on the leg rattles. Typically in these recordings, the *binyege* leg rattles begin to resound after the *ngwara* trumpets or singing. At first they mark the beat with double speed and then continuously vary the basic pattern or use other rhythmic-dance figures. Furthermore, the extent to which these basic rhythmic patterns are performed can change: both in historical recordings and today they can be performed very shortly, and variations or other figures can take over. For this reason, it is sometimes hard to differentiate *runyege* from the similar genres of *iguulya* and *ntogoro* in the historical recordings.

Musical Example 3.2. The patterns played by the two *ngoma* in Tooro *runyege* (after Gerrison Kinyoro): as *ngoma* A keeps the basic pulse, *ngoma* B can perform the patterns *katuruba* or *bangatu*.

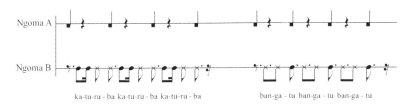

with the last syllable reproducing the final banged sound on the drum. Also the word *bangatu* seems to be more of a mnemonic sequence of syllables than a real word.

Also in Tooro, as in Bunyoro, the *ngoma* B can perform a pattern in either three or four strokes, while the pattern in three strokes remains the basis for the *binyege* rattles. As for the Nyoro rhythmic patterns, Tooro ones can also be performed with slight duration shifts and accent slides or variations. The two main patterns form the basis to develop rhythmic and timbre variations on the *ngoma* and the syncopated patterns performed on the *ngaabi*. Nattiez and Nanyonga-Tamusuza (2003: 959–961) define the basic rhythmic pattern in *baakisimba* as the "immanent structure" of the music and they refer to Simha Arom's notion of "model" as the original structure on which all other variations are based. This is what happens also in *runyege* through the elaboration of the patterns *bitakuli/nkaceka* and *katurumu/bangatu*.

While specific basic rhythmic patterns vary from one area to the other, in *runyege* the *ngoma* B always connects the rhythmic components of the performance: the leg rattles worn by dancers, who follow its basic pattern, and the *ngaabi* long drum, to which the *ngoma* supplies sonic material for possible further elaboration. This means that *ngoma* B drummers have the authority to coordinate the rhythmic parts, as well as the freedom to make variations. At the same time, the other *ngoma* (**A**) defines the meter of music by marking the main pulse, so the drummers have the power to impose the speed they prefer to the whole performance.

All in all, the functions of the two *ngoma* used in *runyege* emerge as fundamental to the genre. Their authority and leadership are features of masculinity—the masculinity inherent in this type of instrument and its performers. From this perspective, in *runyege* music we can find the symbolism of the Uganda drum as power with its temporal, hierarchical, and spatial ramifications in the kingdom. *Ngoma* drums "rule" the performance, by molding

122 ❧ CHAPTER THREE

its pace, establishing the basic rhythmic organization, hence structuring the dance movement, and supplying the material for alternative patterns.

Ngaabi Drumming: Coloring *Runyege* and Masculine Preeminence

Alongside the *ngoma* drums and the *binyege* rattles, the requisite set for *runyege* is completed by the long single-skin cylindrical drum (*ngaabi*). The skin, secured to the upper rim of the *ngaabi* with wooden pegs, was traditionally of monitor lizard (locally called *nsaswa*).[15] The *ngaabi* is played with bare hands while standing and holding the instrument between the legs, sometimes leaning it on a nearby support (Fig. 3.3), while very rarely it is hung on the performer's shoulder. Also the *ngaabi* has a royal equivalent, the *ngaija*, which is slightly shorter and played with bare hands while hanging from a shoulder strap (Wachsmann 1953).

In *runyege*, the *ngaabi* drum rises above the sonic complex because of its shrill, high-pitched sound. It leads the dancers in the motifs they perform and structures their formations on the stage. For this reason, the *ngaabi* drummer exercises an eminently masculine function of leadership and autonomy of choice. In *runyege*, this cylindrical drum normally performs the three-stroke pattern together with the *binyege* rattles when the *ngoma* B performs the pattern in four stokes. In Bunyoro the three-stroke pattern is *nkaceka*, in Tooro *bangatu*. In this function, the *ngaabi* with its powerful sound emphasizes the basic dance step performed by the dancers, which further resonates in their *binyege* leg rattles.

Furthermore, the *ngaabi* performs variations. Some variations can be connected to specific dance motifs, understood as "the smallest unit of dance movement that corresponds with a specific musical idea and a rhythmic unit" (Nanyonga-Tamusuza 2015: 85). Although a *runyege* performance typically follows a development that involves a progressive climax, it is the *ngaabi* drummer who decides whether, when, and how to play a variation or a new musical motif, which the dancers have to follow by performing the corresponding dance motif. The following example (Mus. Ex. 3.4) presents two variations of *ngaabi* as performed in Tooro: a sequence of rapid strokes, the return to the standard *bangatu* pattern repeated twice, and another variation of slapped strokes. The first variation is associated with the men's dance motif of rotating with small steps as

---

15   For several years, the monitor lizard has been classified as an endangered species and the use of its skin has been banned in Uganda. Instrument makers are experimenting with alternatives, using cow hide and other methods, like metal rings, for fixing the skin on the rim of the drum.

Musical Example 3.3. The various patterns performed by *runyege* instruments in Bunyoro and Tooro.

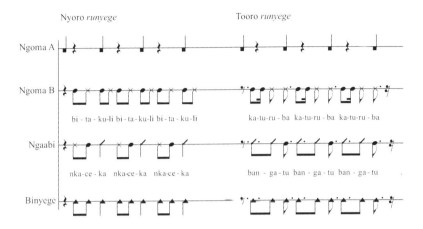

Musical Example 3.4. Some *ngaabi* variations performed in Tooro.

with the *binyege* they perform the same rhythmical pattern of the *ngaabi*. The second variation can be associated with the same pattern used in the previous motif with the *binyege*, while the dancers perform on the spot.

Because of its loud sound, the *ngaabi* also has a leading signaling function. In contrast with the *ngoma*, whose role is to steadily accompany the singing and dancing, the *ngaabi* intervenes in specific moments of the performance to signal a change in the dancers' formation on stage or the transition to a different section of the dance. Indeed, in contemporary performances, various dances that include leg rattles are usually connected in a sort of suite. In these sequences, every dance represents an internal section of the performance, and the connection between the sections is marked by the *ngaabi*. Finally, in the context of festivals and semiprofessional ensembles, new creative dance motifs have emerged and they are accompanied by specific creative *ngaabi* (and *binyege*) patterns. The leadership of the *ngaabi* and its player within the ensemble emerges also with these signals that the *ngaabi* drummer uses to shape the stage design of the dancers and to mark the transition to other dance sections.

My drum instructors and several music teachers referred to *ngaabi*'s role in *runyege* as to "color" the dance: while a whole performance based solely on the basic *ngoma* pattern would be monotonous, the interventions of the *ngaabi* break the repetitiveness and introduce new rhythmic (patterns and variations)—and consequently kinetic (dance motifs)—material in the performance. With its rhythmically relevant motifs that break the monotony and direct the dancing by rhythmically shaping the men's dance steps and leaps, the *ngaabi* rises above the other instruments. The way in which it guides the performance connotes it as a masculine instrument, since decision-making and leadership skills are considered qualities that are possessed by men.

The *ngaabi*'s role as leader is also possible because of its sonic qualities. Not only its volume but also its pitch rises above the *ngoma* and the *binyege*, establishing it as the lead instrument in directing both the accompaniment and the dance. This preeminence of *ngaabi* in *runyege* is similar to that of its Ganda equivalent, the *ngalabi*, in *baakisimba*. As noted by Nanyonga-Tamusuza (2005: 68): "the combination of high pitch, penetrating timbre, greater amplitude, and irregular rhythmic occurrences foregrounds the *ngalabi* relative the *mbuutu* [a Ganda Uganda drum similar to the *ngoma*]." As in *baakisimba* (Nanyonga-Tamusuza 2015), in *runyege* there is a constant dialogue between drummers and dancers, but the *ngaabi*'s sonic preeminence can redirect, change, or stop the dancing.

It is not just its role of freedom in variations and authority in imposing changes in dancing or its loud, penetrating sound that make *ngaabi* an overwhelmingly masculine instrument, its shape also contributes visually to represent and incarnate masculinity. Although it was not mentioned by my research participants, the shape of *ngaabi*, a long cylinder with a bulging upper part, resembles a huge phallus. This association is strengthened by the fact that the instrument is normally played while holding it between the thighs. The *ngaabi* is thus the visual quintessence of virility. According to Veronica Doubleday (2008: 14–15) when musical instruments have a gender identity, performers usually play a "same-gendered" instrument. If a cross-gender relationship with the instrument is established, it is normally between male musicians and female instruments, while "it is uncommon for a woman to play an instrument that has a clearly established masculine identity." Although Nyoro and Tooro women traditionally play neither the *ngoma* nor *ngaabi*, over the last decades this exclusion from instrumental practice has become less rigid and the masculinity entrenched in drums has in part transformed, as I discuss in the next section.

The Changing Masculinity of Drums

Nowadays, some girls and women play the drums at the school festival or in semiprofessional ensembles. Similar to what Sonja Lynn Downing (2019) described for women's and girls' gamelan ensembles in Bali, these experiences challenged the tradition of male-dominated instrumental performance, opening up instrument playing to females who in the past would have been singers or dancers. As noted by Gregory Barz (2004), it was the Ugandan school festival, which includes all-girls schools, that introduced instrument playing for girls. This applied to festival categories such as "traditional folk song" and "traditional folk dance," but also to more innovative ones. The festival category "African instrumental music" (Fig. 3.2), for instance, includes pieces performed by instruments from the various Ugandan cultures grouped as the families in symphonic orchestras and guided by a conductor. It is probably this new genre that has contributed most to the participation of pupils in instrumental playing regardless of their gender. In this festival category, the traditional repertoires locally associated with specific instruments, as well as the gendering of the instruments, have been overcome by a vision that resignifies instrument playing and instrumental music as an educative and creative project that elaborates local elements through musical strategies taken by the symphonic orchestra tradition, especially orchestration techniques and contrasting sections composing the musical piece. By extracting instrument playing from the specific local repertoires with its connected gendered notions, also the masculinity of instruments embedded in local culture was put aside in this festival category. This greatly fostered the access of female pupils to music instruments and also reflected on other festival categories, hence also the drums used to accompany traditional singing and dancing started to be played by girls.

A gender-inclusive approach to instrument playing is supported by some music teachers (int. Clovis Baguma: May 9, 2011) and festival adjudicators (int. Joshwa Kabyanga: August 22, 2018). Notwithstanding this broader vision, the notion that traditional instruments are played by men is still persistent. During my fieldwork, when I asked why women could not play drums, the explanations I was given did not draw on the traditional conception of the drum or the importance of its role in structuring the performance, but rather on physiological and practical considerations. Drums are played only by men because only men have the strength needed to hit and play them. Women have weaker arms and the palms of their hands are soft and delicate, not suited to playing the drum with the energy and stamina required for a lengthy *runyege* performance. The same physical vigor is required for the leg rattles worn by men. These reasons are sometimes still echoed in the primary school context. According to music teacher George Misinguzi (int. June 9, 2011), the *ngaabi* could also be played by a girl, but normally females do not have enough strength compared to their male fellows: "Even if young, a boy is still a boy." Another reason I was given was that women cannot play in the position required for drums because of their ankle-length skirts. The *ngoma* drum is played while seated by holding it between the legs and this requires spreading the legs far enough apart to fit the instrument between them (see Fig. 3.1). Some of my research participants described such a position as awkward and embarrassing for women, for whom decency prescribes that they keep their legs together while seated.

The inconsistency of these explanations emerges when one considers that even young girls are able to play drums, so the strength required to do so is not exclusive to the male body. Furthermore, during rehearsals, the girls and women who play the *ngoma* can do so wearing a skirt, provided it is not too tight, or else they play by leaning the drum on their side. Finally, well-trained school girls can play drums with the same proficiency as their male fellows. This challenges the notion of the feminine ability to play instruments as intrinsically inferior to those of male performers, as is the case with the girls' gamelan ensembles researched by Downing (2019) in Bali.

The explanations I collected for why girls and women do not play drums convey notions not about how they are, but about how society expects them to be: unable to do what men do because physically weak, decent, and chaste in the ways they dress, sit, and behave—habits that are evaluated as proper according to parameters opposite to those applied to men. The reasons given for the exclusion of women from drumming are based more on concrete, physical reasons (be they physiological or practical) than on the cultural symbolism and musical functions of the drums. Naturalizing the normativity of instrument playing as a male activity by regrounding it in some objective conditions rather than on the tradition that the drums themselves carry seems to be a cultural strategy to preserve masculine dominance over feminine access to instrument playing. According to the majority and selective view of tradition that has forgotten *nanga* players, female mediums, and princesses, power, leadership, and authority are masculine, and radically opposed to the features of the hegemonic femininity, which is conceived of as delicate, shy, in need of protection and guidance. The role of women is appreciated in other aspects of performing arts like singing and dancing. As I discuss in chapter 4, especially in dancing elements of femininity are evaluated together with the evidence of stamina in sustaining the physically demanding performance and the body flexibility required for the dance movements of the female part.

Although the opening up of drumming to girls and women signifies a remarkable change in relation to earlier instrumental practice, females still constitute a small minority of drummers and they mostly play the *ngoma* (A), which keeps the main beat but is the less sonically remarkable drum and does not perform the main *runyege* patterns. It is indeed quite rare to see women playing drums in cultural groups where there are also men who can play them. So, besides taking part in the *runyege* dance, in mixed ensembles women typically perform the singing and clapping. When women do play the *ngoma* drums in semiprofessional ensembles, it is normally because there are no men available at that time, like in women's associations (see chapter 6). It is more common that girls play drums not only in all-girls schools but also in mixed schools, but during performances on stage they have to wear masculine costumes, thus representing the gender of the drummer as prescribed by tradition.

During rehearsals, girls who play the drums can be dressed in their usual way, but for the school festival they usually wear the *kanzu*, a long white tunic of Arab origin (Fig. 3.4; see also chapter 5). The *kanzu* is considered traditional men's attire and male performers wear it while playing. According to some teachers, wearing the *kanzu* for performances is an almost compulsory convention for both boys and girls (int. Katusime: June 10, 2011), while others find it acceptable for girls to dress as they normally would when they play *ngoma* (int. Misinguzi: June 9, 2011). Discussing this stage convention with schoolteachers and music instructors, they explained that the *kanzu* is necessary to "respect the culture," to keep to the local customs (int. Baguma: May 9, 2011). The audience should see that it is men who play drums and performers should also be aware of this. This once again reinforces the conception of the *ngoma* drum as a masculine instrument, but on the level of representation, as a stage convention that portrays local tradition. In this sense, it complements on the cultural level the naturalized assumption that females are too physically weak to play. However, the fragility of the custom of drums played exclusively by men is also on display here: it is represented on stage with costumes, while in reality the *ngoma*'s gendered conception is being challenged by the contemporary ensembles and performance contexts. The notion of drums as exclusively masculine instruments appears in this perspective as both conservative and nostalgic, hardly adaptable to the present transformed society and performance contexts. The current ambiguity about females and musical instruments, which rests on both naturalized assumptions about sex and stage conventions representing gender, shows the enduring effort to limit female access to musical instruments in a contemporary performance and

Figure 3.4. From left to right: during a school performance, two boys play the *ngaabi* and the *ngoma* (B), respectively, performing the basic pattern. A girl dressed in *kanzu* keeps the main pulse on the second *ngoma* (A). Hoima (Bunyoro), 2009.

social context that no longer complies with past notions of masculinity and femininity. Since it is evident that girls and women do have enough physical strength to play drums, it is all the more important for patriarchal power to be asserted in other ways—including through normative statements that discourage women from playing drums.

These cultural and naturalized explanations of why drums should be played by men and not by women still have a hold on females and

INSTRUMENT PLAYING IN THE PAST AND TODAY & 129

Figure 3.5. During a school performance, three girls from an all-girls school play drums, including *ngaabi*. Hoima (Bunyoro), 2009.

instrument playing. As the *ngoma*, *ngaabi* cylindrical drums were also traditionally played only by men and even today it is rare that girls or women play them. This happens only when no alternatives are available, such as in all-girls schools (Fig. 3.5) and women's associations. In comparison with the *ngoma*, which is played (especially in the basic beat part) more commonly by females, the gendering of *ngaabi* as a men's instrument is still strong. However, the explanations for why women and girls used not to, and still rarely do, play the *ngaabi* are similar to those for the *ngoma*. First, there is the lack of physical strength necessary to properly hit and play the drum; and then the impossibility of playing it while wearing a long skirt. As for the *ngoma*, the very fact that there are some women and girls who do play it shows that they have enough muscular power. Furthermore, they can do it while wearing a skirt (during rehearsals) or a *kanzu* or, less frequently, another type of tunic when performing on stage (Fig. 3.5). This notwithstanding, the motivations for women not playing the *ngaabi* are stronger than those for the *ngoma*. First, its piercing and powerful sound is associated with greater strength in hitting and playing it and it is hardly conceivable that a woman or a girl would be able to produce such a potent sound. Second, but perhaps more important, its playing position is considered highly inappropriate for women. Besides the never expressed—though striking—association with a phallus, the cylindrical instrument has to be held between the drummer's thighs while playing, and a woman is supposed to sit with her legs together. This explanation, grounded in the playing position of the *ngaabi* being uncomfortable or inappropriate for women, can be found in other musical contexts as well, for instance in the Caribbean, where it was also used to keep women from playing drums, and in North Atlantic cultures, where in the past girls and women were discouraged from playing cellos.

In neighboring Buganda, there is a quite similar conceptualization of the different typologies of drums. Nattiez and Nanyonga-Tamusuza (2003: 968–969; see also Nanyonga-Tamusuza 2005: 63–70) describe the *ngoma* as feminine and the *ngalabi* as masculine, based on their shape and their sonic and rhythmic features. Although the musical attributes of these instruments are the same as the Nyoro and Tooro drums in *runyege,* my research participants have never made explicit reference to their shape as being feminine or masculine. While the appearance of *ngaabi* could implicitly reinforce the ban on women, if the *ngoma* was considered feminine because of its womb shape, as in Buganda, there would be no resistance against women playing it. However, men are still preferred to play the *ngoma* when available and not bad at drumming. Furthermore, while women and girls playing *ngoma* and *ngaabi* in school festivals and ensembles have contributed to eroding the masculinity of these instruments, this gendered conception of the drums remains very strong in the royal context. Indeed, royal drums still symbolize royal authority and continue to be played exclusively by men. For these reasons, I consider the *ngoma* and *ngaabi* as marked by different degrees of masculinity, rather than associated with two different genders.

In this chapter, I have explored instrument playing in the past in relation to contemporary paradigms by focusing on the gender of the performers and the masculinity reflected and attributed to most instruments. Primarily played by men, most musical instruments are gendered as masculine. The only exception is the *nanga* zither, interpreted as a feminine instrument and played by Huma women only. After a progressive disappearance that began in the 1950s, the use of the *nanga* has not yet been revived, thus strengthening the current discourse and representation of musical instruments as traditionally played by men only. By investigating the gender of the drums through their symbolic value within Nyoro and Tooro culture, their playing technique, and their role in *runyege* performance, their masculinity emerges as displayed, articulated, and reasserted. The inclusion of these instruments in the festival system has in part eroded their masculinity, which has been negotiated in recent decades in order to include *runyege* performance in schools and to allow the participation of female performers in music-making. While the access to drums is open to girls in schools and women in women's associations today, the representation of these instruments as masculine continues through the use of costumes aimed at disguising females as males during the performances. This shows once again how the preservation, revival, and presentation of traditional performing arts today is inseparable from reproducing traditional gender as part of the local culture and tradition, but also that the current practice of local culture is flexible enough to adapt to different contexts and to host various forms of agency, competence, and expressiveness of the performers.

My analysis of the drums used in *runyege* has highlighted their important, powerful, and authoritative roles as the epitome of the masculinity associated with most musical instruments, as well as their fundamental musical function in the genre. However, in *runyege* the audience's attention is focused on the dancing rather than on the musical instruments and the gender of the instrumentalists. *Runyege* is indeed conceived of mainly as a dance in the general discourses and the specific festival categories, as well as by the performers themselves. It is on the dance component of the genre that audiences direct their attention, and their appreciation of the women's dancing in the performance as part of the complementary roles prescribed for the two genders is evident, as I discuss in the next chapter.

Chapter Four

Shaking the Hips, Stamping the Feet

The *Runyege* Dance

L: Where and when did you learn to dance?
K: I started in primary school, then continued dancing in secondary and entered a cultural group... I also tried *runyege*, but I was not good at rattling. I am better in *kucweka* [*omugongo*].
L: But would you like to dance *runyege* instead of *mugongo*?
K: I love *mugongo*.
L: Which are the comments when you perform very well?
K: [laughs] Some people said *kacwa basaija mugongo*, "She [can] break men's lower back."
L: And which are the comments when you don't dance well or they don't like the performance?
K: I always dance well.

—Interview by author (L) with Annette Katusime (K).
Masindi: August 23, 2018.

L: How did traditional performing arts enter your life?
M: I learned to dance in primary school. I liked rattling *runyege* and had talent for it. So I continued in secondary school and got involved in a cultural group.
L: What is the significance of *runyege* for you?
M: *Runyege* is my culture. Dancing is preserving and showing our tradition. For me, I can express myself and interact with other performers. It is also good for earning something.

—Conversation between author (L) and Stephen Mugabo (M).
Fort Portal: May 11, 2011.

Today, most *runyege* dancers learn to perform this genre at school and the gifted ones continue by performing in semiprofessional ensembles, as Annette Katusime in MASDRASS (Masindi, Bunyoro) and Stephen Mugabo in Ngabu za Tooro (Fort Portal, Tooro). As chapter 1 mentions, *runyege* dance involves separate dance parts for women and men. In Bunyoro, *kucweka omugongo* describes the women's part, with reference to the fast movement of the lower back and the shaking of the hips. On the other side, men *bateera orunyege*, literally, "they beat the *runyege*," meaning that they shake their ankle rattles by stamping their feet. Annette and Stephen perform *mugongo* and *runyege*, respectively. Annette even tried to dance the *runyege* male part, but was not really good at it or interested in learning it; instead she really loves *mugongo*. Stephen likes to play *runyege* and, on another occasion, told me that he never considered dancing the women's part. For Annette and Stephen, the same as many other adult performers, dancing *mugongo* or *runyege* is a positive and satisfying experience, one that allows them to express themselves, prove their ability, perform for codancers and audience, and possibly gather some extra income when their cultural group is hired for a show. They are confident of their skills ("I always dance well," "I have a talent for it") and sustain them through the engagement in a group, which is today the main context where traditional dances are performed by adults. Beyond the personal value to the dancers, traditional performing arts matter to them—and to audiences and institutions—because *runyege* bears also the fundamental role of representing local identity and culture ("*Runyege* is my culture. Dancing is preserving and showing our tradition"). Along with a sense of belonging, pride, and identity, *runyege* dancing stimulates in the public more material appreciation, such as sexualizing the body of the performer ("She [can] break men's back," associating her skill in dancing with her sexual energy).

When one considers the dance element in *runyege*, multiple issues about its historical dimension, gendered structure, and connections to sexuality emerge. What are its origins and relations to other local dances? How did the performance of gender in dance represent the society in the past and how does it today? Which are the sexual implications displayed, hidden, or negotiated in *runyege*? In this chapter, I first present the variety of dances of Bunyoro and Tooro and contextualize *runyege* among these repertoires. Then I reconstruct *runyege* past performance contexts, which emerge mainly in relation to banana beer drinking, and discuss the cultural importance of banana beer and its connection with the dance origin. Based on my ethnographic work, I proceed to present an analysis of *runyege*'s two separate dance parts according to local narratives. By drawing on interviews and discussions with dancers, dance teachers, and audience members, I further explore the ways in which binary gender is encoded in movement, both

134 & CHAPTER FOUR

individually and through the interactions between the dancing couples, as well as *runyege*'s sexual connotations. Through this discussion, I theorize *runyege* as technique that fosters discourses about gender—a "technology of gender," following de Lauretis (1987: 2–3)—as well as a flexible locus where gender emerges as variously molded by bodily performative practices of repetition and adaptation (Butler 1990).

Runyege and Other Nyoro and Tooro Dances

In Uganda, the same as in other sub-Saharan contexts like Malawi (Gilman 2009: 13), genres comprising different performing arts are usually referred to as "dance." This happens also for *runyege,* which is locally referred to as a dance (*mazina*) and, in the national arena, is included in the "traditional folk dance" category in the school festival. Also, the few texts that deal with *runyege* focus on the dance component of this genre.[1] The centrality of dancing among the Banyoro and the Batooro and its presence in a multiplicity of community and family events was already observed by early European observers who lived for several years in western Uganda, such as Italian explorer Gaetano Casati (1891, II: 48) and Swiss Catholic missionary Ubald Torelli (1973: 522–523).[2]

My research participants described a variety of Nyoro and Tooro dances according to their connection to a specific performance context, their regional origin, or their function.[3] Within the complex of the traditional or

---

1   These are mainly Ugandan university theses and popular publications. The theses by Patrick R. Gafabusa Hairora (2003) and Milton Wabyona (2004) briefly refer to *runyege* in relation to, respectively, *mpango* royal dance and Bagungu's *muzeenyo* dance. The presentation booklet of the Heartbeat of Africa national ensemble (Serumaga 1964) features a map showing some of the Ugandan dances according to the various ethnicities (for Bunyoro *makondeere* and for Tooro *runyege*) and a short description of *runyege* dance. In their booklet presenting the variety of dance repertoires in Uganda, Agnes Asiimwe and Grace F. Ibanda (2008) concisely present *runyege* and *ntogoro* and acknowledge the complexity of transformations and reciprocal influences in dance styles.

2   Torelli's *Notes ethnologiques* were published posthumously in 1973; he actually lived in the Mwenge area (Tooro) from 1903 till his death in 1968.

3   In the ritual context, the dance of the twins (*mazina g'abarongo*) was common to both Batooro and Banyoro and performed at baby twin ceremonies meant to treat and regulate the sacred power of twins (int. Kabutuku: August 30, 2018; Beattie 1962). This kind of function, which involved sexual speech and expressions perceived as vulgar, was severely condemned by Christianity and Islam (Gafabusa Hairora 2003; Mukasa-Balikuddembe 1973). For this

cultural dances (*mazina g'enzarwa*), *runyege* can be considered as a secular or village dance to connote it in relation to the royal or court dance.[4] The latter dance is known as *makondeere* (in Tooro) and *mpango* (in Bunyoro) and, despite the different denominations, is essentially the same in the two kingdoms. This genre, characterized by the accompaniment of the instruments that it is named for (the *makondeere* trumpets or the *mpango* royal drum), is performed at the royal court: in the past, this occurred every month for the New Moon ceremony and, today, the performance happens once a year to mark the anniversary of the coronation of the king (*Mpango*). Unlike village dances, *makondeere/mpango* was, and still is, mainly performed by members of the extended royal family and clan and by individuals that serve the kingship who, unlike most commoners, know how to dance this genre. The dancers perform facing the king or the royal palace because the dance is dedicated to the suzerain and the kingdom. Similar to *runyege,* this genre comprises different dance motifs for men and women (Kahunde 2012a). While male dancers move with wide steps and perform arm gestures representing the use of arrows and shields, female dancers use smaller steps and gracefully wave their *suka* capes. Emerging from the social values of the traditional aristocracy, the male dance part depicts men as brave warriors and protectors of the kingdom and the female dance part displays a conception of femininity as elegant, shy, and discreet. The traditional gender binary also structures this royal dance and molds dance parts as the representation of masculinity and femininity within the aristocracy, similar to what happens in *runyege* among commoners, which I discuss below.

The range of village dances is quite broad and many of them involve the use of the *binyege* leg rattles; for this reason, *runyege* is typically used as an umbrella term referring to all these dances.[5] In Bunyoro, several genres are danced with *binyege*: *ntogoro* and *iguulya* throughout the Masindi and Hoima areas; *kagoma* and the very rare *kalihwa* dance typical of the Bugungu area, near Lake Albert. These dances are named for the feature characterizing them. *Iguulya* refers to the cloth ring worn around the waists

---

reason, twin ceremonies with music and dance are no longer performed, and, as people now feel very uncomfortable talking about this subject, I was unable to gather information about the dance structure and motifs.

4   In Runyoro-Rutooro, no specific denomination defines a division between village and court dances, although *mazina g'ensi,* lit. dances of the land, and *mazina ky'ekikali,* lit. dances of the royal enclosure or court, can be used to specify the difference (int. Kabutuku: August 30, 2018; int. Nyegenya: August 18, 2018).

5   Peter Cooke also documented a Tooro variant of *runyege,* called *kalezi,* which he recorded in Fort Portal in 1966. Cooke's recording remains, to my knowledge, the only documentation of this dance.

of female dancers; *ntogoro* seems to derive from the metallic ankle bracelets worn by women (which are not common today); the term *kagoma* comes from the name of the small double-skin drum that is used to accompany the dance. Details in costumes and instrumentation and different rhythmic patterns used to differentiate these various music and dance genres. However, in present-day performances it can sometimes be difficult to clearly identify them. As discussed in relation to rhythmic patterns, today traditional dances are usually assembled in sequences featuring different genres, where the various rhythmic patterns are alternated or combined while the same costumes and instruments are kept. In addition, Nyoro and Tooro dances with leg rattles share a similar spatial organization of the dancers and conformation involving two dance parts and final couple interaction—all structured around the performers' gender.

The dances of the *runyege* type have been first documented at the beginning of the twentieth century by European observers, such as British traveler and amateur ethnologist James F. Cunningham (1905: 35; cf. also Fig. 1.4) and, later, Swiss missionary Ubald Torelli (1973: 522–523). Although the paternalistic and colonial gaze variously shaping their writings deserves critical consideration, their descriptions of respectively Nyoro and Tooro dances seem to be quite accurate. They indeed show a continuity of performance and main characteristics until today: two lines of dancers facing each other arranged according to gender; two different dance parts for men (using leg rattles) and women (shaking a hide tied around the waist); male and female dancers progressively moving closer and interacting with one another. Conversely, other Nyoro and Tooro traditional dances are rarely performed or have almost disappeared. Some originated from peripheral communities, like Bagungu's (considered part of the Banyoro) *muzeenyo* (Cooke 2001; Wabyona 2004) and Batuku's (considered part of the Batooro) *riiba*.[6] From the 1960s, the dances of the majority of the population have progressively replaced them, as a result of the capillarity of the festival system and the semi-professional ensembles performing the main regional dances. In a similar way, other dances were assimilated to *runyege* and lost their peculiarities, like Banyoro's *rusindi* (also involving rattles) and Batooro's *bw'omu mbaju*.

Of the genres that are not performed anymore, some, like *bw'omu mbaju*, involved just one dancing style, irrespective of the gender of the performers, and others were for men only, like *mirindi* (int. Kinyoro: May 11, 2011). While the historical paths of social and cultural assimilation together with the influence of the school festival led to the disappearance of some genres

---

6   Some of the dances mentioned here can be observed on the YouTube channel of the cultural group Ngabu za Tooro: https://www.youtube.com/user/Engabuzatooro (accessed on April 7, 2022).

and the fusion of others, the present array of traditional dances in Bunyoro and Tooro, both of royal and village origin, only includes genres whose particular arrangement, dance parts, and interactions of the dancers is based on the gender of the performers. The dances still performed today thus convey a notion of local culture in which the traditional gender binary is deeply inscribed and pervasive in its ordering force, but also represented and reproduced in current performances, of which I give an example in the following.

A *Runyege* Performance in Contemporary Tooro

During the time I spent in Bunyoro and Tooro, I attended several *runyege* performances, but none of them was in a participative context nor spontaneously performed. In fact, the performers and elders with whom I talked doubted that informal dancing still takes place today. Nonetheless, *runyege* was danced mainly at wedding parties, school and other competitive festivals, cultural shows, and on occasions of traditional and royal significance, such as the *Mpango*. Apart from the school festival where the performers are pupils, the dancers and musicians were from semiprofessional ensembles composed of young people and adults. Unless they freely participated in a competition with the aim to win a prize or volunteered to perform for the king, these ensembles were hired to perform.

This was the case of a show of the Tooro Kingdom Cultural Troupe, which I attended in a hotel's gardens in Fort Portal, Tooro, in 2012 (**V1**). I knew personally several of the performers because they had participated in my fieldwork in various ways: among them there were Sylvia, my instructor of the *runyege* female part (*nyamuziga*); Stephen, by then my partner, instructor of the *runyege* male part, and research assistant; and other dancers whose rehearsals and performances I had attended. Furthermore, some of the performers were also members of the Ngabu za Tooro association, probably the biggest cultural association in Tooro, of which I had followed the activities for some years.

To boost tourism in Fort Portal town, and specifically attract customers to his premises, in 2012 the owner of the hotel hired Tooro Kingdom Cultural Troupe every Sunday to entertain the hotel's guests as well as other interested individuals, who could attend the show by paying a modest fee. I arrived there early, together with my friends of the ensemble, who needed some time to get ready for the performance. The planned show was a small-scale event in terms of duration, number of performers, and audience. It lasted around half an hour and involved only two dances (*runyege* and *ntogoro*) and an instrumental piece (drums improvisation), while on other occasions cultural groups perform also theatrical sketches, additional dances,

138 &⟩ CHAPTER FOUR

lip singing of popular songs, and even acrobatics. Also, the performers were not numerous (four drummers and ten dancers) and the singing roles were performed by the same drummers and dancers. As on other Sundays, the show took place shortly before sunset and the audience was limited, around ten people (some local and some foreign), plus children who had come to watch the performance once they heard the drums resonating. The chairs for the audience were set on the garden's grass in a semicircular shape around a bonfire. This setting created an ambience more informal than a typical venue where the dance would take place on a stage or a clearly delimited performance space in front of an audience, indeed the ensemble performed in the open space around the bonfire without a clear division from the public.

That *runyege* performance was illustrative of how *runyege* is danced nowadays in western Uganda. It opened with a dancer starting the call of a song and other dancers answering with the chorus while instrumentalists played drums. This and the following songs, all very short, were about joy and love. At the drums—two *ngoma* (performing the fundamental pulse and the basic *runyege* rhythmic pattern) and two *ngaabi* drums (taking different roles in underlining the *runyege* pattern, varying, or giving signals)—were four young men dressed in the white *kanzu* tunic and some with a dark jacket, except for one who would later join the dancers. Dancers performing the men's part wore long black pants, a zebra-striped shirt, and *binyege* leg rattles, while those performing the women's part wore red T-shirts, long skirts of colorful *kikohi* cloth, and short *mucence* raffia skirts around the waist. While the men's part was performed by men, the dancers of the women's part were women, except for one young man who was trans-performing (i.e., dancing a part that was not constructed for his sex/gender; see chapter 6). Different from other performances I saw, the dancer performing the part traditionally prescribed for the other gender did not inspire comments in the audience, composed of white tourists who were probably watching *runyege* performed for the first time. The dancers were initially arranged in a semicircle around the bonfire and dancing on the spot: dancers of the women's part performing small steps and shaking their hips while keeping their arms open on the sides, dancers of the men's parts behind them stamping their feet on the ground in a erect posture with extended arms. After a signal of the *ngaabi* drum, the speed increased and a second song was started by another soloist, my instructor Sylvia, who stood next to the drummers. After this second song, the *nyamuziga* motif, among others, was performed: dancers of the women's parts, with bent legs rotated their parallel feet alternatively toward one side and then to the opposite one; while men dancers performed four lateral steps in one direction and then four in the opposite, each sequence closed by raised hands on one side. Then, a new signal of the *ngaabi* drum transitioned to a third song, during which dancers performed other motifs on the spot. With the beginning of the fourth song, the dancers briefly danced in pairs, as they maintained the initial semicircular formation around the bonfire. At the signal of the *ngaabi*, dancers of the men's and women's part lined up in an alternating row and performed a new dance motif, based on the same rhythmic pattern and footwork as *nyamuziga*, but on every fourth beat one group or the other lowered their upper body, allowing the dancers of the other group to join hands above them. The beginning of the fifth and last song marked the transition to a scattered formation around the bonfire and, when the singing stopped, the main soloist and the performer that had helped with the musical accompaniment joined the dancers who were now arranged in two opposed lines according to the gendered dance parts, as another performer took over the drum that had been left unplayed. The second part of the performance, accompanied by only the drums (besides the leg rattles worn by the men dancers), featured the progressive formation of five dancing couples, which performed one after the other in the space closest to the audience. After all the couples had finished their rapid dance duet, they scattered around the bonfire and continued dancing multiple motifs that, together with advancing and retreating body moves and smiling facial expressions, simulated courtship and attraction. In this phase, while dancers of the men's part advanced with confident body attitudes and smiles toward the performers of the women's part, the latter initially shied away while smiling embarrassedly, and after some danced advances they started to dance more freely with their partners. Finally, a new signal of the *ngaabi* opened the climax of speed, volume, and dance intensity that ended the performance.

In this, like in other contemporary *runyege* performances, the two dance parts—differentiated by footwork, motifs, and role in the couple interactions—are traditionally based on the performers' gender. Their gender is also represented through costumes, especially when a dancer performs the part prescribed for the other gender, a practice that I analyze in chapter 6. Focusing on *runyege* dance as an exemplary element of local culture structured by gender, I now investigate how local interpretations of the *runyege* dance are molded by gender models and concepts by tracing a path which, through the description of *runyege*'s old performance contexts, will bring me to consider the cultural and social value of banana beer, whose preparation is considered by many to be at the origin of *runyege* dance parts.

Runyege's Past Performance Contexts and Banana Beer

Historical sources, such as Casati (1891) and Torelli (1973), mention a variety of occasions when people danced, but they do not directly refer to the specific genre performed. So, in what contexts was *runyege* danced prior to the establishment of the school festival and the formation of troupes (both of which started in the 1960s) and its inclusion in royal ceremonies (begun in the 1990s, after the restoration of the traditional monarchies)?

In connection to old *runyege* dance contexts, most of my research participants mentioned the collective drinking of local banana beer (*tonto* or, rarely, *marwa*). Banana beer was central to Nyoro and Tooro culture in the past, and it is still highly valued today, especially in rural areas and on the occasion of important ceremonies. As I discuss in chapter 1, through *tonto* beer, relations at different levels of Nyoro and Tooro society were established and cultivated, in particular through weddings, harvest celebrations, and parties. Banana beer and dancing marked together important moments of the wedding ceremonies. *Tonto* was an inescapable present donated by the groom's side to bride's during the first phase of the wedding, the *kweranga* (introduction of the groom's family to the bride's), as well as drunk in the final celebration at the arrival of the bide at the groom's household. In old wedding ceremonies, in these moments dances might have been performed (Torelli 1973: 499; int. Kinyoro: May 11, 2011; int. Nyorano: March 03, 2008).[7] Furthermore, banana beer was drunk at the first meal prepared with freshly harvested millet (the staple food in western Uganda) and during *tonto* beer parties, where family, neighbors, and friends celebrated together also with singing, playing, and dancing.[8] Both these events usually happened just after the harvest during the dry season, when there was more free time available and the weather conditions were better. Also, during the dry season, bananas for beer were more abundant and a lot of *tonto* was produced (int. Kinyoro: July 29, 2012). Indeed, *tonto* was prepared only when a good amount of beer bananas was ripe: since it requires an elaborate brewing procedure and it rapidly turns sour, people used to make it in big quantities and consume it soon afterward at gatherings or parties with relatives and neighbors.

Nowadays, banana beer is still produced on a family base but can also be purchased at local markets. While *tonto* is still drunk at ceremonies and cultural occasions or can be consumed in private family gatherings or offered to guests, today beer parties are extremely rare. According to

---

7   Dancing could also take place while the groom's relatives and friends moved from the bride's house to the couple's new home, which is during the second phase of the wedding, *kugaba*, the "give away" (int. Nyorano: March 03, 2008).

8   These community events were also occasions for singing and dancing among other African populations, like the Baganda (Nanyonga-Tamusuza 2005) in Uganda, the Venda in South Africa (Blacking 1985), and the Tsonga in Mozambique and South Africa (Johnston 1973 and 1974).

Figure 4.1. Two gourds decorated with dried banana leaves and containing *tonto* beer are offered, together with crates of sodas, at a wedding in Tooro, 2010.

Mukasa-Balikuddembe (1973), missionary and colonial disapproval of local spiritual practices—considered satanic witchcraft—and their supposed connection with beer parties—condemned because of their excessive consumption of alcohol—had a negative impact on these events and consequently on community-based dancing, which reduced dramatically. During my time in Uganda, I was not able to attend any beer party, but the few among my research participants who had participated in one said that they did not involve participative performances of music and dance anymore but rather played-back music, mainly from local radios. At the weddings I attended, when decorated gourds filled with banana beer were presented as gifts (Fig. 4.1), and later on a portion of the alcohol was consumed by the guests, instead of participative music and dance, the sonic background could involve played-back love songs or a dance or theatrical performance by the hired cultural group (see chapter 2). Although nowadays participative dancing seems not to occur while consuming *tonto*, *runyege* is still connected with celebrations, entertainment, and spending time with friends and family—moments that in the past were associated with banana beer drinking. Significantly, *tonto* preparation emerges as the context in which *runyege* originated not only in Kinyoro's story presented in chapter 1, but also in the narratives of

142 &❧ CHAPTER FOUR

other elders, dancers, and dance trainers. Through their personal or shared views, their linear or controversial interpretations, I continue to explore a path backward, tracing the formation of *runyege*'s two dance parts from the preparation of *tonto* beer.

Brewing *Tonto*, Shaping *Runyege*

In traditional Bunyoro and Tooro, different types of bananas and their derived products were associated with masculinity or femininity. The bananas used to brew local beer belong to particular varieties, distinct from the ones consumed as food—these are cooked (boiled, roasted, or steamed) and usually form the basis of daily meals, or they can be eaten raw as a snack or dessert.[9] In the past, it was men who took care of the family's banana plantation (Torelli 1973: 481), where the various types of banana grew together. While bananas for food were collected, prepared, and cooked by women, bananas for beer were, and are still today, attended by men (int. Kinyoro: July 29, 2012). The connection of bananas for food with women and bananas for beer with men is mirrored in the ancient custom of planting a banana tree for the birth of a baby girl and a beer banana tree for a baby boy (Torelli 1973: 507). Furthermore, being the vehicle of interpersonal relationships (through friendship, family bonds by marriage, etc.) that were traditionally handled by men, *tonto* beer is culturally connoted as masculine.

Today, men are still responsible for the selection of bananas to produce beer, checking and fostering their maturation, digging the *ndeeba* pit in the plantation where they then squeeze the bananas to extract juice, and, finally, adding the sorghum necessary for fermentation. Kinyoro (int. July 29, 2012) reported that the artificial maturation of bananas is a man's task: it takes place through the *numi* fire in the banana plantation. This is symbolically opposed to the fire lit on the three kitchen stones (*mahega*), which is a woman's task, since it is women who are in charge of the kitchen and food preparation. Moreover, squeezing bananas is an activity precluded to women because some believe that they could contaminate the juice with their menstrual blood; hence only men, boys, or in some cases young girls, can stamp

---

9 In the local language, the varieties of bananas for beer are called *mbiira* (known in the *muusa, kisubi, mpurumura, kiterre, nyamaizi, nkenge*, etc. cultivar), bananas cooked as food are *nyamunyo*, and those eaten raw *byenju*. Bananas for beer and for food are quite similar and part of the hybrid species *Musa acuminata x Musa balbisiana* but they are considered different because of their taste and the quantity of juice they can produce, while bananas eaten raw are a variety within the species *Musa acuminata* and have a markedly sweet taste.

THE *RUNYEGE* DANCE & 143

on bananas.[10] A single woman (unmarried, divorced, or widowed) could prepare the bananas to be squeezed, but she was not allowed to stamp on them to mash them, since that beer would be deemed impure and nobody would drink it (int. Kinyoro: July 29, 2012).

In beer production, women had to crumble sorghum (*mugusa*) by smashing the panicles with their feet, and then winnow the cereal in a big flat basket or wicker tray (*rugali*), as they did with millet.[11] So, women were in charge of the preparation of the cereal, but then again it was men who added sorghum to the banana juice in a wooden tub and who checked its fermentation. *Tonto* preparation was also spatially connoted: men brought fruits to maturation and then extracted the juice in the banana plantation while women crumbled and winnowed sorghum in the courtyard.

There are close parallels between *tonto* preparation and *runyege* dance movements. According to Majara Jr. (int. August 12, 2009), who comes from a family of musicians and is himself a music teacher,

> For the men, the [dance] footwork is the making of the banana juice, they step on the bananas—we don't usually do it with hands, we stamp on them. In the banana plantation, they tie the banana leaves to trees on either side of a pit and they begin stamping [on the bananas in the *ndeeba* pit] while they are tied because it is slippery down there. So if you don't hold on to something you will fall over, you will fall in [the banana juice]. If you fell in it, it was a curse, so you would not be allowed to drink it and even your uncles and father would not be allowed to drink that alcohol, that brew you made, because you fell in it ... for this reason, they will tie this side and that side so as not to fall and they will start stamping... So the men [in *runyege*] imitate the making of the juice.

In the men's part, the basic dance steps consist of stamping the soles of the feet on the ground, thus replicating the squeezing of bananas. The posture, slightly bent legs and the upper body leaning forward, which constitutes the standard position of the men's dance part, is the same employed to stamp vigorously on the fruits in the pit. The position of the arms, spread out to the front or to the side, which is the most common position in *runyege*

---

10 Torelli profiles the process of banana beer production as an exclusively male activity; however, he describes a squeezing procedure done with hands instead of feet (Torelli 1973: 470). Roscoe reports that banana squeezing can be done both with hands and with feet (Roscoe 1923: 205–206). According to Mbabi-Katana (int. June 30, 2011), it was possible to squeeze bananas with hands and this would be the case, in the past, if the beer was to be served to a local chief.

11 According to Torelli (1973: 482), a preliminary and rough cereal crumbling was done by men and then women continued with a refined crumbling and winnowing of the cereals.

Figure 4.2. Joseph Kaijumurubi stamping on bananas in the *ndeeba* pit where bananas are mixed with indigenous grass (*sojo*; *Imperata cylindrica*), whose sharp leaves facilitate the squeezing process. Nsorro (Tooro), 2013. Photo by Stephen Mugabo.

dance, is connected to the need to hold onto two ropes made of vegetal fibers tied to nearby banana trees to avoid sliding on the slippery bottom of the *ndeeba* pit.

The correspondence of body posture, position of the arms, and movement of the feet between banana stamping and men's *runyege* dancing is the result of concretization, a procedure that Judith L. Hanna (1979: 37) describes as one of the modalities of meaning communication in dance, which "produces the outward aspect of a thing, event or condition." Furthermore, *runyege* men's dance can be associated with what Anya P. Royce (1977: 204–205) calls mimetic dances, which directly reproduce or imitate actions external to dance.

If the extraction of banana juice by men is mirrored by the main features of their dance part in *runyege*, what about the women's dance part? Women do not wear rattles and their dancing (*mugongo* in Bunyoro and *bw'omu mbaju* or *nyamuziga* in Tooro, see chapter 1) is substantially different from the men's, indeed it is based on small steps connected with waist shaking. Most of the narratives I have been told about the formation of *runyege* focused on the men's part, while explanations of the women's dancing style were less frequent and organic. Some research participants and music teachers told me that the women's dance was also related to *tonto* preparation, specifically with the processing of sorghum (int. Kabutuku: September 5, 2011; int. Majara: August 12, 2009). In particular, Majara saw the shaking of the waist as imitating the act of winnowing: the cloth ring worn by

THE *RUNYEGE* DANCE & 145

Figure 4.3. Left: Herbert Barongo (Bunyoro Foundation Actors Group) performing the men's dance part. Right: detail of his footwork with the *binyege* rattles worn around his calves. Hoima (Bunyoro), 2009.

dancers around their waist would represent the winnowing tray and the position and movement of the hands suggest the rolling of the cereal in the tray:

> When they are making *tonto*, women usually prepare sorghum and, when they are winnowing sorghum, they make this movement [imitates the act of winnowing, emphasizing the hip movement when shaking the tray] …
>
> L: Aren't they seated while winnowing?
>
> Yes, they are. But now they have to imitate the winnowing in dance and they are winnowing this time with their waist. Now, the waist ring is like the tray for winnowing, *rugali*, and then their arms imitate the sorghum.

When I asked Majara if there was also a connection between women's footwork and *tonto* production, he said that it was related to women's cooperation with men in the process of banana beer brewing. Also, according to Vincent Nyegenya (int. June 22, 2011), women's footwork comes from the simple walking of women while helping men and bringing them what they need during the preparation of banana beer. Nyegenya explained that it is the small steps and the hip movement typical of women's walking that originated their basic footwork in *runyege*, the style of footwork that dancers perform at a slow tempo. Alfdaniels Mabingo (2020b: 103–104) reports the

Figure 4.4. Left: Akiiki steps on sorghum panicles to have them release the grains. Kiguma (Tooro), 2018. Right: Adveri shows a *rugali* tray used to winnow cereals. Hoima (Bunyoro), 2009.

story by Mariam Amooti Mugenyi, a Nyoro performer and instructor, about the origin of *runyege* in connection to banana beer preparation and drinking. Also in her narrative the men's part is connected to the squeezing of bananas with their feet, while the women's part comes from their walking with a calabash full of beer and serving the men while kneeling (the latter action recurs in some of women's dance motifs).

On the other hand, Kabutuku (int. August 30, 2018) suggested that women's footwork refers to the crumbling of sorghum cobs by gently stepping on the cereal panicles. I discussed this view with the expert Kinyoro, who has a different opinion on how the women joined in dancing *runyege*, but he described how cereal crumbling was performed anyway and then helped organize a demonstration so that I could see it being done. Millet or sorghum panicles are laid on the ground and women step on them, then, using their feet, they bring the broken parts of the panicles together to create a small mound and, by alternating their feet, continue gently stepping on them to release the grains (int. Kinyoro: August 31, 2018).[12] Kinyoro asked

---

12 Today, it is common to beat the sorghum panicles with a stick before stepping on them, to avoid wounds on the feet.

Figure 4.5. Left: Goretti Basemera (Bunyoro Foundation Actors Group) performs the women's basic dance part. Right: detail of women's basic footwork in *runyege*. Hoima (Bunyoro), 2009.

his daughter-in-law Akiiki to show me how this is done. The small steps made on the balls of the feet to crumble the sorghum generated the alternate lifting of the legs and consequently of the hips. Performed at a faster speed, the whole movement resembles the women's dancing style with steps on the ball of the feet and shaking buttocks. Indeed, Kinyoro concluded that one can find similarities between this process and women's footwork in *runyege*, but his opinion on the women's dance part is different. He maintained that the position of arms and hands does not imitate winnowing because, differently from dancing, while holding the winnowing tray (*rugali*) arms are kept stretched out and palms do not face the ground.

Following Nyegenya's and Kabutuku's interpretations, we can consider the women's footwork as imitating either their walking while helping the men or the processing of sorghum. In either case, the women's dance part can be understood as the result of a process of concretization (Hanna 1979: 37), and therefore as mimetic (Royce 1977: 204–205). On the other hand, if we just acknowledge a general connection between sorghum processing

148   CHAPTER FOUR

and dance, that would suggest a process of stylization or metaphor (Hanna 1979: 37; Hanna 1988: 14–15), especially when the women's cloth rings are seen as symbolizing the *rugali* tray (Majara's view). Thus it could be thought of as an allegorical dance, comprising movements that recall activities to which one wants to refer (Royce 1977: 204–205). A similar codification of everyday gestures and movements into dance through concretization, stylization, and metaphor is described by Nanyonga-Tamusuza (2005) for the *baakisimba* dance. Among the Baganda, this dance was performed in the past by women in the villages and is deeply connected to the feminine activity, clearly reflected by *baakisimba* footwork, of planting new banana sprouts that will generate food for the family.

The narratives I collected about the origin of women's dance movements are all related to *tonto* production. What emerges as a general interpretation is that the roles, based on a binary gender differentiation, of men and women in banana beer production are intertwined with the two distinct *runyege* dance parts. However, there is not a unanimous consensus on the women's dance part. Acknowledging other narratives is important in recognizing the complexity of the dance itself, but also in understanding the process of knowledge transmission and thus of the interpretation of tradition. As I mentioned, Kinyoro did not agree with the idea of the women's dance part deriving from their role in *tonto* preparation. During one of the many afternoons that I spent with him talking about Ugandan music and dance, he told me an alternative narrative about women's dance. Kinyoro (int. May 11, 2011) argued that in Tooro the women's part of the dance did not develop simultaneously with men's *runyege*, but was combined with it later. The *bw'omu mbaju* dance was already widespread in Tooro and, when men started dancing *runyege*, women simply joined in with the dance they already knew, *bw'omu mbaju*. Similar to Nyoro *mugongo*, the *bw'omu mbaju* dance was characterized by small steps and a fast and fluid waist-hip movement, to which the name of the dance ("of the ribs") refers. Today, the term *bw'omu mbaju* seems to have almost fallen into disuse and the term *nyamuziga* is the most commonly used. This literally means "circle" and originally refers to a specific style in the women's dance part, marking the climax of the dance. *Nyamuziga* has thus become per antonomasia the Tooro women's dance part, while *bw'omu mbaju* used to define the more general basic step.

Some of my research participants, like Kagaba (int. May 11, 2011), did not agree with the narrative grounding *runyege* in banana beer production and speculated that it could be a later, intellectual reinterpretation. Most of my research participants supporting the banana beer narrative were music teachers or performers who had studied at the Kabarega Teachers' College in Masindi (northern Bunyoro) or came from the surroundings of Masindi town.[13] Indeed, when I asked Stephen Kabutuku (int. September 5, 2011) how he got to know the origin of *runyege* he said that he had learned it at that Teachers' College, thanks to the teaching of Solomon Mbabi-Katana. At Kabarega College, as in most Ugandan schools and colleges, no textbooks on Ugandan folk music and dance were used, but a fundamental part of the training involved, as it does today, fieldwork about those repertoires. Thus, the students of Kabarega Teachers' College were required to collect information on local music and dance through interviews and, if possible, sound recording in the field. It is likely that this is how accounts of the origins of *runyege* being connected to *tonto* were collected and subsequently incorporated into the college courses. Taking all this into consideration, it seems most probable that the *runyege* connection to banana beer was not a later intellectual, or college-originated, invention. Rather I think most likely that this narrative emerged during early fieldwork conducted in Bunyoro by college students and later was passed on. Nevertheless, it is credible that, as Kinyoro holds, *runyege* as it is in Tooro today developed from two different sources: banana processing for men and *bw'omu mbaju* for women.

Masculinity and Femininity in *Runyege* Dancing Styles

Local gender conceptions emerge as grounded not only in the narratives and interpretations of *runyege*'s origins but also in the local perceptions of the dance itself, views that focus on specific body parts of the dancers and how they move them. Indeed, notwithstanding the local differences in opinion on the origin of *runyege*'s movements, among performers and audiences I found a shared perception of women's and men's dance movements as the expressions of femininity and masculinity.

According to Hanna (1988: 88), in dance the symbolic devices of concretization, stylization, and metonym—which I showed as connoting some of the narratives about the origins of the dance as well as the conception of its movements—underscore notions of manhood and womanhood. In this way, they contribute to the process of "sex role scripting," which she defines as the social construction and dissemination of gender knowledge (Hanna

---

13   Three of my five research participants who connected *runyege* with banana beer production were music teachers who had studied at Kabarega Teachers' College in Masindi (Majara Jr., Gerrison Kinyoro, and Stephen Kabutuku). The other two research participants are Christopher Magezi, a folk musician and dancer from Masindi, and Vincent Nyegenya, a graduate of Makerere College in Kampala, where Mbabi-Katana also taught. The same training was taken by Mariam Amooti Mugenyi, who however was told about the origin of *runyege* dance by her grandmother (Mabingo 2020b: 103).

150 &✦ CHAPTER FOUR

1988: 75). In the case of *runyege*, the gendered differentiation of tasks is clearly reproduced and structured in two separate dance parts that, in turn, strengthen the social divisions and differences between the two genders as they crystallized in the last century. In this sense, *runyege* can be considered a "technology of gender" in the conception of Teresa de Lauretis (1987: 2–3). Building on Foucault's concept of technology of sex, de Lauretis applies this idea to gender, theorizing it as a complex technique, imbricated in social power structures, that involves the elaboration of discourses about gender understood as "the set of effects produced in bodies, behaviors, and social relations [...] by the deployment of a complex political technology." In this perspective, not only is the local gender conceptualization reflected in *runyege*, but *runyege* is also a means that conveys, structures, and models the discourses about gender. This happens in the discursive order, but also on the level of practice since gender becomes inscribed in dancing bodies through the repetition of acts that thus naturalize social and cultural norms, following Pierre Bourdieu's notion of *habitus* (1977). In this perspective, *runyege* emerges also as the space where gender is constructed through its very performance, although its fictional character is reelaborated by most as a natural given. According to Butler (1990), gender is forged through the acting of culturally prescribed and socially approved behaviors and practices. In the case of *runyege*, the social roles and expectations about masculinity and femininity are performed and encoded in dancing.

In order to understand how the gender binary permeates the inner dance structure and the local understanding of the dance parts as expressing hegemonic masculinity and femininity, it is necessary to consider the general development of *runyege* performances and the main features of the two dance parts. As described at the beginning of this chapter, *runyege* normally starts with the dancers performing alone or as a group of fellow men or women usually arranged in two opposite lines. Then, in turns, each man displays his dancing skills and chooses a female partner with whom he briefly dances. The finale usually involves the couples that formed during the performance all dancing together at the same time. Acoustically and visually, a *runyege* performance is a wide crescendo and accelerando that ends with a climax. This rising structure allows the dancers to progressively display their physical skills, as well as their bodies, as the intensity of the performance heightens. The performance structure can be broken down into three segments: the opening, the central part, and the final part with the closing climax. In relation to the different sections of the performance, I identified three main dance styles for men and three for women. By dance styles I mean the different ways, marked by varying degrees of intensity, of dancing the same motif. In the case of the men, the motif is the three-stokes pattern (*nkaceka* in Bunyoro and *bangatu* in Tooro) also played by the *ngoma* B or the *ngaabi* (see chapter 3); while for the women it is a double-step motif connected with the main beat. In these different dancing styles, the main elements of the dance motif (footwork, hand position or gestures, and body movement) have different widths and speeds, hence a diverse emphasis. I illustrate the different styles through analysis based on screenshots of Tooro performers: Stephen Mugabo and Christine Komuhimbo.[14]

The three main styles in men's *runyege* reproducing the three-stoke pattern *nkaceka* or *bangatu* of the drums on the *binyege* rattles have different degrees of speed and intensity. Heterogeneous terms are used to describe these dancing styles in Runyoro-Rutoooro, and I collected different ones from my expert research participants: in Bunyoro, Majara (int. August 12, 2009) and Magezi (int. June 29, 2011; August 19, 2018); in Tooro, Kinyoro (int. May 11, 2011; August 31, 2018).

At the beginning (Dance Ex. 4.1), the men's footwork is in a relatively slow tempo and involves small or on-the-spot steps, with the feet almost shuffling on the ground. The torso is quite upright and the arms are at the sides. Different terms are used to describe this style: *kusigika*, "stand firmly"; *mukutu*, "long knife"; and *kuhonda*, "thresh, pound, crash."

In the central and longest part of the performance (Dance Ex. 4.2), the speed progressively increases. The men lift their feet and stamp firmly on the ground, the upper body is slightly bent to the front, and the arms are open forward. This style is described as *ruseijera* or *kurasa*, "draw a bow, shoot at," referring to the position of the torso and the arms, and *kusimba*, "plant, stick upright in the ground."

In the climax (Dance Ex. 4.3), the men's footwork accelerates even more. The steps are almost jumps, with the knees lifted nearly to the hip level, the upper body is bent forward and the arms can be open forward or stretched upwards. This style is called *munyonyi*, from *nyonyi*, "bird," referring to both the lifted legs and arms, or *kuseesa*, "all of them" or "spread, attack."

In the men's *runyege* dancing, the attention of the performers and the audience is focused on the legs (*maguru*, sing. *kuguru*), whose movement is highlighted by the rattles around the men's calves. As both dance accessories and musical instruments, the *binyege* connect the visual with the aural: the bigger the legs' movement, the louder the rattles' sound; the quicker the jump, the faster the rattles' pattern resonates. The performance of the *muteezi b'ebinyege* ("beater of the rattles," as a male dancer is called) is evaluated on the strength, ability, and energy in his steps and jumps. Men

---

14 Their footwork, and in the case of the women's part, also the waist movement, are slightly different from the Nyoro style of dancing. In particular, in men's footwork Nyoro and Tooro styles alternate the feet differently and, in women's dancing, the waist shaking has a mainly vertical undulation in Bunyoro, while the Tooro one is mostly horizontal.

Dance Example 4.1. Stephen Mugabo showing the men's first dance style in *runyege*. Fort Portal (Tooro), 2018. The notes describe the rattles shaking produced by the footwork corresponding to the *bangatu* pattern of the drums, repeated twice.

Dance Example 4.2. Stephen Mugabo showing the men's second dance style in *runyege*.

Dance Example 4.3. Stephen Mugabo showing the men's third dance style in *runyege*.

have to stamp their feet on the ground with vigor and precision in order to produce a rhythmically correct pattern with the rattles. And long performances require stamina. These elements call for muscular strength and endurance which, in Nyoro and Tooro gender conception, connote a man as a protector of his family, the breadwinner, and a leading figure in society. Furthermore, free movement of the legs, long strides, and jumping are seen as something that pertains to men, since women with their long skirts move with short and dainty steps and are not supposed to jump or sit with their legs spread apart.

Jane C. Desmond (1997) discussed how the cultural embodiment of difference, in particular racial difference, is conveyed in dance. She also connects other categories of identity that are strongly rooted in bodily difference, such as gender, with dance where social distinctions are represented in codified bodily activities. She observes, "By looking at dance we can see enacted on a broad scale, and in codified fashion, socially constituted and historically specific attitudes toward the body in general, toward specific social groups' usage of the body in particular, and about the relationship among variously marked bodies, as well as social attitudes toward the use of space and time" (Desmond 1997: 32). Similarly, in *runyege* the men's dance part represents the cultural and social values attributed to masculinity as incarnated in the male body. This is encoded in the men's dance movements and in the focus on the legs as displaying strength, freedom, and stamina as properties of the male body. Masculinity is thus performed by the dancing male body. This body and its attributes are understood in opposition to the

154 ❧ CHAPTER FOUR

female body, which displays different properties and social meanings in the women's dance part.

The women's dance part *mugongo/bw'omu mbaju* has three main dancing styles, too. The first two styles have local names in Bunyoro (int. Magezi: June 29, 2011; August 19, 2018) and they are also used in Tooro, while the third is more typical of Tooro (Kinyoro: int. May 11, 2011; August 31, 2018). Women's footwork is performed in relation to the main beat of the low-pitched drum (*ngoma* A): for every beat, two steps are performed. From the women dancers' footwork, passing through the legs, derives the undulating lifting of the hips as a natural consequent movement. In a sequence of steps, the hips lift and lower alternatively and generate the wiggling of the hips and the quivering of the buttocks that characterize the women's dance part.[15] In the three women's styles, the footwork and hence the leg and side movement are of different breadths and intensities.

At the beginning (Dance Ex. 4.4), women perform tiny steps on the spot with the soles of the feet: on the main beat, two small steps are performed by the same foot and then, on the following beat, with the other foot. The waist and hips follow the movement of the feet and legs. The arms are open to the side with the palms facing outward. This style is called *kusimba* "stick upright in the ground."

In the central part of the performance (Dance Ex. 4.5), the women perform faster steps on the balls of the feet and the soles and their legs are markedly bent. The resulting waist movement is faster but also fuller because of the bigger movement of the feet (ball–sole), while the arms are in the same position as in the previous style. This style allows the dancers to move quickly through the dancing space and in Bunyoro it is also used, at increased speed, for the climax. Banyoro call this style *omugongo muserebende*, which can be translated as "softly sliding the lower back," highlighting the impressively flexible movement of the dancer's waist and hips.

During the climax (Dance Ex. 4.6), in Tooro the *nyamuziga* style is performed: the legs are apart and bent and the parallel feet rotate alternatively, by shuffling on the ground, toward one side and then to the opposite one, similar to the Twist dance. *Nyamuziga* literally means a "wheel, hoop," and refers to the circular shape of the short raffia skirt when it is lifted by the speed of the dancer's waist rotation. As I mentioned above, this term

---

15 A similar step and waist movement features in the *baakisimba* genre (Nanyonga-Tamusuza 2005). In that dance, however, the step involves the partial rotation of each foot and thus a slightly different hip movement. Furthermore, differently from *baakisimba*, in *mugongo/bw'omu mbaju* the distance between the feet is smaller, the arms are mostly kept open to the side and there is interaction with the male dancers.

Dance Example 4.4. Christine Komuhimbo showing the women's first dance style in *bw'omu mbaju*. Fort Portal (Tooro), 2018. The sequence corresponds to two main beats of the *ngoma* A.

Dance Example 4.5. Christine Komuhimbo showing the women's second dance style in *bw'omu mbaju*.

Dance Example 4.6. Christine Komuhimbo showing the women's third dance style in *bw'omu mbaju*.

originally referred only to this style, but today it is also commonly employed to mean the entire women's dance part in *runyege*.

In *mugongo/bw'omu mbaju*, the attention of performers and the audience is on the women's waists. In the past, various materials could be wrapped around the waist to emphasize its movement: a piece of bark cloth (*rubugo*), an animal hide (*kasaatu*), or dried grass. Today the standard is to use a short raffia skirt (*mucence*) and, especially in Bunyoro, one or two cloth rings (*kiguulya*) around the woman's waist. These elements are not only for decorative purposes; instead, they are an essential element of a good performance. Connected to this, Kinyoro quoted a proverb: *Akahimbisa omuzini nuko akasaatu ka ha kibunu*, "What is good for a dancer is the hide on the buttocks." Indeed, the shaking that the raffia skirt emphasizes draws attention to the dancer's behind. However, when describing women's dance, my research participants usually used the English terms waist and hips. In discussing the part of the body that is referred to as waist or hips, performers, instructors, and spectators provided me with a variety of local terms that in the complex refer to a broader area, including the ribs or sides (*mbaju*), the lower belly or hips (*munda*), the lumbar region or lower back (*mugongo*), and the buttocks (*kibunu*). All these body parts are involved in the shaking emphasized by women's raffia skirts. As anticipated in chapter 1, in the local language these different body parts are referred to by the Nyoro name of the women's dance *kucweka omugongo*, "to break (or to hurry) the lower back"; in the Tooro *bw'omu mbaju*, "of the ribs, of the sides." Furthermore, other expressions point to the flexible and rapid waist shaking during dancing: in Bunyoro the previously mentioned *muserebende omugongo* and in Tooro *matagura*, which can be translated as "it moves up and down." So the most important characteristic of the women's dance part is the flexibility of the abdomen and pelvis, the area of the body that is central in female fertility and sexuality. Indeed, women's elasticity in dance is considered a sign of sexual endurance, fertility, and the strength to bear a pregnancy. Rather than the female dancer's beauty, it is her ability in dancing by displaying extreme flexibility through the fast and frenzied quivering of the hips that defines her femininity and desirability as a partner, in dance and life. This seems to be quite common cross-culturally, from salsa to belly dance, and resonates with Francesca Castaldi's (2006: 82) discussion of female *sabar* dancers in Senegal, when she writes, "The emphasis on motility establishes ideals of beauty and attractiveness that do not depend on body shape and size but on the dancing skills of the subject. Eroticism is expressed through the *sabar* dancing idiom...." Eroticism also emerges from the performers' and audience's focus on female body areas that are sexually connoted. The body, as the repository of naturalized cultural ideas and behaviors, is indeed fundamental in understanding how gender and sexuality are entangled in *runyege* dance.

Embodiment, Gender, and Sexuality: Couple Dancing and *Anyakwine Enambaye Asorole*

The elements that are appreciated in dance performance—for example, strength in the legs for men and flexibility in the waist and hips for women— refer to physical characteristics that most of my research participants considered inherent to two different kinds of bodies: the male and the female one respectively. As in the explanation of why women do not play musical instruments (they are not strong enough), the two dance parts are naturalized: they are commonly understood as the direct result of men's and women's different bodies, meaning what these bodies can physically do and which bodily properties belong to them. In this sense, in *runyege* sexed bodies incarnate a social difference based on gender, as discussed by Desmond (1997). From the Nyoro and Tooro mainstream perspective, a woman is— because of her nature—delicate as well as flexible: she is not as tough as a man, she walks with small steps, keeps her legs together, but while working (digging, weeding, or sweeping) she bends to the ground with ease. Conversely, a man is strong, hard, advances confidently with big and incisive steps, jumps, and climbs when necessary; a man can carry out duties that require great muscular power and his body is perceived as tough because of

158 ❧ CHAPTER FOUR

his physical strength. In other words, femininity and masculinity in *runyege* are perceived as inscribed in two types of bodies that are differentiated by sex and in their physical features (as both appearance and skills) that the dance just enhances. This once again establishes *runyege* as a technology of gender (de Lauretis 1987) as well as a locus of gender performativity (Butler 1990): through the inscription into two different types of bodies of the discourses and practices attributed to the traditional binary, masculinity and femininity are at the same time naturalized and enacted in *runyege*.

In my experience, learning to dance *mugongo/bw'omu mbaju* was neither natural nor intuitive. Indeed, the most difficult thing for me was developing responsiveness and flexibility in the waist-hip area, allowing it to move as a consequence of the movement of the feet and legs. In my first attempts, I tried to imitate the footwork and replicate the quivering of the buttocks of my teacher by shaking them through pelvis and lower back movement. By doing so, my upper body shook as well which was not the correct way to do it and, in addition, I strained my lumbar muscles painfully. Indeed, the women's much-admired flexibility is especially evident in the contrast between the whirling movement of the waist and the still chest. But this was not a natural movement for my female body: it took me some time and practice to understand how I should feel and move in order to dance in the right way. For me, learning the women's dance was physically harder than learning the men's part. Dancing with the *binyege* did not seem so complicated to me once I had learned the basic patterns on the drums. The men's dance part requires stamina to perform for such lengths of time and concentration to move through the different rhythmic patterns and dance motifs, but it did not require my body to get to grips with a completely new movement. My European female body had learned to move differently from Nyoro and Tooro girls and women and I did not have the same skills, in particular that sensibility and flexibility in the waist-hip area. On the other hand, my body and my persona were accustomed to leg stretching and jumping, which made dancing with *binyege* easier for me. In other words, the techniques of the body (Mauss 1973), involving daily activities such as chores, work, and dancing, that since infancy shaped my corporeality have been different from those of most females in Bunyoro and Tooro, both in terms of the body's physical possibilities and of how we conceive our bodies.[16] And, of course, what I did not perceive as "natural" for my body, was considered so by local female performers. So, even if I watched attentively and tried to faithfully replicate the movements of my female teacher, my initial attempts were not

---

16   The importance of the physical and educational experience of dance to shape bodies and prepare them for their role in society has been highlighted also by John Blacking (1985) in regard to the Venda initiation dances.

THE *RUNYEGE* DANCE ❧ 159

quite successful: it was neither physically natural nor culturally intuitive to me to move that way.

My female dance instructors, Sylvia in Tooro and Monica in Bunyoro, were members of local cultural groups and it was thanks to their ensembles that I got to know them. Through the visual and tactile exchanges involved in our lessons both my understanding of dance as embodied practice and of female *runyege* developed. At our dance sessions, they normally helped me to get dressed for dancing, which involved wrapping my lower body in the *kikohi* or another long cloth if I was not wearing a skirt and then tying the cloth ring and the short *mucence* raffia skirt around my hips and pressing them down to the proper position on the lower back. Because of the familiarity with our feminine bodies that developed during dressing and performing together, after some lessons, I asked Sylvia and Monica if I could see and touch their legs as they danced in order to understand how the movement in the lower body was accomplished. Indeed, with the long skirts they wore while dancing, I could see only the footwork and the shaking of the hips accentuated by the *mucence,* and this contributed to my initial wrong understanding that the waist movement was separated from the legs and feet. For them, my request was unusual but they seemed comfortable with it and realized the impact it had on my understanding: seeing and touching how the lifting and rotation of the feet is reflected in the motions of the ankles and knees up to the hips allowed me to reproduce correctly the movements they were showing me. I believe that, because of the feminine intimacy we developed during our lessons, the teaching and learning process was easier, and also the feeling of familiarity and closeness to each other outside the lessons' context benefited from this. As Sally A. Ness (1996: 144) pointed out, "Learning how to embody new forms of movement in cross-cultural encounters exposes in a highly specific way some of one's most personal judgments to others, and in this respect can accelerate a certain kind of body-based intimacy in the production of ethnographic relationships." In my experience, reflexivity about embodiment emerged from coperforming *runyege* dance parts as an essential approach in ethnographic research. It was through learning—observing, imitating, and performing with them—that I reflected on how dancing could be embodied in different physiques. This illuminated my understanding of how the local view of *runyege* dancing parts as possible either for male or for female performers was indeed the naturalization of cultural and social notions of gender. These have been embodied through techniques of the body, as well as shaped and disseminated through discourses on gender as a binary that reflects biological sex.

Bodies—which are trained through both repetitive movements and restrictions on performing other movements according to a dual sexual differentiation that highlights certain physical parts and skills—develop gendered abilities that in turn strengthen the same characteristics (Ahmed 2006; Butler 1990). These features are then perceived as "natural," inscribed in specific sexed body typologies, and make up the ground for a gender binary, while at the same time they intertwine with it. Indeed, ultimately the different characteristics that I described as appropriate to male and female bodies reflect on gendered social behavior. Although female bodies are recognized as physically resistant as well as flexible in their performances of daily work and childbearing and their stamina and suppleness are also displayed in dancing, they are educated and trained to perform only certain movements and avoid others, like spreading legs or jumping, which mark their difference in relation to muscularly stronger bodies of men, who show their greater corporal strength in stamping and jumping *runyege*. Alongside, or derived from, these physical differences between females and males reflected in the dance are local conceptions about the typical character and social position of women and men. A woman is traditionally perceived as kind, shy, and sensitive: her "nature" and character make her unsuitable for decision-making and, for this reason, she has to show deference and respect to men. The hegemonic notion of masculinity defines the man as strong, determined, extroverted, authoritative, and ready to face dangers, decisions, and responsibilities. These opposing characteristics are also present in *runyege*, where the two dance parts reflect the personal and interpersonal characteristics of the Nyoro and Tooro traditional gender binary: men are self-confident and enterprising, women are modest and flexible. This is evident in particular at the moment when, during the dance, couples form. On the one hand, men should confidently compete with other male dancers while choosing the best partner and they should be resourceful and daring in persuading a woman to dance. On the other hand, women should display their shyness, as they normally would with men, but also their graceful embarrassment that in the end makes them accept the dance partner.

In Runyoro-Rutooro, this moment of couple formation and dancing is called *kutongora*, which means "take, choose the best one, or the most mature; choose the dance partner" (Davis 1938: 172). It was, and still is, men who choose their dance partner—not vice versa. Furthermore, in the past when couple formation was not standardized as it is today, *kutongora* happened through an interaction during which a male dancer chose a partner by dancing close to her, looking her in the eyes, and sometimes even touching her on the shoulders or on the sides (int. Kinyoro: May 11, 2011). The expected reaction of the woman dancer would be first to avoid his gaze, coquettishly bending her head, and smiling gently. Later she would agree to dance since a woman was not supposed to refuse a man, as a local adage says (*omusaija tayangwa*, lit. a man is never rejected). So, also at this moment in *runyege*, two distinct dance roles based on a dual gender conception emerge.

Figure 4.6. *Kutongora* performed by two couples of the Bunyoro Foundation Actors Group. Hoima (Bunyoro), 2009.

In the past, *runyege* did not always emphasize courtship dynamics, especially when performed in celebratory contexts. For instance, during weddings when the bride arrived at the bridegroom's family house, it was the groom's relatives and friends who danced *runyege*, but not the wedding couple. However, beer parties were a venue for new encounters and, especially for the youth, they represented an opportunity to find a dance partner who might later become a partner for life (int. Magezi: June 29, 2011). As I mentioned above, it was, and is, proficiency at dancing that makes a performer desirable: the best performers were the most admired and attracted several dance partners. In particular, during the couple formation, boys stamped their feet energetically and lifted them markedly from the ground, thus displaying their stamina, resistance, and skill in rattling—the characteristics that were most appealing for girls. According to Kagaba (int. May 11, 2011), these features in men's dancing were a sign of the strength needed to protect a woman, as well as of sexual power and stamina; but men could also decide to dance less energetically in order not to appear aggressive to female partners. In contrast, when girls accepted a dance partner they smiled openly, accentuated and quickened the

162   &   CHAPTER FOUR

waist movement, their hands kept at the sides at hip level, showing off their flexibility, which had also sexual connotations.

Indeed, sexual allusions were present in *runyege* dance. People danced with the partners they preferred (or by whom they were preferred, in the case of women). The dance movements were intended to be appealing and, in the climax the dancers could touch each other, which does not happen today in school *runyege*. According to Kinyoro (int. May 11, 2011), once the party was about to end someone could say *Anyakwine enambaye asorole*, meaning "who has a dancing partner, can take her away," alluding to the further development of intimacy between the dancing couples. This means that in *runyege* the courtship dynamic could also take the form of sexual seduction and the terms of the approach were not only platonic.[17]

Erotic connotations are apparently absent from the current *runyege* practice, especially in schools—institutions founded by missionaries and developed within a colonial mold, where decades of the national festival have sanitized and partially recodified traditional dances. The process of hiding sexuality was indeed part of the general resignification of traditional repertoires within the Ugandan school system, as documented by Nanyonga-Tamusuza (2003) for *baakisimba* dance, but is common worldwide, in particular when traditional dances are elaborated for performance on stage, as discussed by Shay (2002: 23–24, 42) in relation to state ensembles. This notwithstanding, some elderly research participants are aware of the sexual allusions of *runyege* connected to its past performance practice and some comments on performers, like the one quoted at the beginning of this chapter, involve sexuality. Besides this, sensuality is still perceptible in the *runyege* performances by semiprofessional ensembles, in particular in the dynamic of seduction and couple dancing. Despite this, many of the performers and members of the audience among my research participants denied the presence of erotic connotations in *runyege*, insisting on the cultural value of the dance. The reference to *nzarwa*, as a good, ancient, and morally positive tradition recurs very frequently in the local explanations of present *runyege*, thus represented as a (platonic) courtship dance of the Banyoro and Batooro. This image of *runyege*, however, reduces its multiple past connotations, which only emerge by sifting through layers of historical information and gendered meanings. In this respect, the mainstream representation of *runyege* appears to be the result of a moralization process, one in which both religion and the school system have played a role in sweeping away sexual implications and connections to alcohol consumption. This is the

---

17   Connected with this sexual aspect, according to Kinyoro (int. May 11, 2011) and Kagaba (int. May 11, 2011), over time, but before the inclusion in the school festival, *runyege* in Tooro became a sort of a clandestine dance, performed in secrecy at night by the youth who had escaped the control of their parents.

outcome of revision and obliteration processes started with colonization—marked by Victorian puritan morality and Christian prejudiced condemnation of any custom perceived as immoral according to (sanctimonious) Eurocentric standards—but which continued also after Independence throughout postcolonial times.

While hegemonic discourses erase sensuality in *runyege,* they emphasize the models of femininity and masculinity considered as traditional, even if they are actually the result of the postcolonial elaboration of more complex precolonial models. This is similar to many dual-gender partner dances, such as the waltz, which also contain the representation of "proper" gender roles as well as elements of sexuality and seduction, though camouflaged and "tamed" to be socially acceptable in specific social contexts. What is perhaps peculiar to *runyege,* as well as other Ugandan traditional dances, is that they have been revived after Independence through official and national channels such as school education, the national school festival, and national ensembles, and thus promoted to represent the public image of the country, convey local culture, and pass down heritage to children. For this reason, the obliteration of erotic connotations, which began under the despising colonial and missionary gaze, has been supported also in postcolonial Uganda, in order to build a national image that could be at the same time marked by local culture and appropriate to supposedly desexualized international contexts, as well as to schools.

On the one hand, in the agency of its practitioners and the plural perspectives and understandings of its observers, *runyege* hosts a plurality of meanings, touching the various aspects discussed in this chapter: history and local culture (different opinions on its origins and interpretations of the meaning of dance parts), gender models (various ways in which each performer embodies and enacts gender while dancing, as I discuss in greater detail in chapter 6), and sensuality (old sexual connotations, present ones in couple dancing, and suggestive comments). On the other hand, the pervasiveness of the hegemonic gender binary in *runyege* as told (how men's and women's different activities were incorporated into the dance), embodied (by disciplining and molding the performers' bodies through naturalized posture, movement, and interaction) and represented (displaying quintessential masculinity and femininity) is fundamental in establishing this gender model as traditional and as the reference for local culture, *nzarwa.* In the present practice of performing arts, other structures further reinforce this model, while different features allow spaces of plurality and negotiation: these two aspects are the topics of the next chapters.

Chapter Five

Narrating and Representing Local Culture

Theater in Songs and Dances

> Regarding the *runyege* troupe actors who act a love-story whose words
> are sung by musicians to a drum rhythm, it may be concluded that a
> conscious development from song to drama is emerging.
>
> —Mukasa-Balikuddembe (1973: 382)

In his master's thesis, the late Nyoro theater scholar Joseph Mukasa-Balikuddembe (1973) thus summarized his findings on *runyege*, which emerged from his investigation of the "indigenous elements of theater" in Bunyoro and Tooro. Examining the ceremonies connected to the life cycle, royalty, traditional religion, and local forms of entertainment, Mukasa-Balikuddembe (1973: 368) considered local theatrical expressions as marked by the participation of the audience and a type of theatrical communication that he defined as "unpretentious," in opposition to the mostly elitist Western drama forms. Focusing on a *runyege* performance where the song is about love and courtship, he showed the strict relationship between the song's lyrics and danced action and highlighted its theatrical dimension.[1] Furthermore, he emphasized the connection between acting and telling a story, two fundamental elements of theater that can be found in contemporary performances of traditional genres like *runyege*.

In this chapter, I focus on the drama component of MDD (music, dance, and drama), understood not as theater pieces, but rather in

---

1   This connection is by no means exclusive to *runyege*, but characterizes several genres around the world. For an example of a European traditional genre in which different performing arts are interconnected, see Wrazen 2004.

Mukasa-Balikuddembe's sense of theatrical strategies and practices. In particular, I discuss the paradigms of narration, as the causal development of consequent actions similar to a story, and representation, as including acting, costumes, and makeup. I connect these theatrical devices as found in the traditional practice of singing, instrument playing, and dancing to their contemporary use within the national school festival. In my analysis, the theatrical practices of narrating, costuming, and acting emerge as essential dimensions of performing gender in today's Ugandan traditional repertoires, as it happens in other traditional music and dance contexts, such as in East Java (Sunardi 2015). By exploring the interconnectedness of dramatic strategies and elements with other performing arts, I seek not only to highlight the complexity of *runyege* as a genre, but also to suggest how, along with defined and hegemonic structures and meanings, which I analyze here, there are also possibilities of alternate interpretations that show the flexibility of the genre, as I examine in more detail in chapter 6. According to my interpretation, most renditions at the school festival propose the mainstream discourse about local culture referencing the normative gender binary as it is inscribed in the traditional repertoires still performed today. These are the legacy of village genres in which a strict gender binary—the hegemonic one during colonial time that strengthened and became normative during colonialism—is embedded. In contrast, royal repertoires are not performed in the school festival and remain mostly circumscribed to royal ceremonies, and spirit mediumship repertoires are not performed in contemporary settings, except in highly modified versions. If all the royal and religious repertoires were revived, the complex precolonial gender system—including royal females considered as men, powerful women such as mediums displaying alternative femininities, and the minority masculinity of male spirit mediums—would emerge. The emphasis on village music of the school festival and cultural groups contributes to the reproduction of a discourse on gender as deterministic and univocally binary, where previous multiplicity was flattened during colonization and then absorbed by the postcolonial society. This gender binary is replicated on stage and its pervasiveness is enhanced by the use of narration and representation as theatrical paradigms within the school festival, then assimilated in the cultural groups' practice. However, because of the fictional nature of these paradigms related to the staging of the repertoires, counter-discourses to this gender binary can emerge by exploiting the same stage conventions as well as the very performativity of gender itself (Butler 1990; see chapter 6).

In addition to theatrical paradigms, in the festival system the concepts of authenticity and variety are also operative in shaping the performance choices of teachers and the evaluations of the jury, not only in terms of staging but also musically and choreographically. The ways in which authenticity and variety are negotiated in school performances also contribute to the contemporary definition of local culture. For this reason, along with the discussion of narration and representation as theatrical strategies, I also consider how the festival system has musically and choreutically remodeled the traditional repertoires presented in the previous chapters. In order to understand how these transformations came about and how theatrical paradigms work today, I first take a step back and consider how music education and the school festival developed the main guidelines that have shaped the contemporary practice of traditional performing arts.

Music Education and the School Festival: A System Shaping the Performing Arts

In the 1960s, music education, the school festival, and traditional ensembles started to develop throughout Uganda, and they have progressively become an integrated system operating in the field of traditional performing arts. These repertoires—taught in schools, molded by the festival mechanisms, and then absorbed by cultural groups—feature local cultures as handed down through generations but also as shaped by the contemporary understanding of tradition.

As mentioned in the Introduction, since the 1960s, music education has developed along two main lines that were set out by Peter Cooke and Solomon Mbabi-Katana. Cooke's approach to learning the traditional repertoires directly from the village context and expert musicians is evident in the didactics of teachers' colleges. Mbabi-Katana's educational perspective on folk singing emerging from his numerous anthologies (Mbabi-Katana 1965, 1966, 1973, 1987, and 2002) shaped the learning of traditional repertoires in primary and secondary schools. His method focused on teaching children the meaning and content of songs, in different languages, by dramatizing the lyrics through gestures depicting the sung actions and the interpretation of the various singing characters. Mbabi-Katana's pedagogic vision of traditional repertoires as a means to hand down local culture to the youth is the general approach applied today in teaching traditional repertoires in schools and in performing them within the festival. Lillian Bukaayi (2009), describing the use of marriage songs in Busoga (eastern Uganda), argues that today they are used to instruct children on adulthood in place of the initiation rituals of the past, which are now considered embarrassing. This pedagogic approach implies the use of dramatization as well as other representative devices (especially costumes) in order to better express the content. At the same time, it contemplates the possibility, when necessary, of adapting the meaning and motifs of the lyrics and dances to the young pupils. For instance, some music teachers, like Kinyoro (int. May 11, 2011) emphasized that the language of the songs and the motifs of the dance must be made appropriate for children. Indeed, since the 1960s, wordings considered vulgar or inappropriate (for instance in some *runyege* or twins songs) have been changed, just as dance motifs or interpretations that might allude to sexuality have been removed, as has happened in *runyege* dance. Over time, the repertoires have then crystallized into the modified versions that are now performed at the school festival.

A school festival may be considered a negligible element in the performing arts, but its influence on the Ugandan performative landscape is huge. The festival, an annual event held at a national level, has a history of around sixty years and, since the 1990s, participation is mandatory for all primary and secondary schools, as well as teachers' colleges.[2] The school festival has pushed all schools to include performing arts in their syllabi, mostly with training directed toward the performance at the yearly event. The festival includes several categories: not only the traditional songs and dances on which I focus here, but also African instrument playing, Western singing, drama, and poetry. When one considers both the long history of the institution and the very young average age of Ugandans,[3] the relevance of the festival to millions of schoolchildren and students is clear. Indeed, it is through music education and the national school festival that many, perhaps most, young Ugandans learn traditional performing arts, which they can later choose to continue performing in semiprofessional ensembles.

The school festival, organized by the Ministry of Education, can be understood as a multipurpose state project, in which teachers, trainers, pupils, and communities are all active participants sharing and negotiating its meaning and content. As an educational project, traditional repertoires within the festival are the means through which a continuity with local culture, usually not alive in community practice anymore, is woven. Through singing, playing, and dancing the traditional genres of their region, children and young adults get to know their own culture. In freshly independent Uganda, as in other African countries, such as Malawi (Gilman 2009), this was important in terms of reevaluating postcolonial African identity. Equally

---

2   Since the 2000s, this has partially changed due to the neoliberal policies of the NRM government, which focus on development and "modernity," leading to a new emphasis on subjects such as hard sciences, IT, and tourism to the detriment of humanities (Achieng' Akuno 2009; Reid 2017). As a consequence, many schools, especially secondary institutions, have redirected their resources away from MDD education and tried to avoid participating in the school festival.

3   https://www.statista.com/statistics/447698/age-structure-in-uganda/ (accessed on December 23, 2021).

168   CHAPTER FIVE

central to nation-building was the fostering of the peaceful coexistence of different ethnicities. Through the festival, indeed, performers met and came to know the traditions of other areas of the country, thus constructing a national society conscious of local cultural differences. This was especially emphasized in the first decades of the festival history, when, besides their own repertoires, Ugandan schools had to perform a song or a dance from another region, thus getting to know better another of the country's cultures (Pier 2009).[4] It should be noted that in a national context such as the Ugandan one, where every ethnicity mobilizes performing arts and cultural institutions to obtain visibility and thus access to resources (Reid 2017), the festival reinforces the ethnicization of the repertoires as local heritages belonging to specific groups (Pier 2009 and 2015).

Over the long history of the festival, various performance conventions have emerged. According to Peter Cooke (email October 3, 2012), during the 1960s in a traditional singing performance at festival it was possible to alternate two traditional songs to create some variety. Ugandan musician George W. Kakoma (1970) supported the use of the ternary form in folk singing, where a song (A) is followed by a different one (B) and the repetition (A') of the first one. Nowadays, this form is seldom employed and it is more usual to present a sequence of different songs tied together according to a plot. Narration is indeed the leading principle behind the convention of performing a sequence of songs in the "traditional folk song" category, as I analyze in detail in the following section. Another convention is the use of traditional costumes, makeup, and acting. In dancing, suitable clothes (to allow certain movements), accessories (to enhance the moves), and instruments (rattles) were also used in community practice, but not the makeup. In the early days of the festival, pupils wore their school uniforms for traditional singing, whereas today's traditional costumes and makeup are used to identify different characters on the basis of gender, age, and role, while the story is depicted on stage through acting. The conventional use of costumes, makeup, and acting is guided by the principle of representation, showing the different characters and the development of the action on stage.

The principles of narration and representation in the festival's performances derive from the pedagogical need to clearly communicate and contextualize the meaning of traditional repertoires to young performers and audiences beyond language and cultural barriers. In this sense, they are consciously implemented by teachers and approved by the festival's adjudicating committee. According to the performer and school instructor Kafre (int.

---

4   However, since 2010, the festival guidelines stipulate that only local repertoires from each school's home region are performed, reflecting the recent turn of the education system toward more "spendable" subjects than MDD.

August 20, 2018), "if you sing and act, the message will also be clear to the people that cannot hear the language, just through the actions."

Nowadays the festival, as a competitive event, involves a panel of judges evaluating the pupils' performances. In the grading process, the jury members consider adherence to genre and function as well the styles and features of the traditional repertoires, as they have been cataloged and codified through school education and the same festival practice (Pier 2009 and 2015). The performance is also evaluated in terms of costumes, diversity in the sequence of songs, variety in the danced motifs, and choreography—parameters showing an emphasis on spectacularity. The festival's guidelines, which are updated every year, and the evaluation methods and decisions of the jury are central in shaping performance practice. Indeed, as outlined by Pier (2009), elements of successful performances spread among the schools, and thus stage conventions and performance practice are continually developing and changing through the actions of the teachers, pupils, and adjudication committee. Other competitive events, such as the sponsored Senator National Cultural Extravaganza, have also adopted these conventions, along with the organization model of the school festival (Pier 2009, 2011, and 2015). The performers at these competitions are semiprofessional ensembles, whose members mostly received their training in traditional repertoires at school from instructors who are also sometimes the directors of the group.

The interconnectedness of music education, the school festival, and cultural groups emerges as a system shaping the content and form of traditional repertoires, but also of the local culture that they represent and hand down. Through this system, narration and representation have become paradigms structuring music and dance. Narration is particularly evident in the performance of traditional songs, which is at the center of the following section.

Preserving Tradition, Creating a Story: Narration in Traditional Folk Songs

The principle of narration was institutionalized in the school festival as a paradigm shaping the performance practice; however, the idea of presenting content following temporal and causal development already existed in traditional singing. I discuss this in chapter 1, using the story told by Kinyoro about the origin of *runyege*, in which a song illustrated the banana stamping process, thus driving the story itself. Furthermore, traditional storytelling (*nganikyo*) usually included brief sung interventions that had a fundamental dramaturgical role in developing the story. These songs usually had a dialogical form and could be sung by various characters at different points in the story, thus unfolding the narration. According to Mukasa-Balikuddembe

(1973: 173), the storyteller could also use voice inflection, mimicry, and gestures to dramatize his/her narration. Singing and storytelling are completely integrated into the *bigano* (sing. *kigano*) sung stories or stories in song.[5] However, unlike the linear narration of storytelling, in *bigano* some story elements are implied and the narration can proceed through ellipses, thus making the meaning of some of them obscure.[6] The principle of narration, in the sense of the causal evolution of events, shapes the verbal component of traditional singing in general. For instance, in the solo song *Ke ke kamengo* presented in chapter 2, I remarked on how the lyrics mentioned the subsequent actions needed in the preparation of millet polenta. The same development of the solo parts, as the presentation of the evolution of actions, usually structures call-and-response songs, where the soloist progressively adds new verses in contrast with a repeated chorus.

While narration structured certain traditional genres internally in terms of lyrics, it did not shape their traditional performance practice, that is, which pieces were sung one after the other. In the past, different songs were performed successively following similar content or verbal associations, or according to the changing performing circumstances, thus juxtaposing different topics (int. Kinyoro: May 5, 2011). Conversely, in today's festival performances, the paradigm of narration shapes the staged performance of traditional performing arts. In traditional dances like *runyege*, it can be seen in the carefully staged formation of couples through the courtship process of danced actions. In the "traditional folk song"[7] category, the narration principle is essential. According to the music teacher and adjudicator trainer

---

5   In Bantu-speaking Africa, the radical *-gano* marks several repertoires characterized by narration: for instance, Venda *ngano* sung stories (Blacking 1967), Aka *gano* stories with songs (Kisliuk 2001) and, in East and South-East Africa, the *nthano, ndano,* or *ngano* stories occasionally contain singing (Kubik 1987).
     In Bunyoro and Tooro, people sang *bigano,* especially during the evenings of the harvesting season, when there was more free time to spend together (int. Sabiiti: August 1, 2009; int. Tibamanya: June 27, 2010). The topics of *bigano* are varied, but often feature supernatural events, natural elements, and dangerous animals. Some have an educative purpose, indeed the *bigano* were directed especially at children, who joined in with the chorus.

6   I studied the genres of *nganikyo* and *bigano* mainly through the examples, performances, and explanations that Jane Sabiiti in Bunyoro and Jane Tibamanya in Tooro shared with me. Unfortunately, a deeper analysis of these genres would lead the discussion away from the theatrical strategies in contemporary school and ensemble performances, but these repertoires are highly interesting and worth studying in the future.

7   In the 2011 festival guidelines, this category is also spelled "traditional folksong."

Joshwa Kabyanga (int. August 22, 2018), it was the Ugandan musician Joseph Kyagambiddwa who introduced the idea of a story binding together different pieces in one unified song. This allowed there to be a longer, continuous song that was meaningful to the performers and audience. This approach has become a pillar of traditional singing within the school festival. Indeed, the document "Important Highlights in Each Class" (Ministry of Education and Sports 2011: 5) states: "The story in the song should be relevant and should flow systematically." According to the music teacher and adjudicator trainer Marrion Nyakato (int. June 25, 2011), the story should present an initial problem, further complications in the middle, and a final resolution that is marked by a danced climax. Furthermore, the story should refer to past traditional life, using traditional singing to portray a typical situation from the past.

These are the elements that shape the performance that Kahunga Bunyonyi Primary School from Fort Portal prepared for the 2011 festival. That year, one of the themes for the "traditional folk song" category was work and this school chose to sing about traditional millet polenta preparation. In Kahunga Bunyonyi's performance, we can differentiate seven different pieces of various lengths and internal structures. The narrative development is articulated through a song for grinding millet, two songs describing the operations for the preparation of the millet polenta, a piece depicting the distribution of the meal to the family members, two songs thanking the cook, and the final jubilation with *runyege* dance. The lyrics depict the various steps of food preparation and eating and are illustrated through acted actions on stage, as shown in Table 5.1.

According to the festival's guidelines, the interpretation of the song has to mirror the content and feelings expressed by the lyrics not only by adapting vocal expression but also with facial expression, gesture, and body movement. As described in Table 5.1, the various actions mentioned in the lyrics of Kahunga Bunyonyi's traditional folk song are acted in the different scenes (see Fig. 5.1).

Furthermore, the festival prescribes that costumes, props, and makeup should also be used to bring out the meaning of the song by differentiating and identifying the different characters and setting the scene. On the one hand, the emphasis on costumes, makeup, props, and action on stage fosters a tendency to make the performance as spectacular as possible, for which high marks may be awarded. On the other hand, these theatrical elements, together with the narrative that runs through the song, are understood as pedagogical tools by both teachers and the jury because they allow younger generations to understand old customs that would be hard to grasp without the narration of a story and the representation on stage. So in the performances of traditional folk songs at the national school festival, costumes and

Table 5.1. Structure of the traditional folk song prepared in 2011 by Kahunga Bunyonyi Primary School.

Song	Vocal and instrumental parts	Song's sections and structure	Action on stage
Ceeku ceeku	Two soloists (S1 and S2) singing in unison Two choirs (C1 and C2): C1 performing the line *Kamenjo kaseera bali*, C2 vocalizing Drums in the background	<u>Beginning</u>: 2 verses repeated by the soloists; same 2 verses repeated by the C1 chorus <u>Center</u>: call-and-response form <u>Closing</u>: call-and-response form with the soloists singing *Ahah*	Soloists: millet grinding Other performers: stepping on millet cobs (boys/men), millet winnowing and sifting (girls/women)
Oburo oburo [Millet, millet]	One soloist (S3) One choir Rattles Drums in the background	Call-and-response form	Fetching water and firewood, preparation of the three stones for the cooking fire, lighting the fire, positioning of the cooking pot on it
Eee ee enyungu ehire [Water is boiling]	Three soloists (S1, S2, S3) singing in unison One choir	Call-and-response form	Ground millet is poured in the boiling water and millet polenta (*karo*) is prepared
Ahaa! Ahaa! Abwoli mucumba [Abwooli cooking]	One soloist (S2) One choir Clapping and drums underlining the chorus	Call-and-response form—the solo part is spoken	Millet polenta is distributed in traditional baskets to different family members
Webale kucumba [Thank you for cooking]	Two choirs	Antiphonal form opposing two choirs	The cook is thanked

Itwena, itwena tusiime muno Abwoli [We all thank Abwooli for cooking]	One soloist (S4) Four choirs: C *tutti*; choir (C1); two female choirs (C2 and C3); one male choir (C4) Clapping Drums Rattles	<u>Beginning</u>: verse of the soloist, then repeated by the chorus C *tutti*. <u>Center</u>: call-and-response form with different choruses (C1, C2, C3, C4) answering to the soloist and C *tutti*. <u>Closing</u>: repetition of section C *tutti*, and C3 repeating *Abwoli*.	Thanking of the cook and celebrating through *runyege* dancing when the C *tutti* sings
Tulire twigusire [We have eaten to fullness]	*Tutti* choir Clapping Drums Rattles Ululations	Final verse repeated in unison	Final jubilation and *runyege* dancing

Figure 5.1. Pupils of Kahunga Bunyonyi Primary School rehearsing the "traditional folk song" *Ceeku ceeku* in 2011. In the foreground, Jolly Kabaikya and Resty Kamigisa grind millet while singing the solo of the first piece of the sequence. Costumes and makeup are normally reserved for the stage performance and are not used during rehearsals.

makeup[8] represent the singers' gender, social role, and age traditionally associated with the sung activities.

On stage, Kahunga Bunyonyi Primary School's sung story about millet polenta did not only represent local culture by showing how to prepare and share a traditional meal, but the performers also portrayed the traditional gender binary through costumes[9] and makeup identifying their gendered roles.

---

8   Make up mostly consists of white chalk powder used on hair to whiten it and on the face to draw white beards in order to represent elders.

9   For the stage performance, the girls who played women wore the *kikohi* or *kitambi* long skirt and the *kiteteyi* top; the singers in the choir additionally wore the *suka* cape that allows only restricted movement. Boys who acted and those playing the drums sported T-shirts, short pants, and a cloth tied on one shoulder; boys playing elders wore the white *kanzu* tunic and a jacket. It is worth noting that none of these clothes were worn in pre-colonial times. Back then, people dressed in *rubugo* barkcloth and animal skins. The horizontally striped *kikohi* cloth is an Indian product and the *kanzu* is of Arab origin. These

THEATER IN SONGS AND DANCES ❧ 175

Using costumes and makeup, acted activities and gestures were reproduced on stage as gendered. It is women—as wives and daughters—who grind millet, prepare the polenta, and distribute it while kneeling. It is men—as husbands, clan members, and guests—that first step on the millet cobs, then receive the cooked food and eat it. Food processing and preparation, serving, and kneeling are activities connoted as feminine, while men do not cook but are seated and served food. Acting and costumes present the traditional gender binary in a much clearer way than singing alone could do. The pedagogic purpose of clarifying the content of the folk song through the theatrical devices of acting and costumes thus also mediates a representation of gender. In other words, the handing down of local culture to young generations involves the reproduction of the gender binary perceived as traditional.

By replicating the actions sung in the lyrics as gendered acts—a repetition performed by the pupils in rehearsals and performances, but also a repetition of gendered roles experienced by the audience, teachers, and evaluators attending the performance—the traditional model is established over and over again. Iterated practice inscribes social and cultural norms as *habitus*, incorporated behavior that is seen as "natural" (Bourdieu 1977). Sherry B. Ortner (1996) has shown the implications of a theory of practice applied to gender as informing the daily repeated actions that reproduce gendered power structures thus "making" gender. Judith Butler (1990: 190) specifically discussed gender performativity: "Consider gender… as *a corporeal style*, as an 'act', as it were, which is both intentional and performative, where '*performative*' suggests a dramatic and contingent construction of meaning" [emphasis in the original]. The very performance of traditional folk songs as narrative and gendered sung actions not only represents local culture, as is the declared intention of the school festival, but through iterated bodily acts it also imprints onto young generations the gender model inscribed in the local culture.

Kahunga Bunyonyi is a mixed primary school and, in this performance, girls played women and boys performed as men. However, costumes and makeup are essential tools in representing gender in single-sex schools, where pupils have to play characters of both traditional genders. I will examine this aspect in relation to instrument playing and traditional dances, but first I consider how the musical component of traditional singing is shaped in festival performances through the notions of authenticity and variety.

---

clothes have been worn in Uganda since the nineteenth century and are today perceived as traditional (Reid 2017), especially in opposition to "Western" fashion. The cotton T-shirts are understood as Western, but accepted in this context instead of having the boys performing bare-chested.

Authenticity and Variety Shaping
Traditional Songs: *Ceeku ceeku*

In order to understand how folk songs are interpreted at the school festival, I followed some schools' rehearsals and performances at various levels of the competition. Furthermore, I studied the guidelines and evaluation forms given to the adjudicators (Ministry of Education and Sports 2011), attended an adjudicators' training session (June 25, 2011), and subsequently interviewed the trainers (August 22, 2018). While narration is the basic paradigm structuring folk song performance together with the costumes and makeup that help to convey its meaning, musical elements are equally important and are also evaluated. The adjudicators have to consider musical features—singing style, use of local language and diction, musical phrasing, rhythm, and accompaniment—according to their conformity to local traditional style (Nanyonga-Tamusuza 2003). While "authenticity" is considered a key element in assessing the performance, variety is also highly evaluated. This is why schoolteachers and festival adjudicators continuously negotiate and evaluate the features of the performance according to these two elements. According to Kabyanga (int. August 22, 2018): "[as music teachers] we build the story and create our own song but in relation to a traditional tune, already known, not composed [for the festival] ... but you want to spice up this performance so that it is good enough: it is a competition and you want to excel. So if you leave it as it was without spicing it up, you might not score [highly]. You can add a bit, but in line with the traditional aspects."

We can see these elements applied in Kahunga Bunyonyi's folk song performance discussed above. The first piece of the sequence, *Ceeku ceeku*, is a rendition of the millet grinding song *Ke ke kamengo*, different from the version by Dorothy Kahwa presented in chapter 2. The music teacher that prepared this school performance, Clovis Baguma (int. July 3, 2013), told me that an old lady sang that song for him, with the words *Ceeku ceeku*,[10] then he made it more elaborate with "African tones and dynamics." In comparison to the solo song that I presented, the school version exhibits a more complex structure with three main sections.

At the beginning (section 1, Mus. Ex. 5.1), the two soloists sing the first verse (*Ceeku ceeku, kamengo kasera bali*) twice and Chorus 1 repeats it. In the other versions of this millet song that I recorded, the final part of the verse (*kaseera bali*) was repeated without variations. Kahunga Bunyonyi Primary School's rendition is varied in both the solo and the chorus part. Furthermore, Chorus 2 sings long notes in the background all along. Baguma explained

---

10   The sounds *ke* [ke] and *ce* [tʃe] are both connected with the sound of millet grinding, as I could verify in various versions of this song.

Musical Example 5.1. The initial section (1) of *Ceeku Ceeku* by Kahunga Bunyonyi Primary School.

this second chorus as an element of "African harmony," as the adaptation of the traditional ululation (int. July 3, 2013). Finally, compared to the other millet songs that I recorded, this version is markedly slower. This is probably because this piece opens the sequence, which is constructed like a progressive crescendo and accelerando leading to the closing climax.

In the central and longer part of this piece (section 2, Mus. Ex. 5.2), the original solo form is transformed into a call-and-response. The soloists sing only the first part of the line, which features new lyrics, while the chorus repeats the second part of the line, which is verbally constant (*kamengo kaseera bali*). The soloists hold the final note of their verse for almost the whole length of the following chorus, thus realizing an extensive overlapping that I could not trace either in historical recordings or in the renditions by elders. Indeed, according to Marrion Nyakato (int. August 22, 2018), it was in the festival practice that overlapping was developed by performing longer sustained notes.

In the closing of this piece (section 3, Mus. Ex. 5.3), the main soloist sings *Ahah*—an affirmative expression here meaning that the millet flour is ready—while Chorus 1 answers with the same verse as before and Chorus 2

Musical Example 5.2. The central section (2) of *Ceeku Ceeku* by Kahunga Bunyonyi Primary School.

Musical Example 5.3. The final section (3) of *Ceeku Ceeku* by Kahunga Bunyonyi Primary School.

continues the ululations in the background. Whereas in historical recordings and elders' renditions the volume of singing is normally stable, in this performance there are significant variations. This last part is indeed in diminuendo. Together with the use of ritardando, the overall effect is a progressive fade-out of the song, which leads into the following one, thus allowing the articulation of the sequence. As also noted by Pier (2009), the volume of the singing is one of the parameters evaluated by the adjudicators and it should be functional to the expression of the lyrics' content and shape the internal articulation of the folk song. The use of both diminuendo and ritardando (as well as their opposites, crescendo and accelerando) was introduced in the festival performances most probably under influence of Western classical or church music and meant as means for connecting different musical sections and increasing variety.

While in this first song the drums just mark the beat and are almost inaudible, in the following pieces of the sequence they become louder and louder. In this folk song, like in most performances in this festival category, the volume in both singing and accompaniment increases progressively through the different pieces making up the sequence. This crescendo is carefully planned to reach a final climax, which also involves dancing.

In this folk song, the only instruments played were the drums. However, nowadays it is common to use more instrumentation. According to Nyakato (int. August 22, 2018): "[in the school festival] the accompaniment has changed a bit. Those days in Bunyoro we used only drums and later the tube fiddle to accompany, plus singing, plus yodeling… but now we have included some musical instruments like the xylophone that you can use in your folk song to enrich the accompaniment." Also Kabyanga (int. August 22, 2018) pointed out that: "today because of these competitions, people are trying to add something, to spice up the performances. Now with accompaniment… The way songs were performed ten years ago at the festival, now you find a completely different story in the folk songs. So if you stick to the real real, that this is the way it was and should stay like that, you can't compete…"

In the folk song *Ceeku ceeku*, to break the monotony of the solo song as performed by elders several operations were carried out: the transformation into a call-and-response form, the melodic variations, and the introduction of a second chorus. These are some of the elements that were introduced to "spice up" the song, to use Kabyanga's expression. So the idea of "authenticity" that informs these performances and guides part of the adjudicators' evaluation of the musical features does not mean that the singing has to be exactly as the elders sang. Rather, faithfulness to the old musical style is negotiated in relation to other festival parameters, such as variety. On the other hand, the principle of "authenticity" guides the representation of local culture on the stage, which is portrayed as ancient and traditional mainly by

180 ❧ CHAPTER FIVE

means of theatrical strategies, such as narration. This was explicitly expressed during a lesson to festival adjudicators by Nyakato (June 25, 2011), who declared: "in order to preserve our culture, we have to create a story."

Dressed in a *Kanzu* Tunic: Girls Playing Drums

In discussing instrument playing in chapter 3, I outlined the transformations that have taken place in the gendering of musical instruments and the fact that today women and girls play some of them, despite the traditional conception of the female body as being too weak or unable to perform such tasks. Traditional music education in schools and the national festival played a fundamental role in destabilizing these views. In Uganda, there are many all-girls schools, as well as all-boys, and instruments, drums in particular, are essential in performing traditional songs and dances. Since all schools are supposed to participate in the festival, instrument playing opened up to girls in all-girls schools and later became accepted more generally. While some teachers have conservative stances, thinking that even if girls play drums boys are stronger than them and hence drum better (int. Misinguzi: June 9, 2011), others embrace the idea that pupils of any gender can play well. According to music teacher Clovis Baguma (int. May 9, 2011), if one teaches all the pupils, then girls will also learn to play the drums: the percussion technique is more important than physical strength. In his personal didactic experience in mixed schools, Baguma taught all his pupils and then chose the best ones to play the drums at the school festival, no matter whether they were boys or girls. This is confirmed by Kabyanga (int. August 22, 2018) saying that "culturally, some instruments like the *ndingidi* are only for males. When it comes to school performances, some cultural norms are broken. What is looked at is: what has this person trained in? What can he or she do? So, we are looking at what skills the individual has, not because the individual is male he should perform a male part or she should do female parts because she's female."

To play drums and other instruments on stage during performances of traditional folk songs or dances, girls normally wear the typically masculine tunic *kanzu* or, more rarely, another type of tunic (see Figs. 3.4 and 3.5). This is not because it is more practical than a woman's skirt, rather this costume is employed to represent the masculine gender traditionally associated with drum playing. Whereas costumes in folk singing and dancing illustrate the different characters in the story, instrument players are involved neither in narration nor action. Similar to what happens in the performances of traditional dances, they remain in the background, usually hidden behind the chorus and the main action taking place center stage. The use of costumes for musicians, therefore, is not a didactic strategy meant to clarify the meaning of the song or the dance courtship dynamic.

When I discussed the use of costumes for musicians in the school festival with Kabyanga and Nyakato, Kabyanga said that the festival guidelines do not prescribe the *kanzu* for drummers as mandatory and generally the adjudicators do not focus on that aspect. According to him: "What [adjudicators] want to hear is that the rhythm comes out. And in most cases, in judging the costumes, because there is a costume aspect, they pay very little attention to the musicians and chorus singers. The attention is on the dancers' costumes. What is important is keeping the rhythm on the drums; even if they didn't dress like men, I don't think they would penalize them" (int. August 22, 2018). However, when I asked what would happen if a (male or female) drummer wore typically feminine clothes, both Kabyanga and Nyakato said they wouldn't know because they have never seen it happen, but Nyakato suggested that people in the audience would probably take a picture of that performer with their phones. Indeed, it would be a very unusual thing to see. Reflecting on this, Kabyanga added that "The reason is the cultural aspect. I think that they want to show that it is an item supposed to be performed by boys. I think that should be the whole idea. But the adjudicator doesn't have in mind that he or she should have dressed as a man or a woman...." The importance of respecting local culture by dressing appropriately when playing musical instruments is shared by the music teachers with whom I discussed the role of costumes (int. Baguma: May 9, 2011).

The convention of costumes, as a means of clarifying the role of performers on stage so that the story and the action can be understood, has thus been applied more generally to include performers who have nontheatrical roles, like musicians. Kabyanga explained the role of costumes in the various categories of the school festival: "In the culture, you take that role: when I am dancing the male part, if I am a girl I have to dress like a male because I am playing the role of a man. When I am singing the role of a male, I am turning into a man. So, when I play drums, and culturally drums are masculine, for males ... I dress like a man" (int. August 22, 2018). This use of costumes emerges as a device to reproduce traditional gender by representing drums as instruments played only by men. Correctly interpreting local culture on stage cannot be separated from reproducing the discourse on the traditional gender binary, as I argued for traditional folk songs. By replicating this gendered musical practice through costumes, the image of masculinity as connoted by strength, loudness, and leadership—features associated to drumming in particular—is reinforced. At the same time, this is merely a stage representation of masculinity or, following Butler (1990), a performance of gender in its most theatrical sense. Beneath the white *kanzu* tunic there may be the "delicate" body of a girl playing the drum's skin with determination and skill. This theatrical fiction emerges as limited to the stage, though grounded in the common gender imaginary. Most of the girl-drummers I met did not see playing a drum at the school festival as special. They learned to play it just like other pupils and learning to play the drums is today not gendered—this is true especially for the *ngoma* drum, while there may be some tensions for the *ngaabi* drum (see chapter 3). In the long run, drumming in schools can be instructive in challenging gender determinism and a tool to negotiate traditional femininity for adult women, as I discuss in the next chapter.

Traditional music education in schools and the school festival brought about transformations in access to learning and performing (of instruments or dance parts not corresponding to one's gender, according to the traditional binary), but also in the repertoires themselves. These negotiations between tradition and innovation continuously going on within the festival system, together with the paradigm of representation in traditional dances, are the focus of the following sections.

Runyege on Stage: Conventional Representation between Tradition and Innovation

Relevant to the understanding of the contemporary practice of Ugandan traditional dances is the paradigm of representation that I already mentioned as a theatrical convention at work also in folk songs and instrument playing. By representation I mean the paradigm guiding the set of practices including acting (gestures, body movements, and expressions) and other means (primarily costumes and makeup), which seek to depict not only actions and emotions but also, more broadly, social and cultural dynamics. In the case of the current performances of traditional dances, which are understood as a representation of local culture, the gender binary perceived as traditional plays a major role.

In terms of the acting that takes place in the *runyege* performances at the school festival,[11] the pupils portray the courtship process through the danced advance and retreat strategies inscribed in the genre (Mukasa-Balikuddembe 1973: 382). Indeed, the courting that leads to the formation of couples—including the display of dancing skills, the approach of the male dancers, and the corresponding reactions of the female partners leading to couple dancing—can be understood as acted interaction between the performers. If the

---

11   The category in which *runyege* is performed in the school festival is called "traditional folk dance."

THEATER IN SONGS AND DANCES ❧ 183

gendered dynamic of courtship already inscribed in *runyege* is accentuated, other gendered representations are the result of creative operations triggered by the performance parameters of the festival.

The school festival has indeed introduced new elements into traditional dances, such as "levels,"[12] that have led to the creation of dance motifs, which also involve the paradigm of representation. As a parameter in the school festival for the dance category, the levels are understood as degrees of the vertical posture of the dancer. They include a high level with the standing position, a medium level involving bent legs or kneeling, and a low level with hands on the ground. As I showed in chapter 4, the three traditional *runyege* styles for men and women dancers are all performed while standing, which would correspond to the high level. As is the case for other Ugandan dances (Nanyonga-Tamusuza 2005), in order to stay within the festival parameters and score higher marks, Nyoro and Tooro schools had to invent new dance motifs for *runyege* at the medium and low level.[13] When creating new motifs, music teachers have to consider how to feature different levels while maintaining the main *runyege* features—that is, men shaking leg rattles and women moving their hips. Also, as a performance of traditional dance, local culture should be depicted.

In their 2011 performance of "traditional folk dance," the pupils of Kahunga Bunyonyi Primary School also included in their *runyege* performance a rhythmic motif that had two different dance renditions for female and male dancers and also involved two different levels: the girl danced while kneeling (medium level) and the boy while leaning backward and bearing his weight with his hands on the ground (low level). In this dance motif, the male dancer performed at the low level with an inventive posture that allowed him to shake his leg rattles. The female dancer had a medium level posture that featured the traditional kneeling of women when they address men. This women's motif at the medium level was inspired by an element of local culture, thus recreating tradition through a gendered action that connotes femininity. Variety, as the creation of new motifs, and tradition, as the representation of local culture, combine in this double dance motif.

---

12   I was not able to ascertain how the choreographic technique of levels was included in the parameters for performing folk dances in the Ugandan school festival. The teachers and festival adjudicators with whom I talked did not know when and by whom it was introduced.

13   In every performance at the school festival there are many new motifs. In most of the performances that I observed at the school festival, dance motifs were repeated just three or four times and then followed by another motif. Since the dance speed is high and a performance can last between 6 and 8 minutes, a large number of motifs features in each performance.

184   ❧   CHAPTER FIVE

As is the case for folk songs, variety and authenticity are also negotiated in the staging of traditional dances. New dance motifs at different levels enhance the internal variety of performances, but other strategies also contribute to making the dance diverse and "colorful," a feature that schoolteachers and adjudicators consider to be very important. Internal variety is normally developed by combining different dance genres in a dance suite. Each school can choose to perform just one dance or a sequence of different dances among those identified as originating from their local area.[14] The other element contributing to variety is stage formations, which are the various forms of dancers' groupings on the stage. The dancers can be arranged in the space to create lines or circles, or they can dance in the free mass formation, scattered around the stage, as in the traditional practice (int. Kinyoro: July 29, 2012; Lloyd 1907: 55; Torelli 1973: 523). Other formations, such as serpentine line dancing and forming letters of the alphabet, have been introduced through the festival (Pier 2009 and 2015). The skillful employment of different dance formations on stage avoids monotony and makes the performance more dynamic, as Nyakato (June 25, 2011) pointed out. On the one hand, all these elements—new motifs, levels, the combination of different dance genres, and stage formations—contributing to the energy and dynamism of performances have fostered several transformations not only in Nyoro and Tooro local dances, but in Ugandan dances in general (Nanyonga-Tamusuza 2003 and 2005; Pier 2009). On the other hand, the festival approach to other components of dance performances is more conservative. Once again, authenticity and creativity are combined in the performances of traditional dances at the school festival. The 2011 Ugandan festival guidelines for adjudicators state that the accompaniment should be appropriate to the dance and "authentic," with reference to local traditional repertoires. This means that *runyege* should be accompanied by a set of three drums, clapping, and possibly the *ndingidi* one-string fiddle, as I discuss in chapter 4. Singing should be with a "natural voice" and, in Bunyoro, it may include yodeling. Also, costumes should conform to the codified conventions of traditional clothing, as seen for the "traditional folk song" category.

---

14   Banyoro can thus perform a dance suite including *runyege, ntogoro, iguulya, rusindi,* and *kagoma,* while Batooro can combine local *runyege* and *ntogoro.* In the latter region, just these two dances have been identified as local, although the less well-known *bw'omu mbaju* and *kalezi* also existed, meaning that Tooro schools have few options in combining their dances for the festival. In these dance suites, the rhythmic-dance motifs of one genre can be employed in others, making it difficult to isolate the different genres, as I discuss in chapter 4. On the role of the school festival in defining and cataloguing Ugandan local repertoires, see Pier 2009 and Cimardi 2015 and 2017b.

This blend of conservation and innovation characterizes not only the current performance of traditional repertoires in Uganda, as Nanyonga-Tamusuza (2003) showed for Ganda *baakisimba*, but also is part of a wider trend in the staging of African dances, for example, as described by Franco (2015) and Kiiru (2017 and 2019) for Kenya, and by Castaldi (2006) for Senegal. The negotiation between the notions of authenticity and creativity generally features in the adaptation of folk dances from a participatory context to a presentational format, as argued by Andriy Nahachewsky (1995). Further following Nahachewsky (2001), the Ugandan dances performed today in the school festival or by cultural groups can be seen as instances of the second strategy of theatricalization of folk dances. This strategy is marked by relative freedom of elaboration by the choreographer, who stages the original participatory dance in a frontal and polished performance characterized by a climax structure and the use of musical accompaniment preserving the original model but including changes in instrumentation and dynamics.[15] Furthermore, this mixed format of tradition and innovation shows the hybridity of the cultural forms marking postcolonial times. It is one of the multifaceted results of colonialism, where postcolonial individuals interact in various ways with the heritage of hegemonic powers to reelaborate local expressive practices in a "third space," generating hybrid forms (Bhabha 2004). Globally, the dynamic interrelationship between tradition and modernity has engendered hybrid cultural expressions that involve not only performative arts, but also visual ones and rituals. Néstor García Canclini (2005) discussed a similar tension between tradition and modernity in the context of Latin America, where centuries-long interactions between indigenous populations and local Europeans produced various forms of *mestizaje* or hybridity that challenge not only the very notions of tradition and modernity but also those of subalternity and hegemony, and need to be understood as cultural expressions negotiated by different actors, who are involved in varying historical relations with the nation, the economy, and the mass media.

Returning to the representation paradigm in the Ugandan school festival, the devices allowing the staging of local culture, along with acting, are costumes and makeup. In Nyoro and Tooro schools, the dancers of the women's part have to wear a long skirt (*kikohi*), the short *mucence* raffia

---

15   Nahachewsky (2001) considers three strategies of theatricalizing folk dances. Besides the second type of theatricalization discussed here, the first strategy includes staged performances where most of the original characteristics are maintained and very small adjustments are allowed only if required by the new stage context. The third strategy is based on the inspiration from a motif or central theme of a folk dance that a choreographer freely develops into his or her own composition, which is then performed by a professional ensemble.

186 ❧ CHAPTER FIVE

skirt around the waist, and possibly the *kiguuli* cloth ring. Besides the indispensable *binyege* leg rattles and trousers, the dancers performing the men's part also have to wear the raffia skirt. They can also wear other decorations such as animal skins or a band tied around the forehead. While this apparel is considered traditional, blouses or T-shirts are concessions to modernity and justified by the desire to avoid showing the dancers' naked torso. Music teachers, as well as jury members, consider the costumes fundamental to *runyege* because they are the proper way of presenting local culture (int. Baguma: May 9, 2011; int. Katusime: June 10, 2011; int. Misinguzi: June 9, 2011; int. Nyakato: June 25, 2011). Indeed, it is through costumes and makeup that the prescribed gender of the dancers according to the dance part they are performing is represented on stage. Primary and secondary school pupils are not yet adults, but they dress and act according to the traditional gender binary, as if they were men (dancing with leg rattles and playing instruments) and women (dancing the women's part and singing). Furthermore, it is not uncommon that their sex does not correspond to the gender they are playing on stage. It is *represented* gender that matters in defining the different roles in *runyege* dancing and musicking, not the real gender of the performers. It is not only by means of costumes that gender is represented in school *runyege*. It is through the very configuration of *runyege* as a technology of gender (de Lauretis 1987) as I argue in chapter 4: the gendered connotation of the two dance parts and the courtship interaction of men and women dancers reproduce the traditional gender binary on stage, which in turn becomes embodied by the performers and absorbed by the audience.

Teachers, Pupils, and Audience in the Gendered *Runyege* Field

Some music teachers emphasize that, in school performances, the pupils' sex is not relevant in terms of the part they dance or the instrument they play (int. Baguma: May 9, 2011; int. Kabutuku: September 5, 2011; int. Kagaba: May 11, 2011), as confirmed by festival adjudicator trainers (int. Nyakato and Kabyanga: August 22, 2018). The focus of teachers and adjudicators is rather on the pupils' skillful performance according to the gender of the part they are playing. The many all-girls and all-boys schools in Uganda have to perform their local dance at the festival, which for Bunyoro and Tooro means *runyege* and other two-part rattle dances. Similarly, in Buganda the traditional genre *baakisimba,* which in the past was mainly danced by women, is performed by pupils regardless of their sex (Nanyonga-Tamusuza 2003). In single-sex schools, performing a gendered part that according to the traditional binary does not correspond to the sex of the student comes as a necessity. The costumes and makeup allow for the representation of gendered dance roles and instrument playing as prescribed by local culture. Also, this flexibility between the performer's sex and the gender s/he is portraying on stage is accepted because they are still just boys and girls, not men and women yet. Besides, especially in primary schools, the physical differences between male and female pupils is not evident (int. Baguma: May 9, 2011); and, according to a widespread local understanding, schoolchildren are able to perform both men's and women's parts because their bodies are still malleable since they have not yet fully developed the characteristics marking masculinity (strength in rattling and rigidity in the waist) and femininity (flexibility in the waist and physical resistance but muscular weakness).

In secondary schools, the physical differences between boys and girls become more evident and the audience may notice that sex and gender do not fit the traditional binary molded on biological determinism. When I attended the school festival or chatted with audience members, comments were made expressing surprise at the ability of performers to dance a part that is prescribed for the other gender. On one occasion, a very talented boy performing the women's dance part caught the audience's attention, eliciting comments like "he really dances like a woman," "he moves his waist like a girl!" Many in the audience viewed his performance within the parameters that connected dancing skills to assumptions about the physical capacities of males and females. Males are held to be too rigid, not flexible enough to dance the women's part, and the audience was astonished to see a boy dancing it so well and compared his dancing skills to those of girls and women.

On the part of the pupils, boys and girls have sometimes different attitudes toward performing the dance part prescribed for the other gender. According to music teacher Ramadam Atwooki (int. May 11, 2011), boys do not usually want to dance the women's part because it is feminine and they consider it degrading and embarrassing, unless they are particularly skilled at it. On the other hand, girls are often proud to dance the men's part and they would not be upset if they were called *kanyama*, brawny, because of it. Makleen Namara is a teenager who learned to dance the men's part when she was 10 and has performed it both at the school festival and in a cultural group. She told me that she chose to dance the men's part in primary school following the example of her grandmother, who danced *runyege* in the Mothers' Union group (int. September 1, 2018). Some of Makleen's schoolmates say that she is both a boy and a girl because she can do the activities of both genders. She doesn't care about what they say and described her skill in *runyege* as a talent, a gift from God that she developed through practice. Being good at an activity that is thought of as being just

188 &❧ CHAPTER FIVE

for men is a source of pride for both girls and women, so the comments people make are worth putting up with.

This positive connotation of performing a part prescribed as masculine is most evident in *runyege* dance, whereas, as I described earlier, most girls who play the drums do not perceive it as something exceptional. It is probably because the masculinity of drums has progressively declined, as chapter 3 discusses, but also because gender permeates *runyege* dance in a more pervasive way than it does with instrument playing and it involves the body more completely. Hence, dancing the other gendered dance part is perceived as more challenging and, because of the traditional high status of masculine activities, it represents an accomplishment for girls. Furthermore, the exceptionality of girls interpreting men's roles and boys interpreting women's is evident in some of the reactions of the audience at *runyege* school performances, as I mentioned above. This notwithstanding, most of the teachers and adjudicator trainers with whom I talked minimized the role of the performers' gender and emphasized egalitarian teaching and skill-based roles in festival performances; at the same time, they acknowledged the importance of displaying the traditionally appropriate gender on stage.

This complex of interwoven yet contrasting notions and perceptions of gender in relation to performing arts is grounded in the didactics of local culture through its current theatrical dimension—no longer based in community practice, but still resonant with the traditional gender binary. The situation I have described here is similar to what Louise Wrazen (2010) outlined for the youth of the Polish Górale community in Canada while they learned and performed their traditional repertoires. Wrazen (2010: 53) points out: "Faced with interacting yet conflicting constructs of gendered identity, young participants are essentially being taught by their own community that they have the option to choose how to be both gendered and Górale today. In so doing, the community unwittingly places itself within the processes of transition even while ostensibly promoting its strong associations with the past." Still, in western Uganda, the openness of traditional music learning and performing on stage is mainly limited to the school context. While the performers are school-aged, gender identity is not fixed yet and performing any role is generally seen as unproblematic, whereas expectations become more rigid when the performers are adults. As I discuss in the next chapter, it is a choice of the grown-up pupils how to contextualize their performing skills in the adult world, given both the theatrical devices of current performances and the traditional gender binary still firmly present in the common imaginary.

In this chapter, I considered the current performance practice of traditional repertoires in schools. I analyzed the principles of narration and representation in singing, instrument playing, and dance as fundamental performing devices used to reproduce discourses about local culture and gender. At the same time, I analyzed some of the musical and choreographic changes introduced by the school festival system and discussed them through the concepts of authenticity and variety employed in the festival. Among the theatrical devices, I noted how costumes and makeup allow the young performers to impersonate a gender different from their sex. Festival adjudicators, teachers, audiences, and pupils have various views on this practice, views that highlight the fluid configuration, interpretation, and reception of traditional repertoires in contemporary western Uganda. While most boys do not like to dance the women's part and dress like women, others are satisfied if they can perform effectively. In some cases, girls dressed in masculine clothes perform the men's part with pride, since for them it is a gift and a special talent; in other cases, it is for them normal to be free to play musical instruments, showing how this practice has become common in Ugandan schools. It is again through the use of costumes and makeup as theatrical conventions that some adult performers can challenge the gendered connotation of traditional repertoires and in particular of *runyege*. This is the topic of the next chapter.

Chapter Six

Trans-Performing and Morality in Cultural Groups

"Through our music and dance we preserve good behaviors and good morals."

—(Answer to a question in an anonymous questionnaire submitted to Excel Secondary School students. June 24, 2011)

"When you are given a talent you need to utilize it. God has given me the gift to dance *mugongo*. So, that is my talent. As a man, I used it to dance *mugongo* better than the women."

—(interview with Deosi, a man dancing women's *mugongo*. June 12, 2011)

"When I danced *runyege*, people thought that maybe I am *bwatububiiri* [hermaphrodite]. That's what they thought because it was beyond their understanding, and the way I could do it … very perfectly and energetically."

—(interview with Ruru, a woman dancing *runyege* men's part. August 20, 2018)

From the answers to the anonymous questionnaire I submitted to students in various secondary schools in Bunyoro and Tooro, as well as from numerous other research participants, it emerged that the value given to traditional repertoires as carriers of local culture was often interpreted in moral terms, as repositories of positive examples of customs and modes of behavior, individually and with others. Of course, this understanding of local culture as positive and moral was not universal among the youth nor in the broader society, who also expressed opinions about it as backward and morally ambiguous. However, the understanding of local tradition as morally good seemed to be the prevailing position in Bunyoro and Tooro, especially among persons involved in traditional performing arts, and it dominated discourses of local identity and gender in relation to both the national and international postcolonial contexts. My research participants understood local tradition as indigeneity and old roots, thus tying together spatial and temporal dimensions. As outlined in the Introduction, Nyoro and Tooro identity locates itself in the ancient local, and more broadly African, tradition, in opposition to the West as a foreign dominator whose influence is still present. In this context, a very widespread view is that traditional repertoires convey a model of reference that, on the one hand, is perceived as morally good in opposition to some Western customs that are deemed dissolute (like some aspects of women's emancipation and dressing) and, on the other hand, is reassuring in these contemporary times, troubled by challenging instabilities concerning health, economy, politics, and human relations. In postcolonial Bunyoro and Tooro, the need for morality is felt especially in gender issues, and is grounded in the moral panic initially triggered by the HIV/AIDS pandemic as well as in women's emancipation in some areas of family and social life that is destabilizing patriarchy. The recovery of local culture is thus reassuring and meant to consolidate a past order, conveyed also by traditional performing arts, which are perceived as virtuous. Equally comforting and perceived as ethically good is the common notion of religion (Christianity or Islam) that, in discussions about morality and gender, is also usually evoked as a repository of good models of behaviors, as well as of practices and strategies directed to achieve rectitude also in gender matters, as I discuss later.

As I argue in the previous chapters, historically gender is both inscribed and prescribed in traditional repertoires. At the same time, the gender binary perceived as traditional is both represented and negotiated in the contemporary performances of traditional repertoires. At the core of this binary is biological determinism identifying sex with one of the two possible genders and consequently with normative gender expression (and sexuality). Notwithstanding precolonial conceptions not exclusively based on sexual determinism and recent queer theoretical interventions that have successfully dislocated the socially expected unity of sex, gender identity, gender expression, and sexual orientation, the hegemonic gender model in present Bunyoro and Tooro still rests on the "traditional" binary and on its variants as contemporary forms of masculinities and femininities informed by cisgender heteronormative binarism. From this perspective, it is significant that adults who are able to skillfully perform the dance part traditionally prescribed for the other sex/gender explained this perceived oddity in religious or biological terms. As in the quote from my interview with Deosi, the ability to perform a dance part that is normally perceived as impossible for a performer of the other gender is understood as a "talent" or a "gift" (*kisembo*) given from God (*kisembo kya Ruhanga*), an idea present in both Christianity and Islam, or, in other cases, as an inborn quality, a "talent that one was born with" (*kisembo yahangirwe nakyo*). Conversely, the audience watching men performing a women's dance and vice versa sometimes understands this skill in biological terms, supposing that these performers are hermaphrodite, because of their ability to master something that only people of the other sex/gender are thought to be able to do, as Ruru reported. The need to be morally good informs the recourse to religious or biological references when the gender normativity inscribed in traditional repertoires is challenged or negotiated. In this way, the agency of the competent performer is represented in terms that do not destabilize the local notions of culture and gender, but it is explained as an innate gift that the performer develops through practice. Furthermore, religion, in particular Pentecostalism, also intervenes in the personal lives of some performers to justify and sustain a painful change toward normativity when the social pressure to conform becomes for them unbearable, as I discuss at the end of this chapter.

It is important to note that, in the context of traditional dances like *runyege*, performing a part prescribed for the other gender, which implies dancing skills as well as cross-dressing, is not commonly perceived in terms of (nonnormative) sexuality, in contrast to what could be a common European or American perspective. In my conversations with dancers, members of the audience, and other research participants, the understanding of the performance of the other gender's part centered on the polarities of biology or religion, never on sexuality. Sexuality is indeed a highly private and sensitive topic and never publicly discussed, if not in the context of health (in connection to sexually transmitted diseases or fertility problems) or in relation to the contemporary debates around homosexuality, which usually connect it to westernized and urban environments, like the capital city Kampala, where most LGBTQ+ communities and organizations are based. Sexuality was traditionally a taboo topic and the references to it in performing arts have been, at least superficially, erased, first because of the condemnation of colonizers and missionaries, then through the postcolonial cultural revival that included traditional music and dance in the project of nation-building as well as in schools and, finally, in the recent times marked by concerns about morality. In their present postcolonial understanding as morally good, traditional performing arts are not viewed as carrying sexual meanings, which would be very inappropriate and indecent to display.

In this last chapter, I look at adults performing traditional arts in cultural groups, the semiprofessional ensembles. After contextualizing their activities in the national historical background, I discuss their interpretations of traditional songs and dances. I develop my analysis through a consideration of the complicated negotiations around gender occurring in the performance of traditional songs and dances, also in comparison to school performances, and retrace a sense of morality in these interpretations and in their performers. While current performances of traditional repertoires display a discourse supporting the traditional normative binary, in *runyege* I identify a space for possible counter-discourses. Indeed, in these performances, hegemonic discourses about gender coexist with minority counter-discourses, in which individuals that perform the dance part prescribed for the opposite gender identify. Although my analysis ranges between the polarities of the masculinity and femininity prescribed by the binary perceived as traditional, I want to show how some aspects of this dyad are appropriated, negotiated, or rejected to shape alternative masculinities and femininities that originate from the *runyege* performing space but can also reflect on the dancers' private life. Finally, I examine how the performance of local culture as both a technology of gender and a carrier of positive values contributes to the discussion on morality in contemporary Uganda, also in relation to the role of religion.

Traditional Performing Arts Ensembles: State Companies and Cultural Groups

As discussed in the Introduction, the history of traditional music ensembles in Uganda goes back to the 1960s with the first national ensemble, the Heartbeat of Africa, and runs in parallel with the development of music education in schools and the national festival. Based on the model of the first national ensemble, several others, composed of semiprofessional performers, were established all over the country. By the second half of the 1960s, elements of innovation (in style and choreography) as well as of codification (in costumes) were apparent in the national ensemble's performances of local dances (Hanna 1965; Hanna and Hanna 1968). The successor to Heartbeat of Africa is today the Ndere Troupe, founded in 1984 by Stephen Rwagyezi, which performs repertoires from several regions of the country. Ugandan national ensembles display several typical features that Anthony Shay (2002) found as recurring in state dance companies. First, both the old Heartbeat of Africa and the present Ndere Troupe are based on the "rainbow ethnicity" model; that is, they represent the Ugandan nation as a mosaic of different ethnicities whose main characteristics emerge in different dance genres, styles, and costumes. Their repertoire indeed includes a diversity of traditional genres displayed as representative of the main cultures of the country. Furthermore, they represent the internal variety of each Ugandan culture through the format they adopt to elaborate choreographies for the stage, the suite: in each suite, different dances from one region are juxtaposed, combined, and developed. As typical in state dance companies, in

Uganda dancers are young and come from all over the country (but the majority is from the central region); they are usually already proficient in most of the genres in the repertoire and learn the specific choreographies when they join the national ensemble. Their performance is well coordinated on stage, where different formations are used for creating both variety and spectacularity. Also recurrent in other state dance companies based on the "rainbow ethnicity" model is the treatment of music and costumes in the Ugandan national ensembles. Music is normally played live by musicians, who have become proficient in the repertoires of different ethnicities and mostly remain in the back of the stage; the musical accompaniment is normally adapted to a reduced number of performers or the availability of instruments. Costumes are faithful in depicting local dance attires, but mostly adapted in order to allow wider movements, uniformed in style and fabrics used, and enriched in details.

Ndere Troupe's contemporary shows are highly spectacular and planned in detail to generate interest and attract the mainly foreign audience, with introductions on the meaning of the genres, as well as elaborate and colorful costumes and danced acrobatics. According to late Ugandan music scholar Anita D. Asaasira (2015), Ndere Troupe's audiences in Kampala are middle-class Ugandans and foreign tourists, since the cost of tickets for the show is prohibitive for most Ugandans. In Ndere Troupe's performances, local repertoires are repackaged in "a constructed diversity [that] is a marketing strategy aimed at bringing people together in one place to experience the 'entire' Uganda" (Asaasira 2015: 195). The style of their performances, blending motifs from different genres while at the same time juxtaposing the diversity of ethnicities represented on stage, is then different from the performance modalities of the school festival. Indeed, music schoolteachers usually see cultural groups, in particular the Ndere Troupe, as creative transformers of tradition, while they consider school performances more "authentic" (int. Nyakato: June 25, 2011). However, while the aim of Ndere Troupe's professional performers is to represent Ugandan national diversity in a spectacular way, the performances of local cultural groups display more similarities with the practice within the school festival. Most of the members of local ensembles learned to sing, dance, and play at school (int. Makidadi: February 24, 2008), in the same way as in other East African countries (Barz 2004). Unlike the national troupe, their main source of income is external to these groups' activities and it is in this sense that they may be considered semiprofessional performers. Their focus on the repertoires of their region, the value they give to the internal variety of the performance and to the principle of narration in traditional songs, their conventional use of acting, costumes, and makeup in both singing and dancing show the substantial assimilation of the school festival paradigms into the cultural groups' practice.

The main reason I found among members of cultural groups for engaging in local performing arts is the desire to share and promote their local culture (int. Makidadi: February 24, 2008; Mugabo: May 11, 2011; Mugisa: March 2, 2008; Nyegenya and Banda: February 26, 2008). It is in this capacity that they are hired to enliven cultural functions and weddings and take part in festivals. The wider community, audiences, and music teachers acknowledge the role of cultural groups as active preservers of local tradition. Traditional arts performers are respected and cultural groups, as well as the school festival, are highly valued in the context of a society perceived as rapidly losing its identity and changing for the worse, both culturally and morally, under some negative influences of the West. This widespread view is part of the broader postcolonial discourse in contemporary Ugandan society that sets local/African and foreigner/Western in opposition. In this dichotomic and selective perspective, local culture is understood as a positive heritage of the past, charged with inherent morality, and polarized against foreign habits perceived as dissolute and in conflict with traditional customs. This discourse is applied to a variety of contexts, in particular those involving a reevaluation of gender roles and intimacy: for example, the mentioned policing of women's behaviors or the debate on homosexuality (Vorhölter 2012). However, while this view characterizes the arena of traditional performing arts, it coexists in Ugandan society, and even among the very practitioners and estimators of traditional music and dance, with a positive vision of the West as more prestigious because it is a carrier of wealth and modernity. Foreign customs are similarly viewed as more valuable than local culture. Furthermore, in the contexts where the foreign is identified as a religious model, for instance among certain Christian denominations or Muslim communities, it is also understood as more moral than some local practices that are seen as inherently incompatible with Christianity or Islam.

Besides the role of cultural groups as protectors of local culture, there may be a further level of connoting them and their activities as "good." If we consider sounds and body movement as involved in processes of self-fashioning, of shaping the performer as an individual who introjects models and dispositions encoded in the repertoires, this action can be understood also in ethical or moral terms (Chrysagis and Karapampas 2017: 2–3). Performing traditional repertoires in Bunyoro and Tooro can hence be perceived as morally "good" both at the public level of preserving local culture and at the intimate level of shaping virtuous community members. It is with this in mind that I interpret students' statements such as "Through our music and dance we preserve good behaviors and good morals" in response to my question about their thoughts on traditional music and dance (Anonymous questionnaire submitted to Excel Secondary School students, June 24, 2011).

196 ❧ CHAPTER SIX

Semiprofessional ensembles are normally connected to a local or international NGO, a religious congregation, or a sociocultural or women's association. Their dedication to local culture is indeed usually combined with a commitment in the social and civic field (Pier 2009, 2011, and 2015), an engagement that is often listed in the groups' charter. It is through thoughtfully created theatrical pieces, involving both singing and dancing, that messages about health, gender equality, and education are conveyed. This can be considered as "theatre for development," as defined by Margaret Macpherson (1999): a dramatic piece based on traditional narration forms, together with dances and music, which articulates a message about development. For instance, the role played by local performing arts in the fight against HIV/AIDS in Uganda has been significant, as shown by Gregory Barz (2006). On the other hand, the impact of NGOs' actions and campaigns, especially when internationally funded, is complex and multilayered and usually cannot be reduced to univocally positive or negative readings, in particular when the arts are used for promoting messages and reporting on emergency or catastrophic events, as shown for eastern Congo by Chérie Rivers Ndaliko (2016).

Because of their parallel involvement in preserving local culture and promoting social improvements, the members of cultural groups enjoy the respect of the community. However, even though the community considers them to be cultural ambassadors of good traditional morals, there are sometimes suspicions concerning the morality of the group members. Some research participants alluded to the inappropriateness of the level of intimacy that can develop among the members of a troupe. In particular, some situations are perceived as potentially promiscuous, like changing into—and out of—costumes and spending time together for rehearsals and journeys to venues, where performers sometimes spend the night. It is significant that married women are rarely active dancers in mixed ensembles. In many cases, female performers leave the group after marriage, in part because of pressure from their partner (int. Deosi: June 12, 2011), which is similar to what happens in other countries. For example, women in Malawi who perform in public are undermined as "loose," and some husbands restrict their wives' participation in ensembles (Gilman 2009: 153). In Bunyoro and Tooro, if married women are members of mixed troupes, they tend not to dance: it would be inappropriate for them to dance *runyege*, where their body and waist flexibility would be displayed in front of the audience and male dance partners.

Semiprofessional ensembles have in their repertoire traditional songs and dances from their region. To their performances I now turn my attention, in order to discuss how they present but also negotiate the traditional gender binary.

Cultural Groups Singing Local Culture

Cultural groups are usually more focused on traditional dances than songs and, indeed, it is at the school festival that traditional songs are mostly performed. However, some artists emerging from semiprofessional ensembles have reinterpreted traditional songs. In particular, the association Ngabu za Tooro, founded in Fort Portal (Tooro) in 1999, has championed the local cultural revival of performing arts through its cultural group of the same name. Created in a climate of general enthusiasm for the restoration of the traditional monarchy, the association (Shields of Tooro) seeks to be a protector of local culture. It was initially (1999–2008) funded in cooperation with a Dutch NGO, HIVOS, to lead projects directed at developing local productive activities, supporting cultural promotion especially through women and youth, and contrasting HIV/AIDS (Cimardi 2017a). More recently, it has also relied on crowdfunding for initiatives, such as the candidacy of local cultural heritage for safeguarding at UNESCO.[1] In the words of the Ngabu za Tooro founder and director, Atwoki Rwagweri (n.d.), "we use local culture as [a] catalyst and instrument of social change." Within the activities supported by HIVOS involving the handing down of culture and related to gender are the recording of the traditional song *Ngayaya muhuma wange* and the initiatives reviving the figure of Kogeere, an historical female ruler of Eastern Tooro.

Between 2010 and 2012, *Ngayaya muhuma wange*[2]—credited to Rockamilley Rwamwaro (also known as Rokamela), a member of the Ngabu za Tooro cultural group—was very popular in Tooro and frequently played on local radios, even though the recording was released a few years earlier, in 2006. Its fortune continued for some years and, according to the website bigeye.ug, in 2019 it was chosen as the "most beautiful Ugandan song."[3] In the title of this piece, which is its chorus, *ngayaga* refers to the swaying

---

1   The *mpaako* tradition of the Batooro, Banyoro, Batuku, Batagwenda, and Banyabindi of western Uganda (2013) and the Koogere oral tradition of the Basongora, Banyabindi, and Batooro peoples (2015) have been inscribed in the UNESCO Intangible Cultural Heritage List.

2   The piece can be listened to at these links on YouTube: https://www.youtube.com/watch?v=3QXSMUVairw or https://www.youtube.com/watch?v=zfRLZS20zCU (accessed on April 24, 2022).

3   https://bigeye.ug/ngayaya-voted-the-most-beautiful-ugandan-song-of-all-time/ (accessed on April 24, 2022). In this online article, the piece is described as a "love song [which] praises a woman in all aspects," clearly misunderstanding the perspective of the song, where the dramatization of the lyrics as a duet posits the woman as praising the man, as I discuss in the following.

198 &❧ CHAPTER SIX

movement of the head and torso that women employed while singing, and *muhuma wange* refers to the addressee of the song, which can be translated as "my shepherd" (underlining the pastoralist origin of the man) or "my lord" (emphasizing his aristocratic origins). This is a women's praise and love song known as *nanga*, from the name of the trough zither that women used to accompany their singing of praise and love for their partners. As I mention in chapter 2, the *nanga* zither has not been used for decades in Tooro, if not by the peripheral community of the Basongora. However, some songs are still remembered by Batooro, like for instance *Rwanzira* or *Kowe ens-ama* documented by historical recordings and performed even today.[4] The name *nanga* remains to identify this genre that, like other praise songs such as *bizina by'ente*, is typical of Huma culture. This connotation of *Ngayaya muhuma wange* as connected to pastoralist populations and its denomination as a women's song is found also in the song anthology for schools by Solomon Mbabi-Katana (1965), who presents it as "Basongora Hamitic women's love song."[5] *Ngayaya muhuma wange* in its traditional versions has been very popular in both Bunyoro and Tooro; indeed the oldest examples of this song were recorded in the mid-1960s by Peter Cooke in a primary school and a teachers' college.[6] As Cooke's recordings show, the song was so well known that (and because) it was sung in modern educational contexts, where children and men alike learned and performed it.

In Ngabu za Tooro's *Ngayaya*, the accompaniment, opening with the sound of chirping birds evoking a rural bucolic ambiance, is provided entirely by the synthesizer. However, instead of a timbre recalling the *nanga* zither, other instruments' timbres are used, such as rattles, drums, xylophone, guitar, and flute (the latter in the central instrumental solo). In the historical recordings, as well as the renditions that I documented from the voice of Nyoro and Tooro elders like Abigael Balikenda and Gerrison Kinyoro, the chorus (repeated twice) appears after every two verses of the soloist. The alternating of solo and chorus is doubled in the Ngabu za Tooro's version: in most sections of the song, the solo verses are repeated twice and then the chorus line is

---

4   In comparison with the historical recordings of *nanga* songs accompanied by the zither where the singing is close to speaking, in historical recordings as well as today the songs without accompaniment have a wider melodic extension. The study of accompanied and a cappella *nanga* deserve further attention in the future.

5   With the term "Hamitic" Mbabi-Katana refers to the old and today discredited belief that Bahuma/Bahima people in western Uganda descended from light-skinned populations coming from the northeastern area of the continent.

6   Two performances at Galihuma Primary School in Butiti (Tooro)—one by school children and the other one with a male teacher as a soloist and a pupil choir—and a performance at St. Augustine College in Butoti (in the past part of Bunyoro, now Tooro) by male students.

sung four times. Also, some new verses, interpreted by a male voice, are added in the song. Indeed, in this version, the lyrics are not sung by female voices only, but also by a male one (at the end doubled by a second male voice), thus articulating a sort of love conversation. This can be seen in the lyrics transcribed in the following, where I indicate the female solo as FS, the male solo as MS, and the chorus, which is sung by female voices, as FC.

FS: *Ngayaga*	*Ngayaya*
FC: *Ngayaya ngayaya*	*Ngayaya ngayaya*
MS: *Eh kibuli kyange*	Eh, my flower
FC: *Eh muhuma wange*	Eh, my lord
FC: *Ngayaya ngayaya, muhuma wange* (x8)	*Ngayaya ngayaya*, my lord
FS: *Oli kafunjo k'omu nyanja, muhuma wange* *Niko basikisa emikono yombi, muhuma wange* (x2)	You are like papyrus in the lake, my lord The one that one uproots with two hands,[7] my lord
FC: *Ngayaya ngayaya, muhuma wange* (x4)	*Ngayaya ngayaya*, my lord
FS: *Oli ihuli ly'endisa, muhuma wange* *Abakuzoire kabakatunga, muhuma wange* (x2)	You are the egg of a white bird, my lord Those that made you [your parents] have a lot, my lord
FC: *Ngayaya ngayaya, muhuma wange* (x4)	*Ngayaya ngayaya*, my lord
FS: *Ngonzi ngonzi ningamba naiwe*	Love, love, I am telling you
MS: *Ninkuhurra gamba*	I am listening to you, speak
FS: *Okandogesa enseko y'ensi, muhuma wange*	You bewitched me with herbs,[8] my lord

---

7   A papyrus plant that needs the strength of two hands to be uprooted is difficult to obtain, hence rare.

8   Local herb (*Kyllinga albiceps*) used to make a woman fall in love or make her love long-lasting.

Obu nkurora nseka nyenka,
  muhuma wange
(x2)

FC: *Ngayaya ngayaya,*
  muhuma wange (x4)

MS: *Obw'olinooba ntakunoobere*
  kibuli kyange
Ndyegoromora omu nyanja
  Rweru kibuli kyange
(x2)

FC: *Ngayaya ngayaya,*
  muhuma wange (x4)
FS: *Muhuma wange*

[Flute solo]

FC: *Ngayaya ngayaya,*
  muhuma wange

MS: *Kibuli kyange*

FC: *Ngayaya ngayaya,*
  muhuma wange

MS: *Mawe!*

(x2)

FC: *Ngayaya ngayaya,*
  muhuma wange
FS: *Muhuma wange*

MS: *Mawe*

FC: *Ngayaya ngayaya,*
  muhuma wange

FS: *Muhuma wange*

FC: *Ngayaya ngayaya,*
  muhuma wange (x2)

FC: *Muhuma wange eh,*
  muhuma wange

Every time I see you, I smile alone,
  my lord

Ngayaya ngayaya,
  my lord

If you hate me and I will not hate
  you, my flower
I will drown myself in Lake Rweru,[9]
  my flower

Ngayaya ngayaya,
  my lord
My lord

Ngayaya ngayaya,
  my lord

My flower

Ngayaya ngayaya,
  my lord

Oh, mother!

Ngayaya ngayaya,
  my lord
My lord

Oh, mother!

Ngayaya ngayaya,
  my lord

My lord

Ngayaya ngayaya,
  my lord

Ngayaya ngayaya,
  my lord

---

9   Nyanja Rweru is the Nyoro and Tooro name of the water basin internationally
     known as Lake Edward.

At the beginning of the song, there is a brief exchange of verses between the male (MS) and female (FS) soloists, then only the female solo alternates with the female chorus (FC). In the central part of the piece, the female soloist calls her lover (*Ngonzi, ngonzi, ningamba naiwe*, "Love, love, I am telling you") and the male soloist answers (*Ninkuhurra, gamba*, "I am listening to you, speak"). The female soloist then sings two other verses alternated with the chorus, to which the male soloist answers with two verses, alternating with both the chorus and the female solo. Again, after the flute intermezzo, the male solo—here doubled by a second male voice—alternates the newly composed lines with the chorus and the female solo. The gendered connotation of male and female singers in this rendition has no parallel in historical versions of the song or in those that I heard from elders. In these older renditions, the performers were all female or, in school contexts, all male or with a male soloist and a mixed children choir. In the Ngabu za Tooro's interpretation, the dramatization of the song's lyrics as dialogues between female and male soloists and the new verses created for the male solo strengthen the traditional notions of opposed masculinity and femininity, because the woman praises the man as a shepherd or lord and the man addresses her as a flower (*kibuli*), something beautiful and delicate. On the one hand, this successful version establishes univocally men as the addressees of praising, overcoming the ungendered use of the song in educational contexts where also men performed it. On the other hand, this interpretation also erases the older and traditional gendering of *nanga* songs as feminine by inserting the addressee of the song as a performer. In this way, the male participation in singing can be seen as interference within a feminine space of expression, where masculinity is not compromised by closeness to the feminine, but on the contrary, reinforced as sonic male presence being praised. This rendition of *Ngayaya muhuma wange* offers an example of how the revival of traditional repertoires can be based on a selective interpretation— where the traditional connotation of *nanga* songs as feminine and, later, as gender-neutral is partially lost, while the traditional gender binary inscribed in the genre is reinforced both verbally and dramatically.

The recording of *Ngayaya muhuma wange* has been used by cultural groups during performances on stage, in which the performers mimed to the playback and even acted out the lyrics in the minimal way this specific song allows. The principle of representation through acting and costumes that operates in school folk songs was applied in this case, even if the music was not performed live.[10] In 2010, I attended some weekly shows of the Ngabu

---

10 The members of Ngabu za Tooro preferred playback to live singing of this piece and considered the recorded rendition the best one for different reasons. First, it was a studio recording where rich digital accompaniment provided

za Tooro cultural group and they interpreted the recording of this song on stage, among other pieces. In their performance, four couples (woman-man), dressed in traditional attire, interpreted the song's lyrics while performing the typical *ngayaga* undulation of the head and torso. Since this is a praise song describing thoughts and feelings, there was no action development on stage as in school performances featuring different folksongs in a narrative and dynamic sequence. So, in that case, the acting replicated a possible ancient performance context: a domestic situation in which a woman, properly dressed and seated with legs to the side, praises her man, who is seated next to her—with the addition of the man joining the singing with newly created verses. While there was no real movement of the performers on stage, the interpretation of the song intensified the lyrics' content by dividing verses for men and for women who acted out singing to each other, representing lovers. A similar but more contemporary acted representation appears also in a video of this version of *Ngayaya muhuma wange* uploaded on Youtube.[11] In this video clip, a woman and a man, in modern clothes and seated on a sofa, playback-sing to each other the dramatized lyrics of the song, while the woman sways her head and the man responds to her gestures of intimacy.

Once more, representing local culture on stage, and more recently in video clips, is interwoven with depicting traditional gender and reinforces its binary normativity. Consistent with the recorded audio rendition that does not feature any plucked instrument timbre, the group chose not to interpret or mime on stage the lost practice of women playing the *nanga* zither. This would have meant the recovery—at least on the visual level—of a tradition that disappeared in Tooro and the representation of a purely feminine genre, the only one where women played musical instruments. Instead, the stage and video representation choices followed the lyrics' dramatization where men participate in the singing and receive the praises of devoted women. In this sense, they are exemplary of the dominant discourses on gender and local culture that define femininity as subservient to masculinity. Furthermore, through the dramatization and stage performance also involving male performers and its presentation as a love song, *Ngayaga* clearly posits an example of how, when women behave according to the normative (and selective) understanding of local culture, couple relations are peaceful and affectionate. Lastly, the moral connotation of traditional performing

---

the background for a "clean" and polished singing that would be difficult to accomplish live. Second, there were not enough microphones available for all the singers to sing live but the group's PA system could be usefully employed for playing back the recording.

11   https://www.youtube.com/watch?v=bvuGIUiA9og (accessed on April 24, 2022).

arts reinforces the power of this sonic and visual representation as a positive model for performers and audiences to follow. As a result, the manipulation of a women's tradition in the contemporary cultural revival has produced a song that is considered as a model of "good" behaviors for women and men.

Some other initiatives of the association Ngabu za Toro recovered traditional models to foster women's empowerment. For instance, the oral history about the mythical queen Koogere of Busongora was revived through sensitization campaigns, proposed for recognition by UNESCO,[12] and promoted as a model for women to engage actively in economic and cultural activities that positively impact their community. For some years, communities in Tooro have elected proactive women with the title of Koogere, thus proposing their positive example of female empowerment derived from local culture and, at the same time, increasing their visibility and collaboration opportunities. This initiative was indeed part of the projects, supported by the Dutch NGO, targeting women to promote their active participation in the economic and cultural spheres while following the ideal of Ngabu za Tooro of "local culture as [a] catalyst and instrument of social change" (Rwagweri n.d.).

Considering both cases of *Ngayaya* and Koogere, it is clear that plural ideas of gender inhabit the heterogeneous association of Ngabu za Tooro and are communicated through multifaceted messages, some aspects intentionally promoting notions of women's empowerment, while others more or less intentionally reinforcing traditional gender roles. The new rendition of *Ngayaya* was seen as an opportunity to support youth's artistic skills and passing on of local culture rather than to recover, through sound or representation, the practice of the *nanga* as feminine instrument or singing. In its main aims the song was successful, since Rockamilley Rwamwaro, the male singer to whom the song is credited, got relative popularity and the song has made listeners rediscover and appreciate *nanga* singing and, more generally, traditional Tooro songs. On the other hand, the song did not revive women's past music prerogatives and, conversely, propagated a patriarchal and conservative gender model as well as a selective and conservative version of local culture. These aspects are however coexisting with the examples, also grounded in local tradition and looking at the future, of feminine emancipation supported by the initiatives connected to Koogere.

As extensively shown by Ndaliko's (2016) excellent work on arts in war-devastated yet resilient eastern Congo, the implications of international

---

12   The Koogeere tradition was inscribed in the UNESCO List of Intangible Cultural Heritage in Need of Urgent Safeguarding in 2015: https://ich. unesco.org/en/USL/koogere-oral-tradition-of-the-basongora-banyabindi-and-batooro-peoples-00911 (accessed on November 25, 2022).

NGOs' initiatives are complex to disentangle as they are located at the intersection of different and uneven powers, driven by assorted needs and ideals, and guided by various agendas and priorities, usually (but not exclusively) opposing along the axis Global North/Global South. The role of international funding can be invasive and condition local autonomy if not censor creativity, but it can also effectively support local arts to communicate topical messages when it responsibly builds on the collaboration with local associations (Barz 2006; Ndaliko 2016), as it was the case of many cultural groups I met in Bunyoro and Tooro. An examination of the collaboration between HIVOS and Ngabu za Tooro cannot limit itself to the two cases related to gender messages that I presented and it is beyond my scope here. Echoing Ndaliko's (2016: 155–156) call for NGOs to listen to local communities in order to really meet their needs and plan action strategies, I observe that international associations should be more mindful in mobilizing both creative and traditional performing arts in their projects, which should be based on the careful study of aims and effects in partnership with local associations and communities. The outcomes will most likely be complex and diverse given the different individuals involved. Furthermore, the power of traditional repertoires and gender models in rallying multilayered representations and discourses goes far beyond apparently harmless songs. The success of both *Ngayaya* and Koogere projects is telling of the present value and role of traditional performing arts in Uganda in influencing the idea of tradition and thus of past models to represent the "good" in the present.

Cultural Groups in Women's Associations and *Runyege* Dancing

The main items in the repertoires of semiprofessional ensembles are traditional dances and theatrical sketches. Unlike the school festival's *runyege* performances, cultural groups do not commonly employ stage formations such as letters of the alphabet; rather, they devote more space to dance solos and couple dancing. On the other hand, the cultural groups' *runyege* performances often involve motifs and levels that developed within the school festival, as well as costumes and acting. In these troupes, the traditional separation between men's and women's roles according to their sex is generally respected and it is quite rare to see a man performing a woman's part and vice versa. For retired music teacher Kabutuku (int. September 5, 2011), not respecting the gendered dance division can be tolerated if the cultural group is hired for a presentation or to entertain at a wedding, but a performance at a festival must display the performers' heritage and it should not be misrepresented. This view is shared by the performer and instructor Kagaba (int. May 11, 2011), who thinks that at traditional ceremonies it is disrespectful to change dance parts and that doing so can be degrading, especially for men.

It is generally accepted that ensembles that lack performers of the appropriate gender to perform both dance parts do not have to adhere to the traditional gendered division. This happens in particular with women's associations, which usually have an affiliated cultural group. The members of these associations are not exclusively women and sometimes men are also involved, though women are the majority. Today, women's associations in partnership with NGOs are mainly committed to raising awareness of social, developmental, and gender equality issues, but they can also be devoted to making and selling handicrafts or to group saving and lending in order to support the members' families.

In Uganda, women's associations have a long history and had an extensive impact on the social, cultural, and economical emancipation of many women and on the broader society (Tripp 1998 and 2002). Iris Berger (2014: 9) connected the engagement of female spirit mediums for community well-being as a form of "public healing" in the precolonial era with women's associations established in later decades. The first organized ones, like Mothers' Union (the association of married women of the Church of Uganda), were founded during the colonial time and promoted domesticity as both a value and specific skills; nonetheless they were instrumental in supplying women with practical abilities that became useful for their work outside the household (Tripp and Ntiro 2002). Later, a significant moment for women's associationism started in the late 1980s with the social and political engagement of associations that lobbied the new government for reforms leading to an increased presence of women in politics and a higher education rate for girls. Women's associations devoted to a variety of activities and in general were instrumental in providing women with a space for socialization and engagement outside the family, which could result in augmented social activism, capacity of earning, and new self-confidence in planning wider goals. Women associations also contributed to the development of forms of femininity partially alternative to the main Domestic Virtue model but socially accepted (Bantebya Kyomuhendo and McIntosh 2006), as discussed in chapter 1.

Similar to the approach of most Ugandan women's associations described by Lutwama-Rukundo (2008), the members of women's associations that I met in Bunyoro and Tooro did not describe their activities as impacting exclusively women in order to undermine existing gender relations. Rather, through these associations women can gather forces for implementing projects benefiting the whole society. For example, the associations that emerged from a religious affiliation, like Mothers' Union, sometimes employ traditional dances to attract people to church activities (int. Maseero: April 19, 2011). Other associations use money, which they raise by selling handicrafts or food produced collectively, to support the members' families by paying children's school fees or covering other household expenses (int. members of KCCA: July 2, 2011). At the same time, these associations function as an important space of aggregation and experience for women and this impacts positively on their self-confidence, emancipation, and possibility of affecting public life.

For an association, having a cultural group is another source of income through performing at events and taking part in sponsored projects, as well as a space for women to express sonically and physically their different individualities. Furthermore, an ensemble allows the association to perform newly written shows that convey, in part through traditional singing and dancing, a variety of messages, from health to development, from compulsory education for all children to the fight against domestic violence (Barz 2006; Cooke and Kasule 1999; Pier 2015). Compared to women's gamelan ensembles (*gamelan wanita*) that developed in Bali since the late 1970s from the social movement for women's equality, and where female instrument playing was the main focus in supporting their cause (Downing 2019), contemporary women's ensembles in western Uganda do not emphasize the fact that (most) performers are females in order to promote women's empowerment but, as their associations, they aim at sensitizing to a wide spectrum of themes involving the entire society. The use of performing arts by Nyoro and Tooro women's associations is thus closer to the powerful experiences documented in the Gambia by Bonnie B. McConnell (2019), where women sing to spread messages about health issues that have an impact on the whole community beyond fellow women and, through their use of local forms of musical healing, they also shape contemporary forms of women's empowerment.

As the most representative dance of the Banyoro and Batooro, *runyege* is usually in the repertoire of the cultural groups connected to women's associations and, when dancing it, women also have to take on the men's dance part. Like in the school practice, from whose theatrical conventions cultural groups draw, they use costumes and acting to represent gender, and in particular the opposite gender, on stage. I conceptualize the practice of dancing (or playing) a part that was not constructed for the performer's sex/gender as "trans-performing." It involves the use of costumes to disguise the performer's gendered appearance and interpreting the dance part with different degrees of acting and embodiment of the gendered role being performed. The concept of "trans-performing" is very close to the practices of cross-dressing and cross-gender dancing, as analyzed for instance by Christina Sunardi (2015) in her study of dance in East Java. I prefer to employ the term "trans-performing" to describe a performance dimension that goes beyond the mere use of costumes and includes acting and impersonating characteristics considered as belonging to the other gender, within a system that continues to represent itself as strictly binary. As is the case in East Java, in the Ugandan understanding of these practice in dancing there is no category or term describing cross-gender performing, but only the gendered conceptualization of the dance parts, styles, and costumes. Trans-performing is in fact a category that I created in order to identify practices of dancing and acting as if a member of the opposite gender, which allows me to focus on the gendered implications of this performance practice. I limit the use of "trans-performing" to the practice among adults who act as and imitate the opposite gender characteristics. Acting out gendered attitudes does not normally happen among school pupils, who simply dress as the opposite gender, so they could rather be said to cross-dress.

Women started to trans-perform in all-women groups due to two main factors: the initiation and acceptance of cross-dressing in the school festival, where most women got their training in the opposite dance part, and the burgeoning of women's associations since the late 1990s, especially in connection with social and health projects, which involved performing arts to deliver their messages or as a fund-raising activity. So, this phenomenon emerged from different conditions compared to other global experiences of cross-dressing performers, like those in East Javanese dances where this practice has a long history (Sunardi 2015), but also in *merengue*, where the appearance of cross-dressing is connected with the uncertainty around gender roles resulting from economic transformations (Hutchinson 2016). While in western Uganda women were driven to trans-performing by the very composition of all-female associations rather than by a reaction against existing gender models and relations, this does not mean that this phenomenon is irrelevant for their agency and the forms of femininity conveyed and expressed through these performances.

Women's experiences in trans-performing are varied, founded in different backgrounds, and driven by manifold motivations. For some, trans-performing can be diverting but is limited to contributing to the association's objectives, like for Mary Kasaija, an elderly Tooro member of the Mothers' Union. Some years ago, the Mothers' Union hosted a festival to celebrate an important anniversary. One of the performance categories was traditional dance, so the women of the association, which does not have a permanent cultural group, had to dance the men's part in *runyege*. Mary had never danced *runyege* before, but since the need for performers for the men's dance part had arisen, she quickly learned it and surprised the audience with her energetic performance. For Mary, it was an amusing experience and a very rewarding one because her group won thanks to her performance.

However, it remained limited to that one event, since as a religious person she prefers to sing in the church rather than to perform cultural dances (int. Kasaija: August 3, 2018).

Other women trans-perform when their association's cultural group is hired for an event. This is the case for the Kyomukama Catering and Creative Association (KCCA), a club dedicated to collective fundraising projects based in Kagadi, southern Bunyoro. The association mainly provided catering services and produced handicrafts to be sold; furthermore, when I met them, they were in the process of putting together a cultural group. For some members of the KCCA (int. July 2, 2011), trans-performing was one of the activities—together with being engaged outside the domestic context and earning an income—that allowed them to demonstrate their assertiveness and resourcefulness. In this sense, they embraced a femininity different from the traditionally hegemonic one that saw the man as the breadwinner and the woman dedicated to the home and children. However, members of KCCA did not interpret their trans-performing as purposely challenging gender models or showing that the features of traditional masculinity encoded in *runyege* are shared by women. Indeed, trans-performing was mainly explained by the absence of men to dance with leg rattles rather than as a deliberate choice. Nonetheless, for them, trans-performing was motivating as individual women, had a positive effect on their self-confidence against a model of passive and domestic femininity, and hence supported their active engagement in society through the association.

This positioning, which partially revises the traditional notion of femininity, can be considered as another variation for women, together with the ones of "Service Career" and "Petty Urban Trade," of the "Domestic Virtue model" analyzed by Bantebya Kyomuhendo and McIntosh (2006). This variant is based on associationism in its multiple dimensions, which include feminine sociality; collaboration in shared social, health, or productive projects; participation in a space of activity and engagement outside the household and the family; the possibility of using money by earning or borrowing in turns; and the chance to perform in public, especially by trans-performing in *runyege*. While maintaining their roles of wives and mothers, many female members of women's associations develop their assertiveness and emancipation. This kind of femininity developed through women's associations is generally accepted in Nyoro and Tooro societies, most probably because it has a positive impact on the whole community and does not contest patriarchy. Indeed, when men are members of women's associations, they usually have a supervisory role of some kind. Furthermore, as observed by Pier (2009), when they participate in festivals, the women's groups often ask the cooperation of male skilled performers who usually assume the role of organizing and leading the performances, thus reinstating masculine authority over women.

A number of men are part of another women's association, the Masindi Drama Saving Scheme (MASDRASS), founded for group saving and lending. Within the association there is a cultural group, which was created to participate in the AIDS Support Organization (TASO) projects connected with the Masindi Hospital, in northern Bunyoro. The ensemble devised theatrical sketches to raise awareness of HIV/AIDS, but it is also hired for other occasions and *runyege* is included in its repertoire. Although there are men able to dance in the group, nevertheless, some of the women can and do dance the men's part. It was through their training in the masculine dance part in all-girls schools that they learned how to shake the rattles. In my conversation with them (August 23, 2018), they claimed that they still have the energy to do that, even today when they are wives and mothers. Their attitudes toward rattle dancing are varied. For some, trans-performing is a sort of burden because they don't like the men's part and are better at dancing the women's. For other more skilled performers, it is a source of pride. They interpret their ability to dance as a talent, a gift from God that they have developed from their school training. The audience usually applauds these women's successful performances with a mixture of surprise, curiosity, and laughter. Sometimes people give them nicknames, such as *rusamba masaija*, "kicking (dancing) like a man." The women who dance *runyege* well do not care about these comments driven by the audience's incredulity; instead, they are happy with their accomplished dancing.

I found different levels of awareness and meaning given to trans-performing according to the performer's skill. While some women in this group, and most of the women performing in the KCCA ensemble, knew how to dance with rattles, they were not particularly skilled. They danced *runyege* without particular engagement, as part of the activities of their association, which seemed to represent for them the major catalyst of interest and engagement, as well as source of self-assertiveness. On the other hand, proficient *runyege* dancers were proud of what they described as a gift or a talent, like some of the school-girls mentioned in chapter 5. Pride in something they are surprisingly good at, as the response of the audience confirms, something they developed from an innate gift. Tina K. Ranmarine (2007: 118, 124) discussed training and practice in dance as a way of emphasizing "determined aspirations," hence decision, agency, and attainment, contrasting the idea of skill in dancing as defined by "predetermined possibilities" on the basis of the body structure of the performer. In this sense, the proficiency in dancing obtained through practice can challenge the idea of the body as passively embodying (cultural, racial, sexual) difference. When Nyoro and Tooro women perform *runyege* skillfully, they are using their agency to develop their talent and are aware that displaying it on

Figure 6.1. Rose Mary Kyamuhendo (left) and Maureen Kusima (right) of the MASDRASS group performing the *runyege* men's part. During rehearsals, trans-performing women can wear either trousers or skirts, as in these pictures, while on stage trousers are conventional for dancing the men's part. Masindi (Bunyoro), 2018.

stage shakes the general preconceptions about gender, which see *runyege* as excluded from the "predetermined possibilities" of their gender.

According to Tooro male musician and dancer Kagaba (int. May 11, 2011), today some women choose to dance men's *runyege* to see if they can be as strong as men and have the capability of doing masculine things. Also, I found as a quite common thought that men are smarter than women and that, by dancing like men, women can show that they are on the same level as men. However, from the perspective of trans-performing women, this is not meant to appropriate nor oppose local notions of masculinity or patriarchy, but rather to negotiate some aspects of femininity. In this respect, I found very significant the reflections of Lisa Gilman (2009) about women's political singing and dancing in Malawi. Gilman (2009: 158) argues that, although women could use singing at political rallies to convey their critiques or to demand better civil and economic conditions for women, political venues in contemporary democratic Malawi are free to attend and meant to support politicians; they are not conceived, as it would under be an authoritarian regime, as a place for public criticism, and hence this opportunity is not used. This means that a flexible and open performative context—be it singing and dancing at contemporary Malawian political rallies or *runyege* performances by women in cultural groups—that allows for debate and criticism sometimes is not used so, because it is not deemed as a space for public criticism. Gilman calls for listening to the protagonists' points of view and priorities, rather that insisting in the quest of forms of open debate and resistance, a focus usually dictated by human rights' and feminist theoretical approaches (particularly from the Global North) that privilege action and thus undermine other forms of agency. Gilman (2009: 168–170) builds on Shelly Ortner's (1997) notion of agency as based on the agent's positionality within multiple networks of power, in which she or he can have (and usually has) different priorities and agendas than activists looking at the greater social impact. Like women active in political rallies in Malawi, women engaging in associations in Uganda are driven mostly by individual, domestic, or community-oriented aspirations and goals, which do not involve contesting the whole system, but rather using some of its features to achieve their own priorities and objectives. So, for female performers in Bunyoro and Tooro, trans-performing is not a way to subvert patriarchy. For average-skilled dancers it is usually one source of self-confidence to be found within the association's activities, while women that dance *runyege* with great skill interpret the dance itself as a way of including assertiveness and proactiveness as integral parts of their femininity.

In this sense, while performing *runyege* reproduces the discourses on the traditional gender binary that are embedded in its multilayered meanings, it also allows the presence of a counter-discourse. It is through trans-performing as a device that allows negotiating gender that women stay within the tradition and, at the same time, can partially redefine its assumptions. Respecting the culture and hence locating oneself within a positive moral field remains fundamental for dancers and it is reinforced by the reference to their ability as "a gift from God," which can be understood on two levels. On the one hand, it is a strategic claim for trans-performers that their skill comes from above and for this reason they are entitled to trans-perform, thus circumventing canonical gender prescriptions without being criticized. On the other hand, it is a declaration of the performers as being endowed the characteristics that, through practice, lead them to excel at dancing. With a different awareness from the young performers in schools, adult women can express their agency through trans-performing. Following Butler (1990), it is through the very performativity of *runyege*, including both dancing and the theatrical devices marking its presentation, that individuals express their agency through different forms of interpretation. Besides being a device marked by the use of costumes, trans-performing *runyege* is then a dimension of assertiveness, a space for a counter-discourse challenging the traditional notion of femininity inscribed in this genre as delicate, submissive, and passive. This is resonant with the performance of traditional repertoires as an arena allowing renegotiations of gender, as argued by Sylvia Nanyonga-Tamusuza (2005) for the Ganda genre *baakisimba,* Carol E. Robertson (1993) for the Hawaiian context, and Sydney Hutchinson (2016) for contemporary *merengue.*

In women's associations, trans-performing permits women to contest the traditional notion of femininity inscribed in *runyege*. However—and this is a fundamental aspect—by dancing a genre connoted as positive because it is traditional and performing it with costumes that affirm the traditional gender, women remain within a performative field that is socially acceptable. In fact, their negotiation of traditional femininity is not an open gesture of challenge, but rather operates within the performative space of contemporary *runyege*. This space is marked by stage conventions that allow the fiction of using costumes to represent gender and, for this reason, this practice is socially accepted, similar to cross-dressing in several carnival traditions around the world (Santino 2017). However, not limited to the temporal duration of carnivalesque celebrations and to their peculiar characteristics, trans-performing is closer to cross-dressing practices durably associated with music and dance genres in other cultures. In particular, in her analysis of cross-gender dancing in East Java, Sunardi (2015) shows that this practice does not forcibly aim at subverting hegemonic gender categories but can even reinforce them, since on the representation level it reproduces and reperforms dances according to their traditionally gendered understanding. Indeed, a rejection of cross-dressing could come if a dance was not performed using the costumes and style traditionally considered appropriate for its gendering. However, in East Java women performing masculine dances or styles can adopt a strategy of "layering" where, thanks to theatrical elements such as costumes, makeup, and acted attitudes, the figure of the (masculine) dance character overlaps the one of the (feminine) performer without erasing it, thus allowing female dancers to negotiate different forms of femininity. This way of exercising a type of power that is neither exhibited nor imposed, but rather delicately expressed by moving within the limitations of the (Javanese) patriarchal system is typically feminine, according to Sunardi (2015) and Weiss (2006). In western Uganda, skilled trans-performing women use both their agency and competence to show that other femininities are not incompatible with the tradition that they perform. In the context of women's associations and for their very characterization as such, this can be understood as a general claim for diverse and manifold notions of femininity.

"Trans-Performing" Dancers in Mixed Groups

In mixed semiprofessional ensembles, when dancers trans-perform, it is normally because they want to, not because of a shortage of dancers of the traditionally prescribed gender, as is usually the case in women's associations. Most of trans-performing dancers in mixed groups started to perform the opposite dance part at school and then improved and continued to perform the dance part in which they had specialized in a cultural group. Similar to women in associations, these performers interpret their ability to dance the other gender's part as an innate talent and a gift from God. The reaction of the public to their skilled performances expresses both bewilderment and admiration. The level of interest generated by these dancers means that the ensembles with trans-performers are in greater demand than other groups. On the one hand, this makes it a talent worth exploiting by the performers because, being more sought-after than conventional MDD, it is a good source of income for them and the ensemble as a whole. On the other hand, and for the same reasons, this may lead to negative feelings and envy toward them among the other groups.

While for most of the trans-performing dancers theirs is a talent that should be developed and exploited, the dancers' expressivity in trans-performing has various connotations for the different individuals involved. This resonates with the similar situation in East Java, where performers dance the part or genre prescribed for the other gender within the traditional binary and consider this practice in various ways: from acting during dancing to incarnating characteristics of the other gender in daily life (Sunardi 2015). For some trans-performing dancers in western Uganda, the theatrical component of acting connotes trans-performing as something circumscribed to the stage. In this sense, trans-performing is an activity separated from daily life although it has an (economic or personal) impact on it, as is the case for most members of women's associations. For instance, Deosi, who normally performs the *runyege* women's dance part, considers it a "hobby" (int. June 12, 2011). Although he can also dance the men's part, he prefers the women's part and he feels more confident in that role because he is more skilled at it than at rattling. When he dances on stage he acts like a woman and, in his view, this is important in order to perform his role convincingly, especially during the couple dancing. However, for him, dancing like a woman does not have an influence outside the performance: he thinks that "a man has to behave like a man," as he does himself in his daily life as a married man.

Some performers now in their early 20s got interested in dancing the women's part when they were children and they just carried on. For Kalu, when he joined a cultural group, dancing *mugongo* was easier than the men's

214 ❧ CHAPTER SIX

part and, since he was good at it, he enjoyed it even more (int. August 19, 2018). So he practiced a lot and it became something he excelled at. People made comments about Kalu because he used to spend time with girls to dance the women's part and also because of his way of dressing—characterized by colorful and tight pants, shirts, and scarves—which was deemed eccentric and not very masculine. Tual, another young trans-performing man, started dancing at a mixed primary school and chose to dance women's *nyamuziga*. In his words, "because it's my nature, in my family background. I'm the only [one] boy, we have 18 ladies, only I am a boy. Because I've spent a lot of time with ladies, I've adopted a female character rather than male, as I play and train netball" (int. August 30, 2018). To *nyamuziga* dancing, Tual related his family life among women and netball, a popular sport across the Commonwealth that is generally considered feminine because it emerged as a variation of basketball for women. Tual connected his pleasure in dancing the women's part—something that he feels "in the body," as a part of him—with his way of behaving in his daily life, which is gentle and shy, hence perceived as feminine and not complying with the expected gender expression for men. When trans-performing, Kalu's and Tual's attitude is not connoted by acting as it is for Deosi, but rather by the profound embodiment of the women's dance part. Their experience is of "feeling better" in that role, where they can express themselves more completely. Their gender expression, connoted by a femininity that does not conform to the traditional binary, is then conveyed on stage through the theatrical convention of trans-performing.

A similar experience is shared by Ruru when she dances the men's part. She is a very skilled rattle dancer and besides dancing in a cultural group, she teaches schoolchildren traditional music and dance and composes her own songs. When we first met (int. June 13, 2011), she described her experience, when stamping on the ground while wearing trousers and rattles, as "being a man." In the moment of the *runyege* performance, she expressed the masculinity of the men's dance part as something that she felt deep within her. Elements perceived as masculine also expressed her personality and behavior off the stage. Her appearance (wearing trousers and boots instead of a skirt and heels), her attitude (hanging out in pubs and drinking alcohol, having mostly male friends instead of spending her free time at home in the company of other women), and character (toughness, audacity, self-confidence) are considered mannish by the Nyoro community. Furthermore, in her late 20s, she was not married and did not have any children. Ruru's masculine appearance and behavior recall the characteristics of the *tiguera* presented by Sydney Hutchinson (2016) in her discussion of *merengue típico*: a woman whose gender expression is marked by elements of masculinity. Also, following Judith Halberstam (1998), Ruru's gender expression is shaped by "female masculinity," where traits and attitudes deemed as mannish are strong and evident. The community considers these elements as inappropriate for a woman of her age and is openly or covertly critical of her. However, while Ruru trans-performs within the representational conventions of current *runyege*, her displayed masculinity is accepted. Because of these theatrical conventions, trans-performing is acquiesced as a stage representation by the audience, as well as by coperformers. In this way, trans-performing dancers can at the same time disclose (on stage) and hide (with the costumes and within the *runyege* conventions) alternative masculinities and femininities, as is the case in other Ugandan traditional dances (Nanyonga-Tamusuza 2005) and, more generally, in genres where cross-dressing can be employed, such as *merengue* (Hutchinson 2016). Similar to cross-gender dancing in East Java (Sunardi 2015: 61), in a contemporary Uganda marked by widespread conservatorism and concerns about morality in gender matters, negotiating gender expression through performance constitutes a space for self-expression that is safer than the political and social context.

In this sense, contemporary *runyege* hosts not only the negotiation of femininity in terms of assertiveness as in women's associations, but also counter-discourses about gender expression contradicting the dominant traditional binary and its strict and normative codifications of femininity and masculinity, which mark multiple aspects of the genre. This hazy performative space, which is open to various interpretations for both the audience and the performers, allows Ruru and others to express themselves in a space free from disapproval. It is through gendered body techniques, which they profoundly embody, that personal aspirations, preferences, and self-expressions are mediated and mobilized within represented *runyege*. Embodiment is an essential component in trans-performing dancers' agency to reinterpret the dance and its gendered meanings. Embodied and represented gender are thus integrated in performing, while differently experienced by trans-performing dancers and the audience.

Although the audience accepts these performances, it does not mean that they pass without comment. All the trans-performing dancers that I met told me of surprised reactions to their performances accompanied by various remarks and gossip. Because of the deeply gendered character of *runyege*—where the basic movements of the two dance parts are naturalized as being possible only for the related sexed bodies, the gender of performers is identified by costumes, and the danced interaction is an acted heterosexual courtship—the audience associates trans-performers with the opposite sex/gender according to the traditional binary, which *runyege* as the local genre incarnates. Some young men who trans-perform are derisively called *mukazi* (woman) or *kaisiki* (little girl) with reference not only to their dancing but also to their shy "feminine" manner off the stage (int. Tual: August 30,

2018); others are called *kikazikazi* (feminine male). At times, members of the public are fascinated by trans-performing as being something that challenges nature, almost like a form of acrobatics. Some performers related the comments of some spectators wondering about their "real" biological sex and suggesting that they were a *bwatububiiri*, hermaphrodite (int. Kafre: August 20, 2018; int. Ruru: August 20, 2018). Because of the biological determinism marking gendered *runyege* parts, it is considered "unnatural" that a female can jump and stamp so well, just as it is for a male to be flexible enough to properly shake his waist: their sexed bodies should not be able to do those activities. The very fact that this happens surprises the audience and may be accompanied by enthusiasm for successfully challenging natural and physical constraints. However, the observers' surprise is sometimes manifested as a morbid curiosity concerning the body and the sex of the performer, like in the comments about hermaphroditism suggesting the compresence of two different sexual organs. The incredulity about these performers' biological sex can go to the extent of audience members making bets and codancers wanting to check the dancer's body during costume changes, as shared by Tual (int. August 30, 2018).

As mentioned at the beginning of this chapter, trans-performing in its cross-dressing and acting components is locally understood in relation to the body as the factor determining possible movements and attitudes, not in connection to sexuality. This echoes similar perceptions about transvestism as not forcibly related to sexuality in other global contexts, such as in Mexico (Chávez 2009), in East Java (Sunardi 2015), and in the Dominican Republic (Hutchinson 2016). In particular, Sydney Hutchinson (2016: 151–152) notes that, although among most Dominicans homosexuality is not accepted as a practice nor recognized as a gender identity, cross-dressing performers of *merengue* and other cultural practices are not only tolerated but also appreciated, and "The fact that acceptance of gender play exists alongside condemnation of homosexuality suggests that Dominicans do not always consider sexual orientation and gender performance to be closely linked." Analogous perceptions are common in western Uganda.

Similar to trans-performing dancers in women's associations and to other global cross-dressing cases (Sunardi 2015), trans-performers in mixed groups explain their abilities in religious terms, as something almost miraculous, a gift from God. Perhaps because it is seen as something that in local understanding goes against the physiology of their bodies, religion is mobilized as a legitimizing strategy to explain their skill as a God-given ability. Furthermore, the reference to religion attaches a positive moral value to trans-performing, as it is interpreted as a gift from God—and this "blessing" is confirmed by the audience approval and group's economic success. In line with a moral understanding of their position, trans-performing dancers also express their positive and valuable role as promoters of culture within the positive aura attached to local tradition. Finally, Christian religion is invoked again to sustain transformations in the gender expression of some trans-performing individuals, as I will discuss in brief.

Since trans-performing *runyege* is accepted in the theatrical setting of contemporary performances, most of the dancers dismiss annoying comments made by audiences and coperformers, or at least try not to care. Tida is another trans-performing man, now in his mid-40s, who performs in a cultural group. In his words, "I feel good when I dance *mugongo:* I like it and I feel it. When they are drumming, I start shaking myself even if they have not told me to start [dancing] yet. I just feel it, it is natural" (int. August 22, 2018). Tida has two children and, although the community understands some of his manners in daily life as feminine, he does not care. He came across as an optimist and sure of himself; he said that no one would dare to make unpleasant insinuations in front of him because they fear his reaction.

Despite the general acceptance of trans-performing, some comments convey social tensions around the body and gender. Because of this, even though Tual loves to dance *nyamuziga* and feels it "in his body," he is considering changing to the men's part in the future (int. August 30, 2018). He, like some other trans-performing dancers, does not match the traditional expectations for his gender in terms of clothing, behavior, and relationships in his day-to-day life. Tensions around nonconformity to dominant and normative gender prescriptions increase according to the performers' age and are directed at their daily lives rather than their dancing. Social pressure (by the family and the community in general) is focused on trans-performing dancers who do not have children yet. Indeed, nonnormative gender expressions are tolerated as long as the performers procreate. The production of offspring is certainly central in Nyoro and Tooro culture, but the expectation about having children can also be understood as the community demanding concrete proof of the performer's "nature," of his or her real sex—demonstrated by heterosexual intercourse and the functioning of a person's reproductive capacities according to their biological sex. Alternative masculinities and femininities affect the performers' chances to find a partner and have children, hence social pressure to conform to normative gender becomes stronger, especially when performers are in their 30s and over.

Some of the trans-performing dancers that I have presented here indeed experienced pressing demands from their families and the community to fit the hegemonic forms of masculinity and femininity in their daily lives by finding a partner and having children. Religion, in particular some Christian denominations also active in homophobic campaigns (Sadgrove et al. 2012; Tamale 2007), is once again involved in dealing with social expectations. Faith and praying emerge in the personal stories of some trans-performing dancers, but in this case as the motor and guide for change, to abandon the lifestyle that they had chosen for themselves, and to adjust to normative masculinity and femininity. Religious explanations are not mobilized to legitimize day-to-day deviations from normativity in gender expression and sexuality as it happens, for instance, among East Javanese cross-dressing dancers (Sunardi 2015). Rather, this use of religion is directed to self-transformation and recalls some born-again Christian communities' deplorable practice of prescribing very painful "therapy" intended to "reform" homosexuals. In the personal experiences that trans-performing dancers shared with me, sexuality was not an issue, but rather gender expression was at stake and they presented their turn to religion as a tool enabling them to finally change their personal style and behaviors, not as an imposition from above. However, they narrated how religion marked their struggles while trying to balance their selves with their community's demands, their suffering because of rejecting themselves as inadequate or wrong, and the violence of forcing different ways of being unto themselves. As their distressing stories I report below show, these "changes" involved also abandoning trans-performing, thus depriving them also of the free expression they could enjoy while dancing *runyege*.

For Kafre, a man who used to dance women's *mugongo,* criticism from the community was hard. People laughed at him, at the way, perceived as feminine, in which he behaved in daily life, at the fact that he was too shy to approach girls, and there were rumors that he was impotent (int. Kafre: August 20, 2018). For this reason, women thought that he would not make a good husband and mocked him. Kafre, however, wanted a wife and a family. Although he described the feminine aspects within him as *kyabuzari-ranwa*, inborn, he decided to react since he felt depressed and hated himself because of this condition. So, he forced himself to pray in church for the feminine traits to "go out of me, to behave like a man." Kafre referred to biology to explain gender nonnormativity saying that he was born that way, and used religion as a tool to transform what nature had given him. Biology and religion thus return to discuss gender expression in a different way compared to the dancing talent, which is usually presented as a gift from God, despite what "nature" would prescribe. Kafre finally succeeded in finding a partner and they had a child together; after her premature death, he found another partner, with whom he has two children. Leaving trans-performing was part of his process of change and now he only trains schoolchildren in both *runyege* dance parts. Some of the young people that he trained were able, through performing arts, to get scholarships and continue their education, and this is a source of pride to him. Kafre loved dancing *mugongo* and he misses it, but he said that at least he is now satisfied with what he has accomplished in his personal and public life (int. Kafre: August 20, 2018).

Even self-confident performers reach a point where the social pressure about their gender expression and the expectations to have a family become too much to bear. The second time I met Ruru, the trans-performing woman that I mentioned earlier, she was very different from our first encounter seven years earlier. Ruru comes from a Muslim family, but we met in a Pentecostal church, where she was reading the Bible. I told her that I remembered her dreadlocks and her reggae style songs and she said "Yes, reggae, reggae, rasta rasta. I used to booze so much. But now God changed me, I am no longer drinking [...] now I am saved, that's why I am in a church here. Now I am writing gospel music" (int. Ruru: August 20, 2018). Ruru recounted to me that people commented on her, referring to hermaphroditism and with remarks such as "Why she is not married? How can she get married? Will she box you if you are married to her?" (int. Ruru: August 20, 2018). She responded to the criticism by turning to religion. As God gave her a rare talent for women, being able to dance masculine *runyege* very well, God could also change her nature, make her a proper woman that someone will accept in marriage. It was to adjust to normativity that she converted to Christianity, to praying in the church as Kafre. Furthermore, seeking spiritual and physical refuge in the church, while it may not "change" you, can at least protect you from aggressive questions about whether you are a "good" woman or man. Indeed, local churches, supported by some American evangelical associations, building on the increasing tension around gender and sexuality and the parallel search for morality, have fiercely and publicly condemned nonnormative people, shaming homosexuality (Gusman and Viola 2014; Nyanzi 2014; Sadgrove et al. 2012; Ssebagala 2011; Tamale 2007) and more generally alternative gender expressions. In this sense, by associating themselves to local churches and displaying their faith, some trans-performing dancers chose a position protected from social and religious condemnation. Conversion is not just appearance, but for Ruru it affected many aspects of her personal life, like the clothes she wears. She described her past, when she used to wear trousers and drink alcohol, as not being good, unlike her present life. During our encounter in the church, she was seated in the way considered decent for women (with the knees bent on one side) and with her legs covered by a long skirt. This change surprised me and, when I asked her the reason, she read from the Bible, Deuteronomy 22:5: "A woman must not wear men's clothes, and a man must not wear women's clothes. That is disgusting to the Lord, your God." Conversion also affected her approach to performing arts. She still performs her old songs when they ask her because their message has an important impact on issues such as girls' education, HIV-AIDS prevention, and avoidance of early pregnancies. However, like Kafre, she left trans-performing in cultural groups as part of her religious turn and she now

220 ❧ CHAPTER SIX

focuses on training the youth. Teaching *runyege* rattling is now the only time when she wears trousers—only because they allow the free leg movements required while dancing the men's part. Adjusting to this different lifestyle was hard on Ruru and, at the time of our last encounter, she was struggling to accept these changes through praying. As I respected her distressing but conscious choices, I limited myself to expressing my empathy for her struggles, without criticizing the very need for change or these religious practices.

In this final chapter, I examined contemporary performances and presented some performers of traditional songs and dances in cultural groups. I endeavored to weave together the discussion of gender as represented through these performances and as variously embodied by different performers. In particular, *runyege* dancing has emerged as establishing the traditional binary as well as allowing the expression and embodiment of other forms of masculinities and femininities while trans-performing in women's or mixed ensembles. The notion of morality so important in contemporary Ugandan society characterizes the interpretation of local culture and performing arts as well as of religion, which recurs together with biology in explanations about uncommon gendered performing skills. Besides this, religion is evoked by trans-performing dancers as a force for "fixing" their gender expressions in private life, a change that is usually paired with abandoning trans-performing. Although heavily influenced by social pressure, it is the trans-performing dancers' decision, aiming at feeling better in their communities and protecting themselves from reactionary attacks, to use prayers as a means of personal transformation and the Bible as a reference for their behavior. These sensitive personal stories tell us that, while traditional performing arts both impose the traditional gender binary and allow negotiations of gender expression, they create an inclusive environment mainly on stage because their fluidity is mostly dependent on representation conventions. Even if some positive repercussions of trans-performing can be seen off stage—in particular the impact of these appreciated performances on the cultural group's success and competitiveness compared to other ensembles, other factors—such as age of the performers, parental status, and religiousness—influence their well-being in the community. This considered, a broader social impact of the flexibility intrinsic to traditional performing arts is to be wished to counter currently widespread conservative attitudes and practices.

Postlude

Gendering Culture

While I am writing these pages, the Covid-19 pandemic has been going on for almost three years. As it happened globally, the lockdowns imposed by the Ugandan government in 2020 and 2021 seriously impacted social life as well as the economy. In the cities and towns urban dwellers found themselves in the impossible situation of needing to earn income and purchase food, while in rural areas both food and social relations were less affected because of scattered family-based residents, cultivation of gardens, and local economy. Schools in Uganda remained closed for more than one year with deplorable consequences for a whole generation of students, such as a high school dropout rate and early pregnancies.[1] In addition, like almost everywhere around the globe, cultural life and, with it, live music and dance performances were initially reduced and then prohibited during the lockdowns. Several songs about Covid-19 prevention and sensitization were produced and disseminated through the media, especially at the beginning of the emergency in 2020. Whereas in the past the reaction to HIV/AIDS stimulated the establishment of cultural groups and the production of live performances dealing with this topic, the Covid-19 situation severely restricted live performances of traditional arts, and therefore blocked a space for social and individual expression. It is, however, too early to evaluate the medium- and long-term impact of the Covid-19 pandemic on traditional performing arts, and this can be a fruitful topic for further investigations.

Throughout this book, I have discussed the deep and manifold interconnectedness of gender and traditional performing arts in western Uganda through their complex relations within the local discourses, in terms of representation and embodiment. I have analyzed how the various components of traditional MDD are molded by the hegemonic gender binary in content, structure, and practice. I have traced the continuities between the performance of traditional repertoires in the past and in the present and highlighted the places where the new has split from the old, reconstructed

---

1 https://www.unicef.org/uganda/press-releases/prioritize-re-opening-schools-secure-childrens-well-being (accessed on September 16, 2022).

through historical sources and recordings, as well as from the recollections of elders. I noted how alternative genders have been flattened during the colonial era into what is today understood as the traditional gender binary, essentially represented by the "Domestic Virtue model" for women and its counterpart for men, which was then absorbed by the postcolonial society. Genres connected to figures of strong femininity (spirit medium songs) and repertoires (*nanga* zither pieces) challenging the notion that women "are not supposed to play instruments" have not been included in the revival of tradition that has inspired the school festival. In the practice of cultural groups, moreover, *nanga* songs have been reinterpreted in a way that destroys the femininity of the genre and reinscribes it within the binary connoting other traditional genres. I have considered how singing, instrument playing, and dancing are staged today, at the school festival and in cultural groups' shows, through the paradigms of narration and representation. In addition to formal and musical transformations, I have focused on how gender is reinterpreted in contemporary performances using theatrical devices, seeking to describe both the structural frames and the variety of individual choices and understandings that assign meaning to these performances. In the plurality of individual and intimate nuances that performers, teachers, adjudicators, audiences, and the wider community experience in relation to gender issues in traditional repertoires, I located a dominant discourse about the traditional binary, as well as a space to articulate counter-discourses.

Although officially presented as a traditional MDD identifying Nyoro and Tooro culture, the current performances of traditional repertoires are fluid enough to comply with different cultural and social contexts. In *runyege* especially—as a genre paradigmatic of the whole performing arts complex and profoundly marked by embodiment—the various interests, identities, and feelings of the actors emerge. In school performances, conservative constructions of gender are handed down along with local culture; however, teaching is not normally gendered and this allows pupils to learn while relatively free from gender constrictions. As adults, performers can reinterpret their skills in dynamic elaborations of their gender expressions while participating in cultural groups. For some women in associations, trans-performing is usually a necessity, but, along with other group activities, it contributes to their self-confidence; for other skilled female dancers it is a means to assert that a femininity different from the traditional binary is possible. In either case, even though engaging in these associations and in trans-performing has an impact on women as individuals and as a group, it is not meant to challenge the gender binary. For these women, trans-performing is normally related to their everyday life as married mothers in the sense of boosting their assertiveness and confidence.

For others, however, trans-performing is a meaningful choice, consistent with behaviors in their personal life. In this context, where things go round and round between sex and gender, real life and stage fiction, these performers have found an acceptable way of expressing their nonnormativity. A way of *being* (through a performed representation) and of *feeling* (in their moving bodies) *other* masculinities and femininities. Their trans-performing conveys a counter-discourse to mainstream thinking, because it allows to oppose the moralized traditional gender from the inside while it absorbs the positive values associated with tradition to get a social validation. This is an approach to *runyege* that in the present moralized Uganda is an effective strategy for both inclusion in and evasion of the system for nonnormative individuals. However, theatrical dance forms like *runyege* constitute a special space compared to real life, as Desmond (1999: 318) noted: "Theatrical practice, seen as a space and time set apart from daily action, also provides a potentially utopian arena for the contestation and reimagining of nonnormative renditions of bodily identity ... The meanings that can potentially be generated in such a space are always relationally produced, however, and the utopian potential of theater is counterbalanced by its social designation as the 'not-real'." Similarly, trans-performing is accepted by Ugandan society. However, this is fictional and mainly limited to the stage, while normativity seems imperative in daily life in order to produce offspring and maintain the community. Hence social pressure can crush alternative gender identities and expressions, as the personal stories of some trans-performing dancers have shown.

The experiences of nonnormative trans-performing dancers, and more generally of traditional arts performers, relate in multiple and complex ways to the present social context. Banyoro and Batooro, like other Ugandan populations, are engaged in a traditionalist revival, which is trying to redesignate a sense of local culture and identity in response to the challenges affecting contemporary society. Richard Reid, in his monumental *A History of Modern Uganda* (2017), discusses the importance that Uganda as a nation assigns to the past within the unsettling context of the neoliberal economy and authoritarian state of the present. In his view, tribalism and related violence of the past are feared and rejected in favor of discourses supporting modernity and development, especially by the government but also by the wider society, while at the same time communities invoke the glorious past of traditional and independent kingdoms against the authoritarian NRM government. Reid's interpretation perfectly suits a national perspective, marked by past and present tensions among different ethnicities that are either evoked or dismissed by the government and local communities in relation to the issue at stake. Within this framework, *runyege* as the representative dance of Banyoro and Batooro on the Ugandan stage executes two main functions.

224 POSTLUDE

On the one hand, it works as a tool to pinpoint cultural identity in the multiethnic nation by encapsulating Nyoro and Tooro old and good tradition, also expressed as a conservative gender binary. On the other hand, it is also a channel for modernity in its adaptations to different contexts and reelaborations by diverse performers. In other words, because of its flexibility in conveying multiple meanings, *runyege* constitutes a stronghold and repository of local identity in face of the centralizing state, while it carries the potential to imagine contemporary ways of using Nyoro and Tooro traditional arts in the national cultural market.

I believe that, besides the neoliberal economy and state authoritarianism considered by Reid, the unsettling present in Uganda is also shaped by postcoloniality. The connection with the Global North is still mostly marked by a top-down imposition, which is today experienced through the omnipresent media proposing alternative lifestyles, international NGOs directing local policies, and foreign religious organizations that layer their actions on the colonial past. From this perspective, the reference to the past and tradition is mainly in opposition to the West and is expressed in local culture and indigeneity. In this sense, while there is an impulse toward modernity in government policies and discourses as well as in individual and community entrepreneurship, the engagement in local culture is also lively and cuts across society. This local culture is condensed in the current dynamic role of traditional performing arts—at the same time crystallized and reinterpreted through performance, as well as mobilized in moral terms to face a destabilized present where gendered social identities and relations are perceived as compromised.

According to anthropologist Julia Vorhölter (2012), Ugandans interpret social change as being due to both westernization and neocolonialism and assign different meanings to these two phenomena. Westernization, understood as involving the spread of education, women's emancipation, and human rights, is accepted through negotiations aiming at adapting these issues to local society. This emerged in the quite effective plan of universal primary education implemented by the NRM government and in the massive diffusion of women's associations during the twentieth century, as well as in women's participation in politics (albeit still limited). Criticism of westernization is rather directed toward individuals that mindlessly copy Western habits, undermining local customs. On the other hand, according to Vorhölter, neocolonialism is negatively seen as the forced imposition on Africa of practices and policies perceived as incompatible with the local culture. In this sense, homosexuality, understood as alien and destabilizing the local gender systems and hence order throughout society, is condemned as part of neocolonialism. This view, spread throughout the country, also reflects and is used by President Museveni's demagogy that aspires to set Uganda free from Western influences in order to maintain his hold on power (Tripp 2004). Interestingly, the opposition to what is understood as neocolonialism in gender issues and sexuality has historical roots in the moralized and prudish position on sexuality grounded in missionary and local Christianity and now perceived as local (Ward 2015). This view, developed in relation to the HIV/AIDS pandemic that stimulated the moral panic in the country (Baral 2018; Gusman and Viola 2014) and was particularly supported and disseminated by Pentecostal-charismatic churches backed by US protestant leaders and policies (Bompani and Terreni Brown 2015; Kaoma 2009).

From this articulated perspective combining local postcolonial identities with historical and present external influences, we can better understand the wave of moralism overflowing in Ugandan society. More urgently, this helps explain why Uganda has become notorious for measures impacting on the bodies on women, such as banning skirts that go above the knee (Anti-Pornography Bill, in its initial formulation) and especially for its homophobia (through the nullified Anti-Homosexuality Bill). The condemnation of homosexuality, as well as of progressive forms of women's empowerment, as "imported" and "foreign" has to be related to a parallel engagement in reviving local culture, where many think that a model of "good" and "proper" tradition and gender resides. As I have shown throughout these pages, the traditional heteronormative gender binary is inscribed in the traditional repertoires that are still performed today and this model is reinforced through the current performance modalities. Reproducing local culture as "good" in opposition to foreign practices, perceived as dissolute and contrary to indigenous social values, conveys tradition in terms of (conservative) morality. So, traditional performing arts emerge as reservoirs of sonic, visual, and bodily techniques that educate and shape individuals in ethical ways and whose purpose is to spread the models of gendered morality in the community.

Marked by the discussion of proper roles and behavior for women and the rampant spread of homophobia, current conservative discourses in Uganda are located within a context of expanding tensions concerning gender norms and sexuality generated by encounters with colonial rule and later developed through postcolonial moral crises. In these discourses, local culture is constructed as a positive model of reference. As the intangible heritage shaping local culture filtered through postcoloniality, traditional performing arts are central to the understanding of the discourses surrounding gender in contemporary society. At the same time, gender as a fundamental component and driving force in culture is conveyed, shaped, and represented in these repertoires. Frictions between the "local" gender model, which is established as normative, and alternative ones, marked by the aspiration toward gender equality and individual freedom, also find their expression in performing arts like *runyege*. Possibly, between the semantic interstices of *runyege*, in its flexible stretching between tradition and modernity, an "elsewhere" (De Lauretis 1987: 25) will continue to be located and host, in the margins of hegemony, alternative meanings and models that can reflect on society as a whole.

Appendix I

Glossary of Terms in Runyoro-Rutooro

In this Glossary, I have gathered the Nyoro and Tooro (and some Ganda) terms recurring in this book, except for the words in songs' lyrics, for which a direct translation is provided in the text. In Runyoro-Rutooro language prefixes are fundamental in expressing nominal classes and number for adjectives and nouns, and person and number for verbs, as mentioned in the initial "Note on Language." For this reason, ordering terms alphabetically can be problematic and various solutions have been adopted by different authors (Davis 1938; Ndoleriire et al. 2009; Rubongoya 1999). Here I follow the method adopted by Margaret B. Davis (1938) in her dictionary, which has been very useful for my research, especially to retrieve terms quite uncommon in today's Runyoro-Rurooro. In particular, as I have done throughout this volume, I omit initial vowels since they have a role similar to that of articles; I normally refer to the singular form of nouns and adjectives (and mention the plural when different from the singular); finally, differently from Davis, I list verbs in the infinitive form with the *ku-* prefix, in order to help readers finding the searched verb as it mostly appears in the rest of the book.

Akadinda: Ganda and Soga xylophones and xylophone repertoires.

Amadinda: Ganda and Soga xylophones and xylophone repertoires.

Baakisimba: Ganda music and dance genre.

Bakugarukamu (sing. *mu-*): lit. those who answer; chorus in call-and-response singing, also known as *banukuzi*.

Batebe or *Kalyota:* sister of the Nyoro and Tooro king, female head of the women of the royal clan Babiito.

Banukuzi (sing. *mu-*): lit. those who answer; chorus in call-and-response singing, also known as *bakugarukamu*.

Buhangwa: lit. nature, used to mean local tradition.

Buro: millet; millet polenta.

228 &❧ APPENDIX I

Buswezi: marriage.

Bw'omu mbaju: lit. of the ribs, of the sides; old Tooro dance, then become women's part in Tooro *runyege* dance.

Firimbi: Nyoro whistle.

-gano: root present in several Bantu languages and referring to storytelling or to repertoires combining singing and narrating.

Hima: pastoralist, referred to Bahima pastoralists from Nkore.

Huma: pastoralist, referred to Bahuma pastoralists from Tooro and Bunyoro.

Icumbiro: kitchen.

Iguulya: music and dance genre similar to *runyege* and characterized by cloth rings worn by performers dancing the women's dance part.

Ihega (pl. *ma-*): one of the three stones delimiting the kitchen fire.

Ihuuru: small double-skin cylindroconical drum used in royal music.

Ikondeere (pl. *ma-*): side-blown trumpet used in royal music; the plural form *makondeere* is also used in Tooro to indicate the main royal music and dance genre.

Ikura: lit. wonderful unseen thing, small object inside royal drums.

Irambi: slow and processional part of *makondeere/mpango* royal music and dance.

Iru: referred to Bairu agriculturalists.

Ka: home; family.

Kagoma: small double-skin cylindroconical drum used in village music; music and dance genre of Bagungu communities, characterized by the use of the small drum.

Kalezi: variant of Tooro *runyege*.

Kalihwa: music and dance genre typical of the Bagungo community in Bunyoro.

Kalyota or *Batebe:* sister of the Nyoro and Tooro king, female head of the women of the royal clan Babiito.

Kanzu: men's long white tunic of Arab origin.

Karo (diminutive of *buro*): polenta of millet and cassava flour.

APPENDIX I &• 229

Karonkoronko: tradition (uncommon).

Karukarukaine: tradition (uncommon).

Kasigasigano: tradition (uncommon).

Kasaatu: animal hide (usually goatskin).

Kidongo: arched harp.

Kigano (pl. *bi-*): song connected to a story.

Kiguuli (pl. *bi-*): waist ring made of dried leaves or cloth worn by Nyoro female dancers.

Kikali: royal enclosure, extended royal area, court.

Kikohi (pl. *bi-*): colorful cloth worn by women as a long skirt wrapped around the waist and legs, also known as *kitambi.*

Kinyege (pl. *bi-*): leg rattle; fruit from which the leg rattles are derived.

Kitambi: colorful cloth worn by women as a long skirt wrapped around the waist and legs, also known as *kikohi.*

Kiteteyi: traditional feminine blouse.

Kitiniza: glory, honor, respect, reverence.

Kizina (pl. *bi-*): song, musical piece.

Kubandwa: (passive form of the verb *kubanda*: press down, run into, knock down): lit. to be pressed down; to be possessed by a *mbandwa* spirit; traditional religion in the African Great Lakes region.

Kuceka: to become weak.

Kucweka: to be broken, hasten.

Kucweka omugongo: lit. break the lower back, menstruation; women's dance part in Nyoro *runyege.*

Kudiba: to be left over, remain unsold; become obsolete.

Kugaba or *kugabura:* to give, distribute, contribute; give in marriage (the bride). Term used to refer to the second part of the traditional wedding, involving the departure of the bride from her natal home and her arrival's at the groom's.

Kugana: to sing stories (referred to *bigano*).

Kuganikya: to tell stories.

230 ❧ APPENDIX I

Kuguru (pl. *ma-*): leg.

Kuhonda: lit. to thresh, pound, crash; first dance style in *runyege* men's part, also referred to as *kusigika* or *mukutu.*

Kuhugura: to sing alternating head and chest registers, vocal technique usually referred to as a yodel.

Kujenga: to sing Huma male repertoires, in particular the songs for cattle.

Kulima: to cultivate, dig; to work.

Kulya: to eat.

Kulya engoma: lit. to eat the drum; to become king.

Kisembo: gift; talent.

Kulya: to eat.

Kumpa kitinisa: to give respect (to a man).

Kurasa: lit. to draw a bow, shoot at; second dance style in *runyege* men's part, also referred to as *ruseijera* or *kusimba.*

Kusamba: to kick; to stamp.

Kuseesa: lit. all of them; to spread, attack; third dance style in *runyege* men's part, also referred to as *munyonyi.*

Kusigika: lit. to stand firmly; first dance style in *runyege* men's part, also referred to as *kuhonda* or *mukutu.*

Kusimba: lit. to plant, stick upright in the ground; second dance style in *runyege* men's as well as women's part, for the men it is also referred to as *ruseijera* or *kurasa.*

Kusumikirra: to lead the singing.

Kuswera: to marry (a woman).

Kuswerwa: to get married (by a man).

Kuteera: lit. to beat, strike; to play musical instruments.

Kutongora: to take, choose the best one, or the most mature; to choose the dance partner in *runyege.*

Kuzina: to sing; to dance.

Kyabuzariranwa: inborn.

Kyera: to be white, pure, clean.

APPENDIX I ❧ 231

Kweranga: to announce, introduce; used to refer to the first part of the traditional wedding involving the introduction of the groom to the bride's family.

Kwiri or *Musuga:* brother of the king, head of the men of the Babiito clan.

Manzi: brave man, hero.

Maranga: Canna indica, wild plant whose seeds are used inside *binyege* rattles.

Marwa: banana beer, also called *tonto.*

Matagura: lit. it moves up and down; waist-hip movement typical of the women's dance part in Tooro *runyege.*

Mazina: dance.

Mbaju: ribs, sides.

Mbandwa (pl. *ba-*): spirit/medium of *kubandwa* traditional religion.

Mirindi: a Tooro dance for men only, no longer danced today.

Mpaako: pet name of Lwo origin used in Bunyoro and Tooro, instead of first names, to address individuals with both familiarity and respect.

Mpango (royal drum proper): royal double-skin cylindroconical drum; also Nyoro royal music and dance genre and annual ceremony of the Nyoro and Tooro kingdoms.

Mubandwa (pl. *ba-*): initiated medium in *kubandwa* religion.

Mubaro: the timbric and rhythmic pattern performed on a specific drum.

Mubiito (pl. *ba-*): male member of Babiito royal clan.

Mubiito w'engoma: male member of the royal family, prince.

Mubiitokati (pl. *ba-*): female member of the Babiito royal clan.

Mubiitokati w'engoma: female member of the royal family, princess, in the past gendered as a man.

Mucence: short raffia skirt used in *runyege.*

Mugo (pl. *ba-*): Nyoro or Tooro king's wife.

Mugongo: lower back, lumber region.

Mugusa: sorghum.

232 &❧ APPENDIX I

Muhuma (pl. *ba-*): in the past cattle keeper, today individuals from traditionally high-class families.

Muhuuru: bachelor.

Mujungu (pl. *ba-*): white person, European.

Mukaaga: lit. six; bride wealth.

Mukama (pl. *ba-*): lord, king; god.

Muka: wife.

Mukazi (pl. *ba-*): woman, wife.

Mukondeere (pl. *ba-*): *ikondeere* side-blown trumpet player.

Mukuru (pl. *ba-*): elderly person; *mukuru w'ebikwato:* lit. elder of the royal insignia, custodian of the royal regalia.

Mukutu: long knife; first dance style in *runyege* men's part, also referred to as *kusigika* or *kuhonda.*

Mulimo: (agricultural) work.

Munana: eight.

Munyege: Oncoba routledgei, tree with fruits that are used for *binyege* leg rattles.

Munyonyi: lit. bird-style, from *nyonyi,* bird: third dance style in *runyege* men's part, also referred to as *kuseesa.*

Muranga (pl. *ba-*): handmaid, court female servant; also concubine, according to Davis 1938.

Murongo (pl. *ba-*): twin.

Musaija (pl. *ba-*): man, husband.

Museegu (pl. *ba-*): *nseegu* flute player; assistant of a spirit medium or medium initiator.

Muserebende [*omugongo*]: lit. softly slide; waist-hip movement typical of the women's dance part in Nyoro *runyege,* also used to refer to the second style of women's dance part.

Musigazi (pl. *ba-*): lit. the one remaining [near his father's home], son.

Musumukirizi: lit. the one connecting the words, soloist; also known as *mutongerezi.*

Musuga or *Kwiri:* brother of the king, head of the men of the Babiito clan.

APPENDIX I 𝕤 **233**

Muteezi: lit. beater. *Muteezi w'ebinyege:* beater of the leg rattles, i.e., dancer of the *runyege* men's part.

Mutima: heart, soul. *Mutima w'engoma* (lit. heart or soul of the drum): small object inside a drum.

Mutongerezi: lit. the one leading the song; soloist; also known as *musumukirizi.*

Muzeenyo: music and dance genre of the Bagungu community.

Muzungu (pl. *ba-*): (originally in Ganda language now widely used) white person, European.

Mwana (pl. *ba-*): child. *Mwana bw'ahara:* lit. child of far away, daughters.

Mwenda: nine.

Mwiru (pl. *bu-*). agriculturalist.

Nanga: trough zither; song(s) originally accompanied by the *nanga* zither.

Ndeeba: pit dug in the banana plantation and used to squeeze beer bananas.

Ndingidi: one-string tube fiddle.

Nduuru: joyful ululation.

Ngaabi: single-skin drum with a cylindrical head used in village music.

Ngabu: lit. shield; recitation of heroic deeds.

Ngaija: single-skin drum with a cylindrical head used in royal music.

Nganikyo: traditional tale.

Ngayaya: swaying movement of the head and torso that women used to do while singing *nanga* songs.

Ngoma: common double-skin cylindroconical drum spread throughout Uganda and used in Nyoro and Tooro village music.

Ngoma ny'abahuma: Huma song, in the past performed at Huma weddings in Tooro.

Ngonzi: love.

Ngwara: side-blown trumpet used in village music.

Nsiriba: Tooro whistle.

Nju: house.

Nseegu: composite cone-flute connected to traditional religion.

Ntajemerwa: double-skin cylindroconical drum used in court music.

Nte: cow, cattle.

Ntimbo: single-skin drum with a cup-shaped head used in royal music.

Ntogoro: music and dance genre spread in various variants in Bunyoro and Tooro.

Numi: fire lit in the banana plantation to accelerate banana maturation.

Nyamuziga: lit. wheel or hoop; women's third dance style in Tooro *bw'omu mbaju,* also generically used to mean the women's dance part in Tooro *runyege.*

Nyanja: lake. The Nyoro and Tooro names for some of the African Great Lakes are: Nyanja Mwitanzige (Lake Albert), Nyanja Rweru (Lake Edward), Nyanja Katunguru (Lake George) and Nyanja Kyoga (virtually the only lake in the region that was not named after a member of the British royal family).

Nyina: mother.

Nyin'omukama: lit. mother of the king, queen mother.

Nyineka: household head, owner of a house and head of a family.

Nyinenju. mistress of a house.

Nzarwu: lit. home-born, native, aboriginal; local culture.

Riiba: lit. dove; dance of Batuku community imitating doves.

Rubugo: bark cloth.

Rugali: flat basket or wicker tray used to winnow cereals.

Ruganda (pl. *nganda*): lit. united, clan.

Ruhenda: way of speaking based on metaphors and allegories.

Rumengo: grinding stone (dim. *kamengo*).

Runyege: music and dance genre featuring *binyege* leg rattles.

Ruseijera: second dance style in *runyege* men's part.

Rusindi: one of the Nyoro music and dance genres featuring leg rattles.

Suka: traditional female cape.

Tonto: banana beer, also called *marwa.*

Appendix II

Historical Recordings from Bunyoro and Tooro

The three tables in the following pages present the historical recordings made among the Banyoro and Batooro, some of which are mentioned in this book. Every table gathers the recordings by collection, that is, according to the researcher that realized them. The recordings are listed alphabetically[1] following the title assigned by the collector and accompanied by the place and date or year of recording, as well as the original catalog code. The first time that a place is mentioned, I specify if it is located in Bunyoro or Tooro. The recordings made by Hugh Tracey are preserved at the International Library of African Music (ILAM), at Rhodes University in Grahamstown. The ILAM online archive is still in its implementation stage,[2] but the recordings have been released in the *Sound of Africa Series* of ILAM, first as LP records and later as CDs. The recordings made in Bunyoro and Tooro are featured in the records or CDs no. 132 to 136. The catalog of the series (Tracey 1973a and 1973b) supplies details about Tracey's recordings. The recordings by Klaus Wachsmann and Peter Cooke are mostly unpublished and, together with the accompanying notes, are preserved at the British Library as well as available online, although the listening is limited to the first seconds of the tracks.[3] Copies of the Ugandan recordings from the three collections have also been deposited at MAKWAA, Makerere University Klaus Wachsmann Audiovisual Archive in Kampala.

---

1 The titles and places of recording are mentioned according to the spelling adopted by the three collectors. Hence some orthographic discrepancies in relation to the spelling adopted in this book may occur.

2 https://www.ru.ac.za/ilam/currentprojects/ilamsamaponlinearchive/ (accessed on November 9, 2022).

3 Respectively at these links: http://sounds.bl.uk/World-and-traditional-music/ Wachsmann and http://sounds.bl.uk/World-and-traditional-music/Peter-Cooke-Uganda (accessed on November 9, 2022).

Hugh Tracey Collection

Title	Location	Date	Original catalog code
Abagenyi baizire	Bunyoro District	1950	AMA. TR-132 B - 9
Abagungu	Hoima (Bunyoro)	1950	AMA. TR-133 B - 5
Amarwa tinganywa	Hoima	1950	AMA. TR-132 A - 3
Aramutanga	Hoima	1950	AMA. TR-133 A - 5
Ayahangiri abakazi	Hoima	1950	AMA. TR-133 A - 11
Ayemere Kasunau nwanzi	Bukuku (Tooro)	1950	AMA. TR-135 B - 7
Bwasemera obugenyi ...	Bukuku	1950	AMA. TR-136 A - 6
Choli	Kigumba (Bunyoro)	1950	AMA. TR-132 B - 2
Ekyoma kyabora	Hoima	1950	AMA. TR-132 A - 5
Enanga rwanzira	Bukuku	1950	AMA. TR-135 B - 5
Ilemere abagorra nsonga ilemere	Bukuku	1950	AMA. TR-136 A - 7
Irambi	Hoima	1950	AMA. TR-133 A - 6
Jeni akahongira enyaiya embira	Hoima	1950	AMA. TR-133 B - 7
Kaburora akaiba muhogo	Hoima	1950	AMA. TR-133 B - 4
Kaheru	Bukuku	1950	AMA. TR-136 A - 2
Kawairanga	Hoima	1950	AMA. TR-133 B - 2
Kawamyita wagenda ...	Bukuku	1950	AMA. TR-135 B - 6
Kigara kyamsiriba	Hoima	1950	AMA. TR-132 A - 7
Kitwekize kya Winyi, part I	Hoima	1950	AMA. TR-132 B - 5
Kitwekize kya Winyi, part II	Hoima	1950	AMA. TR-132 B - 6
Kotabijuba	Bunyoro District	1950	AMA. TR-132 B - 8
Kyanda	Bukuku	1950	AMA. TR-135 B - 8
Kyebambi	Hoima	1950	AMA. TR-132 B - 4
Kyenda ali mugenyi	Kigumba	1950	AMA. TR-132 B - 1
Mukunge Stefano	Hoima	1950	AMA. TR-133 A - 12
Muli baripiya	Hoima	1950	AMA. TR-133 B - 3

Musingasingu yakora egali	Kigumba	1950	AMA. TR-133 A - 9
Musingasingu yakora egali	Kigumba	1950	AMA. TR-133 A - 10
Mutitira	Bukuku	1950	AMA. TR-136 A - 1
Nimboroga	Hoima	1950	AMA. TR-132 B - 7
Ntajemerwa	Bunyoro District	1950	AMA. TR-133 A - 1
Ntimbo, webembera Omukama	Hoima	1950	AMA. TR-133 A - 4
Nzaireki akatera empihi	Hoima	1950	AMA. TR-133 B - 6
Obalemege	Bukuku	1950	AMA. TR-135 A - 6
Obugambo bunsemerire ...	Hoima	1950	AMA. TR-132 A - 1
Obundiba ntaizire	Hoima	1950	AMA. TR-132 A - 2
Okuturukya Omukama	Hoima	1950	AMA. TR-133 A - 3
Omukungu nakanyagwe	Hoima	1950	AMA. TR-132 A - 4
Orukobya	Hoima	1950	AMA. TR-133 B - 1
Rukidi	Hoima	1950	AMA. TR-132 B - 3
Rwabazira	Bukuku	1950	AMA. TR-135 A - 5
Rwaflanembe	Hoima	1950	AMA. TR-133 A - 7
Rwakyesiga ensolima	Hoima	1950	AMA. TR-132 A - 6
Rwosere	Kigumba	1950	AMA. TR-133 A - 8
Zali mbogo zali nkanga	Bukuku	1950	AMA. TR-135 A - 7

Klaus Wachsmann Collection

Title	Location	Date	Original catalog code
Abagenyi baizire	Hoima (Bunyoro)	26 November 1954	54.793
Abigambire	Hoima District (Bunyoro)	19 April 1949	49.14
Akabira	Kasule (Tooro)	5 July 1954	54.203
Alimbona n'ente	Hoima District	19 April 1949	49.09
Amakondere song	Nalweyo (Bunyoro)	14 May 1954	54.25
Amakondere song	Nalweyo	14 May 1954	54.27

Amutanga	Hoima District	19 April 1949	49.15
Andererya ya Buganda	Biseruka (Bunyoro)	30 November 1954	54.837
Araire njara	Kasule	5 July 1954	54.211
Aramutanga	Kasule	5 July 1954	54.202
Ayarungire abakazi kakarunga	Mbogwe (Bunyoro)	26 November 1954	54.797
Balimanya	Nalweyo	14 May 1954	54.24
Bambeja	Nalweyo	14 May 1954	54.28
Bamunserekere	Kasule	5 July 1954	54.204
Bigambo biri kweba	Kipolopyo (Bunyoro)	26 November 1954	54.792
Burungi bwa ente	Kitaleesa (Tooro)	?	54.215 b
Cuncururu cu cu cu	Fort Portal (Tooro)	10 July 1954	54.261
Ebigenyi biiziire	Kipolopyo	26 November 1954	54.793
Ekisina kye mpisi	Fort Portal	10 July 1954	54.272
Ekya Busongora …	Kasule	5 July 1954	54.214
Empologoma	Bwanswa	15 May 1954	54.33 b
Empunu 1 and 2	Bwanswa (Bunyoro)	15 May 1954	54.30
Empunu	Bwanswa	15 May 1954	54.31
Enanga ngaju ya omukama …	Fort Portal (Tooro)	10 July 1954	54.267
Enanga ngaju ya omukama … (cont.)	Fort Portal	10 July 1954	54.268
Enanga style song	Kisomoro (Tooro)	9 July 1954	54.234
Endingidi Mbugongo	Butiaba	25 November 1954	54.787
Engabi	Bwanswa	15 May 1954	54.32
Enjogero	Bwanswa	15 May 1954	54.34
Enkooko yange	Kasule	?	54.215 e
Ennumi	Hoima District	19 April 1949	49.03
Ensolima ikaija n'Abajungu	Mbogwe	26 November 1954	54.795
Entabi	Kasule	5 July 1954	54.207
Entuha	Fort Portal	10 July 1954	54.273

APPENDIX II 239

Fishing song	Butiaba (Bunyoro)	25 November 1954	54.778
Galisoigana	Hoima District	19 April 1949	49.04
Guitar song in style of bow-harp	Kisomoro	9 July 1954	54.241
Gwaada	Butiaba	25 November 1954	54.784
Gwosomu megwere	Butiaba	25 November 1954	54.776
Hunting omuso	Bwanswa	15 May 1954	54.39
Ichuma lya luswata	Hoima District	19 April 1949	49.05
Ikangaine ya Kyebambe	Fort Portal	10 July 1954	54.270
Inywena bojo baisiki	Kitaleesa	?	54.215 d
Irambi	Hoima District	19 April 1949	49.01
Irambi	Kasule	5 July 1954	54.201
Irambi	Kasule	5 July 1954	54.205
Irambi	Kasule	5 July 1954	54.206
Kabajwogole	Butiaba	25 November 1954	54.786
Kaboyo 9	Fort Portal	10 July 1954	54.259
Kabusemere obugenyi ...	Kisomoro	9 July 1954	54.243
Kafunjo k'omunyanja	Kitaleesa	?	54.215 a
Kahara niwe ow'omuyaga	Mbogwe	26 November 1954	54.799
Kanusuke ntahe agabera	Fort Portal	10 July 1954	54.264
Karulu warara	Biseruka	30 November 1954	54.832
Kawairanga	Mbogwe	26 November 1954	54.800
Kawangoro	Kitaleesa	?	54.215 c
Kigambo kyentale	Hoima District	19 April 1949	49.08
Kikukule	Bwanswa	15 May 1954	54.36
Kwa - kwakwa	Butiaba	25 November 1954	54.780
Kyawaka	Butiaba	25 November 1954	54.771 and 54.789

Lamellophone song	Biseruka	30 November 1954	54.838
Lumuva	Nalweyo	14 May 1954	54.26
Mayange	Hoima District	19 April 1949	49.06
Mbogo	Hoima District	19 April 1949	49.07
Mirembe	Kasule	5 July 1954	54.210
Mirembeyo	Bwanswa	15 May 1954	54.33 a
Mucakazi	Butiaba	25 November 1954	54.774
Muchecheba	Hoima District	19 April 1949	49.13
Mugara ncuro	Kasule	5 July 1954	54.213
Mujuma ya mugenyi	Fort Portal	10 July 1954	54.269
Mukonderwa	Butiaba	25 November 1954	54.772 and 54.790
Mukunge mulise	Mbogwe	26 November 1954	54.796
Mukunge Stefano	Mbogwe	26 November 1954	54.798
Mukyala Dera	Butiaba	25 November 1954	54.775
Mulime bajwokole	Kipolopyo	26 November 1954	54.791
Munywani wawe ...	Kisomoro	9 July 1954	54.233
Muramu wange nyandera	Biseruka	30 November 1954	54.836
Mwangwangwa	Butiaba	25 November 1954	54.773
Notes of individual amakondeere	Kasule	5 July 1954	54.208
Nshegu	Hoima District	19 April 1949	49.10
Ntimbo	Hoima District	19 April 1949	49.12
Ntimbo	Fort Portal	10 July 1954	54.262
Ntuha	Nalweyo	14 May 1954	54.29
Nyaikya	Fort Portal	10 July 1954	54.263
Nyamalaka yamala kulya	Biseruka	30 November 1954	54.831
Nyama wa Kagoro	Butiaba	25 November 1954	54.777

APPENDIX II ❧ 241

Nyamulimba	Butiaba	25 November 1954	54.782
Obu nkaba nyikalire	Biseruka	30 November 1954	54.834
Ogw'ennimi	Kasule	5 July 1954	54.212
Okutundira Bugangadzi Abaganda	Bwanswa	15 May 1954	54.35
Omugenyi	Hoima District	19 April 1949	49.17
Orunyege team song	Nalweyo	14 May 1954	54.19
Orunyege team song	Nalweyo	14 May 1954	54.20
Orunyege team song	Nalweyo	14 May 1954	54.21
Orunyege team song	Nalweyo	14 May 1954	54.22 a
Orunyege team song	Nalweyo	14 May 1954	54.22 b
Orunyege team song	Nalweyo	14 May 1954	54.23
Orutuha	Hoima District	19 April 1949	49.16
Paddling song or scene	Butiaba	25 November 1954	54.779
Runyanga	Hoima District	19 April 1949	49.02
Rwamaliba ya babito	Fort Portal	10 July 1954	54.266
Song of the Ekizina kya bacwezi …	Fort Portal	10 July 1954	54.265
Song of the enanga ya bacwezi …	Fort Portal	10 July 1954	54.260
Song sung when the baby is suckled	Butiaba	25 November 1954	54.788
Sonoha	Biseruka	30 November 1954	54.835
Twali baisemu	Fort Portal	10 July 1954	54.271
Untitled trumpet set	Hoima District	19 April 1949	49.11
Wambala byoma	Hoima	26 November 1954	54.794
Yadiri kapoli …	Butiaba	25 November 1954	54.785
Yamukeera Kwirina/ Nkutembere tinkutemba	Biseruka	30 November 1954	54.833
Yodelling and flute	Bwanswa	15 May 1954	54.37
Yodelling and flute (cont.)	Bwanswa	15 May 1954	54.38

242 ❧ APPENDIX II

Peter Cooke Collection

Title	Place	Date	Original catalog code
Abairu/Embogo	Butiti (Tooro)	1964–68	PCUG64–8.26.A3 c
Abalwana	Butiti	1964–68	PCUG64–8.25.B9 b
Abanyina bwangye	Butiti	1964–68	PCUG64–8.25. B10 b
Abanyoro balima	Butiti	1964–68	PCUG64–8.25.B5 c
Bainaga	Butiti	1964–68	PCUG64–8.26. A11 c
Bojo kano kasolo ki	Butiti	1964–68	PCUG64–8.26.A3 b
Buhira Iyagwa	Butiti	1964–68	PCUG64–8.26.A13
Bulyera wa Makondere	Butoti (Bunyoro)	1964–68	PCUG64–8.25.B4 b
Bundiba ntaizire kaliba kagambo	Busiisi (Bunyoro)	1 June 1968	PCUG1964–8.34. A6 a, b
Concororonco	Butiti	1964–68	PCUG64–8.26.A8
Cuncubira	Butiti	1964–68	PCUG64–8.26.A1 a
Ekiro kutiire emisinde	Butiti	1964–68	PCUG64–8.26. A11 a
Embogo	Butiti	1964–68	PCUG64–8.26.A3 c
Enjubu	Kisansya (Bunyoro)	1 June 1968	PCUG1964–8.34. B2 a, b
Enkwanzi	Butiti	1964–68	PCUG64–8.26.A2 b
Ensi yaitu Bunyoro	Butoti	1964–68	PCUG64–8.25.B4 a
Enteole	Butiti	1964–68	PCUG64–8.26.A2 c
Fulera we	Butoti	1964–68	PCUG64–8.25.B6 b
Ganembe	Busiisi	1 June 1968	PCUG1964–8.34. A8
Hara Kitara	Butiti	1964–68	PCUG64–8.26. A12 d
Iwe mutooro hinduka orle	Butoti	1964–68	PCUG64–8.25.B6 a
Jawemi Wanjola	Busiisi	1 June 1968	PCUG1964–8.34. A3
Joje na mukama wangye	Butiti	1964–68	PCUG64–8.25. B10 a

APPENDIX II &• 243

Kabusemere	Butiti	1964–68	PCUG64–8.25.B8 a
Kabuyondo	Butiti	1964–68	PCUG64–8.26. A12 b
Kadingidi	Butoti	1964–68	PCUG64–8.25.B5 a
Kaiba karuga Buleremba	Butoti	1964–68	PCUG64–8.25.B6 c
Kaijongoro	Butiti	1964–68	PCUG64–8.26.A3 a
Kalezi dance	Fort Portal (Tooro)	9 October 1966	PC 7, TRACK A, item 2
Kalinadima	Butiti	1964–68	PCUG64–8.26. A11 b
Kansunsuke	Butiti	1964–68	PCUG64–8.26. A12 a
Kunyooma	Butoti	1964–68	PCUG64–8.25.B7 c
Kawaiselya	Butiti	1964–68	PCUG64–8.26.A9
Kikukure	Butiti	1964–68	PCUG64–8.26.A4
Kiwalanganga	Busiisi	1 June 1968	PCUG1964–8.34. A7 a, b
Kowensama	Butiti	1964–68	PCUG64–8.26.A2 a
Masaza ga Bunyoro	Rusembe (Bunyoro)	2 June 1968	PCUG1964–8.34. B4
Mbandwa Nkuligire	Butiti	1964–68	PCUG64–8.26.A5 a
Mbere mwaruga	Butiti	1964–68	PCUG64–8.26.A10
Mixed dances	Fort Portal (Tooro)	9 October 1966	PC 7, TRACK B, item 4
Musenyo dance song	Kisansya	1 June 1968	PCUG1964–8.34. A11
Musenyo dance song	Kisansya	1 June 1968	PCUG1964–8.34. B1 a, b
Mweyanze	Butiti	1964–68	PCUG64–8.25.B8 b
Ndagira nyowe?	Rusembe	2 June 1968	PCUG1964–8.34. B5
Ngayyaya muhuma wangye	Butoti	1964–68	PCUG64–8.25.B7 b
Ngayaya	Butiti	1964–68	PCUG64–8.26.A5 b
Nimbulya	Kisansya	1 June 1968	PCUG1964–8.34. A11
Nyairungi	Butoti	1964–68	PCUG64–8.25.B5 b

Nyambwire	Busiisi	1 June 1968	PCUG1964–8.34. A1
Nyambwire	Busiisi	1 June 1968	PCUG1964–8.34. A2
Obwelinoba (Ngayaya ...)	Butiti	1964–68	PCUG64–8.26. A12 c
Okwerema	Rusembe	2 June 1968	PCUG1964–8.34. B3
Owaitu ni Bunyoro	Butoti	1964–68	PCUG64–8.25.B4 c
Oyonke Nkusereke	Butiti	1964–68	PCUG64–8.26.A1 b
Tiiti Mutitira	Butoti	1964–68	PCUG64–8.25.B7 a
Twabaraga Mugorobe	Butiti	1964–68	PCUG64–8.26.A6
Waiswa omakisa	Busiisi	1 June 1968	PCUG1964–8.34. A4
Wanjegere	Busiisi	1 June 1968	PCUG1964–8.34. A9
Zali mbogo	Butiti	1964–68	PCUG64–8.25.B9 a
Zali mbogo	Butiti	1964–68	PCUG64–8.26. A11 d

Author's Interviews

In this list, I credit the persons that kindly accepted to be interviewed offering their time, knowledge, and patience to answer my questions, and whom I refer to in this book.

I have listed the interviewees by employing first their name in the local language, or their *mpaako* pet name[1] when they use it as a main name; otherwise I have omitted it. I also list what is usually described as a "religious" name, a name of Arabic or English origin connoting religious affiliation. Every research participant agreed to have an interview with me, to be filmed or recorded, and nobody asked for anonymity. However, I chose to protect the privacy of the dancers trans-performing in mixed cultural groups by using pseudonyms because of the increasing intolerance toward individuals not complying with the more and more conservative gender models. In the case of interviews involving two or three people, I list every interviewee in alphabetical order and, in the case of the interview with a whole ensemble, I just mention the group's name. After the name or pseudonyms of the interviewees, I specify the place, region, and date(s) of the interview(s) and I provide some brief information about them that I collected at the time of our meeting.

The documentation of my fieldwork is preserved in my personal archive, comprising audio and audiovisual recordings as well as photographs. I shared these materials with the research participants that requested it. Part of my audio recordings are also deposited at the MAKWAA (Makerere University Klaus Wachsmann Audiovisual Archive) in Kampala.

Atwoki Ramadam. Fort Portal (Tooro): May 11, 2011. Music teacher at Kibiito Secondary School.

Bakondeere ensemble. Kibiro (Bunyoro): March 8, 2008. Group of *makondeere* end-blown trumpet players revived by the late Francis Kiparu.

Bagwara ensemble. Bugambe (Bunyoro): April 13, 2008. Group of *makondeere* and *ngwara* end-blown trumpet players.

---

1   *Mpaako* pet names are only used in Bunyoro and Tooro in Uganda and are considered the polite way to address other people, while using their given names is held as being rude. Some Banyoro and Batooro use *mpako* as one of their main names.

246 &❧ AUTHOR'S INTERVIEWS

Baguma Clovis. Fort Portal (Tooro): May 9, 2011 and July 3, 2013. Music teacher at Kahunga Bunyonyi Primary School, with experience as a member of the jury in school competitions and performer in cultural groups.

Balikenda Abigael. Hoima (Bunyoro): July 28, 2009. Elderly woman related to the Nyoro royal family.

Banda Paul (together with Nyegenya Vincent). Hoima (Bunyoro): February 2, 2008. Secretary of the semiprofessional ensemble Professional Pars.

Bareba Tina. Karuguuza-Kibaale (Bunyoro): June 16, 2011. Field Officer for Forum for Women in Development (FOWODE) in the Kibaale branch.

Bitamale John (with Sebala Leo and Rwakaikara Benezweri). Kagadi (Bunyoro): June 23, 2010. Presenter of a program about local culture on URDT Community Radio of Kagadi.

Bitamazire Aberi. Muuro (Bunyoro): August 13, 2009 and June 29, 2010 (with Korotirida Matama and Godfrey Kwesiga). Elderly musician and dancer, also known as *Ngoma Munana* ("eight drums").

Iraka Japheth. Masindi (Bunyoro): June 28, 2010. Son of a *kidongo* arched harp player, has been teaching for several years in primary schools and is now principal.

Deosi. Hoima (Bunyoro): June 12, 2011. Trans-perfoming dancer in his 40s.

Issa Sunday (with Misinguzi George). Kagadi (Bunyoro): June 14, 2011. Social worker in Bunyoro by the time of my fieldwork, in which he collaborated as my research assistant.

Kabutuku Stephen. Mwibaale (Tooro): September 5, 2011 and August 30, 2018. Music teacher and vice-principal at Kasisi Primary School, near Fort Portal; studied Music Education from Kaberega Teachers' College of Masindi.

Kabuzi Majiiri (with Dorothy Nyakato). Fort Portal (Tooro): August 29, 2011. Elderly woman who used to play the *nanga* zither.

Kabyanga Joshwa (with Marrion Nyakato). Masindi (Bunyoro): August 22, 2018. Trained at Teachers' College in Kyambogo, followed by teaching at the Kabarega Teachers' College in Masindi and training the school festival's adjudicators.

Kagaba Sebastiano. Kacwamba (Tooro): May 11, 2011. Elderly dancer who for many years has worked as instructor in schools and participated in semiprofessional ensembles, like the Ngabu za Tooro.

Kahwa Dorothy. Muuro (Bunyoro): August 13, 2009. Elderly woman who has knowledge of a vast repertoire of traditional songs.

Kafre. Hoima (Bunyoro): August 20, 2018. Dancer in his 40s who used to trans-perform; nowadays he mainly trains pupils in schools and dancers in his cultural group.

Kalu. Hoima (Bunyoro): August 19, 2018. Young dancer who trans-perfoms.

AUTHOR'S INTERVIEWS   ❧   247

Kasaija Mary. Fort Portal (Tooro): August 3, 2018. Elderly woman member of Mothers' Union, in which she performed the men's part in *runyege*.

Katusime Caroline. Hoima (Bunyoro): June 10, 2011. Music teacher at Hoima Primary School and person responsible for the participation of the school in the national festival.

Kinyoro Gerrison. Kiguma (Tooro): September 10, 2010; May 11, 2011; July 29, 2012; August 31, 2018. Retired music teacher and eminent expert of Tooro tradition and performing arts, studied Education at the Kanon Apolo Teachers' College near Fort Portal and Music at the Kabarega Teachers' College in Masindi.

Korotirida Matama. Muuro (Bunyoro): June 29, 2010 (with Bitamazire Aberi and Kwesiga Godfrey). Elderly woman and *mbandwa* medium.

Kyomukama Catering and Creative Association (KCCA) members. Kyomukama (Bunyoro): July 2, 2011. Women's association founded in 2011 to raise money by selling handicrafts, catering services, and through the attached ensemble's performances.

Kwesiga Godfrey. Muuro (Bunyoro): June 29, 2010 (with Bitamazire Aberi and Korotirida Matama). Relative of Korotirida Matama, whom she was training to become a *mbandwa* medium.

Magezi Christopher. Hoima (Bunyoro): March 1, 2008; June 29, 2011; August 19, 2018. Elderly musician, dancer, and music instrument builder. He also cooperates as instructor with several schools and has recently revived a *bakondeere* group.

Majara junior. Masindi (Bunyoro): August 12, 2009. Primary School music teacher. Son of Emanuel B. Majara, musician and music teacher who also participated in Peter Cooke's research in the 1960s.

Makidadi Muhammad. Mparo (Bunyoro): February 24, 2008. Elderly musician and dancer, director of the Bunyoro Foundation Actors Group.

Maseero Dorothy. Rubona (Tooro): April 14, 2011. Elderly Huma woman.

Masindi Drama Saving Scheme (MASDRASS) members. Masindi (Bunyoro): August 23, 2018. Women's association founded to share the members' savings and cooperting with AIDS Support Organization (TASO) connected with the Masindi Hospital, in northern Bunyoro.

Mbabi-Katana Solomon. Buhimba (Bunyoro): June 30, 2011. Late musicologist and expert of Nyoro culture. He taught in Primary Schools, Teachers' Colleges and Makerere University. His numerous publications dealt mainly with music education and East African songs.

Misinguzi George. Kagadi (Bunyoro): June 9, 2011 and June 14, 2011 (with Issa Sunday). Music teacher at Kagadi Modern Primary School.

248 &❧ AUTHOR'S INTERVIEWS

Mugabo Stephen. Fort Portal (Tooro): May 11, 2011; Kampala: March 16, 2012; Fort Portal: August 31, 2018. Dancer, actor, and singer in the semi-professional ensemble Ngabu za Tooro; also worked as my research assistant in Tooro.

Mugisa Daisy. Bujumbura East Village (Bunyoro): March 2, 2008. Director of the semiprofessional ensemble St. Joseph Kolping Troupe.

Muhuruzi George. Hoima (Bunyoro): February 27, 2008 and March 25, 2008. *Mukuru w'ebikwato* (custodian of the Nyoro royal regalia) and great expert of Nyoro traditions.

Namara, Makleen. Fort Portal (Tooro): September 1, 2018. Teenager who learned to dance the men's part when she was 10 and has performed it both at the school festival and in a cultural group.

Nsamba Yolamu. Hoima (Bunyoro): February 25, 2008 and July 31, 2009. Local historian, expert of Nyoro culture, and personal secretary of the Nyoro king.

Nyakairu Kenneth. Fort Portal (Tooro): July 22, 2010. Elderly man expert of Tooro culture, usually hired as master of ceremony in traditional weddings.

Nyakato Dorothy (with Kabuzi Majiiri). Fort Portal (Tooro): August 29, 2011. Elderly woman known for her knowledge about Tooro culture and language.

Nyakato Marrion. Kiryandongo (Bunyoro), lesson to school festival's adjudicators: June 25, 2011; Masindi (Bunyoro): August 22, 2018 (with Joshua with Kabyanga). Music teacher and principal at Army Day Primary School in Masindi; music teacher at Kabarega Teachers' College in Masindi and instructor of school festival's adjudicators.

Nyegenya Vincent. Hoima (Bunyoro): February 2, 2008 (with Banda Paul); June 22, 2011; August 18, 2018. Musician and dancer who studied MDD at Makerere University. He has cooperated as instructor with schools and directed the semiprofessional ensemble Professional Pars.

Nyin'omukama wo Bunyoro (Nyoro Queen mother). Bucunga (Bunyoro): March 26, 2008. Late mother of the current Nyoro king of Solomon Gafabusa Iguru.

Nyorano Ashraf Mugenyi. Hoima (Bunyoro): March 3, 2008. Elderly man expert of Nyoro royal traditions.

Ruru. Hoima (Bunyoro): June 13, 2011; August 20, 2018. Dancer and singer who had a career in pop music and used to trans-perform.

Rwakaikara Benezweri (with Bitamale John and Sebala Leo). Kagadi (Bunyoro): June 23, 2010. Presenter of a program about local culture on URDT Community Radio of Kagadi.

Sebala Leo (with Bitamale John and Rwakaikara Benezweri). Kagadi (Bunyoro): June 23, 2010. Former schoolteacher and presenter of a program about local culture on URDT Community Radio of Kagadi.

Sabiiti Jane (or Janiroda). Duhaga Rusembe (Bunyoro): August 1, 2009. Late primary schoolteacher. Her expertise in traditional song, which she learned in the family environment, was unparalleled.

Tibamanya Jane. Masindi (Bunyoro): June 27, 2010. Retired primary school-teacher. Great expert of traditional songs that she learned during her childhood in her home area near Hoima.

Tida. Masindi (Bunyoro): August 22, 2018. Man in his 40s currently trans-performing in a cultural group.

Tual. Butiiti (Tooro): August 30, 2018. Young man who trans-performs.

References

Achieng' Akuno, Emily. 2009. "Music Education: Policy Development and Advocacy in East Africa." Paper presented at the 3rd IMC World Forum on Music. Tunis, October 17–22.

Agawu, Kofi. 2003. *Representing African Music*. New York and London: Routledge.

Ahmed, Sara. 2006. *Queer Phenomenology. Orientations, Objects, Others*. Durham and London: Duke University Press.

Amadiume, Ifi. 1987. *Male Daughters, Female Husbands. Gender and Sex in an African Society*. London and New Jersey: Zed Books.

———. 1997. *Re-inventing Africa: Matriarchy, Religion, and Culture*. London and New York: Zed Books.

Amselle, Jean-Loup. 1990. *Logiques métisses. Anthropologie de l'identité en Afrique et ailleurs*. Paris: Payot.

Amselle, Jean-Loup, and Elikia M'Bokolo. 1985. *Au cœur de l'ethnie. Ethnies, tribalisme et état en Afrique*. Paris: La Découverte.

Anderson, Lois A. 1967. "The African Xylophone." *African Arts/Arts d'Afrique* 1: 46–79.

Arom, Simha. 1985. *Polyphonies et polyrythmies instrumentales d'Afrique centrale. Structure et méthodologie*. Paris: CNRS–SELAF.

Asaasira, Anita Desire. 2015. "'Performing Uganda': Ndere Troupe's Representation of a Ugandan Identity." In *African Musics in Context. Institutions, Culture, Identity*, edited by Thomas Solomon, 179–209. Kampala: Fountain.

Asiimwe, Agnes, and Grace F. Ibanda, 2008. *Dances of Uganda*. Kampala: Tourguide.

Askew, Kelly M. 2002. *Performing the Nation. Swahili Music and Cultural Politics in Tanzania*. Chicago and London: University of Chicago Press.

Bantebya Kyomuhendo, Grace, and Marjorie K. McIntosh. 2006. *Women, Work, and Domestic Virtue in Africa 1900–2003*. Oxford, Athens, and Kampala: Currey, Ohio University Press, and Fountain.

Baral, Anna. 2018. *Bad Guys, Good Life. An Ethnography of Morality and Change in Kisekka Market (Kampala, Uganda)*. Uppsala: Uppsala University.

Barz, Gregory. 2004. *Music in East Africa: Experiencing Music, Expressing Culture*. Oxford: Oxford University Press.

———. 2006. *Singing for Life. HIV/AIDS and Music in Uganda*. New York: Routledge.

Beattie, John H. 1957. "Nyoro Kinship." Africa 27 (4): 317–340.

———. 1958. "Nyoro Marriage and Affinity." *Africa* 28 (1): 1–22

———. 1960. *Bunyoro: An African Kingdom*. New York: Holt, Rinehart, and Wilson.

———. 1962. "Twin Ceremonies in Bunyoro." *The Journal of the Royal Anthropological Institute of Great Britain and Ireland* 92: 1–12.

———. 1969. "Spirit Mediumship in Bunyoro." In *Spirit Mediumship and Society in Africa*, edited by John Middleton and John Beattie, 159–170. London: Routledge.

———. 1971. *The Nyoro State*. London: Oxford University Press.

———. 1977. "Proverbs in Context: Some Examples from Bunyoro." In *Essays for a Humanist. An Offering to Klaus Wachsmann*, edited by the FPW Festschrift Committee, 83–94. New York: The Town House Press.

Berger, Iris. 1973. *The Kubandwa Religious Complex in Interlacustine East Africa: An Historical Study c. 1500–1900*. Ph.D. diss., University of Wisconsin, Madison.

———. 1981. *Religion and Resistance. East African Kingdoms in the Precolonial Period*. Tervuren: Musée Royal de l'Afrique Centrale.

———. 1995. "Fertility as Power. Spirit Mediums, Priestesses and the Precolonial State in Interlacustrine East Africa." In *Revealing Prophets*, edited by David M. Anderson and Douglas H. Johnson, 65–82. London, Nairobi, Kampala, and Athens: Currey, E.A.E.P., Fountain, and Ohio University Press.

———. 2014. "African Women's Movements in the Twentieth Century: A Hidden History." *African Studies Review* 57 (3): 1–19.

Bhabha, Homi K. 1994. *The Location of Culture*. London and New York: Routledge.

Blacking, John. 1967. *Venda Children's Songs*. Johannesburg: Witwatersrand University Press.

———. 1985. "Movement, Dance, Music and the Venda Girls' Initiation." In *Society and the Dance. The Social Anthropology of Process and Performance*, edited by Paul Spencer: 64–91. Cambridge: Cambridge University Press.

Blanco Borelli, Michelle. 2016. *She Is Cuba: A Genealogy of the Mulata Body*. Oxford and New York: Oxford University Press.

Bompani, Barbara, and S. Terreni Brown. 2015. "A 'Religious Revolution'? Print Media, Sexuality, and Religious Discourse in Uganda." *Journal of Eastern African Studies* 9 (1): 110–126.

Bourdieu, Pierre. 1977. *Outline of a Theory of Practice*. Cambridge and New York: Cambridge University Press.

Brown, Danielle. 2020. "An Open Letter on Racism in Music Studies." June 12. https://www.mypeopletellstories.com/blog/open-letter. Accessed October 10, 2020.

Buchanan, Carol A. 1973. *The Kitara Complex: The Historical Tradition of Western Uganda to the 16th Century.* Ph.D. diss., Indiana University, Bloomington.

Bukaayi, Lillian. 2009. "Gender Power Relations in Soga Marriage Songs." In *Performing Change: Identity, Ownership and Tradition in Ugandan Oral Culture,* edited by Dominica Dipio, Lene Johannessen, and Stuart Sillars, 143–159. Oslo: Novus Press.

Butler, Judith. 1988. "Performative Acts and Gender Construction. An Essay in Phenomenology and Feminist Theory." *Theatre Journal* 40 (4): 519–531.

———. 1990. *Gender Trouble. Feminism and the Subversion of Identity.* New York and London: Routledge.

Casati, Gaetano. 1891. *Dieci anni in Equatoria e ritorno con Emin Pascia.* Milan: Fratelli Dumolard.

Castaldi, Francesca. 2006. *Choreographies of African Identities. Négritude, Dance, and the National Ballet of Senegal.* Urbana and Chicago: University of Illinois Press.

Chávez, Xóchitl C. 2009. "La Feria de Enero. Rethinking Gender in a Ritual Festival." In *Dancing across Borders. Danzas y Bailes Mexicanos,* edited by Olga Nájer-Ramírez, Norma E. Cantú, and Brenda M. Romero, 48–65. Urbana and Chicago: University of Illinois Press.

Chrétien, Jean-Paul. 1985. "L'Empire des Bachwezi. La construction d'un imaginaire géopolitique." *Annales ESC* 6: 1335–1377.

———. 2000. *L'Afrique des Grands Lacs.* Paris: Aubier.

Chrysagis, Evangelos and Panas Karapampas (eds.). 2017. *Collaborative Intimacies in Music and Dance. Anthropologies of Sound and Movement.* New York and Oxford: Berghahn.

Cimardi, Linda. 2008. *La musica reale del Bunyoro.* M.A. thesis, University of Bologna, Bologna.

———. 2013. *Conservare la cultura, creare una storia. Tradizione e genere nella musica di villaggio dei Banyoro e dei Batooro dell'Uganda.* Ph.D. diss., University of Bologna, Bologna.

———. 2015. "From 'Tribes' to 'Regions.' Ethnicity and Musical Identity in Western Uganda." *Perifèria - Revista de recerca i formació en antropologia* 20 (2): 44–59.

———. 2017a. "'Reviving' Tradition through Digital Technologies. Traditional Repertoires and Neo-Traditional Songs in Western Uganda." *Philomusica on-line.* 16 (1): 13–42.

254 ❧ REFERENCES

———. 2017b. "The Construction of Ethnic Identity Through Music in Uganda." In *Making Music, Making Society,* edited by Martí Josep and Sara Revilla Gútiez, 95–122. Cambridge: Cambridge Scholar Publishing.

———. 2019. "Teaching and Performing 'Traditional Folksongs' in Western Uganda Schools." In *Music Traditions, Change and Creativity in Africa. Past and Present,* edited by Giorgio Adamo and Alessandro Cosentino, 111–138. Rome: NeoClassica.

Connell, R(aewyn). W. 2005. *Masculinities.* Second revised edition. Cambridge: Polity Press.

Cooke, Peter R. (ed.). 1966. *Twenty-Four Songs of Uganda.* Kampala: National Institute of Education.

Cooke, Peter R. 1970. "Ganda Xylophone Music: Another Approach." *African Music* 4: 62–80.

———. 1971. "*Ludaya.* A Traverse Flute from Eastern Uganda." *Yearbook of the International Folk Music Council* 3: 79–90.

———. 1995. "Orchestral Melo-Rhythm in Southern Uganda." In *For Gerhard Kubik. Festschrift on the Occasion of his 60th Birthday,* edited by August Schmidhofer and Dietrich Schuller: 147–160. Frankfurt am Main: Lang.

———. 1996. "Music in a Ugandan Court." *Early Music From Around the World* 24: 439–452.

———. 2001. "Uganda." In *The New Grove Dictionary of Music and Musicians,* vol. 26 (revised edition), edited by Stanley Sadie, 34–43. London: Macmillan.

Cooke, Peter R., and Okaka O. Dokotum. 2000. "*Ngoma* Competitions in Northern Uganda." In *Mashindano! Competitive Music Performance in East Africa,* edited by Frank Gunderson and Gregory Barz, 271–278. Dar es Salaam: Mkuki na Nyota.

Cooke, Peter R., and Samuel Kasule. 1999. "The Musical Scene in Uganda. Views from Without and Within." *African Music* 7: 6–21.

Crenshaw, Kimberle. 1989. "Demarginalizing the Intersection of Race and Sex: A Black Feminist Critique of Antidiscrimination Doctrine, Feminist Theory and Antiracist Politics." *University of Chicago Legal Forum* 1: 139–167.

Cunningham, James F. 1905. *Uganda and Its People: Notes on the Protectorate of Uganda, Especially the Anthropology and Ethnology of Its Indigenous Races.* London and Vylibury: Hazell, Watson, and Viney.

D'Hertefelt, Marcel, and André Coupez. 1964. *La royauté sacrée de l'ancien Rwanda.* Tervuren: Annales du Musée Royal de l'Afrique Centrale.

Davis, Mary B. 1938. *A Lunyoro-Lunyankole-English and English-Lunyoro-Lunyankole Dictionary.* Kampala: Uganda Book Shop.

———. 1941. "Lunyoro Proverbs." *Uganda Journal* 9: 115–132.

Decker, Alicia C. 2014. *In Idi Amin's Shadow. Women, Gender and Militarism in Uganda*. Athens: Ohio University Press.

De Lauretis, Teresa. 1987. *Technologies of Gender. Essays on Theory, Film, and Fiction*. Bloomington and Indianapolis: Indiana University Press.

Desmond, Jane C. 1997. "Embodying Difference: Issues in Dance and Cultural Studies." In *Meaning in Motion. New Cultural Studies of Dance*, edited by Jane C. Desmond, 29–54. Durham and London: Duke University Press.

———. 1999. "Engendering Dance: Feminist Inquiry and Dance Research." In *Researching Dance*, edited by Sondra Horton Fraleigh and Penelope Hanstein, 309–333. London: Dance Books.

Dipio, Dominica. 2009. "Reconstructing Traditional Heroism in Contemporary Contexts: The Case of Princess Koogere Atwooki of Tooro." In *Performing Change: Identity, Ownership and Tradition in Ugandan Oral Culture*, edited by Dominica Dipio, Lene Johannessen, and Stuart Sillars, 160–179. Oslo: Novus Press.

Doornbos, Martin S. 1970. "Kumanyama and Rwenzururu: Two Responses to Ethnic Inequality." In *Protest and Power in Black Africa*, edited by Robert I. Rotberg and Ali A. Mazrui, 1088–1136. New York: Oxford University Press.

Doubleday, Veronica. 2008. "Sounds of Power: An Overview of Musical Instruments and Gender." *Ethnomusicology Forum* 17 (1): 3–39.

Downing, Sonja Lynn. 2019. *Gamelan Girls: Gender, Childhood, and Politics in Balinese Music Ensembles*. Urbana: University of Illinois Press.

Doyle, Shane. 2006. *Crisis and Decline in Bunyoro. Population and Environment in Western Uganda 1860–1955*. London: The British Institute in Eastern Africa.

———. 2007. "The Cwezi-Kubandwa Debate: Gender, Hegemony and Precolonial Religion in Bunyoro, Western Uganda." *Africa* 77: 559–581.

Dunbar, Archibald R. 1965. *A History of Bunyoro-Kitara*. Nairobi: Oxford University Press.

Elam, Yitzchak. 1973. *The Social and Sexual Roles of Hima Women. A Study of Nomadic Cattle Breeders in Nyabushozi County, Ankole, Uganda*. Manchester: Manchester University Press.

Epprecht, Marc. 2008. *Heterosexual Africa? The History of an Idea from the Age of Exploration to the Age of AIDS*. Athens: Ohio University Press.

Facci, Serena. 1986/1987. "La musica dei Wanande dello Zaire." *Culture musicali* 10/11: 103–140.

———. 1996. "I Nande e la loro musica." In *Etnografia Nande* III, *Musiche danze, rituali*, edited by Carlo Buffa, Serena Facci, Cecilia Pennacini, and Francesco Remotti, 11–57. Torino: Il Segnalibro.

———. 1998. "*Akazehe* del Burundi: saluti a incastro polifonico e cerimonialità femminile." In *Polifonie*, edited by Maurizio Agamennone: 123–161. Rome: Bulzoni. English edition: 2020. "The *Akazehe* of Burundi: Polyphonic Interlocking Greetings and the Female Ceremonial." Translated by Alessandra Ciucci. *Ethnomusicology Translations* 10: 1–37.

———. 2003. "La rappresentazione del rapporto uomo-donna in alcune musiche africane." In *Enciclopedia della musica* vol. 3, edited by Jean-Jacques Nattiez, 786–810. Turin: Einaudi.

———. 2007. "Dinamiche intorno alla segretezza: tre casi nella musica dei Bakonzo-Banande." *Molimo* 3: 89–103.

———. 2009. "Dances across the Boundaries: Banande and Bakonzo." *Journal of Eastern African Studies* 3: 350–366.

Facci, Serena and Cecilia Pennacini. 2021. "Donne in primo piano. Danze e canti femminili dall'Africa dei Grandi Laghi." In *Sounding Frames: Itinerari di musicologia visuale. Scritti in onore di Giorgio Adamo,* edited by Alessandro Cosentino, Raffaele Di Mauro, and Giuseppe Giordano, 227–245. Palermo: Edizioni Museo Pasqualino.

Fallers, Lloyd A. 1961. "Ideology and Culture in Uganda Nationalism." *American Anthropologist* 63: 677–686.

Fisher, Ruth. 1904. *On the Borders of the Pigmy Land*. London: Marshall.

———. 1911. *Twilight Tales of the Black Baganda*. London: Marshall.

Franco, Susanne. 2015. "Reenacting Heritage at Bomas of Kenya: Dancing the Postcolony." *Dance Research Journal* 47 (2): 4–22.

Fürniss, Susanne. 1991. "La technique du jodel chez les pygmées Aka (Centrafrique)." *Cahiers de musiques traditionnelles* 4: 167–187.

Gafabusa Hairora, Patrick R. 2003. *Cultural Identity: Kinyoro Oral Poetry as an Exposition of Values and View Points*. M.A. thesis, Makerere University, Kampala.

García Canclini, Néstor (ed.). 2005. *Hybrid Cultures: Strategies for Entering and Leaving Modernity*. Minneapolis: University of Minnesota Press.

Gardoncini, Sara. 2010. "Il regno Rwenzururu. I Bakonzo nella modernità." *Africa* 65 (1): 330–350.

Gilman, Lisa. 2009. *The Dance of Politics. Gender, Performance and Democratization in Malawi*. Philadelphia: Temple University Press.

———. 2017. "The Politics of Cultural Promotion: The Umthetho Festival of Malawi's Northern Ngoni." In *Public Performances. Studies in the Carnivalesque and Ritualesque,* edited by Jack Santino, 164–187. Logan: Utah State University Press.

Gilmore, David D. 1990. *Manhood in the Making. Cultural Concepts of Masculinity*. New Haven and London: Yale University Press.

Grau, Andrée. 1993. "John Blacking and the Development of Dance Anthropology in the United Kingdom." *Dance Resource Journal* 25: 21–31.

Gunderson, Frank, and Gregory Barz (eds.). 2000. *Mashindano! Competitive Music Performance in East Africa*. Dar es Salaam: Mkuki na Nyota.

Gusman, Alessandro, and Lia Viola. 2014. "Quando un fatto sociale diventa 'problema sociale.' Un'analisi dell'Anti-Homosexuality Act ugandese tra religioni e *gender studies*." *DADA* 4 (2): 7–28.

Halberstam, Judith. 1998. *Female Masculinity*. Durham and London: Duke University Press.

Han, Enze, and Joseph O'Mahoney. 2014. "British Colonialism and the Criminalization of Homosexuality." *Cambridge Review of International Affairs* 27 (2): 268–288.

Hanna, Judith L. 1965. "Africa's New Traditional Dance." *Ethnomusicology* 9: 13–21.

———. 1973. "African Dance: The Continuity of Change." *Yearbook of the International Folk Music Council* 5: 165–174.

———. 1979. "Toward a Cross-Cultural Conceptualization of Dance and Some Correlate Considerations." In *The Performing Arts. Music and Dance*, edited by John Blacking and Joann W. Kealiinohomoku, 17–45. Le Hague, Paris, and New York: Mouton Press.

———. 1988. *Dance, Sex and Gender: Signs of Identity, Dominance, Defiance, and Desire*. Chicago and London: University of Chicago Press.

Hanna, Judith L., and William J. Hanna. 1968. "Heart Beat of Uganda." *African Arts* 1: 42–45, 85.

Hanson, Holly. 1992. "Queen Mothers and Good Government in Buganda: The Loss of Women's Political Power in Nineteenth-Century East Africa." In *African Encounters with Domesticity*, edited by Karen Tranberg Hansen, 219–236. New Brunswick: Rutgers University Press.

Hood, Made Mantle. 2020. "Separating Intertwined Traditions into Balinese Music and Dance." *The World of Music* 9 (2): 109–129.

Hutchinson, Sydney. 2009. "The Ballet Folklórico de México and the Construction of the Mexican Nation through Dance." In *Dancing Across Borders. Danzas y Bailes mexicanos*, edited by Olga Nájer-Ramírez, Norma E. Cantú, and Brenda M. Romero, 206–225. Urbana and Chicago: University of Illinois Press.

———. 2016. *Tigers of a Different Stripe. Performing Gender in Dominican Music*. Chicago and London: University of Chicago Press.

Ingham, Kenneth. 1975. *The Kingdom of Toro in Uganda*. London: Methuen Young Books.

Johannessen, Cathrine. 2006. "Kingship in Uganda. The Role of the Buganda Kingdom in Ugandan Politics." *CMI Working Paper* 8, Chr. Michelsen Institute: 1–14.

K. W. 1937. "The Procedure in Accession to the Throne of a Nominated King in the Kingdom of Bunyoro-Kitara." *Uganda Journal* 4: 289–299.

Kafumbe, Damascus. 2018. *Tuning the Kingdom. Kawuugulu Musical Performance, Politics, and Storytelling in Buganda.* Rochester, NY: University of Rochester Press.

Kahunde, Samuel. 2012a. "'Our Royal Music Does Not Fade': An Exploration of the Revival and Significance of the Royal Music and Dance of Bunyoro-Kitara, Uganda." Ph.D. diss., University of Sheffield, Sheffield.

———. 2012b. "Repatriating Archival Sound Recordings to Revive Traditions: The Role of the Klaus Wachsmann Recordings in the Revival of the Royal Music of Bunyoro-Kitara, Uganda." *Ethnomusicology Forum* 21: 197–219.

Kaji, Shigeki. 2009. "Tone and Syntax in Rutooro, A Toneless Bantu Language of Western Uganda." *Language Science* 31: 239–247.

———. 2018. "From Nyoro to Tooro: Historical and Phonetic Accounts of Tone Merger." In *Tonal Change and Neutralization,* edited by Haruo Kabuzono and Mikio Giriko, 330–349. Berlin and Boston: De Gruyter.

Kakoma, George W. 1970. "Les traditions musicales de l'Afrique orientale." In *La musique africaine. Réunion de Yaoundé organisée par l'UNESCO:* 75–86. Paris: La Revue musicale.

Kaoma, Kapya. 2009. *Globalizing the Culture Wars: US Conservatives, African Churches, and Homophobia.* Somerville: Political Research Associates.

Karlstöm, Mikael. 1999. *The Cultural Kingdom in Uganda: Popular Royalism and the Restoration of the Buganda Kingship.* Ph.D. diss., University of Chicago, Chicago.

Khamalwa, Wotsuna. 2012. "The Role of Music, Dance and Drama in *Imbalu* Ritual." In *Ethnomusicology in East Africa. Perspectives from Uganda and Beyond,* edited by Sylvia Nanyonga-Tamusuza and Thomas Solomon, 63–70. Kampala: Fountain.

Kibirige, Ronald. 2020. *Dancing Reconciliation and Re/integration: Lamokowang and Dance-Musicking in the Oguda-Alel Post-War Communities of Northern Uganda.* Ph.D. diss., Trondheim, NTNU.

Kiguli, Juliet. 2001. *Gender, Ebyaffe and Power Relations in the Buganda Kingdom: A Study of Cultural Revivalism.* Ph.D. diss., University of Cologne, Cologne.

Kiiru, Kahithe. 2017. "National Competitive Festivals: Formatting Dance Products and Forging Identities in Contemporary Kenya." *Cultural Analysis* 5 (2): 1–28.

———. 2019. "Staging Authenticity: The Limits of Creativity in a National Dance Company." *Jahazi* 8 (1): 45–50.

Kisliuk, Michelle. 2001. *Seize the Dance. BaAka Musical Life and the Ethnography of Performance.* Oxford and New York: Oxford University Press.

Koskoff, Ellen. 2014. *A Feminist Ethnomusicology. Writings on Music and Gender.* Urbana, Chicago, and Springfield: University of Illinois Press.

Kubik, Gerhard. 1960. "The Structure of Kiganda Xylophone Music." *African Music* 2: 6–30.

———. 1962. "The *Endara* Xylophone of Bukonjo." *African Music* 3: 43–48.

———. 1964. "Xylophone Playing in Southern Uganda." *The Journal of the Royal Anthropological Institute* 94: 138–159.

———. 1968. "Music in Uganda. A Brief Report." *African Music* 4 (2): 59–62.

———. 1969. "Composition Techniques in Kiganda Xylophone Music." *African Music* 4 (3): 22–72.

———. 1985. "African Tone-Systems. A Reassessment." *Yearbook for Traditional Music* 17: 31–63.

———. 1987. *Malawian Music. A Framework for Analysis.* Zomba: Centre for Social Research, University of Malawi.

———. 1992. "*Embaire* Xylophone Music of Samusiri Babalanda (Uganda 1968)." *The World of Music* 24: 57–84.

———. 1999. *Africa and the Blues.* Jackson: University Press of Mississippi.

———. 2007. "Nuove ricerche sul campo nel regno di Buganda, 2000 e 2002. Una retrospettiva storica, antropologico-culturale e etnomusicologica." In *Incontri di etnomusicologia*, edited by Giovanni Giuriati, 81–148. Rome: Accademia Nazionale di Santa Cecilia.

———. 2010. *Theory of African Music I.* Chicago: University of Chicago Press.

Kulick, Don, and Margaret Willson (eds.). 1995. *Taboo. Sex, Identity and Erotic Subjectivity in Anthropological Fieldwork.* London: Routledge.

Kwabena Nketia, Joseph H. 1974. *The Music of Africa.* New York and London: Norton.

Lévi-Strauss, Claude. 1969. *Les structures élémentaires de la parenté.* Paris: PUF.

Lloyd, Albert B. 1907. *Uganda to Karthoum. Life and Adventure on the Upper Nile.* London: Fisher Unwin.

Lutwama-Rukundo, Evelyn. 2008. "Dancing to Change. Gender in the Popular Music of Kampala, Uganda." *Glocal Times. The Communication for Development Journal* 11. https://ojs.mau.se/index.php/glocaltimes/article/view/170. Accessed November 7, 2022.

260 &❧ REFERENCES

Mabingo, Alfdaniels. 2017. "Pedagogies of Adaptation: Teachers' Reflections on Teaching Traditional Ugandan Dances in Urban Schools in Kampala, Uganda." In *The Palgrave Handbook of Global Arts*, edited by Georgina Barton and Margaret Baguley, 285–304. London: Palgrave Macmillan.

———. 2020a. "Music as a Pedagogic Tool and Co-Teacher in African Dances: Dissecting the Reflections and Practices of Teachers of Cultural Heritage Dances in Uganda." *Research Studies in Music Education* 42 (2): 231–247.

———. 2020b. *Ubuntu as Dance Pedagogy in Uganda. Individuality, Community, and Inclusion in Teaching and Learning of Indigenous Dances.* Singapore: Palgrave Pivot.

Majefe, Archie. 1991. *Kingdoms of the Great Lakes Region.* Kampala: Fountain.

Makwa, Dominic. 2012. "From 'Entering' and 'Hatching' to Being 'Clothed' into Manhood: Integration of Music, Dance in *Imbalu* Circumcision Rituals among the Bagisu (Eastern Uganda)." In *Ethnomusicology in East Africa. Perspectives from Uganda and Beyond*, edited by Sylvia Nanyonga-Tamusuza and Thomas Solomon, 71–92. Kampala: Fountain.

Mair, Lucy. 1977. *African Kingdoms.* Oxford: Oxford University Press.

Mauss, Marcel. 1973. "Techniques of the Body." *Economy and Society* 2 (1): 70–88.

Mazrui, Ali. A. 1970. "Privilege and Protest as Integrative Factors: The Case of Buganda's Status in Uganda." In *Protest and Power in Black Africa*, edited by Robert I. Rotberg and Ali A. Mazrui, 1072–1087. New York: Oxford University Press.

Mbabazi, Pamela. 2003. *Kikibi Dance of the Bakonzo.* M.A. thesis, Makerere University, Kampala.

Mbabi-Katana, Solomon. 1965. *Songs of East Africa* I. London: Macmillan.

———. 1966. *An Introduction to East African Music for Schools.* Kampala: Milton Obote Foundation.

———. 1973. *Primary School Music, Course I.* Kampala: Uganda Publishing House.

———. 1982. *The History of Amakondere (Royal Trumpet Set) of the Interlacustrine States of East Africa.* Kampala: Makerere University Press.

———. 1984 "The Use of Measured Rhythm to Communicate Messages among Banyoro and Baganda in Uganda." *Selected Reports in Ethnomusicology* V. Los Angeles: University of California: 339–356.

———. 1987. *African Class Music, Course II.* Kampala: Makerere University.

———. 2002. *African Music for Schools, I.* Kampala: Fountain.

Macpherson, Margaret. 1999. "Makerere: The Place of Early Sunrise." In *Uganda: The Cultural Landscape*, edited by Eckhard Breitinger, 23–36. Bayreuth and Kampala: Bayreuth African Studies and Fountain Publishers.

McClain Opiyo, Lindsay. 2015. "Music as Education, Voice, Memory, and Healing: Community Views on the Roles of Music in Conflict Transformation in Northern Uganda." *African Conflict and Peacebuilding Review* 5 (1): 41–65.

McConnell, Bonnie B. 2019. *Music, Health, and Power: Singing the Unsayable in The Gambia*. New York: Routledge.

McMahon, Felicia. 2007. *Not Just Child's Play. Emerging Tradition and the Lost Boys of Sudan*. Jackson: University of Mississippi.

Mendoza, Zoila S. 2008. *Creating Our Own: Folklore, Performance, and Identity in Cuzco, Peru*. Durham and London: Duke University Press.

Ministry of Education and Sports. 2011. "Important Highlights in Each Class." In *Circular no. 03/2011*, Kampala: Ministry of Education and Sports: 4–11.

Miirima, Henry F. (ed.). 2002. *Runyoro-Rutooro Orthography*. Kampala: New Vision.

Morris, Henry F. 1964. *The Heroic Recitations of the Bahima of Ankole*. Oxford: Oxford University Press.

Mudimbe, V.-Y. 1988. *The Invention of Africa*. Bloomington, Indianapolis, and London: Indiana University Press and John Currey.

Mugenyi, Mary R. 1998. "Towards the Empowerment of Women: A Critique of NRM Policies and Programmes." In *Developing Uganda*, edited by Holger Bernt Hansen and Micheal Twaddle: 133–144. Oxford, Kampala, Athens, and Nairobi: Currey, Fountain, Ohio University Press, and E.A.E.P.

Mukasa-Balikuddembe, Joseph. 1973. *The Indigenous Elements of Theatre in Bunyoro and Tooro*. M.A. thesis, University of Dar es Salaam, Dar es Salaam.

Murray, Stephen O., and Will Roscoe. 1998. *Boy-Wives and Female Husbands. Studies in African Homosexuality*. New York: Palgrave.

Musisi, Nakanyike B. 1992. "Colonial and Missionary Education: Women and Domesticity in Uganda." In *African Encounters with Domesticity*, edited by Karen Tranberg Hansen, 172–194. New Brunswick: Rutgers University Press.

———. 2002. "The Politics of Perception as Politics? Colonial and Missionary Representations of Baganda Women, 1900–1945." In *Women in African Colonial Histories*, edited by Jean Allman, Susan Gerger, and Nakanyike B. Musisi, 95–115. Bloomington: Indiana University Press.

Muyanda-Mutebi, Peter. 1996. "An Analysis of Primary Curriculum in Uganda Including a Framework for a Primary Education Curriculum Renewal." *UNESCO report*. https://unesdoc.unesco.org/ark:/48223/pf0000143748. Accessed December 30, 2022.

Nahachewsky, Andriy. 1995. "Participatory and Presentational Dance as Ethnochoreological Categories." *Dance Research Journal* 27 (1): 1–15.

262 &❧ REFERENCES

———. 2001. "Strategies for Theatricalizing Folk Dance." In *Sword Dances and Related Calendrical Dance Events. Revival: Reconstruction, Revitalization. 21st Symposium of the ICTM Study Group on Ethnochoreology,* edited by Elsie Ivancich Dunin and Tvrtko Zebec, 228–234. Zagreb: Institut za etnologiju i folkloristiku.

Nanyonga-Tamusuza, Sylvia. 2002. "Gender, Ethnicity, and Politics in *Kadongo-Kamu* Music of Uganda." In *Playing with Identities in Contemporary Music in Africa,* edited by Mai Palmberg and Annamette Kierkegaard, 134–148. Uppsala: Nordiska Afrikainstitutet.

———. 2003. "Competition in School Festivals: A Process of Reinventing *Baakisimba* Music and Dance of the Baganda." *The World of Music* 45: 97–118.

———. 2005. *Baakisimba. Gender and Dance of the Baganda People of Uganda.* New York and London: Routledge.

———. 2009. "Female-Men, Male-Women, and Others: Constructing and Negotiating Gender among the Baganda of Uganda." *Journal of Eastern African Studies* 3: 367–380.

———. 2015. "Music as Dance and Dance as Music: Interdependence and Dialogue in Baganda *Baakisimba* Performance." *Yearbook for Traditional Music* 47: 82–96.

Nattiez, Jean-Jacques, and Sylvia Nanyonga-Tamusuza. 2003. "Ritmo, danza e sesso: una danza ugandese di iniziazione al matrimonio." In *Enciclopedia della musica* III, edited by Jean-Jacques Nattiez, 957–977. Turin: Einaudi.

Ndaliko, Chérie Rivers. 2016. *Necessary Noise: Music, Film, and Charitable Imperialism in the East of Congo.* New York: Oxford University Press.

Ndoleriire, Oswald et al. 2009. *Runyoro-Rutooro—English Dictionary.* Kampala: Fountain.

Ness, Sally A. 1996. "Dancing in the Field: Notes from Memory." In *Corporealities,* edited by Susan L. Foster, 133–158. London: Routledge.

Nyakatura, John W. 1970. *Aspects of Bunyoro Customs and Traditions.* Nairobi: East African Literature Bureau.

———. 1973. *Anatomy of an African Kingdom.* Garden City: Anchor Press.

Nyanzi, Stella. 2013a. "Dismantling Reified African Culture through Localized Homosexualities in Uganda." *Culture, Health & Sexuality: An International Journal for Research, Intervention and Care* 15 (8): 952–967.

———. 2013b "Homosexuality in Uganda: The Paradox of Foreign Influence." *MISR Working Paper* 14: 1–45.

———. 2014. "Queer Pride and Protest: A Reading of the Bodies at Uganda's First Gay Beach Pride." *Signs* 40 (1): 36–40.

Nyanzi, Stella, and Andrew Karamagi. 2015. "The Social-Political Dynamics of the Antihomosexuality Legislation in Uganda." *Agenda: Empowering Women for Gender Equity* 29 (1): 24–38.

Ortner, Sherry B. 1997. *Making Gender. The Politics and Erotics of Culture.* Boston: Beacon Press.

Oyèrónké Oyĕwùmí. 1997. *The Invention of Women. Making an African Sense of Western Gender Discourses.* Minneapolis: University of Minnesota Press.

Pennacini, Cecilia. 1998. *Kubandwa. La possessione spiritica nell'Africa dei Grandi Laghi.* Turin: Il Segnalibro.

———. 2009. "Religious Mobility and Body Language in Kubandwa Possession Cults." *Journal of Eastern African Studies* 3: 333–349.

———. 2011. "La riscoperta del patrimonio culturale nell'Uganda contemporanea." *L'Uomo* 1–2: 115–137.

Pennacini, Cecilia, and Hermann Wittenberg (eds.). 2008. *Rwenzori: Histories and Cultures of an African Mountain.* Kampala: Fountain.

Perlman, Melvin L. 1962. "Some Aspects of Marriage Stability in Tooro." Paper presented at the conference of the East African Institute for Social Research, Limuru.

———. 1963. *Toro Marriage: A Study of Changing Conjugal Institutions.* Ph.D. diss., Oxford University, Oxford.

———. 1966. "Changing Status and Role of Women in Tooro." *Cahiers d'études africains* 6: 564–591.

Peterson, Derek P. 2016. "A History of Heritage Economy in Yoweri Museveni's Uganda." *Journal of Eastern African Studies* 10 (4): 789–806.

Pier, David. 2009. *The Senator Cultural Extravaganza of Uganda: A Branded African Traditional Music Competition.* Ph.D. diss., The City University of New York, New York.

———. 2011. "The Branded Arena: Ugandan Traditional Dance in the Marketing Era." *Africa* 81: 413–433.

———. 2015. *Ugandan Music in the Marketing Era: The Branded Arena.* London: Palgrave Macmillan.

Ranger, Terence. 1975. *Dance and Society in Eastern Africa 1890–1970: The Beni Ngoma.* Berkeley and Los Angeles: University of California Press.

Ranmarine, Tina K. 2007. *Beautiful Cosmos: Performance and Belonging in the Caribbean Diaspora.* London: Pluto Press.

Reid, Richard J. 2017. *A History of Modern Uganda.* Cambridge: Cambridge University Press.

Remotti, Francesco. 1989. "Capitali mobili." In *Centri, ritualità, potere,* edited by Francesco Remotti, Pietro Scarduelli, and Ugo Fabietti, 107–168. Bologna: Il Mulino.

———. 1993. *Etnografia nande I, Società, matrimoni, potere.* Torino: Il Segnalibro.

Robertson, Carol E. 1993. "The Ethnomusicologist as a Midwife." In *Musicology and Difference. Gender and Sexuality in Musical Scholarship*, edited by Ruth Solie, 107–124. Berkeley: University of California Press.

Roscoe, John. 1915. *The Northern Bantu.* Cambridge: Cambridge University Press.

———. 1923. *The Bakitara or Banyoro.* Cambridge: Cambridge University Press.

Royce, Anya P. 1977. *The Anthropology of Dance.* Bloomington: Indiana University Press.

Rubongoya, L. T. 1999. *A Modern Runyoro-Rutooro Grammar.* Cologne: Köppe.

Rwagweri, Atwoki S. (no date). *Tooro and Her People.* Fort Portal: Ngabu za Tooro.

Sadgrove, Joanna et al. 2012. "Morality Plays and Money Matters: Towards a Situated Understanding of the Politics of Homosexuality in Uganda." *The Journal of Modern African Studies* 50 (1): 103–129.

Santino, Jack (ed.). 2017. *Public Performances: Studies in the Carnivalesque and Ritualesque.* Logan: Utah State University Press.

Scharfenberger, Angela. 2011. "West African Women in Music: An Analysis of Scholarship. Women's Participation in Music in West Africa: A Reflection on Fieldwork, Self, and Understanding." *African Music* 9 (1): 221–246.

Schiller, Laurence D. 1990. "The Royal Women of Buganda." *The International Journal of African Historical Studies* 23: 455–473.

Schoenbrun, David, L. 1993. "A Past Whose Time Has Come: Historical Context and History in Eastern Africa's Great Lakes." *History and Theory* 32 (4): 32–56.

Scott, Joan W. 1988. *Gender and the Politics of History.* New York: Columbia University Press.

Serumaga, Robert. 1964. *Heart Beat of Africa Featuring Uganda Dancers and Musicians.* Kampala: Argus.

Shay, Anthony. 2002. *Choreographic Politics. State Folk Dance Companies, Representation and Power.* Middletown: Wesleyan University Press.

Speke, John H. 1863. *Journal of the Discovery of the Sources of the Nile.* Edinburgh: Blackwood.

Ssebaggala, Richard. 2011. "Straight Talk on the Gay Question in Uganda." *Transition* 106 B: 44–57.

Stacey, Tom. 2008. "The Snows of Rwenzururu and the Kingdom." In *Rwenzori. Histories and Cultures of an African Mountain*, edited by Cecilia Pennacini and Hermann Wittenberg, 7–17. Kampala: Fountain.

Staiti, Nico. 2012. *Kajda. Musiche e riti femminili tra i Rom del Kosovo*. Rome: Squilibri.

Stephens, Rhiannon. 2013. *A History of African Motherhood. The Case of Uganda 700–1900*. Cambridge: Cambridge University Press.

Stone, Ruth M. 2002. "African Music in a Constellation of Arts." In *The Garland Encyclopaedia of World Music* I: *Africa*, edited by Ruth M. Stone, 7–12. New York: Routledge.

Sugarman, Jane C. 1997. *Engendering Song: Singing and Subjectivity at Prespa Albanian Weddings*. Chicago and London: University of Chicago Press.

Sunardi, Christina. 2015. *Stunning Males and Powerful Females. Gender and Tradition in East Javanese Dance*. Urbana, Illinois, and Springfield: University of Illinois Press.

Tamale, Sylvia (ed.). 2007. *Homosexuality. Perspectives from Uganda*. Kampala: Sexual Minorities Uganda.

Taylor, Brian K. 1962. *The Western Lacustrine Bantu*. London: International African Institute.

———. 1998. *Tropic Toro. A Ugandan Society*. Brighton: Pennington Beech.

van Thiel, Paul. 1966–67. "The Music of Ankole: The *Sheegu* Pipeband and the Regalia of the Royal Drum 'Bagyendanwa'." *African Music* 4: 6–20.

———. 1977. *Multi-Tribal Music of Ankole. An Ethnomusicological Study Including a Glossary of Musical Terms*. Tervuren: Musée Royal de l'Afrique centrale.

Tibasiima, Isaac. 2009. "Marriage, Family and Praise Poetry in Toro Society." In *Performing Change: Identity, Ownership and Tradition in Ugandan Oral Culture*, edited by Dominica Dipio, Lene Johannessen, and Stuart Sillars, 121–142. Oslo: Novus Press.

Torelli, Ubald. 1973. "Notes ethnologiques sur les Banya-Mwenge du Toro." *Annali del Pontificio Museo Missionario Etnologico* 27: 461–559.

Tracey, Hugh. 1958 . "Towards an Assessment of African Scales." *African Music* 2 (8): 15–20.

———. 1969. "Measuring African Scales." *African Music* 4: 73–77.

———. 1973a. *The Sound of Africa Series. Catalogue*, vol. I. Roodepoort: International Library for African Music.

———. 1973b. *The Sound of Africa Series. Catalogue*, vol. II. Roodepoort: International Library of African Music.

Tripp, Aili M. 1998. "Local Women's Associations and Politics in Contemporary Uganda." In *Developing Uganda*, edited by Holger Bernt Hansen and Michael Twaddle, 120–144. Oxford, Kampala, Athens, and Nairobi: Currey, Fountain, Ohio University Press, and E.A.E.P.

———. 2002. "Introduction: A New Generation of Women's Mobilisation in Uganda." In *The Women's Movement in Uganda. History, Challenges and Prospects*, edited by Aili M. Tripp and Joy C. Kwesiga, 1–22. Kampala: Fountain.

———. 2004. "The Changing Face of Authoritarianism in Africa: The Case of Uganda." *Africa Today* 50 (3): 3–26.

Tripp, Aili M., and Sarah Ntiro. 2002. "Women's Activism in Colonial Uganda." In *The Women's Movement in Uganda. History, Challenges and Prospects*, edited by Aili M. Tripp and Joy C. Kwesiga, 23–39. Kampala: Fountain.

Turino, Thomas. 2008. *Music as Social Life. The Politics of Participation*. Chicago and London: University of Chicago Press.

Vorhölter, Julia. 2012. "Negotiating Social Change: Ugandan Discourses on Westernisation and Neo-Colonialism as Forms of Social Critique." *The Journal of Modern African Studies* 50 (2): 283–307.

Wabyona, Milton. 2004. *Role of Muzeenyo Dance of the Bagungu People of Uganda*. B.A. thesis, Makerere University, Kampala.

Wachsmann, Klaus P. 1946. "The Namirembe Music Festival and the Future of African Music." *Uganda Church Review* 13: 7–11.

———. 1953. "The Sound Instruments." In *Tribal Crafts of Uganda*, edited by Margaret Trowell and Klaus P. Wachsmann: 311–415. London: Oxford University Press.

———. 1954. "The Transplantation of Folk Music from One Social Environment to Another." *Journal of the International Folk Music Council* 6: 41–45.

———. 1956. "Harp Songs from Uganda." *Journal of the International Folk Music Council* 8: 23–25.

———. 1958. "A Century of Change in the Folk Music of an African Tribe." *Journal of the International Folk Music Council* 10: 52–56.

———. 1961. "The Primitive Musical Instruments." In *Musical Instruments through the Ages*, edited by Anthony Baines, 23–54. Middlesex, Baltimore, and Mitcham: Penguin.

———. 1964. "Human Migration and African Harps." *Journal of the International Folk Music Council* 16: 84–88.

———. 1971. "Musical Instruments in Kiganda Tradition and Their Place in the East African Scene." In *Essays on Music and History in Africa*, edited by Klaus P. Wachsmann: 93–134. Evanston: Northwestern University Press.

Wachsmann, Klaus P., and Russel Kay. 1971. "The Interrelations of Musical Instruments, Musical Forms and Cultural Systems in Africa." *Technology and Culture* 22: 399–413.

Ward, Kevin. 2015. "The Role of the Anglican and Catholic Churches in Uganda in Public Discourse on Homosexuality and Ethics." *Journal of Eastern African Studies* 9 (1): 127–144.

Wegner, Ulrich. 1990. *Xylophonmusik aus Buganda (Ostafrika)*. Wilhelmshaven: Florian Noetzel.

———. 1993. "Cognitive Aspects of *Amadinda* Xylophone Music from Buganda: Inherent Patterns Reconsidered." *Ethnomusicology* 37 (2): 201–241.

———. 1995. "Musikinstrument, Spieltechnik und Wahrnehmung. Ein Kiganda Holm-Xylophon aus der Sicht der Kognitionsforschung." *Studia instrumentorum musicae popularis* 11: 27–35.

Weiss, Sarah. 2006. *Listening to an Earlier Java. Aesthetics, Gender and the Music of Wayang in Central Java*. Leiden: KITLV Press.

Williams, F. Lukyn. 1936–37. "The Inauguration of the *Omugabe* of Ankole to Office." *Uganda Journal* 4: 300–312.

Wong, Deborah. 2015. "Ethnomusicology without Erotics." *Women and Music: A Journal of Gender and Culture* 19 (1): 178–185.

Wrazen, Louise. 2004. "Men and Women Dancing in the Remembered Past of Podhale Poland." *Anthropology of Eastern Europe Review* 22 (1): 145–154.

———. 2010. "Daughters of Tradition, Mothers of Invention: Music, Teaching, and Gender in Evolving Contexts." *Yearbook for Traditional Music* 42: 41–61.

Wymeersch, Patrick. 1979. *Ritualisme et fonction des tambours en Afrique interlacustre*. Rome: Istituto italo-africano.

Websites

https://www.statista.com/statistics/447698/age-structure-in-uganda/. Accessed December 23, 2021.

https://www.youtube.com/user/Engabuzatooro. Accessed April 7, 2022.

https://www.youtube.com/watch?v=3QXSMUVairw. Accessed April 24, 2022.

https://www.youtube.com/watch?v=zfRLZS20zCU. Accessed April 24, 2022.

https://bigeye.ug/ngayaya-voted-the-most-beautiful-ugandan-song-of-all-time/. Accessed April 24, 2022.

https://www.youtube.com/watch?v=bvuGIUiA9og. Accessed April 24, 2022.

https://ich.unesco.org/en/USL/koogere-oral-tradition-of-the-basongora-banyabindi-and-batooro-peoples-00911. Accessed November 25, 2022.

https://www.unicef.org/uganda/press-releases/prioritize-re-opening-schools-secure-childrens-well-being. Accessed September 16, 2022.

https://www.ru.ac.za/ilam/currentprojects/ilamsamaponlinearchive/. Accessed November 9, 2022.

http://sounds.bl.uk/World-and-traditional-music/Wachsmann. Accessed November 9, 2022.

http://sounds.bl.uk/World-and-traditional-music/Peter-Cooke-Uganda. Accessed November 9, 2022.

Index

Note: Page numbers in italics indicate illustrations.

Abubakar, Bakar, 7
"African harmony," 177
Agawu, Kofi, 26
AIDS, xxii, 14, 191, 225; educational
    programs about, 196, 197, 209,
    219, 221; support organization
    for, 209
Albanian Presba people, 48–49, 51, 91
Alituha, Moses, *119*
allegorical dances, 148
alliterative harmony, 92n14
Amadiume, Ifi, 16
Amin, Idi, 1, 71
Anti-Homosexuality Act, xxi–xxii,
    12–14, 225
Anti-Pornography Act, xxii, 73, 225
anyakwine enambaye asorole, 157–163
Arom, Simha, 121
Asaasira, Anita D., 194
Asiimwe, Agnes, 134n1
Atwooki, Ramadam, 187
"authenticity," 22, 194; innovation
    and, 182–184; variety and, 165–
    166, 175–180, 184–185

baakisimba dance, 18, 24, 148, 162,
    185, 186, 212
Babiito clan, 55
Bacwezi (demigods), 50, 106n5
Baguma, Clovis, 125, 176, 180
bakondeere ensembles, 101–102
Balikenda, Abigael, 198
Ballet Folklórico de México, 11, 19–20

banana beer, 41–45, 87, 139–142,
    141; gender and, 45, 91, 142–144;
    gourds of, *141*; production of, 140,
    142–149, *144–147*
banana juice (*nsande*), 41–42
Bantebya Kyomuhendo, Grace, 16,
    57; on Domestic Virtue model,
    59–61, 71–72, 208
Bantu languages, 2
Bareeba, Tina, 72
Barongo, Herbert, *119*, *145*
Barz, Gregory, 125, 196
Basemeera, Alice, 7
Basemera, Goretti, *147*
Beattie, John, 49, 55, 61; on bride-
    wealth, 77, 81
Berger, Iris, 53, 59, 205
bigano (story-songs), *35*, 87, 164, 170
bigeye.ug website, 197
binyege (leg rattles), *39*, 112, 209–
    210, *210*; for drinking songs,
    88n10; female dancers with, 208–
    210, *210*; making of, 36–38, *37*;
    male dancers with, 35, 36, 44, *145*,
    152–153, *161*; musical notation
    of, xv; *ngaabi* drums and, 112,
    122–124, *123*
biological determinism, 58, 62, 187,
    191–192, 216
bitakuli rhythm, 118–120
Bitamazire, Aberi, 78–80; *Kamut-
    waire* sung by, 83–86, *85*; *Kyera
    maino* sung by, 79–80, *81*

270 ❧ INDEX

Bitamazire, Joy Katusabe, 92, *93*
Bituli bambi (song), 97–100, *99*
bizina by'ebijungu (Western music), 10
bizina by'ente. See cow-praising songs
bizina by'enzarwa (local music), 10
Blacking, John, 158n16
blacksmiths, 41, 91
Bourdieu, Pierre, 150
bridewealth (*mukaaga*), 33, 52,
    68–71, *69*, 75; Beattie on, 77, 82;
    colonial gender model of, 59, 61;
    Nyakairu on, 96. *See also* weddings
Brown, Danielle, 29
Buganda, 24; Kingdom of, 1, 5,
    54–55; xylophone music of, 25
Bukaayi, Lillian, 166
"bull name," 96
Bunyoro Foundation Actors Group, 8,
    119, 145, 147, 161
Bunyoro Kingdom, xix, xx, 2–5, *3*
Butler, Judith, 16–17, 150, 175, 181
bwatububiiri. See hermaphroditism
bw'omu mbaju dance, 136, 148, 154–
    158, *155–156*

Caribbean music, 46, 157
Casati, Gaetano, 134
Castaldi, Francesca, 157
cattle raising, 2, 51, 90; songs of,
    34n3, 90, 95–100, *99*
Ceeku ceeku (song), 176–180,
    177–178
Central African Republic, 101, 109
Chrétien, Jean-Pierre, 95, 96
Christianity, 191, 194; evangelical,
    14, 56–57, 219; marriage in, 82;
    Pentecostal, 14, 192, 219, 225;
    "religious" names of, 245; sexuality
    and, 13–14, 52, 57, 225; trans-
    performers and, 192; twins cer-
    emony and, 134n3
circumcision (*imbalu*), 47

clothing, 103, 174n9, 186; costumes
    and, 139, 194; "miniskirt bill,"
    xxii, 225. *See also kanzu* tunic
Congo. *See* Democratic Republic of
    Congo
Connell, R. W., 48
Cooke, Peter, 20, 25, 88, 198; on cat-
    tle-praising songs, 95n15; on *kalezi*
    dance, 135n5; on music education,
    166, 168; recordings of, 109, 235,
    242–244t
couple dancing, 157–163, *161*, 204
courtship dance, 38–41, *39*, 161, 162,
    183
Covid-19 pandemic, 221
cow-praising songs (*bizina by'ente*),
    34n3, 90, 95–100, *99*
culture, 15, 204–212, *210*; folk songs
    and, 197–204; tradition versus, 10;
    "tribal," 21n5. *See also nzarwa*
Cunningham, James F., 136

dance motifs, 122, 124
Davis, Margaret B., 10, 86
de Lauretis, Teresa, 150, 226
Democratic Republic of Congo
    (DRC), 2, *3*, 87, 95, 109, 196,
    203–204
Desmond, Jane C., 153, 157, 223
diversity, 19, 168; "rainbow ethnicity"
    and, 23, 193, 194
divorce, 71
"Domestic Virtue model," 57–62, 71,
    208, 222. *See also* gender roles
Doubleday, Veronica, 117, 124–125
Downing, Sonja Lynn, 126
drinking songs, 87n8
drums, 112–117; *binyege* leg rattles
    and, 112, 122–124, *123*; construc-
    tion of, 37, 114; female players of,
    125–131, *128, 129*, 180–182, 188.
    See also specific types

ekikebi dance, 40
enthronement anniversary. *See Mpango*
Epprecht, Marc, 13
ethnomusicology, 24–26, 29–30
evangelicals, 14, 56–57, 219. *See also* Christianity

Facci, Serena, 5, 18, 114
Fallers, Lloyd A., 3–4
feminism, 16, 26–28, 191. *See also* women's rights
fiddle. See *ndingidi*
firimbi whistle, *109, 112*
Fisher, Ruth, 80–82
flutes (*nseegu*), 104–105, 105t, 198, 201
folk dances, 9; gender roles in, xx–xxi, 32–34; sexual allusions in, 17, 133–134; social value of, 190–191
folk songs: "authenticity" of, 176; of cultural groups, 197–204; judging criteria of, 170–171, 176; narration in, 169–175, *174*; structure of, 172–173t; variety shaping of, 176–180, *177–178*; yodeling in, 89
Foucault, Michel, 150

Gafabusa Hairora, Patrick R., 134n1
Gambia, 59, 206
gamelan ensembles, 25, 126, 206–207
Ganda, 4, 212. *See also* Buganda
García Canclini, Néstor, 185
gender issues, 5–8, 12–15, 62–63; under Amin, 71; colonial, 56–61; education and, 60; and folk dance, xx–xxi, 32–34; hermaphroditism and, 190, 192, 216; with instrument making, 37–38; and instrument playing, 27–28, 101–105, 110–111; intersectionality of, 17–18; postcoloniality and, 15–18, 28, 34, 70–75, 222–226;

precolonial, 34, 48–56, 56t; questionnaire on, 32–34; researchers of, 26–28; with *runyege*, 32–34, 45–48, 87, 90, 143–157, 186–189, 222–223; spirit mediums and, 52–54, 58–59; women's rights and, 12, 71–73, 78n2, 195, 224. *See also* sexuality
gender roles, 90–92; in agricultural work, 90–91; biological determinism and, 62, 187, 191–192, 216; in cattle raising, 90; debates over, 12–15; "Domestic Virtue model" and, 57–62, 71, 208, 222; drum players and, 125–131, *128, 129*, 180–182; in millet-grinding song, 174–175; "propriety" and, 33, 46n10, 126; "scripting" of, 47, 149–150; Victorian, 52, 57. *See also* trans-performers
gendering culture, 15, 45–48, 62–63, 186–188, 221–226
Gilman, Lisa, 11, 15, 210–211
Global North/Global South, 204
glossary, 227–234
Grau, Andrée, 46
grinding song, 92–95, *93, 94*, 170–175, 172–173t, *174*
Guinean national ballet, 22
Gusman, Alessandro, xxi–xxii, 14

Hairora, Gafabusa, 46
Halberstam, Judith, 214–215
Hanna, Judith L., 45, 47, 144, 149
Heartbeat of Africa ensemble, 22–23, 134n1, 193
hermaphroditism, 190, 192, 216
Hernández, Amalia, 20
HIV disease. *See* AIDS
HIVOS (Dutch NGO), 197, 203, 204
homophobia, 13–14, 217–218, 225

272 ❧ INDEX

homosexuality, 12–14, 56n20, 195; conformity pressures on, 192, 218–219, 222–226; legislation against, xxi–xxii, 12–14, 225. *See also* sexuality
hoquetus (interlocking) technique, 101, 110
hunting songs, 91n13
Hutchinson, Sydney, 212, 214–216
hybridity, 185

Ibanda, Grace F., 134n1
iguulya, 108, 135–136
ihuurru (small royal double-skin drum), 105t
ikondeere (royal side-blown trumpet), 105t
ikura (wonderful unseen thing), 114
imbalu (circumcision), 47
Indonesian gamelan ensembles, 25, 126, 206–207. *See also* Java
initiation rituals, 166
innovation, 182–186. *See also* "authenticity"
instrument making, 37–38
instrument playing, 101–105, 109–114, *111*
interlocking (hoquetus) technique, 101, 110
International Library of African Music (ILAM), 235
intersectionality, 16–17, 221
interviewee list, 245–249
Islam, 13, 191, 194; "religious" names and, 245; trans-performers and, 192; twins ceremony and, 134n3

Jamal, Salim, 8, 118
Java, 21, 58, 165, 212; cross-dressing in, 216, 218; gamelan ensembles of, 25, 126, 206–207

Kabarega Teachers' College, 149
Kabutuku, Stephen, 44, 118; on gendered dance roles, 204; on *run-yege*'s origins, 146, 149
Kabyanga, Joshwa, 125, 171, 176, 179, 180–181
Kagaba, Sebastiano, 148, 161, 205, 210
kagoma (small double-skin drum), 105t, 108, 136
Kahunde, Samuel, 24–25
Kahunga Bunyonyi Primary School, 171–180, 172–173t, *174, 177–178*, 183
Kahwa, Dorothy, 92–95, *94*
Kaijumurubi, Joseph, *144*
Kakoma, George W., 168
kalezi dance, 135n5
kalihwa dance, 135
Kampala, 19
Kamutwaire (song), 83–87, *86*
Kanyooma, 112
kanzu tunic, 127, *128*, 138, 174n9, 180–182
karonkoronko, 10
karukarukaine, 10
Karungi, Sylvia, 8
Kasaija, Mary, 207–208
Kasangaki, Harriet, 5
kasigasigano, 10
Katusime, Annette, 132, 133
Ke ke kamengo (millet grinding song), 92–95, *93, 94*, 170, 176
Kenya, *3*, 19, 23, 185
Kibiro group, 101n2
kigano (sung story), *35*, 87, 170. See also *bigano*
kikazikazi (feminine male), 216. *See also* trans-performers
Kinyoro, Gerrison, 8, 41–42, *43*, 167; *Bituli bambi* sung by, 97–100, *99*; on drum rhythms, 112, 118, 120,

121; on *Ngayaya muhuma wange*, 198; on *runyege* origins, 169; on women's *runyege* dancing, 146–148

Kiparu, Francis, 102

Kitara Complex, 2

Kitara Empire, 1–2, 5, 50n14

kizina (musical piece), 34, 35

kizina ky'ente, 97

Kogeere, 197

Komuhimbo, Christine, *155–156*

Koogere, queen of Busongora, 197n1, 203, 204

Koskoff, Ellen, 29–30, 106

kubandwa music, 59

Kubik, Gerhard, 95

kucweka omugongo, 156

kuhugura (yodeling), 84, 88–89, 179

kujenga, 34n3

kusimba style, 154, *155*

kutongora, 160–162, *161*

kweranga (bride's introduction), 78

Kwesiga, Godfrey, 78; *Kamutwaire* sung by, 83–86, *85*; *Kyera maino* sung by, 79–80, *81*

Kyagambiddwa, Joseph, 171

Kyera maino (song), 79–83, *81*

Kyomukama Catering and Creative Association (KCCA), 208, 209

lamellophones, 101n1

Lawrence, Jeremy C. D., 3–4

leg rattles. See *binyege*

LGBTQ+ community, 12–14. *See also* homosexuality

literacy, 10

Lloyd, Albert B., 36, *39*, 112

Lord Resistance Army (LRA), 26

Luganda language, 68n1, 74

lullabies, 92, 95

Lutwama-Rukundo, Evelyn, 205

Mabingo, Alfdaniels, 22, 145–146

Macpherson, Margaret, 196

Magezi, Christopher, xx, 8, 38, 108; with *binyege* leg rattles, 36, *37*; on *runyege*, 39, 118, 149n13

mahuurru (double-skin drum), 105t

Makerere University, 5, 19n4

makondeere (royal side-blown trumpets), xix, xx, 24–25, 110; gender/race issues and, 101–103; *ngwara* and, 37, 105t, *111*

Malawi, 11, 15, 19, 134; performing arts of, 23, 38, 196; political rallies in, 210–211

maranga (*Canna indica*) seeds, 36, *37*

marriage, 60, 83–87, *85*; bride's farewell song after, 79–83, *81*; Bukaayi on, 166; Christian views of, 82; courtship dance for, 38–41, *39*, 161, 162, 183; divorce and, 71; mediums and, 53; monogamous, 71; polygamous, 61; precolonial, 49. *See also* weddings

Masindi Drama Saving Scheme (MAS-DRASS), 209

matagura, 157

Matama, Korotirida, 78; *Kamutwaire* sung by, 83–86, *85*; *Kyera maino* sung by, 79–80, *81*

mazina g'abarongo (dance of the twins), 134n3, *135*

Mbabi-Katana, Solomon, 20, 24–25, 88, 198; on banana beer production, 143n10; on music education, 166; on *runyege*'s origins, 149

mbira (lamellophone), 101n1

McConnell, Bonnie B., 206

McIntosh, Marjorie Keniston, 16, 57; on Domestic Virtue model, 59–61, 71–72, 208

McMahon, Felicia, 96

MDD. *See* music/dance/drama

274 ❧ INDEX

mediums. *See* spirit mediums
merengue, 212, 214–215
Mexico, 11, 19–20
Middleton, John, 3–4
Miirima, Henry F., xiii
millet beer, 47
millet grinding song, 92–95, *93*, *94*,
170–175, *172–173*t, *174*
mimetic dances, 144, 147–148
mirindi dance, 136
Misinguzi, George, 126
monogamy, 71
Morris, Henry F., 99n18
Mothers' Union, 187, 205–207
mpaako, 197n1, 245
Mpango (enthronement anniversary),
xix–xxi, 9, 62, 102; kings' mother
and, 117
mpango (royal double-skin drum),
105, 114, 135; names of, 115. See
also *ngoma*
Mugabo, Stephen, 7–8, 29, 40n6,
118; on men's dance styles, *152–
153*; on *runyege dance*, 132, 133
Mugenyi, Mariam Amooti, 146
mugongo (lower back), 132, 133, 154–
158, *155–156*, 213–214, 217, 218
Muhuruzi, George, 66, 69–70
Muhuruzi, John, 66–70, 73–75
Muhuza, Moses, *119*
mukaaga. *See* bridewealth
Mukasa-Balikuddembe, Joseph, 49,
140–141, 164–165, 169–170
multiculturalism. *See* diversity
munyege tree (*Oncoba routledgei*), 36,
37
Murray, Stephen O., 13
murungi (good/beautiful person), 86
muserebende omugongo, 157
Museveni, Yoweri, xix, 1; anti-gay
legislation of, 12n2; on women's
rights, 12, 78n2

music/dance/drama (MDD), 30–34;
Mukasa-Balikuddembe on, 164–
165; paradigms of, 34–36, *35*, 165,
221–222; school festivals of, 9,
18–24, 166–169, 183
musical transcription, xv
muzeenyo dance, 136
Mwanga (Ganda king), 56n20

Nahachewsky, Andriy, 185
Namara, Makleen, 187
Namirembe Music Festival, 21
nanga (trough zither), 62, 105–107,
105t, 222; poems for, 96; songs
for, 198, 201–202
Nanyonga-Tamusuza, Sylvia, xv, 5, 18,
121, 124; on *baakisimba* dance,
148, 185; on female drum players,
130; on traditional repertoires, 212
National Resistance Movement
(NRM), 1, 4, 72; educational policies of, 224; neoliberal policies of,
167n2, 223–224
Nattiez, Jean-Jacques, 121, 130
Ndaliko, Chérie Rivers, 196, 203–204
Ndere Troupe (Kampala), 23–24, 67,
193, 194
ndingidi (one-string fiddle), 37, 38,
104, 110–111, *111*
neocolonialism, 13, 14, 224–225;
definition of, xxii; homosexuality
and, 224–225; women's rights and,
72–73, 224
neoliberalism, 14, 26, 167n2,
223–224
Ness, Sally A., 159
New Moon ceremony, 115, 135
ngaabi (single-skin drum), 27, 105t,
107, 117, *119*, 122–125, *123*;
binyege leg rattles and, 122–124,
123; construction of, 122; female
players of, 125–131, *129*; gender

issues and, 122, 124; playing position of, *119*, 124, 129–130; whistles and, 112

ngabu poems, 96

Ngabu za Tooro troupe, 7, 8, 133, 136n6, 137, 197–204

ngaija (royal single-skin drum), 105t, 122

nganikyo (fable), *35*, 169

Ngayaya muhuma wange (song), 197–202

ngoma (double-skin drum), 105t, 107, 112, 114–117, *119*; communication by, 116; female players of, 125–131, *128*, *129*; gender issues and, 102, 117, 118; rhythmic patterns of, 117–122, *119*, *121*

ngwara (side-blown trumpets), 37, 105t, *111*. See also *makondeere*

nkaceka rhythm, 118–120, 122

Nkore Kingdom, 1n1, 5

NRM. *See* National Resistance Movement

nsande (banana juice), 41–42

nseegu (flutes), 104–105, 105t, 198, 201

ntajemerwa (royal double-skin drum), 105t, 115. See also *ngoma*

ntimbo (royal single-skin drum), 105t

Ntiro, Sarah, 60

ntogoro, 134n1, 136

Nyakairu, Kenneth, 8, 96

Nyakato, Marrion, 171, 177, 179, 181, 184

nyamuziga dance, 148, 154–156, *156*, 214

Nyanzi, Stella, 13, 14

Nyegenya, Vincent, 8, 118, 145, 149n13

nzarwa (local culture), 9–11, 15, 162, 163, 221–226

Obote, Milton, 1

obw'omu mbaju dance, 120

oli songs, 96

omugongo muserebende style, 154, *155*

Ortner, Sherry B., 175

Oyēwùmí, Oyèrókè, 16, 77

Pennacini, Cecilia, 53

Pentecostalism, 14, 192, 219, 225. *See also* Christianity

performing arts. *See* music/dance/drama

Perlman, Melvin L., 52, 60

Peru, 19–20

Peterson, Derek R., 4

"Petty Urban Trade," 71, 208

Pier, David, 26, 169, 179, 208–209

pluralism. *See* diversity

polygamy, 61

pornography, xxii, 73, 225

postcoloniality, 4, 19–22, 224; gender and, 15–18, 28, 34, 70–75, 222–226; local identity and, 191, 192, 195; neoliberalism and, 26; performing arts and, 163, 185

pottery, 91

Presba people (Albania), 48–49, 51, 91

"rainbow ethnicity," 23, 193, 194

Ranmarine, Tina K., 209

rattle dances, 107. See also *binyege*

Red Cross, 5–6

Reid, Richard, 223, 224

"religious" names, 245

riiba dance, 136

Robertson, Carol E., 212

Roscoe, John, 3–4, 55, 75n3; on banana beer production, 143n10; on blacksmith songs, 91

Roscoe, Will, 13

Royce, Anya P., 144

Rubongoya, L. T., xiii

rumengo (grinding stone), 92, *93, 174. See also* millet grinding song

runyege, 28, 35–36, *39*, 104–108, 105t; as courtship dance, 38–41, *39*, 161, 162, 183; dancing styles of, 149–157, *152–153, 155–156*; emic narratives of, 41–45; female drum players in, 125–131, *128, 129*; female's footwork in, 144–148, *146, 147*, 154–157, *155–156*; gender issues and, 32–34, 45–48, 87, 90, 143–157, 186–189, 222–223; historical recordings of, 104, 109–114, 120n14, 235, 236–244t; hybrid nature of, 15; *iguulya* versus, 108; *Kamutwaire* song and, 86–87; Magezi on, 108; male's footwork in, 143–144, *144, 145*, 151–154, *152–153*; musical notation of, xv; origins of, 41–45, 143–149, 169; performance contexts of, 40, 87, 89–90, 132–134, 13/–140; as performing arts paradigm, 34–36, *35*; sexual allusions in, 17, 133–134, 161–162, 192; staging of, 182–186; standardization of, 107, 108; theatrical elements of, 164–166; *tonto* production and, 143–148, *144, 146*; Tooro performance of, 137–139; types of, 134–137; women's groups and, 204–212, *210*

Runyoro-Rutooro language, xiii, 2, 7–8, 227–234

Rwagweri, Atwoki, 197

Rwagyezi, Stephen, 193

Rwamwaro, Rockamilley (aka Rokamela), 197, 203

Rwanda, 2, *3*, 97, 105n4

sabar dancers, 157

Sabiiti, Jane, 8, 170n6

salsa, 157

samba music, 42n7

Schoenbrun, David L., 58

school festivals, 9, 18–24, 183; Cooke on, 168; female drummers in, 125–131, *128, 129*; music education and, 166–169; nation-building and, 167–168

semiprofessional ensembles, 18–19, 22–23, 133, 169; female drum players in, 127; sponsors of, 196

Senator National Cultural Extravaganza, 169

Senegal, 19, 23, 185

"Service Career," 60

sex workers, 61

sexuality, 195; anti-gay legislation and, xxi–xxii, 12–14, 225; colonial religions and, 13–14, 52, 57, 225; conformity pressures on, 192, 218–219, 222–226; in couple dancing, 157–163, *161; runyege* dancing and, 17, 133–134, 161–162, 192; *sabar* dancing and, 157. *See also* gender issues; homosexuality

Shay, Anthony, 22n6, 193

Solomon Gafabusa Iguru I, king of Bunyoro, xix

Sound of Africa Series (ILAM), 235

spirit mediums, 2, 52–54, 58–59, 105

Ssebagala, Richard, 13n3

St. Joseph Kolping Troupe, 67

Stephens, Rhiannon, 58

storytelling, 18, *35*, 169–175, *172–173*t, *174. See also* music/dance/drama (MDD)

Sugarman, Jane, 29

Sunardi, Christina, 50–51, 206, 212

Sunday, Issa, 5–8, *69*, 101n2

Tamale, Sylvia, 13
Tanzania, 2, *3*
theater. *See* music/dance/drama (MDD)
Tibamanya, Jane, 170n6
Tibasiima, Isaac, 49n13, 96
tonto. See banana beer
Tooro Kingdom, 2–5, *3*
Tooro Kingdom Cultural Troupe, 137–139
Torelli, Ubald, 87–88, 112; on banana beer production, 143n10; on blacksmith songs, 91; on folk dances, 134
Tracey, Hugh, 25, 236–237t; on cow-praising songs, 95n15; on *nanga* songs, 106n5; recordings of, 109, 112–113, 120n14, 235, 236–237t; yodeling examples of, 88n11
trans-performers, 138, 190–193, 208, 212–220, 222–223; costumes of, 139; definition of, 207; homophobia and, 13–14, 217–218, 225; Kagaba on, 205, 210. *See also* gender roles
Tripp, Aili Mary, 60, 72
trumpets. See *makondeere*; *ngwara*
Turino, Thomas, 15, 19, 101n1
twins' songs, 59, 167

Uganda, 24–26; Church of, 205; constitution of, 4; demographics of, 32; map of, *3*; school closures in, 221. *See also* Heartbeat of Africa ensemble; National Resistance Movement
"Uganda drum." See *ngoma*
Ugandan Red Cross Society, 5–6
ululation, 177, 179
Umthetho Festival (Malawi), 11
Universal Primary Education, 72

Victorian morality, 52, 57

Viola, Lia, xxii, 14
virilocality, 83
Vorhölter, Julia, 224

Wabyona, Milton, 134n1
Wachsmann, Klaus, 25; on cow-praising songs, 95n15; on hunting music, 91n13; on *ndingidi*, 110; recordings of, 109, 112–113, 120n14, 235, 237–241t; on "Uganda drums," 114, 117; on yodeling, 88
waltz, 163
Ward, Kevin, 14
weddings, 75–78, 110, *141*; Anglican, 69–70; gender balance in, 70–75, *73*; gift exchange at, 44; living together versus, 73; *nanga* songs and, 106n5; Nyoro, 66–70, *69*; postcolonial, 70–75, *73*; precolonial, 49. *See also* bridewealth; marriage
Weiss, Sarah, 29, 212
women's associations, 59, 61, 224; cultural groups in, 204–213, *210*; instrument playing in, 103, 111, 127, 129; trans-performers in, 216–217. *See also* semiprofessional ensembles
women's rights, 12, 71–73, 78n2, 195, 224. *See also* gender issues
Wong, Deborah, 17
Wrazen, Louise, 188

xylophones, 25, 84n7, 104n3, 179; interlocking technique for, 101n1, 104n3

yodeling (*kuhugura*), 84, 88–89, 179

Zimbabwe, 15, 19, 23–24
zither. See *nanga*

Printed in the United States
by Baker & Taylor Publisher Services

.